D0435204

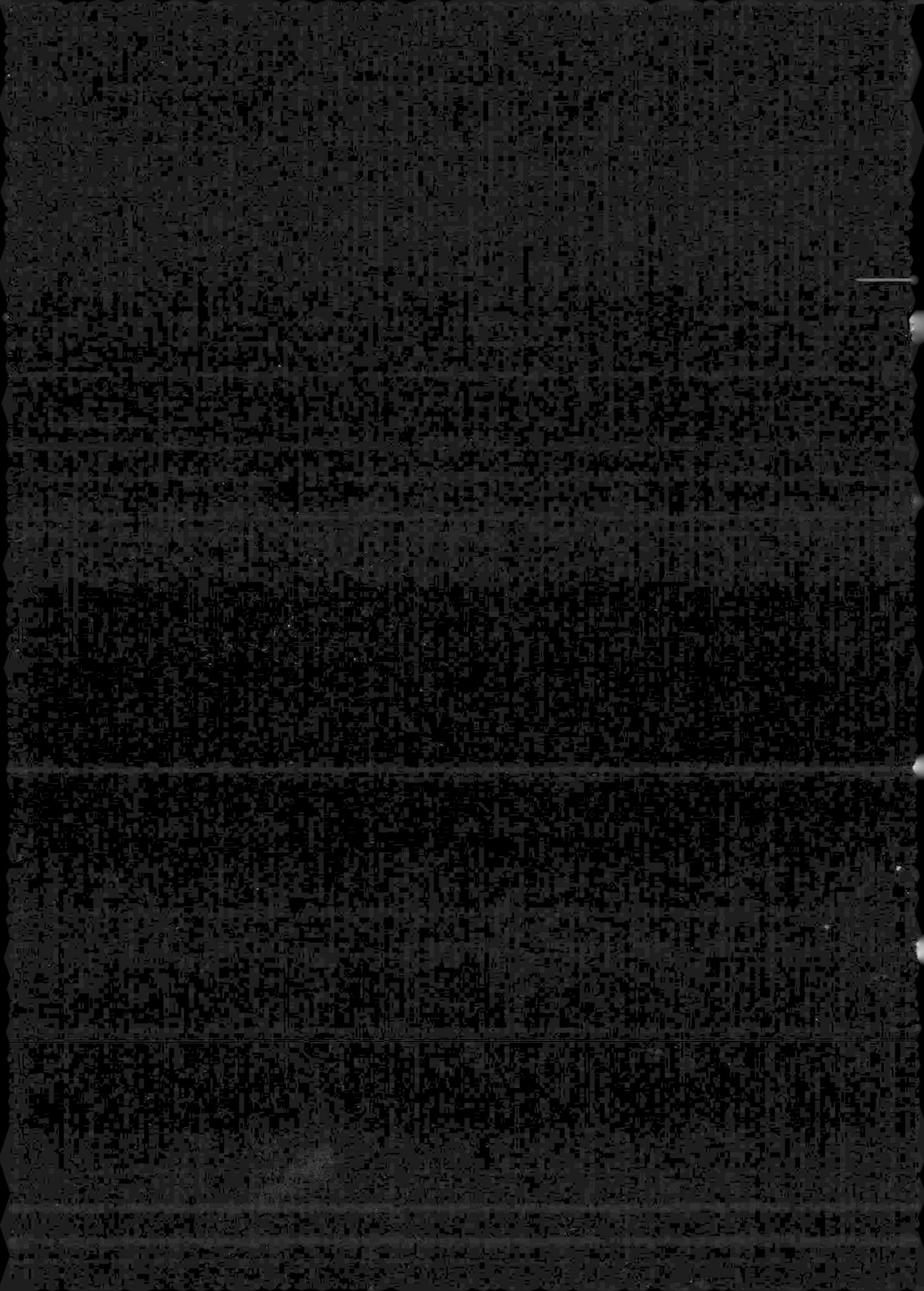

1001 PEOPLE WHO MADE AMERICA

BY ALAN AXELROD

NATIONAL GEOGRAPHIC
WASHINGTON, DC

For Anita and Ian

Preface

History as a succession of events is at most only half-history. The rest is all about the people behind the events. The English essayist and historian Thomas Carlyle understood this, writing back in 1840. "For, as I take it," he declared, ". . . History . . . is at bottom the History of the Great Men who have worked here."

Change "men" to "men and women," and we've almost got it right. But that still leaves the troublesome word *great.*

There are a handful of American men and women just about everyone would agree deserve to be called great—but probably not a thousand, let alone a thousand and one. Among the people who made Amcrica, some were great, some were good, others just lucky, and some downright bad, mistaken, unfortunate, and even evil. But they all merit inclusion in this book because what they did, what they made, what they thought—and what they caused others to do, make, or think—shaped our nation and who we are today.

The makers of America include the roster of notables any schoolteacher would recognize—Jefferson, Lincoln, and the like—but they also take in figures from our cultural and pop-cultural life, from the underworld of crime, from the struggle for civil and minority rights, from politics, business, sports, entertainment, literature, and art. They range from Jesse James to Al Capone, Harriet Beecher Stowe to Betty Friedan, Harriet Tubman to Martin Luther King, Jr., George Washington to George W., John Jacob Astor to Bill Gates, John L. Sullivan to Muhammad Ali, Stephen Foster to Elvis Presley, Edwin Booth to Marlon Brando, Washington Irving to Thomas Pynchon, Gilbert Stuart to Andy Warhol. Also among those nominated are the land's most consequential record breakers, including the best, the worst, the greatest, and even the meanest.

This book is arranged alphabetically rather than chronologically, but, in terms of chronology, you should know that we begin long before there was a United States or even a place called America. The first figure on our time line is Bjarni Herjulfsson, the first European to lay eyes on the New World, back in 986. He was not an American—How could he have been?—but, because he was the first to see America, he had had an impact on our part of the world, so he deserves a place in these pages. And that brings us to another criterion for inclusion. You don't have to be an American to have had a hand in making America. So readers will find a good many outsiders here—explorers, mostly—whose doings were somehow very important to who we are. And being dead is no necessary for inclusion, either. Readers will find in this book plenty of people who, as of 2006, were very much with us.

Yet I still haven't really answered a question readers have a right to ask. How did I happen to choose each of the 1,001 people in this book?

First, by reading a lot of history. That has given me a good idea of who's who and who was who in the American story. The majority of people in this book are the people a majority of historians think should be in such a book as this. That is, they are here by consensus.

Now, consensus is a valuable tool of knowledge, but, taken alone, it is pretty dull. So I have also looked beyond it to include some people who speak directly to me, who seem to me—as an American—important to America. My hunch is that a lot of readers will agree with my choices, but, even if they don't, they'll find value in arguing with me about them.

So much for content. Here are two points concerning form.

First: 1,001 people in a book the size of your hand leaves precious little space to spend much time with any one person. For each figure profiled, I've tried to nail the essence in under a hundred words: who, what, when, and how—then on to the next.

Second: The alphabet can be an awful tyrant. A to Z, after all, is always A to Z. But that doesn't mean the reader has to knuckle under, starting with A and not stopping till Z. Go backwards or sideways, if you like. You cannot lose your way. This book is the collective biography of America. It's meant to be stimulating, entertaining, and revealing from all points of view and at any angle. Dig in where you will.

Abbey, Edward (1927–1989) Novelist, journalist, lecturer, and university professor "Cactus Ed" Abbey wrote about the American West and the environmental problems created by human exploitation of the region. Abbey often called for radical methods to remedy environmental ills. His 1975 novel *The Monkey Wrench Gang,* about a group of environmental vigilantes, inspired the founding of the Earth First! organization.

Abernathy, Ralph David (1926–1990) A close associate of Martin Luther King, Jr., Abernathy was a key activist in the Montgomery Bus Boycott of 1955–1956, which began when Rosa Parks refused to yield to a city ordinance segregating public transportation. After King's assassination in 1968, Abernathy became leader of the Southern Christian Leadership Conference (SCLC) and carried on the fight for racial equality.

Acheson, Dean (1893–1971) A brilliant graduate of Yale and of Harvard Law School and private secretary to Supreme Court Justice Louis Brandeis, Acheson, as undersecretary of state from 1945 to 1947, persuaded the Senate to approve U.S. membership in the newly created United Nations. He was the dominant force in shaping the Cold War policy dubbed in 1947 the "Truman Doctrine," which pledged economic and military assistance to any nation fighting the expansion of Communism. With Secretary of State George C. Marshall, Acheson formulated and promoted the Marshall Plan, for the post World War II relief and rebuilding of Europe.

Adams, Abigail (1774–1818) Married to John Adams on October 25, 1764, Abigail advised her husband, supported the Revolution of which he was a prime architect, and took on the solo management of the family farm and Adams's business affairs, not only preserving but increasing the family fortune. As her husband began work with Jefferson on the Declaration of Independence, Abigail asked him to "remember the ladies and be more generous and favourable to them than your ancestors."

Adams, Ansel (1902–1984) This photographer's meticulously crafted large-format photographic landscapes of the American West—especially of the nation's great National Parks—awakened in many Americans both a love for the photographic art and the wild beauty of the continent's natural environment.

Adams, Henry (1838–1918) Great grandson of John Adams, Henry Adams was a journalist, historian, novelist, and educator whose 1906 autobiography, *The Education of Henry Adams*, presented himself as the typical man of the dawning 20th century, struggling to move from a world defined by faith and custom into one both shaped and torn by science and technology, a world in which absolute certainty has yielded to relativism and doubt. The book is one of the great spiritual and intellectual testaments of American literature.

Adams, John (1735–1826) The son of a shoemaker and farmer, Adams became a highly successful lawyer in Massachusetts and was among the first great champions of American independence. He was a leading member of the Continental Congress (1774–1777), author of his state's constitution (1780), signer of the Treaty of Paris ending the American Revolution (1783), first American ambassador to Britain (1785–88), vice president under George Washington

(1789–97), and the nation's second president (1797–1801). A radical in the Revolution, Adams was a conservative force after it.

Adams, John Quincy (1767–1848) Son of John Adams, J. Q. Adams was a formidable diplomat who, as secretary of state under President James Monroe, formulated the Monroe Doctrine, by which the president served notice on all European powers that any attempt to colonize or interfere with any state in the Western Hemisphere would be treated as an attack on the United States. As a president, Adams was a visionary, who proposed creating a national university and a national astronomical observatory, creating a federal trust for the western territories, and using federal funds to build national roads. Unique among U.S. presidents, Adams went on to serve in the House of Representatives from 1831 until his death, taking a strong stand against slavery.

Adams, Samuel (1722–1803) Bostonian Sam Adams inherited a one-third interest in his father's prosperous brewery and ran into the ground. Although incapable of managing money, Adams was highly skilled at politics, founding the Sons of Liberty, most influential and radical of Boston's many political clubs. In 1765, Adams organized Massachusetts opposition to the oppressive Stamp Act, thereby sowing the seeds of revolution. After 1770, Adams was chief architect of intercolonial "committees of correspondence," which coordinated the developing revolution, and in 1773, was the prime instigator of the Boston Tea Party. Adams helped mastermind the 1781 Articles of Confederation, precursor of the Constitution.

Addams, Jane (1860–1935) In 1889, Jane Addams and her friend Ellen Starr founded Hull House in the immigrant slums of

Chicago. This institution offered hot meals, child care services, tutoring in English, and many classes in vocational and other subjects—all with the goal of tending to the physical and intellectual needs of the community as well as creating a community in which residents themselves worked together to improve their lives. In 1931, Addams became the first American woman to receive the Nobel Peace Prize. She also worked vigorously for labor laws to protect children and women and was a founding member of the National Association for the Advancement of Colored People (NAACP) and the American Civil Liberties Union (ACLU).

Adler, Dankmar (1844–1900) Adler immigrated to the United States from Prussia in 1854 and settled in Detroit, where he began his study of architecture in 1857. He then moved to Chicago, worked as a draftsman, and, in 1881, partnered with Louis Sullivan to create the most famous and influential firm in American architecture, which, among other things, brought the skyscraper to prominence as the great characteristic American building style.

Adonis, Joe (1902–1972) Born Giuseppe Antonio Doto in Naples, this supremely vain Mafioso took the name Joe Adonis when he rose to power in the New York gangs. Finally brought before the Senate's Kefauver crime committee, he became the poster boy of American organized crime and was deported to Italy on January 3, 1956, where he settled into a lavish Neapolitan villa—until Italian police picked him up for questioning in 1972. He died in their custody of (according to them) a heart attack.

Agassiz, Jean Louis Rodolphe (1807–1873) Swiss-born Agassiz immigrated to the United States in 1846 and became professor of natural history at the Lawrence Scientific School of Harvard University. One of the great scientists of the 19th century, Agassiz established a museum of comparative zoology at Harvard and opened the field of ecology to generations of scientists. His teaching method, radical in its day, emphasized personal contact with nature rather than instruction from books and lectures.

Agnew, Spiro T. (1918–1996) The son of Greek immigrants, Agnew became governor of Maryland in 1967, then accepted nomination for the vice presidency in 1968, earning wide public recognition for his alliterative speeches denouncing anti-Vietnam War protesters and other opponents of the Nixon administration as "nattering nabobs of negativism" and "hopeless, hysterical hypochondriacs of history." In 1973, he was accused of extortion, bribery, and income-tax evasion while governor of Maryland. He resigned as vice president on October 10, 1973, pleaded no contest to a tax charge, paid a $10,000 fine and "served" three years of unsupervised probation.

Albright, Madeleine (1937–) With her family, Albright fled her native Czechoslovakia after the Nazi occupation (she learned late in life that her family was Jewish) and earned degrees from Wellesley College and Columbia University (M.A. and Ph.D). President Bill Clinton appointed her ambassador to the United Nations in 1993, then secretary of state in 1997.

Alcott, Amos Bronson (1799–1888) Innovative educator, vegetarian, abolitionist, and advocate of women's rights, Alcott developed with Ralph Waldo Emerson the Transcendentalist school of philosophy, which sought to penetrate to higher spiritual truths by the close study of the natural world. This philosophy profoundly influenced American literature and art throughout most of the 19th century.

Alcott, Louisa May (1832–1888) Second daughter of the Transcendentalist philosopher Amos Bronson Alcott, Louisa May Alcott realized that her highly spiritual but totally impractical father was bringing the family to financial ruin; she therefore embarked on a career as a an author of books for young people, producing a string of hits, including *Little Women* (1868–1869), about the coming of age of four daughters during the era of the Civil War. Frail and overworked, Alcott died just two days after her father.

Alger, Horatio (1832–1899) The son of a Unitarian minister, Alger graduated with Phi Beta Kappa honors from Harvard in 1852 and enrolled in Harvard Divinity School. He preached until 1866, when he was forced out of his Brewster (Massachusetts) pulpit by charges of sexual misconduct with local boys. Alger fled to New York City and began writing books about desperately poor lads who, by virtue of hard work and courage—"pluck and luck"—rise to great wealth. During three decades, he wrote more than 100 enormously successful rags-to-riches novels purveying the profoundly influential mythology of anything-is-possible in America.

Ali, Muhammed (1942–) One of the greatest athletes in history, Ali was three-time world heavyweight boxing champion. He was also a compelling champion of civil rights, a protester against the Vietnam War, and a dedicated member of the Black Muslims (Nation of Islam). He was born and raised in Louisville, Kentucky, where he was encouraged by a local white police officer, Joe Martin, to train at a neighborhood gym. Clay went on to win an Olympic gold medal at age eighteen (which he later renounced in protest over racism in the United States) and went on to a spectacular professional career. Influenced by Malcolm X, he converted to Islam (as a "Black Muslim") and stirred controversy by adopting a Muslim name, Muhammad Ali. In 1966, during the Vietnam War, he refused to accept conscription in the U.S. Army and was stripped of his heavyweight title. His many supporters saw this as a bold act of civil disobedience.

Allen, Ethan (1738–1789) This rambunctious Vermonter fought in the French and Indian War, then raised a local militia called the Green Mountain Boys (1770), which he led in the capture of British Fort Ticonderoga, New York (May 10, 1775) during the revolution. A subsequent attempt to take Montreal (September 1775) failed miserably.

Altgeld, John Peter (1847–1902) As Democratic governor of Illinois (1893–1897), Altgeld reformed the state's penal system and promoted strict child labor laws, but when he courageously pardoned (June 26, 1893) German-American anarchists unjustly condemned to death for involvement in Chicago's Haymarket Riot of May 4, 1886 (in which seven Chicago policemen were killed), he destroyed his political career. Out of office, he returned to the private practice of law with his partner, Clarence Darrow.

Ames, Oakes (1804–1873) At 16, Ames took over his family's modest shovel-manufacturing business and transformed it into a multimillion-dollar business triumph, for which he became nationally known as the "Ace of Spades." Anxious to complete the floundering transcontinental railroad, Abraham

Lincoln asked Ames to oversee financing the massive project. The result was the founding of Crédit Moblier, whose investors essentially paid themselves to build the railroad at inflated prices. The Union Pacific-Central Pacific got built, but the Crédit Moblier scandal destroyed Ames's reputation.

Anastasia, Alberto (1902–1957) Emigrating from Italy in 1919, Anastasia became the chief executioner of the Giuseppe Masseria gang, then founded "Murder, Inc.," an underworld murder-for-hire enterprise. By the late 1940s he was boss of one of New York's infamous Five Families of organized crime—until he himself was gunned down in a barber's chair at the city's Park Sheraton Hotel.

Anderson, "Bloody Bill" (1840–1864) After one of his sisters was killed and another crippled in the collapse of the Kansas City jail in which Union forces held them, Anderson (and 100 men under his command) joined William C. Quantrill's Confederate raiders in rampaging through Kansas. His most infamous deed was the brutal murder in Centralia, Missouri, of 24 unarmed Union soldiers. When 150 Union cavalrymen gave chase, Anderson and his gang ambushed them, killing and scalping 116, then cutting off noses and ears as souvenirs.

Anderson, Marion (1897–1993) Born in Philadelphia, Marion Anderson earned fame in the black community as a church singer. She went on to study classical voice, and performed in opera houses and concert hall throughout Europe, only to be turned down in 1939 by the Daughters of the American Revolution (DAR) when she sought to perform at Washington, D.C.'s DAR-owned Constitution Hall. Eleanor Roosevelt promptly resigned from the DAR, and persuaded Secretary of the Interior Harold Ickes to arrange a free outdoor concert at the Lincoln Memorial. Anderson performed on Easter Sunday to an audience of 75,000.

Anthony, Susan B. (1820–1906) Born into a politically and socially progressive Quaker family, Anthony became deeply committed to the abolition movement before the Civil War. She was also active in the temperance movement and, after meeting Amelia Bloomer and Elizabeth Cady Stanton, in the cause of women's suffrage as well. Rebuffed in 1852 when she attempted to speak at a male-dominated temperance meeting in Albany, she immediately organized a rival Woman's New York State Temperance Society and used the organization to campaign for women's rights.

Armour, Philip (1832–1901) A Chicago meat packer, Armour innovated mass slaughtering and butchering techniques, recycled waste products, perfected the canning of meat, and pioneered the use of refrigerated transportation—even exporting meat to Europe. He used his enormous profits for philanthropy, founding in Chicago the Armour Mission and the Armour Institute of Technology, later called the Illinois Institute of Technology.

Armstrong, Louis (1901–1971) Born poor in New Orleans, trumpeter and vocalist Armstrong was one of the jazz pioneers who brought the music up North—and to the world at large. He transformed jazz from band music to a popular art form suited to intense and exuberant solo expression.

Armstrong, Neil (1930–) Ohio-born Armstrong got his pilot's license at age 16 and went on to become a naval aviator with an academic background in aeronautical engineering.

He flew in the Korean War (earning three Air Medals) and in 1962 joined the U.S. space program. On July 16, 1969, Armstrong (with Edwin E. "Buzz" Aldrin, Jr., and Michael Collins) ascended in Apollo 11 and, four days later, at 4:18 p.m. (EDT), Armstrong piloted the lunar landing module *Eagle* to the moon's surface. At 10:56 p.m. (EDT), July 20, 1969, he descended *Eagle*'s ladder, planted his foot in the lunar dust, and broadcasted: "That's one small step for [a] man, one giant leap for mankind."

Arnold, Benedict (1741–1801) Born in Norwich, Connecticut, Benedict Arnold served as a teenager in the French and Indian War (1754–1763) and, during the American Revolution (1775–1783), compiled a brilliant combat record, but became embittered when he was passed over for promotion. In 1779, he married Margaret Shippen, the daughter of a prominent Philadelphia Loyalist. Accustomed to affluence, his bride encouraged Arnold to spend freely, and he was soon buried in debt. Arnold saw the British as a means of gaining both military promotion and ready cash. He offered them the plans of Patriot fortifications at West Point, New York. After his treachery was discovered, Arnold was commissioned a brigadier general in the British army and caused havoc in Virginia and his native Connecticut.

Astaire, Fred (1899–1987) Born Frederick Austerlitz in Omaha, Nebraska, Astaire started dancing in vaudeville at age four, then teamed with his sister, Adele. He made a screen test for MGM in 1932, eliciting from studio head Louis B. Meyer the comment, "Can't act, can't sing. Balding. Can dance a little." Despite this, he was cast in *Dancing Lady* (1933) then was teamed with Ginger Rogers in RKO's *Flying Down to Rio*. The picture launched his cinematic dancing career, which extended into the late 1950s and featured a uniquely elegant tap style in which Astaire seemingly danced on air.

Astor, John Jacob (1763–1848) Born in Waldorf, Germany, Astor opened a fur shop in New York City in 1786, having "learned" the fur trade at sea, on the ship that brought him to America. A boldly energetic entrepreneur, he sent fur traders to the far corners of the North American continent, creating the American Fur Company—the nation's first business monopoly—in the process amassing a great fortune (which financed the building of much of early 19th-century New York City) and motivating the exploration and initial settlement of the Far West.

Attucks, Crispus (1723?–1770) Almost nothing is known about the life of Crispus Attucks, except that he was a black man (perhaps partly Natick Indian) and very likely had been a fugitive from slavery since 1750. In 1770, he became the first of five Americans killed (three died instantly, two died later of their wounds) in the confrontation between British soldiers and Bostonians known as the "Boston Massacre" of March 5, 1770. This fugitive slave is generally counted as the first to fall in the cause of liberty.

Audubon, John James (1785–1851) Audubon was born in Santo Domingo (modern Haiti) and lived for a time in France before he immigrated to the United States in 1803. He pursued various business ventures in the States, but his true passion was studying, drawing, and painting birds. His masterwork, *The Birds of America*, based on firsthand exploration and observation, was published between 1827 and 1838 with an extraordinary five-volume text titled

Ornithological Biography accompanying it. His work is treasured by scientists as well as lovers of art and birds, and he was one of the first Americans to receive international acclaim for cultural and scientific achievements.

Austin, Stephen F. (1793–1836) In 1821, Moses Austin (1767–1821) secured a land grant from Mexico to establish a colony in the Mexican state of Texas. He died before the project began, and it was his son, Stephen, who founded in 1822 a colony of several hundred families on the Brazos River. This became the core of the American settlement of Texas, which resulted ultimately in the colony's war for independence (1836) and the United States-Mexico War (1846–1848).

Bacon, Nathaniel (1647–1676) Bacon, a Virginia planter who advocated unlimited territorial expansion of the colony, led what some have labeled the "first American revolution," an unauthorized military expedition against the Indians in 1676. When Governor William Berkeley opposed him on the grounds that it would trigger a major Indian war, Berkeley rose against him and the Virginia House of Burgesses. He attracted a substantial popular following, but succumbed to disease at the very height of the rebellion, causing the movement to collapse.

Baez, Joan (1941–) The daughter of a physicist, Baez was at the forefront of the "folk revival" of the 1960s, capturing a new, youthful audience for traditional American music. Through this music, she protested racial injustice and the Vietnam War. Baez was in the vanguard of "hippie" culture.

Baker, Josephine (1906–1975) After growing up fatherless and poor in St. Louis, Baker toured with a Philadelphia dance troupe at age 16, then broke into Broadway. She went to Paris in 1925 and created a sensation with her "*danse sauvage.*" Becoming a French citizen in 1937, she worked with the resistance and Red Cross during World War II and also entertained Allied troops. After the war, Baker adopted babies of various nationalities to create what she called a "rainbow tribe . . . an experiment in brotherhood."

Bakker, Jim (1941–) Jim Bakker was born James Orson in Muskegon, Michigan, and took the last name of his wife and partner Tammy Faye Bakker when he began his rise as a preacher and evangelist. He founded the PTL (Praise the Lord) Club, which grew into an internationally popular and influential television ministry, and Bakker became famous as a "televangelist." In 1989, he was convicted on 24 counts of fraud and conspiracy for bilking hundreds of thousands of contributors of millions of dollars. Released from prison in 1994, he started a new television show in 2003.

Baldwin, James (1924–1987) Born into poverty in Harlem, Baldwin became a revivalist preacher at age 14, graduated from high school, and embarked on a period of self-education that led to his first novel, the autobiographical *Go Tell it on the Mountain* (1953), the first of many eloquently incisive works dealing with race in America. Baldwin emerged not only as a major literary talent, but a stirring voice in the Civil Rights movement.

Ball, Lucille (1911–1989) Lucille Ball started her career in film, but truly entered the American consciousness in 1951 as the screwball wife of a nightclub bandleader on *I Love Lucy.* From 1951 to 1955—the original run of the show—*I Love Lucy* commanded two-thirds of America's televiewers.

Baltimore, George Calvert, First Baron (1578/79–1632) Persecuted as a Catholic in England, Baron Baltimore was also spurned in the new American colony of Virginia, so petitioned King Charles I for a grant on Chesapeake Bay, where he could found a refuge for Catholics. He pleaded his case eloquently, but died before the grant was made. It was left to his son actually to found the colony—an important early step in what would become an American tradition of religious freedom.

Bari, Judi (1949–1997) A long-time political and social activist, Bari began working as a carpenter in Northern California. While building luxury homes with old-growth redwood, she became concerned about the future of the redwood forest and joined the radical environmentalist organization Earth First! She enlisted the aid of the loggers themselves to stop reckless and rapacious logging practices and organized a mass non-violent protest called Redwood Summer, which resulted in the preservation of Headwaters Forest, the last unprotected redwood wilderness in California and prompted many logging companies to end the practice of redwood clearcutting.

Barnum, Phineas T. (1810–1891) Just 15 when his father died, P. T. Barnum had to support his mother and five siblings. He started publishing a newspaper in Danbury, Connecticut, and was arrested for libel three times. To him, this proved the potential profitability of sensationalism and in 1834, having moved to New York, he earned notoriety—and cash—presenting one Joice Heth, an elderly black woman, as the 161-year-old nurse to George Washington. This exhibition evolved into such attractions as the Barnum Museum, spectacular concerts, and, of course, a three-ring circus in partnership with

James A. Bailey. The Barnum and Bailey Circus was billed, characteristically, as the "Greatest Show on Earth."

Barton, Clara (1821–1912) Born in North Oxford, Massachusetts, Clara Barton discovered her life's work when, beginning at age 11, she nursed her brother through a two-year convalescence from injuries sustained in a bad fall. During the Civil War, she persuaded the military establishment to allow her to work as a battlefield nurse. The soldiers called her the "Angel of the battlefield." In 1870, while touring Europe, Barton became involved in the International Red Cross movement and, on her return to the United States in 1873, worked toward creating an American Red Cross, which she founded in 1877.

Bartram, William (1699–1777) A self-educated naturalist, Bartram counted Benjamin Franklin among his best friends and earned an appointment as royal botanist for the American colonies. His pioneering work included scientific expeditions into the Alleghenies, Carolinas, and other areas of the continent, and he was the first American to hybridize flowering plants, creating near Philadelphia an internationally renowned botanical garden. Bartram's son, also named William, often accompanied his father and published in 1791 *Travels*, a masterpiece of literate scientific writing.

Baruch, Bernard (1870–1965) Starting out as a Wall Street office boy, Baruch became wealthy as a stock market speculator and was appointed chairman of the War Industries Board by President Woodrow Wilson during World War I. After the victory, he served as Wilson's top adviser in negotiating the Treaty of Versailles. Baruch later served President Franklin Roosevelt as an adviser during World War II and was instrumental after that war in formulating United Nations policy regarding the control of atomic energy.

Beamer, Todd (1968–2001) A New Jersey resident who worked for the Oracle software company, Todd Beamer was one of 37 passengers aboard United Airlines Flight 93 out of Newark and bound for San Francisco. When Islamic extremists hijacked the airliner as part of a cluster of suicide attacks in which hijacked planes were crashed into New York's World Trade Center and the Pentagon, Beamer and other passengers fought back, attempting to wrest control of the airplane from the terrorists. Over an open cell phone connection, Beamer was heard to say "Let's roll," apparently as a signal to the other passengers. The phrase became a verbal icon of heroic resistance on this day. Beamer, the other passengers and crew, as well as the hijackers were killed when Flight 93 crashed in rural Pennsylvania.

Beard, Charles A., and Mary R. (1874–1948; 1876–1958) The Beards met and married as college students and, both together and separately, wrote groundbreaking works of American history and social history, including the coauthored *Rise of American Civilization* (1927), perhaps the most influential work of American history published in the 20th century. Both of the Beards were lifelong activists for liberal social causes, and Mary Beard was a pioneering scholar of women's history.

Beecher, Catharine (1800–1878) Eldest daughter of revivalist preacher Lyman Beecher, Catharine Beecher worked to advance the cause of public education in America and to define and establish the role of women in American society. Although she was a fierce advocate of equal rights for women, her most influential book, *A Treatise on Domestic Economy* (1841), was an effort to define and standardize homemaking practices and to exalt domestic values, founded on the proposition that a woman's place is in the home—the arena from which she could most profoundly influence American society.

Beecher, Henry Ward (1813–1887) The eighth of the thirteen children of revivalist preacher Lyman Beecher, Henry Ward Beecher earned national renown for his oratorical eloquence and his enlightened, even scientific approach to religion and society, which included advocacy of woman suffrage, the theory of evolution, and scientifically based analysis and criticism of the Bible.

Belasco, David (1853–1931) Either as playwright or producer, David Belasco was associated with no fewer than 347 plays. The vast majority were undistinguished as literature, but were great commercial successes. The association of his name with an actor or a play guaranteed a full house. He innovated production techniques, emphasizing sensational realism, lavish production values, and special effects (mostly with lighting). Routinely transforming unknown actors into stars, Belasco pioneered American show business as truly Big Business.

Bell, Alexander Graham (1847–1922) Born in Edinburgh, Scotland, Bell immigrated to Canada and then to the United States, where he worked on developing and popularizing his father's innovations in teaching the deaf and mute to speak. Bell was well established as a pioneering audiologist when he began working on a means of transmitting sound by electricity. The result in 1876 was the telephone, patented on March 7, 1876. Bell prevailed through a blizzard of patent suits, became wealthy (as principal stockholder of the Bell

Telephone Company), then continued upon a life of invention, creating the photophone (which transmitted sound via light), conducting medical research, continuing to innovate techniques for teaching speech to the deaf, improving Edison's phonograph, experimenting with flight, developing the principles of sonar detection, and creating a hydrofoil craft that set a 70-mile-per-hour speed record in 1919.

Bellamy, Edward (1850–1898) Son of a Baptist minister, Bellamy was strongly moved by social inequality and the plight of the poor. In 1888, he published *Looking Backward*, a novel set in Boston in the year 2000 that depicted America under a utopian socialism built on cooperation, brotherhood, and industry suited to human need. The book was a million-selling bestseller and catapulted Bellamy to international celebrity. Visionary and often naïve, his utopianism had a powerful effect on late 19th-century reform and Progressive politics.

Bellow, Saul (1915–2005) Born in Quebec of Russian-Jewish émigré parents, Bellow was raised in the poor neighborhoods of Montreal and Chicago and began to write realistic, darkly comic novels in which characters struggle to find purpose and ethical stability in a world alternately indifferent and entangling. Bellow was awarded the Nobel Prize for Literature in 1976 and was a distinguished university professor.

Benjamin, Judah (1811–1884) Born in St. Croix, Judah was taken to Charleston, South Carolina, in his early youth and became an American citizen. He practiced law and became the first professing Jew elected to the U.S. Senate in 1852 (he was reelected 1858). An advocate of slavery, he left the Senate when South Carolina seceded from the Union and was named attorney general in the Confederate government, then secretary of war, and, finally, secretary of state (February 7, 1862). He fled to England after the Civil War, set up a law practice there, and in 1872 rose to become a queen's counsel.

Bennett, James Gordon (1795–1872) Born in Scotland, Bennett immigrated to American in 1819, taught school, then worked as a journalist. On May 6, 1835, he founded *The New York Herald*, printing it in a cellar. He was aggressive in gathering news, which ranged from the first Wall Street financial article ever printed (June 13, 1835) to sensational reports of fires, murders, and war. He developed many of the techniques of modern reporting, and he was the first newspaper publisher to make extensive use of the telegraph. He illustrated his paper extensively and even included a society page.

Benton, Thomas Hart (1889–1975) Missouri-born Benton was the son of a famous Congressman. He did newspaper cartooning as a young man, then studied serious art in Europe and at the Art Institute of Chicago. Turning his back on the prevailing Modernist styles, he traveled through the rural South and Midwest, capturing people and landscapes and emerging as the foremost of the Regionalists, who transformed the humble American scene into memorable art.

Berle, Milton (1908–2002) Born Milton Berlinger in New York, Berle earned his living as a vaudevillian, movie actor (in silent films and talkies), nightclub comic, and marginally successful radio comedian until he was tapped in 1948 to host the *Texaco Star Theatre* on the fledgling medium of television. Berle proved to be a comic sensation, perfectly suited to "the tube" and so popular that his presence drove sales of television sets and was instrumental in establishing the medium. He was justly dubbed "Mr. Television."

Berlin, Irving (1888–1989) Born Israel Baline in a part of Russia that is now Belarus, Berlin was the son of a Jewish cantor, who immigrated with his family to New York in 1893. Berlin worked as a street singer after his father died in 1896 and wrote his first song in 1907. Despite a lack of formal musical education, Berlin emerged as a leader in the creation of the American popular song and the Broadway musical. He is widely considered the greatest of American popular songwriters.

Bernays, Edward L. (1891–1995) Born in Vienna—a nephew of Sigmund Freud—Bernays came to the United States when he was a year old, earned a degree in agriculture, became the editor of a medical journal, tried his hand at producing plays, then went on to create the great American public relations industry by harnessing psychology and other social sciences to shape public opinion at the behest of various clients.

Bernstein, Carl (1944–) With Bob Woodward, Carl Bernstein made journalism history—and changed American history—with investigative reporting in the *Washington Post* of the Watergate break-in, which led directly to the resignation of President Richard M. Nixon in 1974. With Woodward, he also coauthored a book in Watergate, *All the President's Men* (1974), and an inside account of the collapse of the Nixon presidency, *The Final Days* (1976).

Bernstein, Leonard (1918–1990) Handsome and charismatic, Leonard Bernstein earned international fame as a conductor (especially of the New York Philharmonic from 1958 to 1969) and a composer, who achieved great success in musical theater (*On the Town, Wonderful Town, West Side Story*, and others) and in classical composition. Bernstein was also an accomplished pianist and an influential musical educator, host of a distinguished televised series of "Young People's Concerts," and the author of two important texts, *The Infinite Variety of Music* (1966) and *The Unanswered Question* (1976), taken from his 1973 Harvard lecture series.

Berrigan, Daniel (1921–) Inspired in part by his activist brother Philip (also a Catholic priest), Daniel Berrigan wrote poems and essays as a means of social protest against injustice and war (his was one of the most eloquent voices in protest of the Vietnam War during the 1960s and 1970s). He defined the role of the clergy in the struggle for social justice.

Berryman, John (1914–1972) Berryman had a distinguished career as a professor of English at Wayne State University, Harvard, Princeton, and the University of Minnesota while also developing a unique style of surreal confessional poetry into which he wove a profound understanding of American history and mythology. Some have called Berryman a 20th-century Walt Whitman.

Bethune, Mary McLeod (1875–1955) Born in Maysville, South Carolina, one of 17 children of former slaves, Bethune sought an education at the Maysville Presbyterian Mission School, the Scotia Seminary, and the Moody Bible Institute, then founded in 1904 the Daytona Normal and Industrial Institute for Negro Girls, which later became Bethune Cookman College. Bethune founded the National Association of Colored Women and during the administration of

President Franklin D. Roosevelt served as director of Negro Affairs in the National Youth Administration. Later, she was a consultant on interracial affairs and understanding at the conference that created the charter of the United Nations.

Beverley, Robert (c. 1673–1722) A Virginia plantation owner, Beverly wrote *The History and Present State of Virginia* in 1705 to promote the further settlement of his colony. The book is a minor literary masterpiece and was one of the first internationally popular works by an Amcrican author.

Bierstadt, Albert (1830–1902) Bierstadt was born in Düsseldorf, Germany, but made his career in America, earning international renown for his epic canvases depicting the wonders of the American West, including (most famously) *The Rocky Mountains* (1863). Based on sketches he made in the field, the works were painted in his New York studio, became icons of a romantic vision of western magnificence, and earned the artist a fortune.

Big Foot, Chief (ca. 1825–1890) Called by the Miniconjous Si Tanka (Spotted Elk) and known to whites as Big Foot, this chief was a diplomat who sought peace among the tribes and peace with whites. He was killed by Seventh Cavalry troopers at Wounded Knee, South Dakota, while on a mission to avert a final war between the whites and the Sioux.

Billings, William (1746–1800) A tanner by vocation, Billings was a self-taught musician and composer who wrote hymns, anthems, and psalms of great vitality. His tunes have become part of the American folk tradition, and he is generally considered America's first important composer.

Billy the Kid (1859/60–1881) Born Henry McCarty (or possibly William H. Bonney, Jr.) in the slums of New York City, Billy the Kid became an outlaw during the range wars of New Mexico and earned, even during his brief life, a legendary reputation as a gunfighter, credited by many sources with having killed 27 men before Sheriff Pat Garrett killed him in his twenty-first year.

Birdseye, Clarence (1886–1956) Trained as a naturalist, Birdseye became a fur trader in Labrador, working there in 1912 and 1916. He observed that many Labradoreans froze food during the winter as a way of preserving it. This inspired him to experiment with quick-freezing method, and in 1924, he became a founder of General Seafoods Company, marketing his first quick-frozen foods in 1929. Almost single-handedly, Birdseye created the frozen food industry.

Bishop, Hazel (1906–1998) Hazel Gladys Bishop graduated from Barnard College in 1929, did graduate work at Columbia University, and became a chemist in a dermatologic laboratory and then for two oil companies. Experimenting at home, she created in 1949 a novel long-lasting lipstick, which she advertised as "kiss-proof." This became the basis of Hazel Bishop, Inc., one of the best-known names in American cosmetics.

Black Hawk (1767–1838) Ma-ka-tai-me-she-kia-kiak—Black Hawk—was chief of the so-called "British Band" of the Sauk and Fox tribe of Illinois, Wisconsin, and Iowa. His resistance to white settlement of Indian land ceded to the government by a fraudulent 1804 treaty triggered the Black Hawk War of 1832, which resulted in the massacre of many of his followers.

Black, Hugo (1886–1971) As associate justice of the U.S. Supreme Court from 1937 to 1971, Black championed the Bill of Rights as an absolute guarantee of civil liberties. Equally important was his argument that the Fourteenth Amendment extended the authority of the Bill of Rights to state governments as well as the federal government, neither of which was to be allowed to impinge upon individual freedom.

Blackmun, Harry A. (1908–1999) Associate justice of the United States Supreme Court from 1970 to 1994, Blackmun earned his greatest fame as a jurist when he wrote the majority decision in *Roe v. Wade* (1973), declaring that a woman's right to abortion is guaranteed by the constitutional right to privacy. The decision unleashed decades of national controversy.

Blaine, James G. (1830–1893) Republican congressman and senator, Blaine was secretary of state under President James A. Garfield and, again, under Benjamin Harrison. In this post, he called for an inter-American conference to prevent wars in the Western Hemisphere. This became the Pan-American Conference, which Blaine chaired and which launched the Pan-American Movement—a set of alliances and reciprocity treaties between the United States and the countries of Latin-America.

Blake, Eubie (1883–1983) James Hubert "Eubie" Blake was born in Baltimore and earned fame as an African-American ragtime composer and performer. His longtime partnership with lyricist-singer Noble Sissle began in 1915 and produced a series of musicals, including the 1921 *Shuffle Along*, generally regarded as the first American musical written, produced, and directed by blacks. His most famous song is "I'm Just Wild About Harry."

Blackstone, Harry (1885–1965) Born Harry Bouton in Chicago, "The Great Blackstone" began his stage career as a teenage magician and became the most famous magician of his day, mentor to a generation of magicians.

Bloomer, Amelia (1818–1894) Bloomer was born Amelia Jenks in Homer, New York, and began publishing in 1849 *The Lily: A Ladies Journal Devoted to Temperance and Literature,* a newspaper for women believed the first to be edited entirely by a woman. By the early 1850s, Bloomer was among the best-known advocates of women's rights, but also championed reform of women's dress in the form of full-cut pantaloons under a short skirt. This article of clothing allowed greater freedom of movement. Originally called "Turkish trousers," the pantaloons became famous as "bloomers."

Boas, Franz (1858–1942) Boas was born and educated in Germany, but earned his greatest fame as professor of anthropology at Columbia University (New York City) from 1899 to 1942. During this period he developed the relativistic approach to anthropology, which focused non-judgmentally on the variety of human cultures, and which became the preeminent definition of the field. Boas taught a generation of great American anthropologists, including Margaret Mead.

Boesky, Ivan (1937–) Boesky rose to fame and wealth as an arbitrageur—essentially a stock trader who bet on the outcome of corporate takeovers. Boesky's tactics were characterized as brazen, and, as it turned out, were based on tips he received from corporate insiders, a form of "insider trading" in violation of federal law. His plea bargain in the mid 1980s became iconic of the era's corporate greed—and he himself earned additional notoriety for a 1986 speech at the

University of California, Berkeley, in which he proclaimed "I think greed is healthy. You can be greedy and still feel good about yourself."

Bogart, Humphrey (1899–1957) Son of a prominent New York physician, Bogart became a journeyman stage actor in the 1920s then found greatness as ruthless killer in the 1935 Sherwood Anderson play *The Petrified Forest.* This brought him film roles—typically playing gangsters—followed by two iconic starring turns, in *High Sierra* and *The Maltese Falcon* (both 1941). For many fans, his portrayal of Rick Blaine in *Casablanca* (1942) remains his masterpiece: the sensitive "tough guy" as altruistic hero.

Bok, Edward (1863–1930) Born in the Netherlands, Bok grew up poor in Brooklyn and rose to edit the *Ladies' Home Journal* from 1889 to 1919. In this position he wielded great moral and social influence, using the pages of the magazine to champion everything from woman suffrage to wildlife conservation. He refused advertising from the makers of ineffectual or harmful patent medicines, an action that spurred passage of the Pure Food and Drug Act.

Boone, Daniel (1734–1820) Boone was born in Pennsylvania but moved to the North Carolina frontier and made his living as a far-ranging hunter and trapper. Contrary to popular belief, he did not "discover" Kentucky, but he did explore and settle a part of it, blazing a trail through Cumberland Gap, thereby opening Kentucky and the rest of the trans-Appalachian West to widespread settlement. Always courageous, always resourceful, Boone fought in the French and Indian War as well as the Revolution, laid claim to vast tracts of wilderness, and earned legendary fame even during his lifetime—yet he failed financially and died in relative obscurity on the Missouri frontier.

Booth, Edwin (1833–1893) A member of America's most celebrated theatrical family, Edwin Booth rose to become the most acclaimed American actor of his day and was judged a tragedian equal to the finest English actors. His phenomenal success was dogged by drink and by the crime of his brother, John Wilkes Booth, who murdered Abraham Lincoln on April 14, 1865.

Booth, John Wilkes (1838–1865) No name is more infamous in American history than that of John Wilkes Booth, a matinee idol, whose sympathies with the Confederate cause in the Civil War prompted him to assassinate Abraham Lincoln on April 14, 1865. After shooting the president as he watched a performance at Washington's Ford's Theatre, Booth made his escape and remained at large for eleven days until, cornered in a Virginia tobacco barn, he was fatally shot.

Borden, Lizzie (1860–1927) The daughter of a successful Fall River (Massachusetts) businessman, Lizzie Borden lived with her father and stepmother. On August 4, 1892, the couple was found brutally murdered—bludgeoned and hacked, possibly by an axe. Lizzie (who had tried to purchase poison the day before the slayings) was indicted for both murders but acquitted (because of inadequate circumstantial evidence) after a trial that created an international sensation. Despite the verdict, most Americans believed her guilty, and she lived out her life as a pariah. Histories, novels, plays, and an opera have been written about Lizzie Borden, but the most famous "literary" product was a children's rhyme: "Lizzie Borden took an axe / And gave her mother forty whacks; / And when she saw what she had done / She gave her father forty-one."

Bork, Robert H. (1927–) A strict constructionist (believer that law should be guided by the framers' original understanding of the U.S. Constitution), Bork served as solicitor general in Richard M. Nixon's Department of Justice from 1972 to 1977. President Nixon elevated him to acting attorney general in 1973 after Attorney General Elliot Richardson and Deputy Attorney General William Ruckelshaus both resigned rather than obey Nixon's order to fire Watergate Special Prosecutor Archibald Cox after Cox demanded the president's tapes of Oval Office conversations. Bork obeyed the order and fired Cox in the infamous "Saturday Night Massacre," which hastened the president's downfall. In 1987, President Ronald Reagan nominated Bork to the Supreme Court. After an intensely heated debate, the Senate rejected his nomination.

Bourke-White, Margaret (1906–1971) White (she later added her mother's maiden name to make Bourke-White) turned her photographic hobby into a profession as an industrial photographer and then as a photojournalist working for *Fortune* and then for *Life.* She photographed extensively in Depression-era America and in Germany and the Soviet Union before World War II, then covered the bloody Italian campaign during the war. She accompanied Patton's Third Army into Germany and documented the horrors of the concentration camps. After World War II, she photographed Gandhi in India and served as a correspondent in the Korean War.

Bowie, Jim (1796?–1836) Born in Kentucky, Bowie became a Louisiana sugar planter and a New Orleans man-about-town.

Reportedly, he decided to move to Texas (then a Mexican possession) after killing a man in a duel. He became a Mexican citizen, obtained land grants from the Mexican government, then joined other American colonists in resisting Mexican attempts to curb the influx of American settlers. He joined the Texas independence movement and was co-commander (with Colonel William B. Travis) in the defense of the improvised fortress at the Alamo (in San Antonio) when it was overrun by forces under Mexican dictator Santa Anna on March 6, 1836. Bowie was slain with the other Alamo defenders and was immortalized in ballad, song, and (later) film and television portrayals. His name is also memorialized in the fearsome broad-bladed knife he (or his brother, Rezin) invented: the Bowie knife.

Bradbury, Ray (1920–) Beginning with his first published story in 1940, Bradbury used highly inventive science fiction as an instrument of social criticism. *The Martian Chronicles* (1950) is a science fiction classic that evokes an idyllic Martian civilization corrupted by greed-driven explorers and exploiters from Earth, while *Fahrenheit 451*(1953) depicts a society in which technology has displaced imagination, love, liberty, and free thought, and in which reading has become a capital crime and books objects fit solely for burning.

Braddock, James J. (1905–1974) After rising rapidly in a prizefighting career that began in 1926, Braddock lost a title bout in 1929, then, during the Great Depression, descended into poverty and obscurity, only to reemerge by defeating heavyweight champ Max Baer on June 13, 1935, capping a comeback so fast and so startling that sports writer Damon Runyon dubbed him the "Cinderella Man." Braddock was a hero to millions of hard-pressed men and women in

Depression-era America, who learned that you can be down without being out.

Bradford, William (1590–1657) As governor of the Massachusetts Plymouth colony for three decades, Bradford played a critical role in the colony's survival and early growth. His *History of Plymouth Plantation,* which covers the colony from its founding in 1620 to 1647, is a remarkable window into early American settlement and Puritan religious passion.

Bradley, Omar N. (1893–1981) Bradley commanded 12th Army Group in the European Theater during World War II, earning promotion to five-star rank and, because of his straightforward approach, disdaining ceremony and the trappings of lofty rank, earning from journalist Ernie Pyle the sobriquet of "The G.I. General." After the war, Bradley was named the first chairman of the U.S. Joint Chiefs of Staff (1949–1953).

Bradstreet, Anne (c. 1612–1672) Born Anne Dudley in England, she was 16 when she married Simon Bradstreet and, at 18, sailed with him (and other Puritans) to a new life on Massachusetts Bay. While bearing and raising eight children, Anne Bradstreet wrote some of the first English-language poems in North America. A number of these were first published (in England) in 1650 as *The Tenth Muse Lately Sprung Up in America,* but the very best—a series entitled *Contemplations*—remained unpublished until the 20th century.

Brady, Mathew (1823–1896) Brady opened a daguerreotype studio in New York City in 1844 and another in Washington, D.C., in 1848. In 1852, he opened a famous and successful gallery in New York, in 1852. The wealthy, powerful, and prominent came to Brady for portraits—which endure as valuable historical documents—but it is on the work of his staff of some twenty photographers during the Civil War that Brady's greatest fame rests.

Brandeis, Louis (1856–1941) As a young man, Brandeis earned a reputation as "the people's attorney," often fighting the interests of big finance and big business, especially trusts and monopolies. The reform-minded Woodrow Wilson appointed him to the Supreme Court in 1916—he was the first Jew to sit on the high court—and he embarked on a twenty-three-year career in which he steered a brilliant middle course between government authority and individual liberty.

Brando, Marlon (1924–2004) Born in Omaha, Brando moved to New York City in 1943 to study acting at the famed Dramatic Workshop of Stella Adler. Here he imbibed his first lessons in "the method," an approach to acting first developed by the Russian Konstantin Stanislavski, by which an actor learns actually to feel the emotions he wishes to portray. The following year he made a successful Broadway debut in *I Remember Mama,* then in 1947 gained national attention with his electrifying portrayal of Stanley Kowalski in Tennessee Williams's *A Streetcar Named Desire* and repeated his role on screen in 1951. From this point on, he was generally considered the most influential actor of his generation.

Brant, Joseph (1742–1807) Called Thayendanegea by the Mohawks, Brant was educated at Moor's Charity School for Indians in Lebanon, Connecticut, and converted to the Anglican church. Well versed in the English language and in history, he became an interpreter for an Anglican missionary and coauthored a Mohawk translation of *The Book of Common Prayer* and the Gospel of Mark. Believing that American independence would result in the usurpation of all Indian land, Brant fought on the side of the British during the American Revolution, visiting terror upon the New York frontier. After the war, however, he become an advocate for peace between whites and Indians and settled on a land grant in Canada.

Braun, Wernher von (1912–1977) In youth, Wernher von Braun became fascinated with rocketry and in the 1930s studied the subject under a grant from the German military. By the mid 1930s, Braun was directing rocket research for the German government and during World War II developed the V-2 long-range ballistic missile, which was used against London and other targets. After the war, Braun surrendered to U.S. troops, and despite his Nazi affiliations, was allowed to immigrate to the United States, where he became chief of the U.S. Army ballistic missile program. Later, he was named director of the NASA George C. Marshall Space Flight Center in Huntsville, Alabama. Braun directed much of the early U.S. space program, specializing in the development of booster systems, including the one that sent American astronauts to the moon.

Brice, Fanny (1891–1951) Brice was a lovably homely stage comedienne, who shot to fame as a result of her 1921 star turn in the Ziegfeld Follies, when she debuted the torch song "My Man." Her vaudeville, Broadway, and film career made her one of the most successful comediennes in American entertainment history, and her life was the subject of a hit 1964 musical, *Funny Girl,* which catapulted Barbra Streisand to stardom in the role of Brice.

Bridger, Jim (1804–1881) Bridger spent two decades, from 1822 through the early 1840s, tramping through the vast wilderness bounded by Canada, the Missouri River, the Colorado-New Mexico border, Idaho, and Utah, in search of new peltries (fur-trapping grounds). He was the first white man to see the Great Salt Lake (1824), and in 1843, he established Fort Bridger in southwestern Wyoming, which served as rendezvous for trappers and as a way station Oregon Trail "emigrants" bound for the far West.

Brooks, Gwendolyn (1917–2000) Born in Topeka, Kansas, Brooks grew up in Chicago's black ghetto and began publishing poetry in the 1930s in *The Chicago Defender,* a black newspaper. Her first book appeared in 1945. Brooks wrote about daily life in Chicago's black community and in 1949 became the first African-American poet to win the Pulitzer Prize. She was named poet laureate of Illinois in 1968.

Brooks, Van Wyck (1886–1963) Brooks was a prolific historian of American literature and culture, who created a sensation in 1908 with his first book, *The Wine of the Puritans,* which, instead of praising the Puritan forefathers, blamed them for stunting American culture. Taken together, his writings outline the history of American literature from its beginnings to his own day.

Brown, Charles Brockden (1771–1810) In his short life, Philadelphia-born Brown wrote six important early American novels—including two classics of "Gothic" fiction, *Wieland* and *Edgar Huntley*—and published and edited important early periodicals. His fiction shows profound psychological insight, which prefigured the great work of later American novelists such as Nathaniel Hawthorne and

Herman Melville, but he was perhaps even more important to the nation's literature and culture as the first American writer to earn a living solely from literary pursuits.

Brown, John (1800–1859) John Brown was active in the vicious guerrilla war between antislavery and proslavery settlers in Kansas. On May 24, 1856, he led a raid against a proslavery settlement at Pottawatomie Creek, in which five men were hacked to death with sabers. After this, he came east, and on October 16, 1859, raided the federal arsenal at Harpers Ferry, Virginia (now in West Virginia), intending to arm local slaves for an uprising he hoped would trigger a universal slave rebellion. A small force of U.S. Marines (led by army officer Robert E. Lee) attacked the raiders on the 17th, wounding Brown and killing two of his sons as well as eight other followers. Brown was tried for murder, inciting a slave insurrection, and treason. He was hanged on December 2, 1859. Abolitionists regarded him as a martyr, and the raid, trial, and punishment hastened the coming of the Civil War.

Brubeck, Dave (1920–) Brubeck started playing jazz in 1933, then studied with modern classical giants Darius Milhaud and Arnold Schoenberg. He combined his jazz background with his modernist training to produce "third-stream" jazz, combining elements of traditional jazz and African-rooted music with avant-garde classical techniques. Since the late 1940s, Brubeck has been one of the most influential and admired of American pianists and composers and is universally regarded as a jazz great.

Bryan, William Jennings (1860–1925) Nebraska's Bryan was thrice defeated for the presidency (1896, 1900, 1908), but was renowned as an electrifying orator who championed such Populist causes as the popular election of senators, the introduction of a graduated income tax, the creation of a Department of Labor, the institution of Prohibition, and the passage of woman suffrage. A great campaigner, he was perceived as a man of the people, especially in rural America, but was also feared by some as a demagogue. A religious man, he volunteered to assist the prosecution in the 1925 trial of schoolteacher John T. Scopes for having violated Tennessee law by teaching the theory of evolution. Although Scopes was convicted, Bryan was intellectually shredded by defense counsel Clarence Darrow, fell ill shortly after the trial, and died.

Brzezinski, Zbigniew (1928–) Born in Poland, Brzezinski was the son of a diplomat, who, posted to Canada on the eve of World War II, was unable to return to Poland. Brzezinski left Canada to study at Harvard and became a U.S. citizen in 1958. He taught political science at Harvard and Columbia, served as an adviser to presidential candidates John F. Kennedy and Lyndon B. Johnson, and was named National Security Advisor to President Jimmy Carter. A strong anti-Communist, Brzezinski played key roles in the ongoing normalization of relations with the People's Republic of China, the conclusion of the SALT II arms control treaty, the brokering of the Camp David Accords that brought peace between Israel and Egypt, the encouragement of democratic reform in Eastern Europe, and the elevation of human rights to prominence in U.S. foreign policy.

Buchanan, James (1791–1868) As U.S. president from 1857 to 1861, Buchanan drifted badly in a weak effort to find a compromise in the conflict between the North and the South.

His failure of leadership helped make the Civil War inevitable. Most historians rate him as one of the worst American presidents, if not the worst. He also has the distinction of being the only bachelor to serve in the White House.

Buffett, Warren (1930–) An extraordinary investor—founder of the Berkshire Hathaway investment firm—the Nebraska-based Buffett was long known as the "Oracle of Omaha" and amassed a personal fortune that made him the second wealthiest man in the world. In June 2006, Buffett became America's foremost philanthropist by announcing his intention to contribute some 10 million Berkshire Hathaway shares (worth about $30.7 billion) to the Bill and Melinda Gates Foundation. This, the largest single charitable gift in history, makes the Gates Foundation history's largest charitable organization.

Bunche, Ralph (1904–1971) After earning graduate degrees from Harvard University in 1928 and 1934, Bunche created the Howard University (Washington, D.C.) Department of Political Science. He served in the OSS (Office of Strategic Services) and Department of State during World War II, then was instrumental after the war in planning the United Nations, of which he eventually served as undersecretary general. In 1949, he mediated a truce in the first Arab-Israeli War, for which he was awarded the 1950 Nobel Peace Prize.

Burke, James (1925–) As CEO of Johnson & Johnson from 1976 to 1989, Harvard-educated Burke presided over a major period in his company's growth, but he entered into national prominence by his response to the Tylenol poisoning crisis of 1982. During September of that year, seven people in the Chicago area died after swallowing cyanide-laced Tylenol capsules. Instead of waiting for government authorities to take action, Burke ordered the removal of all Tylenol products from store shelves nationwide and even initiated a recall program to buy back Tylenol directly from consumers. Some 31 million bottles of medicine were thus recalled, representing about 100 million retail dollars. Burke's bold and selfless action saved lives and enabled Johnson & Johnson to restore public confidence in the product after introducing the tamper-resistant packaging that is now industry standard.

Burnham, Daniel (1846–1912) Working in Chicago after the great fire of 1871, Burnham not only designed much of the city's new commercial architecture, but pioneered the science of urban planning, providing for the city a comprehensive vision of development that had a profound impact on the American urban landscape well into the 20th century.

Burr, Aaron (1756–1836) Burr served on George Washington's staff during the American Revolution, but he was transferred after irritating the commander in chief. He became a prominent New York attorney, then entered politics, tying in 1800 with Thomas Jefferson in electoral votes for president. Thanks to Alexander Hamilton's determined opposition to Burr, Jefferson won and Burr (under the then-prevailing election laws) became vice president. In 1804, Hamilton again worked against Burr—this time depriving him of the governorship of New York—and Burr (still sitting as vice president) killed Hamilton in a duel. After warrants were issued for Burr's arrest, he fled to Philadelphia. He conspired with U.S Army general James Wilkinson to invade Mexico, establish an independent government there, and (possibly) foment the secession of the American West to join the empire they would found. Burr was arrested, tried for treason in

1807, acquitted, but publicly ruined. He fled to Europe, returned to New York four years later, practiced law, and wasted his fortune.

Burroughs, John (1837–1921) Burroughs combined science with the sensibility of a poet to produce 27 books on the flora and fauna of the Hudson River Valley. He was an important influence on the first great conservationist president, Theodore Roosevelt. A close friend of Walt Whitman, he wrote the first biography of the poet in 1867.

Bush, George H. W. (1924–) A naval aviator during World War II, successful businessman, Congressman, ambassador to the United Nations (appointed by Richard Nixon), director of the CIA, then vice president under Ronald Reagan, Bush defeated Democrat Michael Dukakis in 1988 to become president. Bush led a coalition of nations against Saddam Hussein's Iraq in the first Gulf War in 1990–1991. Despite a jump in his popularity after the quick victory in that war, Bush was defeated by Democrat Bill Clinton largely because of Bush's failure to reverse a slide in the American economy.

Bush, George W. (1946–) Son of President George H. W. Bush, George W. served as governor of Texas then eked out an electoral college victory (the contested outcome was decided by the Supreme Court) over Democrat Al Gore for the presidency in 2000. Bush's presidency was defined by the "War on Terror," which began with the horrific September 11, 2001, terrorist attacks on the World Trade Center in New York and the Pentagon. Bush quickly went to war against the Afghanistan-based terrorist organization called al-Qaeda and the Islamic fundamentalist Taliban government that supported it there. Far more controversially, he went to war (in 2003) against Iraq for the purpose of toppling the regime of Saddam Hussein. The Iraq War, together with the administration's response to Hurricane Katrina, which devastated New Orleans and the Gulf Coast in 2005, led many Americans, including some members of his own party, to question Bush's leadership and effectiveness.

Bush, Vannevar (1890–1974) An electrical engineer, Bush invented in 1931 the Differential Analyzer, an advanced electromechanical computer. When World War II began in Europe in 1939, Bush persuaded President Franklin D. Roosevelt to create the National Defense Research Committee (with Bush as chair) to organize defense-related scientific research. Bush next chaired the even more powerful Office of Scientific Research and Development, which oversaw development of radar and the atomic bomb, among many other war-related technologies. Vannevar Bush was arguably the most powerful scientist of his time.

Bushnell, David (1742–1824) A student at Yale College during 1771–1775, Bushnell demonstrated that gunpowder could be detonated underwater. This gave him the idea of building what he called a "water machine": the world's first combat submarine. A pear-shaped vessel made of oak and reinforced with iron bands, the *Turtle* (as witnesses dubbed it) was 7 1/2 feet long by 6 feet wide and was operated by a crew of one, who could submerge the vessel at will by pulling a hand-spring valve that flooded a compartment in the hull and then could surface again by operating a foot pump. The *Turtle* could place an explosive mine below the waterline on the hull of an enemy ship. The mine was timed to explode after the *Turtle* had retreated to safety. The Patriots used Bushnell's *Turtle* a few times in the American Revolution, but without success.

Byrd, William (1674–1744) William Byrd of Westover would be remembered (if at all) as just another colonial Virginia planter were it not for his diaries, which—with often bawdy wit—provide an intimate look at life on the southern British plantations. In addition to his principal diary, he kept an encrypted shorthand version, which reveals much about the nefarious romantic life of a southern planter. In 1728, he produced *History of the Dividing Line*, a remarkably biting satire recording his experience as a surveyor of the North Carolina–Virginia boundary.

Byrne, Jane (1934–) Jane Byrne was was appointed Chicago's head of consumer affairs by mayor Richard J. Daley in 1968. Fired in 1977 by Mayor Michael Bilandic (who had succeeded Daley upon his death), Byrne campaigned to unseat him and won election. She served from 1979 1983, when she was defeated in the Democratic primaries by Harold Washington, Chicago's first African-American mayor.

Byrnes, James F. (1879–1972) A self-taught South Carolina lawyer, Byrnes was a congressman from 1911 to 1925 and a senator from 1931 to 1941. During World War II, he served President Franklin D. Roosevelt as a dynamic adviser and administrator and was dubbed "assistant president for domestic affairs" during his tenure as director of war mobilization (1943–1945)—a most powerful office. From 1945 to 1947, he was secretary of state.

Cabot, John (1450–ca.1499) Born Giovanni Caboto in Italy, Cabot sailed for England's Henry VIII in 1497 and 1498 and discovered the Labrador coast of Newfoundland (which he mistook for China), thereby establishing the basis for the British claim to Canada.

Cabrini, Frances Xavier (1850–1917) Born in Italy, this nun founded the Missionary Sisters of the Sacred Heart in 1880 and sailed with them in 1889 to the United States, where she began mission work among poor Italian immigrants. She subsequently traveled throughout North America, South America, and Europe, founding 67 mission houses in addition to schools, hospitals, and orphanages. She was naturalized as a U.S. citizen in 1909, and was canonized on July 7, 1946.

Cage, John (1912–1992) The son of an American inventor, Cage pursued the serious study of music and included among his teachers Arnold Schoenberg and the American innovator Henry Cowell. Cage experimented with a wide variety of instruments and techniques, simultaneously expanding the musical vocabulary and paring it down to its essentials. A pioneer of aleatory music, in which chance figures prominently, Cage pushed the frontiers separating musical expression from random noise, even producing in 1952 one work, *4?33?*, in which the performer sits silently before his instrument and his audience for exactly four minutes, thirty-three seconds.

Calder, Alexander (1898–1976) The son and grandson of prominent sculptors, Calder created what he called the mobile, a form of abstract kinetic sculpture, the elements of which are balanced and/or suspended, so that they move in response to wind or (in some works) an electric motor. In addition to this highly influential form, Calder produced elegant stationary sculptures (which he called stabiles) and, most delightfully, an array of imaginative wire figures, many of which he arranged into an expansive miniature circus.

Calhoun, John Caldwell (1782–1850) South Carolinian by birth, Calhoun was a congressman, secretary of war, vice president from 1825 to 1832, a senator, and secretary of state. He is best known for his defense of the doctrine of states' rights, arguing that the U.S. Constitution was a compact among the states, which were sovereign, so that any state could nullify an act of Congress by pronouncing it unconstitutional. "Nullification" effectively protected slavery by disallowing—in the absence of a Constitutional amendment (which required ratification by two-thirds of the states to pass)—federal laws intended to curb slavery. Calhoun's nullification doctrine also implied the right of states to secede from the Union and thereby provided a theoretical basis for the formation of the Confederacy and the start of the Civil War.

Calley, William (1943–) On March 16, 1968, U.S. Army lieutenant William L. Calley's platoon marched into the South Vietnamese hamlet of My Lai, reputedly a Viet Cong stronghold. In an atrocity recorded by U.S. Army photographers, the platoon massacred 347 unarmed civilians, including women, old men, and children. After an army cover-up was exposed by Vietnam veteran Ronald Ridenhour, several soldiers were tried by court martial, of whom only Calley was convicted on March 29, 1971. Many Americans saw My Lai as a microcosm of the Vietnam War, in which U.S. "defenders of democracy" were slaughtering the innocents; others saw Calley as a victim, thrust into a war without clear direction from policy makers. Calley was released in September 1974 after a federal court overturned his conviction.

Camp, Walter (1859–1925) Team captain (head coach) of the Yale football team, Camp introduced a host of innovations that transformed what had been essentially a form of English rugby into the modern game of American football.

During the 1880s, his innovations became widely accepted, and he is generally credited as the inventor of the American form of the game.

Candler, Asa Griggs (1851–1929) Candler was an Atlanta druggist who, in 1887, bought the formula for Coca-Cola, at the time an obscure soda fountain beverage. Candler developed an improved manufacturing process and marketed Coca-Cola so skillfully that it became an enterprise of global proportions—probably the most universally recognized product of America.

Capone, Al (1899–1947) Born to Italian immigrant parents, Capone grew up in Brooklyn and, from youth, rose in New York's criminal gangs. A razor fight in a saloon resulted in his nickname, "Scarface." By the 1920s, Capone became organized crime boss of Chicago, which made him the most powerful and famous criminal in the United States. Despite crimes of corruption and violation of Prohibition, gambling, prostitution, and other laws—even despite gangland murders (most infamously the St. Valentine Day's Massacre of February 14, 1929)—Capone evaded prosecution until he was finally convicted on charges of income tax evasion in 1931. He was imprisoned, but released in 1939 because of advanced syphilis.

Capra, Frank (1897–1991) Born in Italy, Capra grew up in Los Angeles and directed his first films in the early 1920s. In 1934, his *It Happened One Night* won an Academy Award and typified his gently satiric, slyly sentimental comic style, which presented naïve heroes who embody optimistic American "populist" values—founded on essential selflessness and decency—that invariably enable them to triumph over shrewder, more cynical opponents. Favorite Capra films include *Mr. Smith Goes to Washington* (1939) and *It's a Wonderful Life* (1946).

Carey, Henry (1793–1879) This pioneering economist and sociologist founded the "American school" of economics, based on supremely optimistic notions of steady—indeed, unstoppable—economic progress and the possibility of productively harmonizing diverse economic interests.

Carmichael, Stokely (1941–1998) Born in Trinidad, Carmichael immigrated to the Bronx in 1952 and, while a student at Howard University, became active in the Civil Rights movement. By the mid-1960s, Carmichael was in the forefront of young African Americans who had grown impatient with the non-violent philosophy of Martin Luther King, Jr. and espoused a more militant approach to social and racial justice he dubbed "Black Power." During the late 1960s, he became vocal in protest against the Vietnam War and other examples of what he deemed American tyranny and repression. He moved to Guinea, West Africa, in 1969, and, after changing his name to Kwame Toure, helped found the All-African People's Revolutionary Party, dedicated to Pan-Africanism.

Carnegie, Andrew (1835–1919) Born poor in Scotland, Carnegie immigrated to the United States in 1848, went to work at 12 as a bobbin boy in a cotton factory, then became a messenger in a telegraph office two years later. He worked his way up to private secretary and personal telegrapher for the superintendent of the Pennsylvania Railroad Company in 1853. Within a very few years, he rose to superintendent of the railroad's Pittsburgh Division. Through shrewd investment he came to control what became the Carnegie Steel Company, which he sold to United States Steel for $250,000,000 in 1901. Arguing that it was the duty of the wealthy to improve society, Carnegie used his enormous wealth to endow educational and other foundations, including a program to build and stock libraries in cities and towns across America.

Carrier, Willis H. (1876–1950) While working as an engineer for the the Buffalo Forge Company in 1902, Carrier invented a system that simultaneously controlled temperature and humidity. He explained the theory behind his system in a 1911 technical paper, "Rational Psychrometric Formulae," which marked the birth of modern air conditioning, and his company, Carrier Corporation, founded in 1915, was the first manufacturer of the equipment. Air conditioning made it possible to work in all climates and proved essential to many precision manufacturing processes.

Carson, Kit (1809–1868) Christopher Houston "Kit" Carson was born near Richmond, Kentucky, and grew up in Missouri. At 16, he joined a Santa Fe trading caravan and from 1827 to 1842 lived in the Rockies as a fur trapper and mountain man. In 1842, he served as a military guide in Oregon and California and, during the Mexican War, was a courier. After the war, Carson settled in Taos, New Mexico, where he served from 1853 to 1861 as Indian agent to the Utes. With the outbreak of the Civil War, Carson became colonel of the First New Mexico Volunteer Cavalry and fought Confederates as well as Apaches and Navajos. Earning a national reputation as an Indian fighter, Carson was nevertheless an impassioned advocate for the rights of Native Americans.

Carson, Rachel (1907–1964) Rachel Carson's dramatic and elegiac *Silent Spring* (1962) made the American public aware of the dangers of widespread pesticide use and is frequently cited as the popular manifesto that launched the environmental movement of the 1960s and 1970s. Federal legislation restricting the use of DDT and other pesticides had its origin in her book.

Carter, Jimmy (1924–) James Earl Carter, Jr. (Jimmy) Carter was a liberal Georgia politician who entered the White House in 1977, inheriting a severe economic recession from Presidents Nixon and Ford, then leading the country through an energy crisis, which included gasoline shortages. Added to the president's problems was the Iran hostage crisis, which began on November 4, 1979, and did not end until Carter left office. Despite such foreign affairs triumphs as brokering the Camp David Accords, which brought peace between Israel and Egypt, and an array of domestic initiatives, Carter's presidency was widely perceived as a failure, and he was not elected to a second term, losing to Ronald Reagan in a landslide vote in 1980. After leaving office, he began working on behalf of human rights and other causes. His diplomatic efforts earned him the Nobel Prize for Peace in 2002.

Carver, George Washington (1861?–1943) Born a slave, Carver worked odd jobs while he obtained two college degrees and became director of the department of agriculture at the Tuskegee Institute in 1896. He spent the rest of his life at this pioneering African-American institution doing agricultural research, which resulted in finding new uses for the peanut (including peanut butter and a host of manufactured goods) and the soybean. By expanding southern agriculture beyond cotton, Carver's work was a boon to white as well as black southern farmers.

Cash, Johnny (1932–2003) Cash achieved early fame as a Country and Western singer-songwriter beginning in the mid 1950s and overcame drug addiction to bring this genre to a new height with his "Man in Black" persona, which celebrated sincerity and the rebellious spirit. He and his music identified with society's outcasts, and he loved especially to perform for prison inmates. Beginning in 1961, he often appeared in performance with his wife, the Country and Western great June Carter Cash (1929–2003), who died shortly before him.

Cassady, Neal (1926–1968) Cassady never wrote a novel or a poem, but he was a driving force behind the "Beat Generation" of writers during the 1950s and early 1960s, figuring as a principal character in the novel *Go* (1952) by John Clellon Holmes, considered the first work of "Beat" literature, and in the most famous Beat novel, Jack Kerouac's *On the Road* (1957), as well as other works. He had been raised by an alcoholic father on Denver's skid row and grew into a thief and con artist. He met Kerouac and the poet Alan Ginsberg in 1946 and served as the subject-catalyst for them and their circle—the embodiment of the sensitive outlaw spirit, born of America, yet apart from it. He died of exposure and acute alcoholic intoxication in Mexico in 1968.

Cassatt, Mary (1844–1926) Born in Pittsburgh, Cassatt was tutored privately in art in Philadelphia and attended the Pennsylvania Academy of the Fine Arts from 1861 to 1865, then studied in Europe. She became associated with the French Impressionist school and first exhibited—with great success—

at the Paris Salon of 1872. Cassatt is best known for her magnificent and much-loved depictions of mothers and children.

Cather, Willa (1873–1947) Born in Virginia, Cather moved with her family at age 9 to frontier Nebraska, where she imbibed the life of the immigrant settlers of the Great Plains. She graduated from the University of Nebraska and made her way as a journalist, then earned her first literary fame with stories from the Nebraska frontier, *O, Pioneers!* (1913) and *My Antonia* (1918). Her 1922 *One of Ours* was awarded the Pulitzer Prize.

Catt, Carrie Chapman (1859–1947) Successor to Susan B. Anthony as president of the National American Woman Suffrage Association, Catt was a brilliant and inspiring organizer, who mounted the culminating public campaign that finally achieved passage and ratification of the Nineteenth Amendment, giving women the vote in America.

Chambers, Whittaker (1901–1961) Born Jay Vivian Chambers in Philadelphia, this left-wing journalist took his mother's maiden name, Whittaker, in the 1920s. In August 1948, he testified to a committee of Congress that State Department official Alger Hiss had been a fellow member of a Communist spy ring in Washington, D.C., during the 1930s. The accusation and the Hiss trial that followed became the focal points of an American "red scare" that persisted through the mid 1950s, brought the anti-Communist "witch hunts" of Senator Joseph McCarthy, and precipitated the rise of then-Congressman Richard M. Nixon.

Champlain, Samuel de (1567–1635) Champlain is generally acknowledged as the founder of Quebec and, in what is now the United States, explored widely in northern New York and the eastern Great Lakes. He did much to develop the French fur trade in eastern North America and generally to consolidate French holdings in the New World. New York's Lake Champlain is named in his honor.

Channing, William Ellery (1780–1842) A Congregationalist minister, Channing founded Unitarianism, a liberal take on Christianity that advocated a rational approach to Scripture and religious belief. Linked to this was Channing's advocacy of Transcendentalism, a philosophy whose most famous exponent was Ralph Waldo Emerson and that proposed the essential unity of all creation and the innate goodness of humankind. Channing exerted a profound influence over 19th-century American religion, philosophy, and literature.

Chanute, Octave (1832–1910) Born in Paris, Chanute was brought to the United States as a child. He was a civil engineer most of his life, but during his sixties set up a glider camp on the shore of Lake Michigan near Chicago, where he and colleagues made over 2,000 flights in gliders of Chanute's design. Chanute and his work had a profound influence on Orville and Wilbur Wright, with whom he carried on a long correspondence.

Chaplin, Charlie (1889–1977) Chaplin was born to London music hall entertainers and made his stage debut at age five. While touring the United States with a stage company in 1913, Chaplin made his first comic short for Mack Sennett. This one-reeler was unremarkable, and Sennett asked Chaplin to come up with a more marketable film persona. The result, in 1914, was the figure of the "Little Tramp," who was destined to become an icon of silent film comedy and even survived into the talking-picture era, culminating in the 1936 *Modern Times.* Most film historians consider Chaplin the greatest film comic of all time and one of the most important figures in the history of cinema.

Chase, Salmon Portland (1808–1873) Chase was a lawyer, politician, and abolitionist who served in Abraham Lincoln's cabinet as secretary of the Treasury from 1861 to 1864. He was skilled in the role of financing the war, but he also worked behind Lincoln's back to steal the 1864 presidential nomination from him. On the death of Supreme Court chief justice Roger Taney, Lincoln disposed of Chase by nominating him to the court. He served as chief justice from 1864 to 1873, presiding with fairness over the Senate impeachment trial of President Andrew Johnson in 1868.

Chavez, Cesar (1927–1993) Born in Mexico, Chavez grew up as a migrant laborer in Arizona and California, becoming an organizer of oppressed migrant labor in 1958. In 1962, he founded the National Farm Workers Association (NFWA), which made great strides in organizing migrants to improve pay and working conditions. He was catapulted to national prominence when he led, beginning in 1965, a strike and nationwide boycott of California grapes. The boycott brought much support for the plight of the migrant and resulted in bargaining agreements with growers.

Cheney, Dick (1941–) Cheney was a conservative Republican politician who served six terms as U.S. Representative from Wyoming and was secretary of defense under President George H. W. Bush (1989–1993), overseeing the military invasion of Panama (1989) and the first Persian Gulf War

(1990–1991). As vice president in the administration (2001–) of George W. Bush, Cheney was popularly perceived as a shadow president, who wielded unprecedented decision-making power. Many saw Cheney—not Bush—as the chief architect of the "war on terror" that followed the attacks of September 11, 2001, and the prime instigator of Operation Iraqi Freedom.

Chennault, Claire L. (1890–1958) An innovative—even maverick—military aviator, Chennault retired from the U.S. Army Air Corps in 1937 and was hired by Chinese Nationalist leader Chiang Kai-shek as his aviation adviser. During the Sino-Japanese War (which began in 1937), Chennault organized the Chinese air force and in 1941 created the American Volunteer Group (AVG), better known as the Flying Tigers, a squadron of volunteer U.S. pilots. With the most modest of resources, Chennault's aviators, trained in combat techniques he developed, achieved an extraordinary record against the much more numerous air forces of the Japanese. With U.S. entry into World War II, the Flying Tigers were incorporated into the U.S. Army Air Forces as the China Air Task Force (later, the Fourteenth Air Force), and Chennault returned to active duty as the unit's commander. Once again, Chennault performed tactical miracles against superior forces.

Child, Julia (1912–2004) Born Julia McWilliams, Child served in World War II as a member of the U.S. Office of Strategic Services (OSS) in Ceylon (today, Sri Lanka), then spent six years after the war in Paris, where she attended the famed Cordon Bleu cooking school. She subsequently founded a school of her own and, in 1961, published *Mastering the Art of French Cooking*, a runaway bestseller and enduring classic that brought French cookery into mainstream American culture. From 1962 through the mid 1990s, she was the star of several popular television cooking shows and became an international celebrity, as famous for her on-screen good-humored exuberance as for her cooking.

Child, Lydia Maria (1802–1880) Child was a pioneering abolitionist author, whose 1833 *An Appeal in Favor of That Class of Americans Called Africans* contained a comprehensive history of slavery and appealed not only for abolition but for equality of education and employment for blacks. The first book of its kind, its publication created a sensation. Child continued to campaign for abolition until the end of the Civil War, after which she wrote *An Appeal for the Indians* (1868) and other works advocating just treatment for Native Americans.

Chisholm, Shirley (1924–2005) The daughter of immigrant parents from British Guiana (now Guyana) and Barbados, Chisholm grew up in Brooklyn, where she later taught school and became active in the civil rights movement and in Democratic politics. She was elected to Congress in 1968—the first African-American woman to serve in the House—and was a powerful liberal voice in that body until her retirement in 1983. She subsequently became a lecturer and college professor.

Chomsky, Noam (1928–) Noam Chomsky's 1955 work, entitled *Transformational Analysis,* established "transformational grammar." This theory holds that grammar is not merely learned but grows from an innate human faculty for understanding the grammatical structures of language. During the 1960s and 1970s, Chomsky, already famed as a linguist, became known for his strident political activism, first directed against the Vietnam War and then more generally critical of American foreign policy. He is regarded as one of the most important voices of the American left.

Chopin, Kate (1851–1904) Chopin wrote about what she knew best: the colorful people in and around New Orleans in the late 1800s, but she is best remembered today for her 1899 novel *The Awakening*, a story about the sexual awakening of a young wife and mother, who seeks to escape stifling social convention by abandoning her husband and children. Condemned in its own time, it was rediscovered in the 1950s and is considered a precursor of modern feminist literature.

Chrysler, Walter P. (1875–1940) Chrysler's first job was as an apprentice in a railroad machine shop; from this, he worked his way up to the presidency of the Buick Motor Company in 1916. After building Buick into the strongest unit of General Motors, Chrysler resigned to become director of the Willys-Overland Company and of Maxwell Motor Company, Inc., which he transformed into the Chrysler Corporation in 1925. For his new company, Chrysler personally designed a car with the first commercially available high-compression engine. Chrysler became the only major domestic competitor of Ford and GM.

Church, Benjamin (1639–1718) Born in Plymouth, Massachusetts, Church was one of New England's ablest military commanders and was instrumental in defeating the forces of Indian chief King Philip in King Philip's War (1675–1676)—in proportion to population, the deadliest war in American history.

Church, Frederick (1826–1900) Church was one of the greatest of the Hudson River School painters, who specialized in magnificent panoramas. In addition to portraying great romantic American scenes (such as *Niagara*, 1857), Church painted in North and South America as well as Europe.

Clark, George Rogers (1752–1818) Although the battles fought on the settled East Coast are the most famous engagements of the American Revolution, most of the fighting took place in the interior, on the frontier, and George Rogers Clark was one of the leading American commanders in this theater. His victories were largely responsible for Britain's cession of the Old Northwest to the United States in the Treaty of Paris, which ended the war.

Clark, Mark W. (1896–1994) After graduating from West Point in 1917, Clark served in France during World War II. His biggest assignment during World War II was as commander of Fifth Army, the principal force fighting the Italian Campaign, which proved far more costly than anticipated. British prime minister Winston Churchill called Clark the "American Eagle."

Clark, William (1770–1838) Younger brother of American Revolution hero George Rogers Clark, William Clark served in the U.S. Army before he was handpicked by Meriwether Lewis in 1803 as co-captain of the expedition to explore the Far West. He proved a magnificent choice.

Clay, Henry (1777–1852) Clay was born in Virginia, but lived most of his life in Kentucky, which sent him to the House of Representative (1811–1814, 1815–1821, 1823–1825) and the

Senate (1806–1807, 1810–1811, 1831–1842, 1849–1852). In a struggle to find a compromise on the slavery issue and thereby avoid civil war, Clay became the chief promoter of the Missouri Compromise (1820), the compromise tariff of 1833 (which ended the Nullification crisis that threatened secession), and the Compromise of 1850, another effort to reconcile the claimed rights of free and slave states.

Cleveland, Grover (1837–1908) The only president to serve two discontinuous terms (1885–1889 and 1893–1897), Cleveland is remembered as that rarest of commodities of the so-called "Gilded Age": an honest politician. He approached the presidency as a genuine conservative, believing that the chief executive's function was mainly to check the excesses of the legislative branch. He won a majority of popular votes for reelection, but came in second to Republican Benjamin Harrison in the Electoral College.

Clinton, Bill (1946–) Clinton grew up poor in Arkansas but went on to become a Rhodes Scholar. As a young man, he deeply admired John F. Kennedy and resolved to embark on a life of public service. He served five two-year terms as Arkansas governor, then survived a sex scandal to win election as president in 1992. Through two terms, this moderate, centrist, and business-friendly Democrat presided over the nation's longest peacetime economic expansion. In 1998, however, a new sex scandal—a liaison with White House intern Monica Lewinsky followed by the president's efforts to cover it up—resulted in his impeachment by a Republican-controlled Congress. Voting along party lines, the Senate failed to obtain the two-thirds majority necessary for removal from office, and Clinton was acquitted in 1999.

Clinton, DeWitt (1769–1828) As a New York state legislator, Clinton promoted the construction of a canal across New York State to link the Northeast coastal trade with the Great Lakes via Lake Erie. He won legislative approval in 1816 to finance the canal, and his election as governor in 1817 ensured that he would be able to oversee the enormous project personally. The opening of the canal on October 25, 1825, made New York City a key trading port with the Midwest and opened the American frontier to eastern commerce.

Clinton, Hillary Rodham (1947–) Hillary Rodham was an attorney and advocate of children's rights, who, in 1975, married Bill Clinton, three years before he was elected governor of Arkansas. Hillary Clinton was active in children's rights during her husband's gubernatorial tenure, and she played a major strategy and public role in his 1992 campaign for the presidency. She was an active first lady, heading up the Task Force on National Health Care and working on other initiatives. Opinions about her tended to break down along party lines and she was often vilified by members of the conservative press. During the Monica Lewinsky scandal that rocked the Clinton presidency, she remained firmly behind her husband. In 2000, Hillary Clinton was elected junior senator from New York and, as of 2006, is thought to be the leading contender for the Democratic party's presidential nomination in 2008.

Cobb, Ty (1886–1961) A Georgia native, Tyrus Raymond Cobb was dubbed the "Georgia Peach." During 24 seasons in the American League, he scored of 2,245 runs (surpassed in 2001 by Rickey Henderson), stole 892 bases (surpassed in 1979 by Lou Brock), and achieved a lifetime batting average of .366 (unsurpassed as of 2006). A great ball player, Cobb was a miserable human being, outspoken in his racism and misogyny and often given to violence.

Cochise (d. 1874) Cochise was widely admired by the Chiricahua band of the Apaches, which he led in a fierce resistance against the incursions of white settlers in the Southwest during the 1860s. Feared and respected by all, he was given the posthumous honor of having an Arizona county named for him.

Cody, Buffalo Bill (1846–1917) William F. "Buffalo Bill" Cody was a buffalo hunter, an army scout, and an Indian fighter, but he earned international renown for his Wild West Show (officially called Buffalo Bill's Wild West and Congress of Rough Riders of the World), which debuted in 1883. The show dramatized the American West and made an enduring contribution to the image of the West in American history and mythology.

Cohan, George M. (1878–1942) Cohan was born into a vaudeville family, with whom he performed from an early age. Before the end of the 19th century, he was writing vaudeville skits and debuted his first full-length play in 1901. A pioneer of the American musical theater, Cohan had an unbroken string of hits from 1901 (*The Governor's Son*) to 1937 (*I'd Rather Be Right*). Of his many songs, the most famous include "You're a Grand Old Flag," "Mary's a Grand Old Name," "Give My Regards to Broadway," and "I'm a Yankee Doodle Dandy." His "Over There," occasioned by U.S. entry into World War I in 1917, earned Cohan a Congressional medal in 1940.

Cohn, Roy (1927–1986) A New York prosecutor, Roy Cohn came to prominence in helping to prosecute the espionage trial of

Julius and Ethel Rosenberg (1951) and as counsel to Senator Joseph McCarthy's Senate committee investigating reputed Communist infiltration of the U.S. government. A ruthless opportunist, Cohn wielded significant power for a time, but was almost universally disdained.

Cole, Thomas (1801–1848) Cole was born in England and immigrated to Philadelphia, then settled in 1826 in Catskill, New York, on the Hudson River. This became his base for many painting trips along the Hudson River and its valley. His romantic sensibility created large canvases that evoke the mystery of the American forestland, and his example inspired a number of followers, who were the first great American landscape painters.

Colfax, Schuyler (1823–1885) Colfax was an Indiana newspaper publisher who became a Republican Congressman and was in the forefront of Radical Reconstruction after the Civil War, favoring harsh treatment of the former Confederacy. He served as vice president during the first term (1869–1873) of Ulysses S. Grant, but in 1872 (while still sitting as vice president) was implicated in the massive Crédit Moblier scandal, involving the financing of the transcontinental (Union Pacific-Central Pacific) railroad. Although never prosecuted, Colfax became a symbol of corruption during the era popularly known as "The Gilded Age."

Colt, Samuel (1814–1862) Colt was serving as a sailor when, to pass the time, he whittled a wooden model of handgun he later perfected as a revolver. His first practical design was patented in England and France in 1835 and in the United States in 1836. The new design was slow to catch on, and Colt's first factory failed in 1842, but after the U.S. government ordered 1,000 of the weapons for use in the U.S.-Mexican War, Colt reestablished his business and became the manufacturer of the most famous handgun in America—the "gun that tamed the West."

Colter, John (ca. 1775–1813) Colter was a member of the Lewis and Clark Expedition (1803–1806) and joined Manuel Lisa's fur trading enterprise in 1807, traveling into the region of present-day Yellowstone National Park in search of fur. He was the first white man to see and describe the area. Colter was celebrated for his hair's-breadth escapes from Indian captivity and combat.

Coltrane, John (1926–1967) As a saxophonist, bandleader, and composer, John Coltrane was highly influential on jazz, creating spiritually charged and musically adventurous improvisatory solos of unprecedented length and complexity. More than any musician before him, Coltrane introduced free improvisation into American jazz.

Columbus, Christopher (1451–1506) The Italian-born Columbus was already an experienced mariner when he managed to persuade King Ferdinand II and Queen Isabella I of Spain to fund his first voyage in 1492. His plan was to sail west to reach spice- and gold-rich Asia; instead, in one of the most famous mistakes in history, he encountered North America. Although the Viking Leif Eriksson had discovered the continent some 500 years earlier, Columbus's four voyages were the first to excite among Europeans a desire to explore, settle, and exploit the New World. For this reason, Columbus is traditionally credited with the "discovery" of America.

Coolidge, Calvin (1872–1933) A taciturn New Englander, Coolidge was not the typical outgoing American politician. He served in Massachusetts politics, becoming governor in 1918. His hard line against striking Boston police officers ("There is no right to strike against the public safety by anybody, anywhere, any time.") gained him national prominence and selection as Warren G. Harding's running mate in the presidential elections of 1920. When Harding died in office in 1923, Coolidge stepped in and did much to clean out the corruption that had characterized that administration and rebuilt American confidence in the presidency. Despite his tight-lipped approach—"Silent Cal," he was called—Coolidge won election in his own right in 1924.

Cooper, James Fennimore (1789–1851) The scion of a prominent upstate New York family, Cooper is reputed to have become a novelist at his wife's urging. He had complained about a British novel he had just read, claiming that he could do better. Susan De Lancy Cooper dared him to do just that, and he wrote *Precaution* (1820), largely in imitation of Jane Austen. He found his life's subject in a series of five novels—collectively called the Leatherstocking Tales—that featured a frontier guide and scout named Natty Bumppo. In *The Pioneers* (1823), *The Last of the Mohicans* (1826), *The Prairie* (1827), *The Pathfinder* (1840), and *The Deerslayer* (1841), Bumppo emerged as an archetypal man of the frontier, a character of mythic proportions.

Cooper, Peter (1791–1883) In 1830, Cooper built the locomotive "Tom Thumb" for the fledgling Baltimore and Ohio Railroad. An engine capable of pulling passengers and freight over the railway's hilly route, the Tom Thumb enabled the commercial success of the B&O and launched the American railroad industry. Cooper went on to contribute to other manufacturing enterprises, including the production of the world's first structural steel beams. Grown wealthy, he used much of his fortune to create in 1859 New York's Cooper Union, which offered free courses in science, engineering, and art. The institution continues to thrive today.

Copland, Aaron (1900–1990) Copland grew up in Brooklyn, the son of Russian-Jewish immigrants. By the age of 15 he decided to become a composer and in 1921 studied with the famed teacher Nadia Boulanger in Paris. His early avant-garde, abstract style matured into a vigorously American expression, replete with elements of jazz, folk songs, and spirituals, but also uniquely modernist. For such works as the ballets *Billy the Kid* (1938) and *Appalachian Spring* (1944)—among many others—he gained enduring recognition as a representative American classical composer.

Copley, John Singleton (1738–1815) Copley was born in Boston and created his early portraits there, including *Boy with Squirrel* (1766), which was praised by the great British painter Sir Joshua Reynolds and thus became the first work of American art to be publicly appreciated in Europe. With opportunities limited in America, Copley settled permanently in London in 1775 and turned his attention to painting historical subjects.

Corbett, Boston (1832–1894?) Corbett immigrated to New York with his family in 1839 and became a hatter in Troy, New York. Like many in that trade (who were exposed to high levels of mercury), he suffered symptoms of mental illness, became a religious zealot, wore his hair long in imitation of

Jesus, and (in 1858) castrated himself with scissors in order to avoid the temptations of prostitutes. He joined the Union Army in the Civil War and, on April 24, 1865, was one of 26 cavalrymen pursuing John Wilkes Booth after the assassination of Abraham Lincoln. Corbett and the others ran Booth to ground on April 26 in a Virginia tobacco barn. The soldiers set the barn on fire to smoke Booth out, but when Corbett saw Booth silhouetted by the flames, he shot him with a Colt revolver. Paralyzed, Booth died within hours. Corbett was arrested for disobeying orders, but the charges were dropped by Secretary of War Edwin M. Stanton and Corbett was awarded $1,653.84 as his share of the bounty on Booth. Corbett died in obscurity, having suffered from mental illness for the rest of his life.

Corey, Giles (1612–1692) Accused during the infamous Salem witch trials of wizardry, Corey defiantly refused to enter a plea. English common law required a plea before a trial could proceed; to obtain the plea, the law prescribed pressing with weights until it was obtained. Corey, 80 years old at the time of his accusation, endured two days during which more and more rocks were laid on him. Reputedly, he refused to speak, except for his final words: "More weight." Because he was not tried, his estate passed to his heirs and was not confiscated by Massachusetts. He figures as an early American example of refusal to yield to injustice.

Coronado, Francisco (1510–1554) Coronado was a Spanish conquistador who explored the American Southwest in search of the fabled seven cities of gold. These he did not find, but he explored the vast magnificence of the American Southwest and was the first European to behold the Palo Duro Canyon of Texas and the Grand Canyon of Arizona.

Costello, Frank (1891–1973) Costello was four years old when his family emigrated from Italy and settled in New York. He became a gang member and, during Prohibition, engaged in bootlegging and gambling in New York, Florida, Louisiana, and elsewhere. He moved up the syndicate ladder during the 1930s and, after World War II, was instrumental in financing the newly developing Las Vegas casino industry. During this period, he moved freely among New York politicians and legitimate businessmen, whom he variously corrupted. Costello was targeted by Senator Estes Kefauver's organized crime committee in the early 1950s and was convicted first of contempt of Congress and then of income tax evasion. While out on bail in 1957, a rival crime boss shot him, he recovered, served out his sentence, but never regained his power in organized crime.

Coughlin, Charles (1891–1971) Born in Canada, Coughlin was ordained a Catholic priest in Detroit and began in 1930 experimenting with radio-broadcast sermons and religious lessons for children. His popularity exploded, and he became the first electronic-media evangelist; however, his shows became increasingly political. At first he attacked President Herbert Hoover and supported Franklin D. Roosevelt, but then turned on Roosevelt with diatribes protesting the New Deal, warning against Communism, and railing against the influence of Jews in government and business. His magazine, *Social Justice*, was banned for violating the Espionage Act and closed down in 1942, the same year that Church authorities ordered him to stop broadcasting.

Cox, Archibald (1912–2004) A distinguished American jurist, solicitor general in the Kennedy administration, and law professor, Cox accepted appointment in May 1973 as the first special prosecutor assigned to investigate the Watergate affair. When Cox pressed to obtain Richard M. Nixon's secret tapes of White House conversations, the president ordered Cox to be fired. Attorney General Eliott Richardson and his deputy, William Ruckelshaus, both resigned rather than obey the order, which was carried out by Solictor General Robert Bork on October 20, 1973, in the so-called "Saturday Night Massacre." Cox responded with simple dignity: "Whether ours shall be a government of laws and not of men is now for Congress and ultimately the American people to decide."

Cox, Ida (1896–1967) Georgia native Ida Cox sang in the choir of the African Methodist Church in Cedartown before she left home to tour with traveling minstrel shows. In the 1920s, she began making "race records" (recordings by black performers, mostly marketed to a black audience) that helped inaugurate the era of classic female blues. She was a sensation among black and white audience alike and was billed on tours as the "Sepia Mae West."

Coxey, Jacob (1854–1951) A socialist politician from Ohio, Coxey is best remembered as the leader of what was popularly called Coxey's Army. In 1894 and again in 1914, he marched at the head of bands of unemployed men from his hometown of Massillon, Ohio, to Washington, D.C., to demand that Congress vote funds to create jobs for the unemployed. Coxey's two "armies" were never large, and he was widely ridiculed in his own time, but the idea of creating public works jobs for the unemployed became a cornerstone of FDR's New Deal during the Great Depression of the 1930s.

Crane, Hart (1899–1932) This poet created rich, visionary lyrics that portrayed and even celebrated life in industrial

America. His most ambitious work, *The Bridge* (1930), used the magnificent Brooklyn Bridge as a central image on which to build an epic myth of the American experience. The result was one of the greatest American poems since Walt Whitman's 19th-century masterpiece, *Song of Myself.*

Crane, Stephen (1871–1900) In his short life, Stephen Crane worked as newspaper reporter while creating a new, lean realistic style of fiction, culminating in his masterpiece, *The Red Badge of Courage* (1895), a depiction of the Civil War so authentic that most readers thought it autobiographical. Crane inspired a generation of American realistic novelists, including Ernest Hemingway.

Crazy Horse (1842?–1877) One of the great Native American military leaders, this Oglala Sioux chief led the militant resistance to white settlement of Indian lands on the Great Plains. He is most famous for his victory over George Armstrong Custer and the Seventh Cavalry at the Little Bighorn on June 25, 1876, in which Custer and his entire command fell. After years of fighting, Crazy Horse surrendered to General Crook in Nebraska on May 6, 1877. He was subsequently killed in a scuffle with his soldier-jailers.

Creel, George (1876–1953) Creel was a crusading journalist who, when the United States entered World War I in 1917, created for the administration of Woodrow Wilson the Committee on Public Information and fashioned it into a powerful propaganda machine, which made use of traditional and emerging media to shape American public opinion in favor of the war. Unprecedented, Creel's efforts were a model for government propaganda and for the emerging American public relations industry.

Creeley, Robert (1926–) Creeley dropped out of Harvard in his senior year, worked in India and Burma, lived variously abroad, and began writing poetry. In 1955, Creeley received a B.A. from the experimental Black Mountain College in North Carolina, joined the faculty, and edited the *Black Mountain Review*, which became the leading venue for some of the most innovative American poetry and prose of the intellectually fertile 1950s.

Crèvecoeur, Hector St. John de (1735–1813) Born Michel-Guillaume-Saint-Jean de Crèvecoeur in France, Crèvecoeur served as a military officer and mapmaker in Canada, then traveled widely in the Ohio and Great Lakes region and became an American citizen in 1765. Caught up in the American Revolution—spurned by Patriots and Loyalists alike—he returned to Europe in 1780. Two years later, in London, using his American name, J. Hector St. John, he published *Letters from an American Farmer*, an optimistic vision of the young American democracy, which became an international bestseller and is still considered one of the best analyses of the American character ever written.

Crittenden, John J. (1787–1863) After Abraham Lincoln's election in 1860, Crittenden desperately sought a compromise that would avert civil war by proposing a set of resolutions collectively called the Crittenden Compromise, which would have protected slavery but prohibited its spread beyond the current slave territories. This last-ditch effort to prevent the war failed, after which Crittenden worked successfully to save his state of Kentucky for the Union. One of his sons became a major general in the Union Army, while another served at the same rank in the army of the Confederacy.

Crockett, Davy (1786–1836) With an education that amounted to no more than three months' tutoring from a backwoods neighbor, Tennessean Crockett fought in the Creek War during 1813–1815, earning a reputation as a fearless Indian fighter, which helped to propel him in 1821 to the Tennessee legislature. There he fashioned his popular political persona and, in fact, showed great flair for spinning out amusing tales and homely metaphors, which found their way into a highly profitable series of almanacs and an 1834 *Autobiography.* Crockett served three terms in the U.S. House of Representatives, but after his defeat in 1835 he bade farewell to Washington—"You can all go to hell. I'm going to Texas"—and was among the Alamo defenders slain by Santa Anna on March 6, 1836.

Cullen, Countee (1903–1946) Born in Louisville, Kentucky, Cullen grew up in New York's Harlem, where he won a citywide poetry competition then went on to New York University (B.A., 1925), winning there the prestigious Witter Bynner Poetry Prize. He was soon published by all of the important literary magazines, and his first collection of verse, *Color*, appeared in 1925, before he finished college. Cullen was one of the most active writers of the Harlem Renaissance, a literary and artistic movement in this predominantly black neighborhood during the 1920s that for the first time brought the work of African-American writers, artists, and musicians to broad American audience.

Cunningham, Merce (1919–) Cunningham began to study dance from age 12 and joined Martha Graham's dance troupe in 1939. He began choreographing for her in the 1940s and pushed the limits of modern choreography by developing dances of pure movement, removed from programmatic or narrative implications. From this, he went on to create "choreography by chance," in which dances were created from a vocabulary of movements, which were assigned sequence random methods, including the toss of a coin. Cunningham founded his own dance company in 1952.

Currier, Nathaniel, and James M. Ives (1813–1888) Currier was a New York lithographer, who hired Ives as a bookkeeper in 1852 and made him a partner in 1857. As the firm of Currier & Ives, the pair produced the most popular lithographs of the 19th century. In an era before journalistic photography, film, and television, they satisfied the public appetite for visual depictions of important current events, and they also supplied images of famous people (both current and historical) and scenes of Americana and humor. Their company, run by their sons, endured until 1907, when other technologies made their prints obsolete. Today, the enormous volume of Currier & Ives images provides a unique window on 19th-century America.

Custer, George A. (1839–1876) Custer graduated from the West Point in 1861 at the bottom of his class, but distinguished himself in Civil War combat so spectacularly that, at 23 he became brigadier general of volunteers—the youngest general officer in the army. During the war, he acquired a reputation for recklessness; nevertheless, he was dashing and aggressive, pursuing Robert E. Lee so relentlessly at the end of the war that he surely hastened the Confederate's surrender at Appomattox Courthouse on April 9, 1865. After the war, Custer served in the West, fighting Indians. His career and his life came to an end on June 25, 1876, at the Little Bighorn River, Montana Territory, when, anxious to attack a band of Sioux, he failed to make reconnaissance and fell into a brilliantly executed ambush. He and some 200 men were overwhelmed and killed.

Czolgosz, Leon (1873–1901) The son of Polish immigrants, Czolgosz worked for the American Steel and Wire Company, was fired for striking, and became a confirmed anarchist. On August 31, 1901, he moved from Ohio to Buffalo, New York, rented a room near the site of the Pan-American Exposition, which he knew that President McKinley was scheduled to visit. On September 6, armed with a pistol that he had concealed in a handkerchief, Czolgosz went to the exposition, assumed a place in a line of McKinley well-wishers, and shot the president twice at point-blank range at 4:07 p.m. McKinley died on September 14.

Daley, Richard J. (1902–1976) Elected mayor of Chicago every four years from 1955 to 1975, Richard J. Daley was the last of the big city bosses, wielding tremendous power by controlling patronage jobs but also by managing the city with a high level of competence that stimulated growth at a time when many large American cities were in decline. Daley's dictatorial style caused much outrage—especially for the brutal measures taken against demonstrators during the 1968 Democratic National Convention held in the city—but the mayor also commanded great loyalty from the majority of Chicagoans. His son, Richard M. Daley, became mayor in 1989 and, as of 2006, is still serving.

Darling, Jay Norwood "Ding" (1876–1962) "Ding" Darling was born in Norwood, Michigan, and raised in Sioux City, Iowa. He earned early national fame as a Pulitzer Prize-winning political cartoonist, who worked principally for the *Des*

Moines (Iowa) Register, but his most enduring legacy was as a founder of the Cooperative Wildlife Research Unit at Iowa State College (later Iowa State University), which set the pattern for similar research units all over the nation. He created the first federal duck stamp in 1934, sales of which enabled the purchase of two million acres of national waterfowl habitat.

Darrow, Clarence (1875–1938) Through a long legal career, Darrow earned a reputation as a brilliant attorney defending liberal causes and unpopular people. He was one of the defenders of the Haymarket rioters charged with murder (May 4, 1886); he defended socialist labor leader Eugene V. Debs, charged with contempt of court for his leadership of the great Pullman Strike (May–July 1894); he secured acquittal for International Workers of the World (IWW) leader William D. ("Big Bill") Haywood on murder charges; he defended antiwar protestors in World War I; he saved the infamous child murderers Richard Loeb and Nathan Leopold from execution in 1924; and, in 1925, he defended teacher John T. Scopes, who had violated Tennessee state law by teaching the Theory of Evolution.

Davis, Angela (1944–) Davis was a Marxist philosophy professor who became an advocate of black revolution during the 1960s and 1970s. When she espoused the cause of another black revolutionary, George Jackson, she was charged in 1970 with kidnapping, murder, and conspiracy for her suspected complicity in an attempted escape and abduction from a California courtroom. An all-white jury acquitted her. In 1991, Davis was named professor of the history of consciousness at the University of California, Santa Cruz.

Davis, Benjamin Oliver Jr. (1912–2002) Davis was born in Washington, D.C., the son of Benjamin Oliver Davis Sr., first general officer in the U.S. Army. He graduated from West Point in 1936, as the sole African American at the academy having suffered ostracism by the corps of cadets. Trained at the segregated flight school established at Tuskegee Institute in Alabama, Davis led the legendary Tuskegee Airmen in combat during World War II. After the war, in 1954, he became the first African-American general in the USAF. In 1971, he was named assistant secretary for the department of transportation.

Davis, Benjamin Oliver Sr. (1877–1970) Davis was born in Washington, D.C., and studied at Howard University, which he left in 1898 to serve as a lieutenant of volunteers in the Spanish-American War. After the war, he reenlisted in the regular army as a private, rising through the ranks to become in 1940 the segregated U.S. Army's first African-American general. After World War II, he served as assistant inspector general of the army until his retirement in 1948. His son, Benjamin Oliver Davis Jr., became the first black general in the U.S. Air Force.

Davis, Jefferson (1808–1889) A hero of the United States-Mexican War (1846–1848), a U.S. Representative, and secretary of war under Franklin Pierce, Davis, a Mississippian, accepted appointment as president of the Confederate States of America in 1861 and served as such throughout the Civil War. After the war, he was held in prison by the federal government for two years before he was charged with treason. The government dropped its case in 1868, however, and Davis returned to private life, becoming a president once again—this time of a Memphis, Tennessee, insurance company.

Davis, Stuart (1894–1964) Philadelphia-born Davis was the son of a graphic artist and newspaper art editor. The graphic designs young Davis grew familiar with as a child influenced his mature abstract painting style, which combined Cubism (inspired by Picasso, Cezanne, and Braque) with elements of American commercial art. This combination, innovative and idiosyncratic at the time, became highly influential on later modern American art movements, including the Pop Art movement of the 1960s.

Dayton, Jonathan (1760–1824) At 27, Dayton was the youngest member of the U.S. Constitutional Convention. He rose to become speaker of the U.S. House of Representatives and went on to develop huge portions of the Ohio territory, especially the area that later became the state of Ohio. This earned him the honor of having a major Ohio city named for him, even though he was implicated in Aaron Burr's grandiose scheme to establish an empire in the American West. Like Burr, Dayton was indicted for high treason; unlike him, he was never prosecuted.

Dean, John (1938) Dean earned his law degree in 1965 from Georgetown University and in 1970 became President Richard M. Nixon's White House counsel. In 1972 Nixon appointed Dean to investigate the "possible involvement" of White House personnel in the break-in at Democratic National Headquarters in Washington's Watergate complex. Refusing President Nixon's request that he fabricate a report denying an investigation cover-up, Dean soon turned against his boss, revealing to federal investigators all he knew about Watergate. Two months after Nixon fired Dean on April 30, 1973, Dean testified publicly before the Senate Select Committee on Presidential Campaign Activities, revealing in detail how the White House had systematically obstructed justice following the Watergate break-in. Imprisoned briefly for his role in Watergate, Dean told all in the confessional memoir *Blind Ambition* (1976).

Debs, Eugene (1855–1926) Debs revolutionized the concept of the American labor union when he organized workers by industry rather than by craft. After becoming president of the American Railway Union in 1893, he united railway workers from various crafts, thereby creating the nation's first industrial union. He led the union in the great Pullman strike of 1895, for which he was given a six-month jail sentence. During this time, he read the works of Karl Marx and became a confirmed socialist, convinced that the essence of the labor movement was a struggle between classes. Between 1900 and 1920, he ran for U.S. president five times as a member of the Socialist Party.

Decatur, Stephen (1779–1820) Decatur became a national naval hero in 1804 when he led an expedition into Tripoli harbor to burn the U.S. frigate *Philadelphia*, which had fallen into Tripolitan hands during action against the Barbary pirates. During the War of 1812, he compiled a magnificent record against the ships of the mighty British fleet. After further victories against Barbary pirates in 1815, he famously replied to a toast in his honor: "Our country! In her intercourse with foreign nations may she always be in the right; but our country, right or wrong." He met his death in a duel with a former officer in whose court martial he had been involved.

Deere, John (1804–1886) After working as a blacksmith in his native Vermont, Deer moved west and set up a smithy at Grand Detour, Illinois. Kept busy repairing plows broken by the tough prairie soil, he hit upon radical design improvements, finally producing a plow of his own in1836 with a hard steel share shaped like ship's prow. It was the plow that broke the plains—enabling the productive agricultural exploitation of vast tracts of the prairies and Great Plains, thereby opening much of the West to homesteading settlement.

De Forest, Lee (1873–1961) De Forest was fascinated by mechanics and technology and, as a teenager, was a tinkerer and amateur inventor. De Forest defied his father, who wanted him to study for a career in the clergy, and instead earned a Ph.D. in physics. In 1902, he founded the De Forest Wireless Telegraphy Company, inventing in 1907 the Audion vacuum tube, capable of more sensitive radio reception than existing vacuum tubes. This enabled the live broadcast of radio and also led to such inventions as radar, television, and early computer systems. It was the key electronic component prior to the invention of the transistor in 1947 and ushered in the modern electronic age.

de Kooning, Willem (1904–1997) Born in the Netherlands, de Kooning was active in the New York art scene of the 1950s and became a leading exponent (with Jackson Pollock) of abstract expressionism, abstract painting closely allied to so-called "action painting," a revolutionary style in which spontaneity and chance figured in dynamic compositions that seemed to reflect the high energy of life at mid 20th century.

Deloria, Vine, Jr. (1933–2005) Born near the Pine Ridge Oglala Sioux Indian Reservation in South Dakota, Deloria studied for the Lutheran ministry but earned a law degree instead and served as Executive Director of the National Congress of American Indians. He published his first book in 1969, *Custer Died for Your Sins: An Indian Manifesto*, which attacked Indian stereotypes and took a fresh look at the history of white American western expansionism from the Native point of view. It was the first of his twenty books on historical and cultural issues relating to Native Americans, with emphasis on education and religion.

De Mille, Agnes (1905–1993) The daughter of a playwright and niece of director Cecil B. DeMille, Agnes George De Mille brought into modern American dance elaborate elements of dramatic narrative and incorporated American themes, folklore, popular culture, and folk dance into a new vocabulary of choreography, which transformed modern ballet into choreographic drama and storytelling.

DeMille, Cecil B. (1881–1959) The son of a playwright, DeMille started his career as an actor and got into directing movies in 1914. He developed the genre of the Hollywood spectacle, which used an army of extras playing on vast movie sets to tell epic stories, often of a religious nature. His original silent versions of *The Ten Commandments* (1923) and *The King of Kings* (1927) were seen by an estimated 800 million people. Critics did not consider DeMille a cinematic artist, but his commercial success propelled him through a 50-year career in which he directed and/or produced 70 films, culminating in his 1956 remake of *The Ten Commandments.* All contemporary "special effects" mega-budget Hollywood entertainments trace their ancestry to the films of "C.B."

De Soto, Hernando (1496/95–1542) One of the most famous of the conquistadors, De Soto participated in the Spanish conquests of Central America and Peru and explored a vast swath of what would become the southeastern United States.

He was the first European to lay eyes on the Mississippi River (south of modern Memphis, Tennessee). Succumbing to fever, he was buried along that river's bank.

DeVoto, Bernard (1897–1955) DeVoto wrote in every genre—fiction, criticism, and journalism—but he is best known as a magisterial historian of the American West. De Voto was not only immersed in the western past, but was deeply concerned about the region's future, and his monthly column for *Harper's Magazine*, "The Easy Chair," served to make the nation's public aware of the precious value of the western lands and the necessity for faithful stewardship of them.

Dewey, George (1837–1917) Dewey began the Battle of Manila Bay, Philippines, before 6:00 a.m. on May 1, 1898, with the words (directed to the captain of his flagship): "You may fire when ready, Gridley." Dewey destroyed the Spanish fleet without losing a single man. In March 1899, Congress created a new rank expressly for him—admiral of the navy, the highest rank ever held by a U.S. naval officer.

Dewey, John (1859–1952) Working mainly at the University of Chicago, Dewey was a pioneer of philosophical pragmatism, which holds that ideas are essentially tools to be used in the solution of problems encountered in the environment. A typically American approach to intellect, the philosophy gave rise to what Dewey called functional psychology and to a pragmatic program of progressive education, which stressed interaction with the world on a practical, physical level as the best means of developing a child's mind.

Dewey, Thomas E. (1902–1971) Dewey's unsuccessful runs for the White House in 1944 (against FDR) and 1948 (against

Truman) overshadow his early success as a New York prosecutor. Between 1935 and 1937, his prosecution of organized crime in New York resulted in 72 convictions out of 73 prosecutions. In 1942, he was elected to the first of three terms as New York governor and was a powerful Republican political leader.

Dickey, James (1923–1997) Dickey earned his literary reputation as a poet (the 1965 *Buckdancer's Choice* is his best-known collection) and critic, but he became a popular literary sensation with his 1970 novel *Deliverance*, a horror-adventure narrative of canoeing down a Georgia river. He transformed the bestselling novel into a screenplay, which was produced in a 1972 film of the same name.

Dickinson, Emily (1830–1886) Dickinson was born and died in Amherst, Massachusetts. Outwardly, she led an uneventful life. Inwardly, she experienced intense physical and spiritual passion, which found expression in nearly two thousand lyric poems of striking modernity. Her fame was entirely posthumous, the work of her lifetime not published until well after her death.

Dickinson, John (1732–1808) Dickinson's 1767–68 *Letters from a Farmer in Pennsylvania, to the Inhabitants of the British Colonies* crystallized colonial resistance to the oppressive Townshend Acts (1767) and thereby advanced the cause of independence. He served as a delegate from Pennsylvania in the Continental Congress during 1774–1776 and helped draft the Articles of Confederation (1776–1777), under which the revolution was fought. Dickinson served as Delaware delegate to the Constitutional Convention (1787) and was instrumental in defending and promoting the completed document.

Dillinger, John (1902–1934) Dillinger spent most of his adult life as a criminal—primarily a bank robber—and gained the dubious distinction of becoming the first man placed on the FBI's Ten Most Wanted list. Dillinger was the subject of a long FBI manhunt, which culminated in Chicago, when FBI agents ambushed him in front of the city's Biograph Theater, shooting him down on July 2, 1934.

Disney, Walt (1901–1966) An animator by vocation, Walter Elias Disney created the animated character of Mickey Mouse in the 1928 short *Steamboat Willie* and used its success to build a cartoon and entertainment empire, which came to encompass television and two theme parks, Disneyland, which opened in Anaheim, California, in 1955, and Walt Disney World, in Orlando, Florida, shortly before his death. The company Disney founded and built expanded far beyond cartoons and theme parks to become one of the world's great entertainment corporations.

Dix, Dorothea (1802–1887) A schoolteacher since the age of 14, Dix was asked in 1841 to teach a Sunday school class in the East Cambridge (Massachusetts) House of Correction. While there, she was appalled by the inhumane treatment of the mentally ill, who were jailed with criminals and without regard to age or sex. They were often left naked, in darkness, sometimes chained, frequently flogged. Dix began a campaign to reform the treatment of the mentally ill, and in 1843 submitted to the Massachusetts legislature a detailed report of conditions in the state's institutions. Over the next 40 years, Dix inspired legislators in 15 states and Canada to establish state hospitals for the mentally ill. Her work spread to Europe as well. By the time of the Civil War, Dix had earned such a formidable reputation that she was made superintendent of nurses for the Union army.

Dodge, Grenville Mellon (1831–1916) Dodge served as an engineer during the Civil War, building bridges and railroads for the Union war effort, then, from 1866 to 1870 was chief engineer for construction of the Union Pacific Railroad, which provided an overland rail link from coast to coast. From 1873 on, Dodge engineered nearly 9,000 miles of railway in the American Southwest.

Dole, Sanford (1844–1926) Dole grew up in Hawaii, the son of American Protestant missionaries. After a mainland education, he practiced law in Honolulu (1869–1887) and served in the Hawaiian legislature, He led a reform movement to adopt a constitution in 1887 and in 1893, acting on behalf of American sugar interests in Hawaii, helped engineer the overthrow of Queen Liliuokalani and obtain annexation by the United States. When U.S. president Grover Cleveland blocked annexation and demanded the restoration of Liliuokalani, Dole and others created the Republic of Hawaii (1894). As president of the republic, Dole continued to seek annexation, which came in 1900. President William McKinley named Dole territorial governor.

Donnelly, Ignatius (1831–1901) Born in Philadelphia, Donnelly settled in Minnesota, where he won election as lieutenant governor and congressman (1863–1869). He left the Republicans in the 1870s to form a succession of liberal third-party movements representing farmers and working men and opposing bankers and financiers, whom he attacked as public enemies. Donnelly wrote a series of highly popular visionary novels, including *Atlantis* (which portrayed the origin of civilization in the lost continent of Atlantis), *Ragnarok: The Age of Fire and Gravel* (which related certain gravel deposits to an ancient near-collision of the earth and a comet), and, most important, *Caesar's Column* (1891), a futurist work that predicted radio, television, and poison gas and that pictured the United States in 1988 ruled by a financial oligarchy that tyrannizes over a downtrodden working class.

Donovan, William "Wild Bill" (1883–1959) Trained as a lawyer, Donovan served with distinction in World War I and earned the Medal of Honor. Between the wars, he returned to the law, serving as a district attorney and as assistant U.S. attorney general as well as practicing privately. On the eve of World War II, President Franklin D. Roosevelt called on Donovan to create a central intelligence service for the United States. This became the Office of Strategic Services (OSS), of which Donovan was named chief on June 13, 1942. Throughout World War II, the OSS collected foreign intelligence, carried out counterpropaganda operations, and, most daringly, covert actions in enemy and occupied countries. After the war, the OSS served as a model for the Central Intelligence Agency (CIA).

Doolittle, James H. (1896–1993) Doolittle was an aviation pioneer, who combined seat-of-the-pants daring with advanced academic study of aeronautics (earning an MIT doctorate). He served as an army pilot in World War I, established a number of aviation speed records between the wars, then resumed active military service in World War II. Shortly after the U.S. entered the war, as Japan moved from triumph to triumph in the Pacific, Doolittle led an extraordinary raid on Tokyo and other Japanese cities using 16 twin-engine B-25 bombers launched from the deck of the aircraft carrier *Hornet*—on the face of it an impossible feat. The April 18, 1942 raid was successful, and although it had all the earmarks of a suicide mission, most of the aircrews, including Doolittle, returned.

Dorr, Thomas (1805–1854) A lawyer by profession, Dorr served in the Rhode Island legislature (from 1834) but failed to reform the conservative state constitution, which was essentially unchanged since Rhode Island had been established as a colony in 1663. In 1841, Dorr founded the People's Party, which, acting on its own, called a convention, drafted and adopted a new constitution, and, on May 3, 1842, held elections that installed Dorr as governor. A small war broke out, and Dorr, tried for treason, was sentenced in 1844 to life imprisonment. He was released after serving a year.

Dos Passos, John (1896–1970) After graduating from Harvard in 1916, Dos Passos volunteered as an ambulance driver in World War I and, like many young men of his age, was emotionally scarred by the experience, becoming one of the so-called "Lost Generation." After the war, Dos Passos became deeply involved in the struggle for social justice, culminating in his efforts to save the Anarchists Nicola Sacco and Bartolomeo Vanzetti, charged with murder. After their execution in 1927, he set to work on his masterpiece, the epic trilogy *U.S.A.*, which depicts America as "two nations," one of the wealthy and the other of the poor.

Douglas, Stephen A. (1813–1861) An Illinois politician, noted orator, and leader of the Democratic Party in the years before the Civil War, Douglas sought compromise in the slavery issue by arguing for popular sovereignty, whereby the citizens of each territory would, when applying for statehood, vote their territory free or slave without intervention by the federal government. This (among other things) became the subject of the seminal Lincoln-Douglas debates of 1858, which eloquently articulated the crisis facing the nation on the brink of civil war. Douglas defeated Lincoln in his bid for the Senate.

Douglas, William O. (1898–1980) Douglas graduated from Whitman College in Walla Walla, Washington, in 1920, and worked his way cross country in 1922 to enroll in Columbia University Law School. He graduated second in his class, practiced corporate law briefly, taught, worked for the Securities and Exchange Commission, and in 1939 was appointed to the Supreme Court by Franklin Roosevelt. Douglas was an uncompromising defender of the Bill of Rights, especially free speech and the rights of those accused of crimes. His views made him a target of conservatives.

Douglass, Frederick (1818?–1895) Raised a slave, Douglass escaped to New York in 1838 and soon earned fame for his eloquent personal perspective on the evil of slavery. He became an abolitionist lecturer and in 1845 wrote a stirring autobiography, *The Narrative of Frederick Douglass,* which was published in its final form as *The Life and Times of Frederick Douglass.* Douglass, a strong advocate of the enlistment of black troops, served Abraham Lincoln as an adviser during the Civil War. After the war, he became a champion of women's rights, and he served in several high-level U.S. government posts—the first African American to do so.

Dreiser, Theodore (1871–1945) Born poor in Terre Haute, Indiana, Dreiser became a newspaper reporter, then started writing fiction, beginning with *Sister Carrie* (1900), the story of a small-town girl who uses men to transform herself into a successful actress. Devoid of Victorian moral judgments, the novel proposed that Carrie's career was the product of nature: she was naturally stronger and more adaptable than the men she used. Dreiser's "naturalism" culminated in his masterpiece, *An American Tragedy* (1925), which used the rise and fall of a man convicted of murder as a microcosm of success and failure in America. Condemned by conventional religious and political leaders of his day, Dreiser helped clear the way for a bold new American literature.

Dubinsky, David (1892–1982) Born in czarist Russia, Dubinsky became a labor leader there and was exiled to Siberia for his "subversive" activities. He escaped and immigrated to the Untied States, where he became president of the International Ladies' Garment Workers Union (ILGWU), which he transformed into a giant organization—growing it from 45,000 to 450,000 members—and a model international union, which pioneered housing, pension plans, and health benefits for its members.

Du Bois, W.E.B. (1868–1963) The first African American to earn a Ph.D. (in sociology, from Harvard, 1895), Du Bois hoped that sociology could be used to win the social changes that would bring equality of treatment and opportunity for the races in America. Disillusioned in this belief, he organized the so-called Niagara Movement, which opposed the "accommodationist" view of Booker T. Washington, who was willing to trade social equality for expanded economic opportunities for black Americans. Arguing that both were immediately necessary, DuBois was instrumental in transforming the Niagara Movement into the National Association for the Advancement of Colored People (NAACP) in 1909. Du Bois edited the NAACP's important magazine, *The Crisis*, a position that made him for some two decades the most influential leader of black America.

Dulles, Allen (1893–1969) The younger brother of Secretary of State John Foster Dulles, Allen Dulles served during World War II, from October 1942 to May 1945, as chief of the Office of Strategic Services (OSS) branch in Bern, Switzerland, where he was effectively America's head spymaster in Europe. After the war, Dulles was instrumental in creating the CIA, of which he became director in 1953, overseeing the agency's expansion during the height of the Cold War.

Dulles, John Foster (1888–1959) A career diplomat, Dulles was one of the architects of the United Nations. In 1953, President Dwight D. Eisenhower appointed him secretary of state. He served until illness forced his resignation in 1959. As secretary, Dulles formulated much of the policy that would guide the United States through the Cold War. Some condemned him as inflexible, but others saw his unwavering firmness as critically important in containing the expansion of international communism.

du Pont, Eleuthère-Irénée (1771–1834) Born into a prominent French family, E.I. du Pont learned the explosives business at the French gunpowder works before he immigrated to America in 1800. He found American gunpowder to be of low quality and high price, and built a gunpowder plant in 1802 near Wilmington, Delaware, producing a much-improved product, which made him a fortune, especially during the War of 1812. This led to the founding of E.I. du Pont de Nemours and Co. in 1833, which became one of the world's great chemical manufacturers in areas ranging from explosives to plastics.

Durand, Asher (1796–1886) Durand made his early living as an engraver. After touring Europe in 1840–1841 and studying the work of the old masters, he returned to America and began painting Hudson River, Adirondack, and New England landscapes, rendering them precisely but with a generous Romantic sensibility. Among the founders of the Hudson River School of landscape artists, he was one of the first American painters to work directly from nature out-of-doors.

Durant, Will and Ariel (1885–1981 and 1898–1981) Will Durant married his student, Ada Kaufman (whom he called Ariel), while he was teaching at the Ferrer Modern School in New York in 1913. The couple collaborated on the massive eleven-volume *Story of Civilization* (1935–1975), which became perhaps the most popularwork and genuinely authoritative work ever published on philosophy and history, bringing these subjects to a wide audience of general readers.

Duryea, Charles and J. Frank (1861–1938 and 1869–1967) When bicycle mechanic Charles Duryea saw a stationary gasoline engine at a state fair in 1886, he got the idea of using it to power a carriage. He drew up designs, and in 1891 he and his brother Frank built an automobile and an engine in a Springfield, Massachusetts, loft. There is a dispute as to when the vehicle was finally completed, but it made its first run on the streets of Springfield on September 22, 1893.

Dylan, Bob (1941–) Born Robert Zimmerman in Duluth, Minnesota, Dylan reinvented himself as a latter-day Woody Guthrie and made a sensation during the folksong revival of the early 1960s with his 1963 album, *Freewheelin' Bob Dylan.* Combining folk traditions with a uniquely contemporary sensibility, a charismatic stage presence, and often brilliantly poetic lyrics, Dylan was hailed by many as the Shakespeare of his generation. In 1965, he introduced electric instruments, which outraged folk fans, but opened up a new form of expression that partook of rock and roll. Dylan has remained an enduring voice in American popular music—commercially very successful, yet also well apart from corporate music making and marketing.

Eakins, Thomas (1844–1916) This Philadelphia-based painter produced portraits with psychological penetration worthy of a great novelist. In these works, and in depictions of such outdoor sports as swimming and boating, he brought the realist style to its greatest height of expression.

Earhart, Amelia (1897–1937) Earhart served as a military nurse during World War I and as a social worker after the war. In 1920-1921, she defied her family by learning to fly and in 1928—as a passenger—was the first woman to fly across the Atlantic. She piloted a plane solo across that ocean on May 20–21, 1932, setting a record time of 14 hours 56 minutes. Celebrated worldwide, she flew solo from Hawaii to California in 1935, the first aviator to complete that route successfully. In 1937, with navigator Fred Noonan, she set out on a round-the-world flight, only to vanish in the central Pacific. No trace of her, Noonan, or their Lockheed Electra has ever been found.

Eastman, George (1854–1932) In 1880 Eastman founded the Eastman Dry Plate and Film Company to manufacture dry photographic plates of his own invention. This improvement over the clumsy wet plate system was followed in 1888 by the introduction of what he called the Kodak—two nonsense syllables Eastman thought mimicked the sound of the camera's shutter—which was a simple box camera anyone could use. Eastman's advertising slogan said it all—"You press the button, we do the rest"—and photography for the masses was born.

Eastman, Max (1883–1969) A philosophy professor at Columbia University, Eastman edited *The Masses*, a radical political and literary journal whose editors were tried twice in 1918 for opposing America's entry into World War I. After the war, Eastman edited *The Liberator*, another popular radical magazine, then traveled to the Soviet Union in 1922 to see firsthand the effects of the Bolshevik Revolution. Appalled by what he believed was a betrayal of the Communist ideal, he wrote a series of anti-Soviet books, and in 1941 became a roving editor for *The Reader's Digest*, the only mainstream periodical he ever worked for.

Ebbers, Bernard (1941–) Bernard "Bernie" Ebbers was born in Canada to the family of a traveling salesman. He started in business as the operator of motels in Mississippi and in 1983 invested with others in the newly formed Long Distance Discount Services, Inc (LDDS). Named CEO in 1985, he presided over the acquisition of more than 60 other independent telecommunications firms to create WorldCom in 1995. The explosive expansion of WorldCom attracted many investors, but in 2005 Ebbers was convicted of fraud and conspiracy for spectacularly overstating the financially strapped company's earnings—at a cost to investors of $180 billion. Ebbers was sentenced to 25 years.

Eckert, J. Presper (1919–1995) With his University of Pennsylvania professor, John W. Mauchly, Eckert created, in

1946, ENIAC (Electronic Numerical Integrator and Computer), the first all-electronic (not electromechanical) digital computer. Commissioned by the U.S. government, it was used primarily for military applications and contained, in rudimentary form, all of the circuitry employed in modern computers.

Eddy, Mary Baker (1821–1910) Raised in the Congregational church, Mary Baker Eddy suffered from chronic, debilitating disease until 1866, when she claimed to have been suddenly healed as a result of reading the New Testament. This inspired her to create a new religion, Christian Science, in which spiritual faith is linked to physical healing. The religion grew rapidly and now has about 2,500 congregations in 70 countries.

Edison, Thomas Alva (1847–1931) Almost certainly the most famous inventor in the world, Edison held 1,093 patents, an international record that remains unbroken to this day. His inventions include the phonograph, the incandescent electric light, the elements of the electric power industry, and the basic constituents of motion picture technology, among much else.

Edwards, Jonathan (1703–1758) A Connecticut clergyman and religious philosopher, Edwards was an orator of electrifying spiritual eloquence, whose most celebrated sermon, "Sinners in the Hands of an Angry God" (1741), had his congregation writhing with a sense of hellfire. His preaching stimulated the " Great Awakening," a mass religious revival that swept America during the mid eighteenth century. Edwards was the forerunner of the modern American evangelist preachers.

Ehrlich, Paul R. (1932–) A Philadelphia-born zoologist who served as Bing Professor of Population Studies at Stanford University, Ehrlich writes about the dangerous impact of runaway population growth on the United States and the world and is the author of the best-selling *The Population Bomb,* published in 1968, which warned of the collapse of civilization unless world governments institute policies to control population growth.

Ehrlichman, John (1925–1999) Ehrlichman was officially assistant for domestic affairs in the administration of President Richard M. Nixon, but his mission was, in effect, to selectively insulate the president from the public and from other members of the government. Early in the administration, Ehrlichman created a covert and illegal team of operatives he called the Plumbers, because their role was to stop information leaks. They also illegally acquired political intelligence. Ehrilchman resigned in April 1973, during the Watergate scandal, and was subsequently convicted of conspiracy, perjury, and obstruction of justice, for which he served 18 months in prison.

Eisenhower, Dwight D. (1890–1969) Born in Texas and raised in Kansas, "Ike" Eisenhower graduated from West Point in 1915 and rose through the U.S. Army to become Supreme Allied Commander, Europe, during World War II. From this position, he coordinated the Allied victory over fascist Italy and Nazi Germany. After the war, he served briefly as president of Columbia University, returned to active duty as supreme commander of the newly formed NATO forces, then ran for president on the Republican ticket in 1952. Elected by a landslide over Democrat Adlai E. Stevenson, he served two terms, during which the United States experienced a decade of business and economic expansion as well as a certain postwar complacency, despite the early ferment of the civil rights movement at home and the ongoing Cold War.

Eliot, T. S. (1888–1965) A native of St. Louis, Eliot was educated at Harvard but lived his literary life in England, where, during the 1920s, he became a leading light of the "modernist" movement in poetry. His lyrical yet challenging works explore the alienation of 20th-century humanity and search for answers in a spiritual wasteland. His masterpieces include the long poems *The Waste Land* (1922) and *The Four Quartets* (1943)—the latter earning him the Nobel Prize for Literature in 1948.

Ellington, Edward Kennedy "Duke" (1899–1974) Washington-born Duke Ellington was the elegant embodiment of big band jazz, a great pianist, and perhaps the most prolific jazz composer in history. The ensemble sound he created has never been duplicated, and his compositions combined classical tone poem traditions with swing-era jazz. While Ellington was a great jazz symphonist, he also wrote some of the most memorable songs in the pop repertoire, including "Sophisticated Lady," "Satin Doll," "Don't Get Around Much Any More," and "Prelude to a Kiss."

Ellison, Ralph (1914–1994) Educated at Alabama's Tuskegee Institute, Ellison began writing for publication in the late 1930s, publishing his only finished novel, *Invisible Man,* in 1953. The semi-realistic, semi-surrealistic novel tells the story of an idealistic Southern black youth who seeks opportunity in Harlem and joins the struggle against white oppression, only to find that he is "invisible," ignored by blacks and whites alike. The book won the National Book

Award. Ellison produced little else during the rest of his literary career, but *Invisible Man* secured his legacy as an acutely poetic analyst of what it means to be black in America.

Ellsberg, Daniel (1931–) Employed by the RAND Corporation "think tank" as a military analyst during the Vietnam era, Ellsberg was one of the authors of a top secret study commissioned by President Lyndon Johnson's secretary of defense, Robert McNamara, analyzing the process and circumstances by which the United States became involved in the Vietnam War. Ellsberg turned against the war and in 1971 leaked the top-secret study to the *New York Times.* The so-called "Pentagon Papers" revealed the Vietnam War to have been the product of official deceit and deception, combined with tragic miscalculation and misjudgment, during the administrations of four American presidents. The document galvanized the antiwar movement and caused many Americans to lose their trust in the integrity of government.

Ellsworth, Oliver (1745–1807) A Hartford, Connecticut, lawyer during the American Revolution, Ellsworth resolved a major obstacle to approval of the new U.S. Constitution by coauthoring with Roger Sherman the Connecticut Compromise—or Great Compromise—of 1787, which synthesized the Virginia Plan (favoring representation in Congress based on population) and the New Jersey Plan (favoring equal representation for every state). Ellsworth and Sherman proposed a bicameral Congress, in which representation in the House of Representatives would be based on population and representation in the Senate apportioned equally among all states. Ellsworth went on to write the Judiciary Act of 1789, which established the federal court

system, and he served as the nation's third chief justice of the Supreme Court (1796–1800).

Emerson, Ralph Waldo (1803–1882) Trained as a Unitarian minister, Emerson pursued instead a life as a man of letters and a philosopher, the leading exponent of Transcendentalism, which posited the unity in nature of all creation, the innate goodness of man, the primacy of intuitive insight over received wisdom and logic, and the belief that a close experience of the natural world would reveal the deepest spiritual truths. Inspired by these beliefs, Emerson wrote excellent poetry and some of the most beloved essays in American literature. As a philosopher, he earned an international reputation. As a man of letters, he encouraged other American writers to create a genuinely original American literature, free from the bonds of tradition and imitation.

Equiano, Olaudah (Gustavus Vassa) (c. 1745–c. 1797) Kidnapped in Benin, Africa, at age 11 or 12, Equiano was enslaved and sent to America. Eventually freed by his master, he went to England, where he became an abolitionist, lecturing on the cruelty of the British slave owners of Jamaica. British abolitionists funded publication of his 1789 autobiography, *The Interesting Narrative of the Life of Olaudah Equiano,* a dramatic account of his abduction and his first voyage via the "Middle Passage" to the West Indies and America. His book was the most widely read work by an African American prior to the Civil War and did much to awaken the world to the suffering of slaves.

Eriksson, Leif (fl. 11th century) The Norse explorer Leif Eriksson—Leif the Lucky—is generally believed to have

been the first European to land in North America, when, about A.D. 1000, he spent a winter in Newfoundland at a place he called Vinland (from the abundance of grapes there), establishing the first North American European settlement at present-day L'Anse aux Meadows.

Ervin, Sam (1896–1985) Ervin was a Democratic senator from North Carolina from 1954 until 1974. At the beginning of his Senate career, he served on the Senate committee that censured the anti-Communist "witch hunter" Senator Joseph McCarthy, but it was for his work at the culmination of his career, as chairman of the Senate Select Committee to Investigate Campaign Practices, known as the "Ervin Committee," that he is best known. It was this committee that publicly investigated the Watergate scandal and brought down the presidency of Richard M. Nixon in 1974.

Evans, Walker (1903–1975) On assignment for the Resettlement Administration (later renamed the Farm Security Administration [FSA]) beginning in 1935, Walker recorded in breathtaking detail the lives of people hit by the Great Depression. He produced intensely moving documents of pride and poverty, which convey as much about the human spirit as they do about the hardships of an era in America.

Evers, Medgar (1925–1963) Evers was an African-American businessman who became an NAACP leader in Mississippi, organizing voter-registration drives and other civil rights initiatives. On June 12, 1963, just hours after President John F. Kennedy delivered a broadcast on civil rights, Evers was gunned down in front of his Mississippi home. The murder made him a national figure, underscored Kennedy's pronouncements, and focused national

attention on civil rights and social justice. White segregationist Byron de La Beckwith was arrested and charged with the murder, but was freed in 1964 after two hung-jury trials. He was finally convicted in a third trial in 1994.

Exner, Judith Campbell (1934–1999) Born Judith Inmoor in New York and raised in Los Angeles, she married an actor (William Campbell), divorcing him in 1958 after she became romantically involved with Frank Sinatra, who introduced her to presidential candidate John F. Kennedy in 1960. She was having an affair with JFK when Sinatra next introduced her to Chicago mob boss Sam Giancana, with whom she also had an affair. Reputedly, Exner served as a liaison between Kennedy and Giancana, who is believed to have delivered critical votes in the 1960 presidential election. (Campbell's name changed again when she married golfer Dan Exner in 1975.)

Fall, Albert (1861–1944) Albert Fall became a symbol of national political corruption rampant in the administration of President Warren G. Harding. He was Harding's secretary of interior from 1921 to 1923. In 1924, a Senate investigation revealed that Fall had taken a bribe to lease to private oil interests naval oil reserve lands in Wyoming's Teapot Dome reserve and other reserves in California. The Teapot Dome Scandal rocked the nation, and Fall, convicted of bribery in 1929, served nine months of a one-year sentence.

Falwell, Jerry (1933–) Jerry Falwell is among the highest-profile figures of the American religious right, a Fundamentalist Baptist pastor and televangelist, whose moral and political pronouncements regularly generate much controversy. In 1971 he founded Liberty University and in 1979 the Moral

Majority, a political action committee (PAC) that pursued an agenda of evangelical political lobbying.

Farmer, James (1920–99). Farmer led the Congress of Racial Equality (CORE) and introduced into the civil rights movement such tactics as nonviolent sit-ins (to force the integration of segregated restaurants and other places) and Freedom Rides (to force the integration of bus stations in the South). These tactics came to symbolize the civil rights movement during its height in the early 1960s and helped bring about passage of the Civil Rights Act of 1964 and the Voting Rights Act of 1965.

Farnsworth, Philo T. (1906–1971) Television was not a single invention, but the result of many innovators, foremost among them Vladimir Zworykin and Philo T. Farnsworth. In 1927, Farnsworth transmitted an electromechanically scanned image—it was (perhaps hopefully) a dollar sign—composed of 60 horizontal scan lines. Based on this, he submitted the first of his 165 television and other electronic patents.

Faubus, Orval (1910?–1994) One of several segregationist southern governors during the 1950s, Faubus garnered national attention when, in 1957, he called out the Arkansas National Guard to prevent African-American children from attending Little Rock Central High School pursuant to a federal desegregation order. Unwilling to allow a governor to defy federal law, President Dwight Eisenhower federalized the Arkansas National Guard, ordered them to stand down, and sent members of the 101st Airborne Division to Little Rock to escort and protect black students enrolling in the school. Faubus responded by shutting down Little Rock Schools for the next two years.

Faulkner, William (1897–1962) William Faulkner drew on his experience of the American South, especially his native Mississippi, to create a fictional universe of remarkable depth and richness. He took an intensely local approach that illuminated fundamental and universal human issues, and he did so in a bravura narrative style that combined the timeless elements of traditional storytelling with avant-garde literary modernism, including dazzling shifts in time, place, and the consciousness of his characters. He was awarded the Nobel Prize for Literature in 1950.

Felt, W. Mark, Sr. (1913–) Reporters Bob Woodward and Carl Bernstein received much of the information that allowed them to expose the Watergate scandal that undid the Nixon presidency from an insider source known only as "Deep Throat." In May 2005, thirty years after the revelation of the scandal, W. Mark Felt finally revealed himself as the whistlesblower. During part of the investigation of the Watergate candal (1972–1974), Felt was the FBI's associate director, its second in command.

Ferraro, Geraldine (1935–) A member of the House of Representatives, Ferraro was selected in 1984 by Democratic Party presidential candidate Walter Mondale as his running mate. Mondale was defeated by incumbent president Ronald Reagan.

Field, Marshall (1834–1906) Born on a Massachusetts farm, Field became a dry-goods store errand boy, but rapidly metamorphosed into a talented salesman. He moved to Chicago in 1856 and went to work for a mercantile concern, in which he became a partner. From here, in 1865, he joined the merchandising firm of Potter Palmer, which became Field, Leiter and Company in 1867 after Palmer withdrew. The following year, Field and Leiter opened their first department store, which, in 1881, became Marshall Field and Company. Field created the modern department store, adopting as his motto "Give the lady what she wants." He revolutionized retailing in the United States.

Fillmore, Millard (1800–1874) Fillmore was elected vice president in 1848, ascending to the presidency on the death of President Zachary Taylor in July 1850. He served out Taylor's term, which ended in 1853. Fillmore sought to appease the South by insisting on strong federal enforcement of the Fugitive Slave Act that was part of the Compromise of 1850. This not only alienated the North, spelling the end of the Whig Party, but served to galvanize the abolition movement, giving rise to a militant, radical antislavery faction and bringing the nation closer to civil war.

Finster, Howard (1916–2001) A native of Summerville, Georgia, Howard Finster was a "born again" Christian who became a Baptist pastor and created folk art under what he claimed was the inspiration of God, who enjoined him to preach the gospel through an art assemblage called "Paradise Garden" and some 46,000 individual pieces of art. The incredibly prolific Finster incorporated a dazzling array of images in his art, which included paintings and three-dimensional works, appropriating pop culture icons (especially Elvis Presley), historical figures (Lincoln and Washington), and renderings of more conventional religious images. During the 1970s, his work began to receive national recognition, and he emerged as the first of the so-called "outsider artists," artists who are not part of the academic or commercial art establishment.

Firestone, Harvey (1868–1938) An early believer in rubber tires, Firestone drove the first rubber-tired buggy in Detroit. He moved to Chicago in 1896 and opened a retail tire business before relocating to Akron, Ohio, in 1900, where he exploited his patent on a device that applied rubber tires to carriage wheel channels. This led to his founding the Firestone Tire & Rubber Company, which became the giant of the industry and earned Firestone a reputation as the man who put America on tires.

Fischer, Bobby (1943–) Born in Chicago, Fischer dropped out of high school at 16 to devote himself to chess. In 1958, he became the youngest grandmaster in history, but rose to international celebrity even beyond the world of chess when he became the first native-born American to win the title of world champion, defeating Soviet grandmaster Boris Spassky. After he refused in 1975 to defend his title against another Soviet challenger, Anatoly Karpov, he was stripped of his championship and withdrew into obscurity for two decades, reemerging to defeat Spassky in a private rematch in 1992.

Fitzgerald, Ella (1917–1996) After winning amateur talent contests in New York, the youthful Fitzgerald joined the Chick Webb orchestra in 1935. Webb nurtured the girl's talent, even becoming Fitzgerald's legal guardian after the death of her mother. When Webb died in 1939, Fitzgerald led the band until it broke up in 1942. From this point on, Fitzgerald had a solo career that spanned another five decades. Her range as a singer was unparalleled and the lyric mellowness of her voice unequalled. Many critics consider her the greatest female vocalist who ever sang jazz.

Fitzgerald, F. Scott (1896–1940) Fitzgerald enjoyed early success for his novels and short stories depicting the "Jazz Age" of the Roaring Twenties, but his masterpiece, *The Great Gatsby* (1925), now recognized as one of the greatest of American novels—a poignant study of love, passion, and the American dream—was a commercial failure during Fitzgerald's lifetime. Fitzgerald and his exciting but mentally unbalanced wife, Zelda, led lives that were by turns fabulously glamorous and desperately frantic. They were, during the 1920s, one the world's most celebrated couples.

Flagg, James Montgomery (1877–1960) From 1892 on, Flagg was one of the nation's most prominent and successful illustrators, his work adorning most popular magazines. Especially celebrated for stylish and buxom young ladies, he became even more famous for his depictions of Uncle Sam on World War I and World War II "I Want You" recruiting posters.

Flagler, Henry M. (1830–1913) Flagler made a fortune partnering with John D. Rockefeller in creating the Standard Oil Company, but he is best known as a real estate entrepreneur and developer, who purchased several railway lines in Florida in 1886, combined them as the Florida East Coast Line, then built a chain of luxury hotels along the railroad. From this, modern Florida developed as a tourist, leisure, and retirement Mecca.

Flanagan, Father Edward J. (1886–1948) Born in Ireland, Flanagan immigrated to the United States in 1906 and became a Roman Catholic priest. In 1917, he founded the Home for Homeless Boys in Omaha, Nebraska, then expanded it, leaving downtown Omaha to establish Boys

Town, ten miles west of the city in 1921. Flanagan directed the growth of Boys Town into a genuine community for orphans and troubled youths. Here, boys between 10 and 16 were transformed by love and understanding into productive citizens in a "town" with a mayor, council, schools, chapel, post office, cottages, gymnasium, and vocational training facilities. The world's most famous orphanage, Boys Town continues to operate today as Girls and Boys Town.

Ford, Betty (1918–) Wife of Gerald Ford, 38th president of the United States, Betty Ford became addicted to pain relievers, entered a treatment center, and then founded the Betty Ford Center to treat others with addictions. Ford's public courage in discussing her addiction removed much of the moral stigma from addictive disorders and changed the way many Americans viewed drug and alcohol problems.

Ford, Gerald (1913–) A Michigan Congressman, Ford was appointed vice president by Richard M. Nixon after the resignation in disgrace of Vice President Spiro T. Agnew in 1973. When Nixon resigned in 1974 as a result of the Watergate scandal, Ford became the nation's only unelected chief executive. His conciliatory personality contrasted with the combative demeanor of President Nixon, and he professed a desire to heal the nation after Watergate—although many denounced his blanket pardon of the former president. Ford failed in his bid for election in his own right, losing to Democrat Jimmy Carter in 1978.

Ford, Henry (1863–1947) Raised on a Michigan farm, Henry Ford grew up more interested in machines than crops and livestock. He began working as a machinist and was drawn to the newly developed internal combustion engine. This led to his tinkering together his first automobile, which, in 1899 spawned the Detroit Automobile Company (later the Henry Ford Company). But it was in 1908, with the introduction of the Model T, that Ford began the simultaneous transformation of industrial production—indeed, the very nature of work—with the modern assembly line and the transformation of America: its habits of consumption, its manner of living, its culture, and its landscape. The widespread availability of private transportation in the form of affordable automobiles remade America from a collection of cities, isolated villages, and farms, into a new form of civilization networked by roads and driven by a new ethic of personal freedom.

Ford, John (1895–1973) Born Sean Aloysius O'Feeney in Maine, Ford moved to Hollywood in 1914, became a prop man for a film studio, changed his name, and directed his first movies in the 1920s. As a director, he was noted for brilliant cutting, which put the emphasis on action without ever compromising sharp and colorful characterization. Some of his most notable films—*The Grapes of Wrath* (1940), *How Green Was My Valley* (1941), and *The Quiet Man* (1952)—won Academy Awards for direction and emphasized social themes, but he is even better remembered as a master of the western genre, with such classics as *Stagecoach* (1939), *My Darling Clementine* (1946), *The Searchers* (1956), *The Man Who Shot Liberty Valance* (1962), *How the West Was Won* (1962), and *Cheyenne Autumn* (1964).

Forrest, Edwin (1806–1872) One the great tragedians of the 19th-century American stage, Forrest started a feud with the English actor William Macready, which triggered in May 1849 the Astor Place riot in New York City as a mob of Forrest partisans stormed the Astor Place Opera House, where Macready was appearing. Twenty-two persons were killed and 36 wounded. Forrest's reputation was another casualty of the riot. Two years later, he stirred a fresh scandal when he sued his actress wife for divorce on grounds of adultery. He lost, but obsessively appealed for 18 years, during which time he became a recluse. Forrest's experience is an early example of the nation's limitless appetite for scandal.

Forrest, Nathan Bedford (1821–1877) Self-taught in everything, including the military art, Forrest was commander of great skill and daring, considered by William T. Sherman the most dangerous man in the Confederacy. His philosophy of combat was simple: "Get there first with the most men" (often misquoted as "Get there firstest with the mostest"). His reputation for ruthlessness was certified by his role in the Ft. Pillow Massacre (April 12, 1864), in which more than 300 African-American troops were slaughtered after they surrendered. Following the war, Forrest organized the original Ku Klux Klan, serving for a time as its Grand Wizard.

Frankenthaler, Helen (1928–) Strongly influenced by the work of Arshile Gorky and Jackson Pollock, Frankenthaler developed her own style of abstract expressionism, creating ethereal works by applying thinned oil paints onto unprimed canvas in a stain technique that broke with the heavy application of paint (impasto) in vogue among other abstract expressionists. Frankenthaler's lyrical works inspired the next generation of painters, the so-called color-field painters, including Morris Louis.

Frankfurter, Felix (1882–1965) Born in Vienna, Austria, Frankfurter immigrated to the United States with his family in 1893. Earning his law degree from Harvard, he was a brilliant scholar and adviser to presidents, beginning with Woodrow Wilson during the negotiation of the Treaty of Versailles. Appointed to the Supreme Court in 1939 by Franklin D. Roosevelt, Frankfurter was a passionate advocate of what he called "decency of government," but was above all an advocate of judicial restraint, believing that judges should adhere to precedent over their own opinions.

Franklin, Benjamin (1706–1790) Franklin earned national and international fame as a printer, publisher, author, inventor, scientist, diplomat, and charming wit. Self-educated, he had a tremendous breadth of knowledge and achievements. He was celebrated as a font of homely wisdom with his enormously popular *Poor Richard's Almanacs*; he was a driving force behind the American Revolution; he was a diplomat of extraordinary skill, instrumental in negotiating the Franco-American alliance during the revolution; he was an entrepreneurial innovator (a pioneer of the insurance industry); he was a brilliant author; he was an internationally respected scientist (especially for his early work on electricity); and he was an inventor. Bifocals, the Franklin stove, and the lightning rod were among his best-known inventions, but his greatest invention was himself. In his justly celebrated *Autobiography*, Franklin mythologized his own life, presenting himself as an illustration of all that was possible in America for one who applied wit, sound ethics, imagination, and a willingness to work.

Frelinghuysen, Frederick Theodore (1817–1885) Frelinghuysen graduated from Rutgers College in 1836, studied law under his uncle, then began practicing in 1839. He was a founder of the Republican Party in New Jersey. Appointed to the U.S. Senate to fill a vacancy in 1866, he was defeated for the Senate in 1869 but was elected for a full six-year term beginning in 1871. President Chester A. Arthur appointed him secretary of state in 1881. Frelinghuysen forged strong commercial ties with Latin America, acquired Pearl Harbor, Hawaii, for a U.S. naval base—giving America control over much of the Pacific—and opened diplomatic relations with the "hermit kingdom" of Korea in 1882.

Frémont, John C. (1813–1890) Frémont explored and mapped much of the Far West during the 1840s in the course of surveying potential routes for a transcontinental railroad. During the U.S.-Mexican War (1846–1848), Frémont was instrumental in breaking California away from Mexico. A committed abolitionist, he ran unsuccessfully in 1856 as the first Republican presidential candidate, then served (with little success) as a Union general during the Civil War.

Freneau, Philip (1752–1832) Freneau was a schoolmaster and divinity student before the American Revolution, during which he used his considerable poetic talent to compose acid satires mocking the British and Tories. He joined the New Jersey militia in 1778 and was captured by the redcoats in 1780. He recounted his POW experience in a bitter poem titled *The British Prison-Ship* (1781). After the war, Freneau worked as a partisan journalist promoting the liberal orientation of such leaders as Thomas Jefferson against the more conservative Federalism exemplified in John Adams. As a poet, Freneau stood well above most of his American contemporaries.

Frick, Henry Clay (1849–1919) Frick made his fortune by building and operating coke ovens beginning in 1870 and supplying the steel and iron industry with the coke needed for the blast furnaces that refined raw ore. As chairman of Andrew Carnegie's steel interests (1889), Frick built the company into the world's largest manufacturer of steel and coke. In 1892, during the Homestead (Pennsylvania) steel strike, Frick was shot and stabbed by the anarchist Alexander Berkman, but recovered and went on to create the United States Steel Corporation. Frick used part of his great fortune to amass one of the great private art collections in the world. He bequeathed the collection and the Manhattan mansion housing it to the city of New York as a museum.

Friedan, Betty (1921–2006) While working as a journalist, Friedan wrote *The Feminine Mystique* (1963), which asked why so many modern American women were frustrated in traditional roles. The book created a sensation and launched the modern feminist movement. Friedan went on to cofound the National Organization of Women (NOW) in 1966, dedicated to achieving equality of opportunity for women.

Frost, Robert (1874–1963) Frost was born in California but lived most of his life in New England, which was the setting for much of his poetry. Although his work was in some ways backward looking—often portraying rural life in New England and always composed in traditional rhymed verse—Frost tackled timeless issues of the human condition and was a virtuoso of American colloquial speech. His realist sensibility and his lyrical style made Frost the most popular of 20th-century American poets.

Fuller, Margaret (1810–1850) Fuller was a part of the literary circle that gathered around Ralph Waldo Emerson, with whom she shared an enthusiasm for the Transcendentalist philosophy, which saw divine inspiration in all objects of nature. During 1839–1844, Fuller led classes (she called them "conversations") for women on the subjects of literature, education, mythology, and philosophy. Her purpose was to enrich the lives of women and to bring them to a place of social equality. Her *Woman in the Nineteenth Century* (1845) is regarded as an important feminist work.

Fuller, R. Buckminster (1895–1983) Best known as the inventor of the geodesic dome, an elegant multipurpose structural design patented in 1953, Fuller advocated engineering and design on self-sustaining ecological principles that exploited renewable resources in order to ensure the future of the planet he called "Spaceship Earth." Fuller's genius was the application of visionary design to immediate, practical needs.

Fulton, Robert (1765–1815) Fulton's first ambition was to become a painter, but failing to win critical and commercial success, he turned to engineering and invention instead. He designed a system of inland waterways and canals, a practical submarine, a steam warship, and, most famously, in 1808, a sidewheel steamboat called the *North River Steamboat of Clermont*—but popularly dubbed the *Clermont*—which plied the Hudson as the first practical steam-powered vessel.

Galbraith, John Kenneth (1908–) Raised in Toronto, Galbraith did his advanced work in economics in the United States and served as an adviser to President John F. Kennedy as well as his ambassador to India from 1961 to 1963. Galbraith challenged conventional economic wisdom by calling for less consumer spending and more spending on government programs. His policies shaped the Democratic agenda of JFK and Lyndon Johnson and contributed to the modern concept of the American welfare state.

Gallatin, Albert (1761–1849) Born in Switzerland, Gallitin immigrated to the United States when he was nineteen. He was a vigorous anti-Federalist and ally of Thomas Jefferson, who appointed him the nation's fourth secretary of the Treasury. Gallatin introduced a new simplicity in government, which drastically reduced the public debt. He was instrumental in implementing Jefferson's ideal of a minimized federal administration.

Gallaudet, Thomas (1787–1851) Gallaudet founded the first American school for the deaf in the belief that persons with this disability could be fully educated and had a right to such an education. After graduating from Yale in 1805, Galludet studied institutions for the deaf in Europe, then returned to the United States in 1816 and founded the American Asylum for Deaf Mutes at Hartford, Connecticut, obtaining for this a land grant from the U.S. Congress—the first instance of federal aid to the disabled. Galludet's school became the nation's principal training center for instructors of the deaf. Gallaudet's 1825 *Plan of a Seminary for the Education of Instructors of Youth* included a proposal for the special education of the disabled and for the professional training of teachers of all types of students. In 1856, Amos Kendall founded a small school for the deaf and the blind in Washington, D.C.; later headed by Gallaudet's son, it was named Gallaudet College in 1893 to honor Thomas Gallaudet. It is now Gallaudet University.

Galloway, Joseph (1731–1803) In 1774, this distinguished Philadelphia attorney introduced the Galloway Plan, which proposed a union between the discontented American colonies and Britain. The plan provided for greatly expanded home rule, including a colonial president general (appointed by the king) and a locally voted colonial legislature, which would function in the manner of the House of Commons. The Continental Congress debated the plan for a single day, then rejected it by a single vote. This narrow rejection was a major step toward revolution.

Gallup, George (1901–1984) Gallup was a journalism professor, who, in 1932, was hired by an advertising firm to conduct public-opinion surveys on behalf of its clients. This led to his developing a system of public opinion survey, the "Gallup Poll," which had a profound impact on corporate marketing and political campaigning. Gallup founded the American Institute of Public Opinion (1935), the British Institute of Public Opinion (1936), and the Audience Research Institute, Inc. (1939).

Gardner, John (1933–1982) A respected university professor and poet, Gardner's enduring literary reputation rests largely on a single work, *Grendel* (1971), which retold the Old English story of Beowulf—from the point of view of the monster, whose situation, perceptions, and emotions are remarkably and profoundly human.

Garfield, James A. (1831–1881) Garfield, who served with distinction in the Union army during the Civil War, was an Ohio representative and Senator before he was elected president in 1880. Inaugurated on March 4, 1881, he was shot in the back on July 2, 1881, by a disgruntled office seeker, Charles J, Guiteau. Garfield lingered until September 19, 1881. His long incapacity raised critical constitutional questions concerning the circumstances under which the vice president should assume the role of the chief executive.

Garland, Hamlin (1860–1940) Garland was born on a Wisconsin farm and moved with his family to Iowa and then the Dakotas. As an adult, he embodied his experiences in autobiographical novels and short stories that chronicle the hardships—both physical and economic—of pioneer life. His masterpiece is *Main-Travelled Roads* of 1891.

Garrett, Pat (1850–1908) Garrett was born in Alabama and settled in Texas and New Mexico, where he worked as a cowboy and buffalo hunter before becoming deputy sheriff then sheriff of Lincoln County, New Mexico. His fame rests solely on his having tracked and shot down the legendary outlaw Billy the Kid at Fort Sumner, New Mexico, on July 14, 1881.

Garrison, William Lloyd (1805–1879) In 1831, Garrison started publishing *The Liberator*, which emerged as the most radical of American abolitionist journals. In its pages, Garrison called for an immediate, unconditional end to slavery, and in 1832 founded the New England Anti Slavery Society, also becoming the following year a founding member of the American Anti Slavery Society. Uncompromising in his views, Garrison in 1844 called for the peaceful secession of the free northern states from the states of the slaveholding South.

Garvey, Marcus (1887–1940) Born in Jamaica, Garvey, mostly self-taught, traveled in Central America, lived in London from 1912 to 1914, then returned to Jamaica, where, with others, he founded the Universal Negro Improvement and Conservation Association and African Communities League, or Universal Negro Improvement Association (UNIA). The principal goal of the organization was to create, in Africa, an independent black governed nation. Meeting with little success in Jamaica, Garvey brought the UNIA to the United States in 1916, establishing branches in New York's Harlem and black neighborhoods in other northern cities. Between 1919 and 1926, when he was jailed for mail fraud, Garvey was hailed as the "Black Moses" for having awakened the African-American community to the possibilities of self-determination.

Gary, Elbert (1846–1927) A powerful corporate attorney and noted jurist, Elbert Gary was elected chairman of U.S. Steel after its merger with Federal Steel in 1901. For the next 26 years, he presided over the enormous growth of the steel industry and was the personification of a captain of American industry. When U.S. Steel created a company town around its principal mills in Indiana in 1906, it named it Gary, after the chairman.

Gates, Bill (1955–) Gates founded a company—Microsoft—that developed and controlled the most important operating systems of the emerging personal computer (PC). With MS-DOS (Microsoft Disk-Operating System) and, later, Windows, Microsoft held the software keys to the personal computer. This made Gates one of the wealthiest men in the world (at times, *the* wealthiest) and simultaneously one of the world's most admired, envied, and sometimes hated business titans. In 2000, Gates and his wife, Melinda, established the Bill and Melinda Gates Foundation, which rapidly became the richest philanthropic organization in the world—and attracted in 2006 the largest single philanthropic gift ever made, $30.7 billion in stock from Warren Buffet, which more than doubled the foundation's already spectacular $29 billion endowment.

Gates, Daryl (1926–) As chief of the Los Angeles Police Department (LAPD) from 1978 until 1992, Gates introduced law enforcement innovations of national significance, including the DARE (Drug Abuse Resistance Education) and Community Resources Against Street Hoodlums (CRASH) programs and, most important of all, the SWAT (Special Weapons And Tactics) concept. His hard-charging leadership style, however, was often viewed as excessive, and his paramilitary approach to policing was seen by some as brutal and inappropriate. Most serious were charges of institutionalized racism within the LAPD. His controversial police career ended in 1992, after he seemingly failed to take necessary steps to quell the worst race riots in Los Angeles history. Gates's embattled career dramatized many of the challenges of law enforcement in modern America.

Gatling, Richard Jordan (1818–1903) About 1862, this American inventor developed the Gatling gun, the direct precursor of the modern machine gun. For better or worse, it was a major step in the efficiency of infantry weapons and—especially in its later development as the machine gun—would have a profound effect on modern warfare.

Genêt, Charles Edmond (1763–1834) Sent by revolutionary France as an emissary to the United States, Genêt sidestepped President Washington and the U.S. government by conspiring to involve American citizens directly in France's ongoing war against Britain. This strained Anglo-American relations and set the stage for a major crisis in Franco-American relations. But it also successfully tested President Washington's determination to uphold and defend United States sovereignty.

Genovese, Vito (1897–1969) After immigrating to the United States from Naples in 1913, Genovese became active in New York gangs, rose to control those gangs, then fled to Italy in 1937 to avoid U.S. prosecution. He became an illicit financier of Benito Mussolini and smuggled narcotics into the United States. Returned to the States after World War II, he again rose to prominence as organized crime's "boss of all the bosses" in the New York area. Convicted on smuggling and narcotics charges in 1959, he was imprisoned, but continued to rule the underworld from his cell. His reign was finally ended by a fatal heart attack, while still in custody.

George, Henry (1839–1897) In 1879, George published *Progress and Poverty*, in which he proposed the so-called single tax. Government, he wrote, should be financed by a state tax on "economic rent"—the income from the use of the bare land, not any improvements on that land—and all other taxes should be abolished. The idea took fire as the country struggled to recover from the major panic and depression of 1873–1878, and George became a celebrity. His ideas continue to serve as the basis for many ambitious tax reform schemes.

Geronimo (1829–1909) Geronimo, whose Indian name was Goyathlay ("One who yawns"), led his band, the Chiricahua Apaches, in a highly effective guerrilla resistance to reservation confinement. Geronimo was the last great leader of the Apaches, who had resisted white colonization of their homeland since the days of the Spanish conquistadors. Geronimo led raids and resistance from the early 1860s until his final surrender in 1886. His name was memorialized by U.S. paratroops in World War II, who used "Geronimo!" as their jump cry.

Gerry, Elbridge (1744–1814) A signer of the Declaration of Independence, Gerry was vice president during the second term of James Madison. His name is memorialized in the term "gerrymandering"—dividing electoral districts for partisan political advantage—a practice first associated with Gerry's administration as governor of Massachusetts (1810–1812).

Gershwin, George (1898–1937) Born in Brooklyn, Gershwin was one of the most important of all popular American composers. He wrote highly successful Broadway musicals, which included some of the most beautiful of American popular songs (many with lyrics by brother Ira), and also major orchestral compositions, the most famous of which is *Rhapsody in Blue*, which successfully combines elements of the classical piano concerto with 1920s jazz. He called his 1935 *Porgy and Bess* an "American folk opera." Filled with beautiful music, it featured an all African-American cast.

Gershwin, Ira (1896–1983) Born in Brooklyn, Ira Gershwin became most famous as the lyricist who collaborated with his composer brother, George, on more than 20 Broadway musicals. After George Gershwin's death in 1937, Ira served as lyricist to such greats as Kurt Weill, Jerome Kern, Harry Warren, and Harold Arlen. Witty, lyrical master of the American colloquial idiom, Gershwin was among the very greatest of popular lyricists.

Getty, J. Paul (1892–1976) Getty owned a controlling interest in the Getty Oil Company and in hundreds of other firms. He was celebrated for his eccentricity—an extravagant, irascible, and unsettled character who married and divorced five times—and for his fabulous art collection, which became the basis of the J. Paul Getty Museum, built at Malibu in 1953, expanded in 1974, then transformed in 1997 into the spectacular Getty Center, which houses the art collection and other philanthropic activities.

Giancana, Sam (1908–1975) Giancana was Chicago's top syndicate boss from 1957 to 1966, and was reputedly tapped by John F. Kennedy's father, Joseph P. Kennedy, to exert his influence among labor unions to swing the 1960 election in favor of JFK. In 1975, Giancana was gunned down in his Oak Park (Illinois) home by unknown assailants shortly before he was scheduled to appear before the U.S. Senate Intelligence Committee to testify concerning his alleged involvement in a CIA plot to assassinate Cuba's Fidel Castro in the early 1960s.

Gilbreth, Frank and Lillian (1868–1924 and 1878–1972) Frank Gilbreth was trained as an engineer and his wife, Lillian (neé Moller) as a literary scholar. Together, they pioneered the science of time-motion study, the analysis of the motions and the amount of time required to carry out specific industrial tasks. Their 1911 *Motion Study* was groundbreaking and made them the world's first consulting "efficiency experts." The Gilbreths raised 12 children, two of whom, Frank Bunker Gilbreth, Jr., and Ernestine Gilbreth Carey, described how their parents applied their efficiency methods to family rearing in the popular 1949 memoir *Cheaper by the Dozen,* which became a hit film the following year.

Gillespie, Dizzy (1917–1993) John Birks Gillespie—called Dizzy—was a jazz trumpet virtuoso, bandleader, and innovative composer who developed bebop—or bop—out of big band swing popular in the 1930s and 1940s. The new style was greatly accelerated and made use of often wild chord progressions and syncopated rhythms so rapid that only a virtuoso could play them. Bebop—whose heyday extended from the mid 1940s to the early 1960s—was *the* sound of modern jazz.

Gilman, Charlotte Perkins (1860–1935) In fiction and nonfiction, Gilman critically analyzed the role of women in American society at the turn of the 19th century and concluded that they were generally oppressed emotionally, intellectually, culturally, and economically. Her 1898 *Women and Economics* was a manifesto calling for the economic liberation of women, including from the unreasonable demands of everything from time-worn social convention to motherhood itself. Her radical feminism was rediscovered in the 1960s at the height of the modern women's movement.

Gingrich, Newt (1943–) Speaker of the House of Representatives from 1995 to 1999, Gingrich was associated with the Republican "Contract with America," which addressed such issues as welfare reform, term limits, tougher crime laws, and a balanced budget law, and which helped conservative Republicans gain 54 House seats and take control of the House for the first time since 1954. For a time, Gingrich, wholly identified with the new conservative agenda, was the most powerful Speaker in recent history, but his decline was as precipitous as his rise, and he lost the Speakership amid ethics questions and after the poor Republican showing of 1998.

Ginsberg, Allen (1926–1997) Ginsburg grew up in Paterson, New Jersey, the son of noted poet Louis Ginsberg. Influenced less by his father than by the likes of William Carlos Williams—an exponent of free verse and narrative poetry in a lyric vernacular—and Walt Whitman, Ginsberg created a new form of free verse, wild, ecstatic, angry, and richly inventive, in his modern autobiographical epic *Howl* of 1956, which is considered one of the central poems of the so-called Beat movement in American literature.

Gist, Christopher (1706–1759) Gist was a trader, frontiersman, and explorer based in western Maryland and highly regarded by colonial authorities as a wilderness guide and an interpreter/negotiator influential with the Indians. In 1753, he joined George Washington, at the time a colonel of the Virginia militia, in an expedition against French "invaders" of the Ohio Valley, which was claimed by the English. Gist was an invaluable mentor to Washington in the ways of the frontier and in Indian diplomacy.

Giuliani, Rudolph (1944–) Giuliani was an attorney who, as U.S. attorney for the Southern District of New York (appointed in 1983), earned a reputation as a tough, savvy prosecutor. He ran for mayor of New York in 1989, was defeated, but emerged victorious in 1993, the first Republican mayor of the city in twenty years. He pledged major reforms of the city's finances and law enforcement, and he presided over a period of financial recovery and substantially reduced crime. Although some objected to what they regarded as his authoritarian manner, most New Yorkers—and most of the nation—were greatly impressed by Giuliani's strong, efficient, and compassionate leadership during the September 11, 2001, terrorist attacks on the World Trade Center and afterward.

Glasgow, Ellen (1873–1945) A lifelong resident of Richmond, Virginia, Glasgow had a long career as a novelist, in which she chronicled life in the American South as it made its uneasy transition from the traditions of the 19th century to the demands of the 20th. Her *The Romantic Comedians* (1926), *They Stooped to Folly* (1929), and *The Sheltered Life* (1932) are extraordinary chronicles of the slow decay of Southern aristocracy in a modern industrial civilization. Her final novel, *In This Our Life* (1941), was awarded a Pulitzer Prize.

Glenn, John (1921–) A Marine Corps aviator, Glenn was one of the seven original Mercury astronauts and the first American to orbit the earth (February 20, 1962). Glenn was elected to the U.S. Senate from Ohio in 1974 and was reelected three times. At 77, on October 29, 1998, he returned to space as a "payload specialist" aboard the shuttle *Discovery,* thereby becoming the oldest person ever to travel in space.

Godkin, E. L. (1831–1902) Born in Belfast, Ireland, Godkin came to the United States in 1851, practiced law in New York City, and in 1865 founded *The Nation*, which became the leading political review in the United States and was highly influential in bringing about all manner of major political reform.

Goethals, George Washington (1858–1928) A U.S. Army engineer, Goethals directed construction of the Panama Canal from 1907 until its opening in 1914, when Goethals became the first governor of the U.S. Canal Zone.

Goldman, Emma (1869–1940) Goldman immigrated to the United States from her native Russia (where she had been a radical activist) in 1885 and became active in socialism, but increasingly gravitated toward anarchism. She was arrested and imprisoned on several occasions and in 1906 founded an anarchist periodical, *Mother Earth*, which she published until the U.S. government suppressed it in 1917. Jailed during World War I for her activities in opposition to the war, she was deported to the Soviet Union as a Communist in 1919. She was appalled by the effects of the Russian Revolutions, but continued to espouse anarchism. Her autobiography, *Living My Life* (1931), is a classic of political dissent.

Goldwater, Barry (1909–1998) Republican U.S. senator from Arizona (1953–1964 and 1969–1987), Goldwater lost the presidential contest to Democrat Lyndon B. Johnson in 1964. Goldwater was the embodiment of hardline conservatism in a time of emerging liberalism.

Gompers, Samuel (1850–1924) A pioneering American labor leader, Gompers was the first president of the American Federation of Labor in 1886. Having arrived as an immigrant from England in 1863, he settled in New York, where he worked as a cigar maker. Naturalized in 1872, Gompers took the national organization of cigar makers out of the Knights of Labor and made it the basis of the AFL. He served as the president of the federation from 1886 to 1924 (except for 1895).

Goodman, Andrew (1943–1964) With fellow Congress of Racial Equality (CORE) volunteers Michael Schwerner and James Chaney, Goodman was murdered on June 21, 1964, on a back road in Mississippi while working for CORE's Mississippi Summer Project to register black voters in the segregated South. A white Manhattan native, Goodman was driven by a passion for social justice.

Goodman, Benny (1909–1986) Bandleader and jazz clarinet virtuoso, Goodman was a master of swing—the musical sound of the 1930s and 1940s, featuring fast, syncopated rhythms that were meant to be danced to. Goodman's band featured a who's who of American jazz, including guitarist Charlie Christian, trumpeter Harry James, drummer Gene Krupa, vibraphonist Lionel Hampton, and pianist Teddy Wilson. Some of Goodman's most memorable tunes were arranged by orchestration genius Fletcher Henderson.

Goodnight, Charlie (1836–1929) A Confederate veteran, Charlie Goodnight returned to Texas after the Civil War, rounded up and branded as much free-ranging cattle as he could, and in 1866, with partner Oliver Loving, drove 2,000 longhorns from Belknap, Texas, to Fort Sumner, New Mexico, to feed U.S. Army troops there. It was a hot, dry distance of some 500 miles, and the partners lost 400 head on the trail—300 from thirst, another 100 trampled to death when they finally reached the watering hole—but they were paid the spectacular sum of eight cents a pound for the stringy meat, netting a profit of $12,000. The Goodnight-Loving Trail they blazed became one of the most heavily trafficked routes in the Southwest, was the foundation of the trail-drive industry, and gave employment to the most celebrated and beloved worker in American industry, the cowboy.

Gore, Al (1948–) Gore was vice president under Bill Clinton (1993–2001) and, before that, a Tennessee representative and senator. In 2000 he defeated Republican George W. Bush in the popular vote for president of the United States, but in a hotly disputed election decided by a Supreme Court ruling, he was defeated in the Electoral College. A longtime champion of environmental causes, Gore emerged in the first decade of the

21st century with a mission to raise the awareness of the dangers posed by global warming.

Gorgas, William (1854–1920) A U.S. Army surgeon, Gorgas was responsible for health and sanitation in Havana during the period of the Spanish-American War. Confronted by endemic yellow fever, he proved by experiment that the disease was transmitted by the bite of a certain mosquito. By taking measures to control the mosquito population, he eliminated yellow fever from Havana, then was sent in 1904 to Panama, where the disease was defeating efforts to build the Panama Canal. Gorgas not only eradicated yellow fever from the Canal Zone, he also drastically reduced the prevalence of another mosquito-borne endemic disease, malaria.

Gorky, Arshile (1904–1948) Born Vosdanik Adoian in Armenia, Gorky took his pseudonym from the Russian word for "bitter," which was also the pseudonym of a writer he much admired, Maxim Gorky. The name reflected the horrors of his childhood during the Turkish genocide of Armenia—a fate he narrowly escaped by immigrating to the United States. Here he developed a dashing, dramatic style that built on the surrealist tradition and laid the foundation for abstract expressionism. Gorky thus emerged as one of the great pivotal figures in American art.

Grady, Henry (1850–1889) A journalist, Grady bought a quarter interest in *The Atlanta Constitution* newspaper in 1879, which he used as a platform from which he promoted the industrialization and modernization of the South. His work on the newspaper and as a popular orator helped transform the South, defeated and economically depressed following the Civil War, into fertile ground for new industrial investment and development.

Graham, Billy (1918–) Graham was ordained as a Southern Baptist minister in 1939 and, after World War II, began preaching fundamentalist sermons on radio. By 1950, he was nationally famous. Eminently telegenic, he appeared on TV as that medium developed, and also toured the country in revival crusades. Immensely popular, he also had the ear of every U.S. president since Harry S. Truman.

Graham, Martha (1894–1991) Graham was a driving force in American modern dance for half a century, creating a new style of expressive choreography with works "designed to reveal the inner man" by expressing primal emotion and the spiritual and emotional essence of what it is to be human. Her work was sometimes based on Greek myth and drama, but was also rooted in America, as in her collaboration with the great American composer Aaron Copland on the ballet *Appalachian Spring* (1944), perhaps her most famous work.

Grant, Ulysses S. (1822–1885) U.S. Grant failed at every enterprise he attempted except soldiering. After winning victories in the western theater of the Civil War, he was promoted by Abraham Lincoln to general-in-chief of the Union Army, which he led to a costly victory in the Civil War. Hailed by many as a bold leader and great strategist, he was condemned by some as a "butcher," a man always willing to spill the blood of others. Grant was elected president of the United States in 1868 and served two terms (1869–1877), his administration notorious for its corruption—although he himself was regarded as a scrupulously honest man. After leaving the White House, Grant failed in business and was on the verge of abject poverty when Mark Twain, who had a controlling interest in a publishing company, offered him a fortune for his memoirs. The result was a masterpiece of autobiography and history, completed just four days before Grant succumbed to cancer of the throat.

Greeley, Horace (1811–1872) Greely raised himself from Vermont printer's apprentice to founder in 1841 of the *New York Tribune*, which became the liberal voice of abolitionism, woman suffrage, and general political reform. Greeley set a high journalistic standard in news-gathering and public-spirited moral purpose. He was the original American "crusading journalist."

Greenhow, Rose O'Neal (1815–1864) The widow of a prominent physician and historian, Rose O'Neal Greenhow was a popular Washington, D.C., hostess who was connected at the very highest levels of government. A Maryland native, her sympathies were wholly with the South during the Civil War, and she used her social position and considerable sexual allure to obtain important military intelligence that proved especially valuable in the First Battle of Bull Run. In August 1863, she traveled to Europe as an unofficial agent of the Confederacy, obtained funding for the Confederate cause there, but was drowned on October 1, 1864, weighed down by gold coins sewn into her clothing, after her boat sank off Wilmington, North Carolina, while she was attempting to evade a Union naval blockade.

Greenough, Horatio (1805–1852) Greenough contributed two things to American art and culture. The first was his monumental neoclassical sculpture of George Washington—the first work of art commissioned by the federal government (1832)—which is now at the National Museum of Art in Washington, D.C. The second was his groundbreaking writing on aesthetic theory, in which he set out the relationship between architecture and decoration, proposing that "form follows function." Although articulated before the mid 19th century, this became the basis of Functionalism, the ideal on which so much modern architecture and industrial design is based.

Gregory, Dick (1932–) Born Richard Claxton in St. Louis, Gregory rose from the ghetto to become a nationally successful comic in the 1960s, who delivered biting satire targeted against racial prejudice. His comedy added a new dimension to the Civil Rights movement, raising the consciousness of black as well as white Americans. By the 1980s, Gregory had left the comic stage and became an entrepreneur in the field of nutrition.

Griffith, D. W. (1875–1948) Often judged the first great genius of American film direction, Griffith pioneered many of the staple techniques of modern film making, including the use of dramatic camera angles, camera movement, lighting effects, and, most of all, effective pacing and storytelling through skillful editing. His masterpiece, the 1915 epic *Birth of a Nation*, was both praised for its ambition and artistry and condemned for its racist vision of the Civil War and its aftermath.

Grimké, Sarah (1792–1873) and Angelina (1805–1879) The Grimké sisters were born in South Carolina and knew the evils of slavery first hand. They left the South, settled in Philadelphia, became Quakers, and worked with abolitionist leader William Lloyd Garrison in the campaign against slavery. Angelina Grimké wrote an *Appeal to the Christian Women of the South* in 1836, urging southern women to help persuade their men to end slavery. Soon after, Sarah Grimké wrote *An Epistle to the Clergy of the Southern States.* The sisters lectured nationwide and attempted to unite the cause of women's rights with the struggle against slavery.

Grinnell, George Bird (1849–1938) In its obituary, *The New York Times* called Grinnell the "father of American conservation." Born in Brooklyn and educated at Yale (from which he earned a Ph.D. in paleontology), he served as a naturalist on a number of western expeditions and was the natural history editor, then publisher-owner, of *Field and Stream*, which he used to conduct a series of pioneering conservation campaigns that promoted the protection of Yellowstone National Park and moved Congress to create Glacier National Park. Grinnell founded the first Audubon Society and was a founder (with Theodore Roosevelt and others) of the Boone and Crockett Club. Grinnell was also a renowned student and historian of the Plains Indians.

Grosvenor, Gilbert H. (1875–1966) Hired by Alexander Graham Bell as an editorial assistant on the magazine of the National Geographic Society (of which Bell was president), Grosvenor became its editor, transforming it from a modest scholarly journal (circulation 900) into a popular illustrated magazine that reached some 2,000,000 subscribers. Elected president of the Society in 1920, Grosvenor was responsible for mounting many major geographical expeditions throughout the world. The National Geographic Society and its magazine became celebrated American institutions.

Groves, Leslie R. (1896–1970) Groves was an officer in the U.S. Army Corps of Engineers. In 1940, he was put in charge of building the Pentagon, at the time the largest office building in the world. His next major assignment was as military director of the Manhattan Project, which researched, designed, and built the atomic bombs that ended World War II.

Guthrie, Woody (1912–1967) Guthrie traveled the country by freight train during the Great Depression, composing and singing folksongs that gave lyric voice to the lives of the economically downtrodden and dispossessed and that also expressed the somewhat sentimentalized ideals of American labor and populism. Best known among his more than 1,000 songs was "This Land Is Your Land," which became an anthem of the Civil Rights movement during the 1960s. Guthrie was a major influence on the folk music revival of the 1960s, on Bob Dylan in particular, and on American popular music generally.

Haig, Alexander (1924–) Haig was a career military officer who served in the Korean and Vietnam wars. He was military assistant to Henry Kissinger (when he was Nixon's national security advisor), then became White House Chief of Staff at the height of the Watergate scandal from May 1973 until September 1974. Haig proved a great crisis manager, who (many believe) kept the government running while Nixon struggled with Watergate. After serving as supreme commander of NATO from 1974 to 1979, Haig was appointed secretary of state by Ronald Reagan in 1981. He made a major gaffe when, after the March 30, 1981, assassination attempt on Reagan, Haig declared that he was "in control" in the White House, asserting—unconstitutionally—that he was third in succession to the presidency. Haig resigned in 1982.

Haldeman, H. R. "Bob" (1926–1993) An advertising executive, Haldeman worked on President Nixon's election campaigns and served as his White House chief of staff from 1969 to 1973. His power was great, since he largely determined who would and who would not see the president. Haldeman was deeply implicated in what Nixon's inner circle called "dirty tricks" designed to undermine or destroy the administration's opponents. During the Watergate scandal, Haldeman resigned, was convicted of perjury, conspiracy, and obstruction of justice, and served 18 months of a 30-month sentence.

Hale, Nathan (1755–1776) Hale was a Connecticut schoolteacher who served as militia captain in the revolution and volunteered to conduct espionage behind the British lines in Long Island, New York. Captured, he suffered the fate of a spy: hanging. Long-accepted tradition has it that his final words were, "My only regret is that I have but one life to lose for my country." This was a close paraphrase of a line from *Cato* by the eighteenth-century British playwright Joseph Addison, which the Yale-educated Hale may well have read—or which may have been supplied by some contemporary Patriot myth maker.

Hall, G. Stanley (1844–1924) Hall began his academic career intending to study for the ministry, but switched to philosophy and then to psychology. His early research used specially formulated questionnaires to study child development and concluded that mental growth proceeded in an evolutionary manner roughly analogous to the course of biological evolution proposed by Charles Darwin. Hall integrated modern psychology into the most advanced currents of scientific thought of his age, successfully incorporating into his work both Darwin and Freud.

Hamilton, Alexander (1755 or 1757–1804) Hamilton was of illegitimate birth in Nevis, British West Indies. After serving as a staff officer to General Washington during the American Revolution, he rose to become a New York delegate to the Constitutional Convention of 1787 and was a prime contributor to *The Federalist Papers* (1789–1795), which helped ensure that the new Constitution would achieve ratification. Under President Washington, Hamilton was the first secretary of the treasury and was responsible for a fiscal policy that established the credit of the infant nation on a sound basis. He was an ardent champion of a strong central government, which put him at odds with Washington's secretary of state, Thomas Jefferson, who favored a more radical democracy. Hamilton was killed in a duel (July 11, 1804; he died the next morning) with his chief political foe, Aaron Burr.

Hammerstein, Oscar (1847–1919) His memory overshadowed by the fame of his lyricist son, Hammerstein immigrated from Germany to the United States when he was a teenager and became a cigar maker. He also moonlighted as a theater manager and, in 1889, built his own theater, to which he brought the greatest actors and singers of the day. While he produced shows in all genres—including drama, comedy, vaudeville, and musical comedy—his greatest passion was grand opera, the production of which he revolutionized by introducing an unprecedented degree of genuine theatricality. By the end of his life he had built eleven theaters, ten of them in Manhattan.

Hammerstein, Oscar, II (1895–1960) Son of the major American opera impresario for whom he was named, Oscar Hammerstein studied law, but soon became an author and lyricist for the musical comedy stage, writing between 1920 and 1959 all or most of 45 musicals. His most notable collaborations were with composer Richard Rodgers, with whom he wrote (among others) *Oklahoma!* (1943), *Carousel* (1945), and *South Pacific* (1949), all landmarks in popular musical entertainment.

Hammon, Jupiter (c. 1720–c. 1800) Hammon was a slave on Long Island, New York, whose masters allowed him to attend school. Deeply religious, he wrote his first published poem, "An Evening Thought. Salvation by Christ with Penitential Cries," on Christmas Day 1760. Printed early the next year, it was the first piece of literature published in the United States by an African American.

Hancock, John (1737–1793) A prosperous Boston merchant, Hancock was a major leader of the independence movement and the president of the first and second provincial congresses in 1774 and 1775. The first to sign the Declaration of Independence in 1776, he wrote his name large—large enough, he said, so that King George and his ministers could read it all the way from London.

Hardin, John Wesley (1853–1895) During 1868–1877, Hardin earned notoriety as an incorrigible Texas gunslinger, killing at least 21 men in duels and ambushes. Apprehended in Florida in 1877, he was convicted and sentenced to 25 years at hard labor. He was pardoned in 1894, but soon fell to thievery. On August 19, 1895, John Selman, a policeman and fellow thief, shot him in the back of the head as he drank at the bar of the Acme Saloon, El Paso. The shooting was motivated by a personal feud, but Selman was acquitted of murder.

Harding, Warren Gamaliel (1865–1923) A genial Ohio politician, Harding was chosen by a caucus of party insiders (legend has it, in a "smoke-filled room") as the Republican presidential candidate in 1920. His promise of a "return to normalcy," after the strenuous reforms of President Woodrow Wilson's two terms and U.S. involvement in World War I, appealed to the American people, who sent him to the White House by a landslide. His administration was characterized by conservative isolationism, rampant corruption, and even sexual scandal (Harding had a mistress). The president died, in California, during a trip to Alaska in 1923. Many historians consider him the least competent president in U.S. history.

Harlan, John Marshall (1833–1911) Harlan served as an associate justice of the U. S. Supreme Court from 1877 until his death, earning a reputation as one of the high court's great dissenters. He dissented most forcefully from the majority on issues of civil rights for African Americans, arguing that the equal rights of blacks were guaranteed by Thirteenth, Fourteenth, and Fifteenth Amendments. His opinions would not be vindicated until the mid 20th century, years after his death. His grandson, also named John Marshall Harlan (1899–1971), also served on the Supreme Court (1955–1971).

Harriman, W. Averell (1891–1986) President Franklin Roosevelt sent Harriman him to Britain and the Soviet Union to manage U.S. aid to these allies during World War II. From 1943 to 1946, Harriman served as ambassador to the Soviet Union, then, briefly, as ambassador to Great Britain (April to October 1946). He was Harry S. Truman's secretary of commerce from 1947 to 1948, and—except for a period as governor of New York from 1954 to 1958—served Truman, John F. Kennedy, and Lyndon B. Johnson in various high-level capacities. As JFK's assistant secretary of state for Far Eastern affairs (1961–1963), he helped negotiate the Nuclear

Test-Ban Treaty, and as LBJ's ambassador-at-large, he headed the U.S. delegation to the Paris peace talks in an effort to end the Vietnam War during 1968–1969. His greatest influence during the Cold War period was in advising presidents on U.S. Soviet policy.

Harris, Joel Chandler (1848–1908) A Georgia journalist, Harris earned national fame as a humorist, beginning with his 1879 story, "Tar Baby," told in African-American dialect by a slave named Uncle Remus and introducing the characters of B'rer Fox and B'rer Rabbit. This was the first of many stories Harris later published in a long series of "Uncle Remus" books, beginning with the 1880 *Uncle Remus: His Songs and His Sayings.* Not only did these stories become popular American classics, Harris developed a passionate interest in African-American folklore, which he did much to collect, preserve, and present to both black and white America.

Harrison, Benjamin (1833–1901) The grandson of the ninth president, the short-lived William Henry Harrison, Benjamin Harrison defeated incumbent Democrat Grover Cleveland in 1888, winning an electoral majority but losing the popular vote by a margin of more than 95,000. Harrison was man of impeccable conscience, whose moderate Republicanism moved him to sign into law the Sherman Antitrust Act of 1890, which curbed monopolies. In foreign affairs, Harrison presided over a general expansion of U.S. influence abroad. His rival Cleveland defeated him in 1892—thereby becoming the only U.S. president to serve two non-consecutive terms.

Harrison, William Henry (1773–1841) An army officer who served as governor of Indiana Territory, Harrison negotiated treaties that acquired from the Indians millions of acres during 1802–1809. When tribes under the Shawnee Tecumseh resisted, Harrison led forces that defeated them at the Battle of Tippecanoe (November 7, 1811), near Lafayette, Indiana. This victory provided the first memorable slogan in a U.S. presidential campaign in 1840: "Tippecanoe and Tyler, too!" (John Tyler was Harrison's running mate.) Harrison was 67 when he was elected. On a frigid March 4, 1841, he took the oath of office and delivered the longest inaugural address in history (nearly two hours). He took a chill, fell ill, and died exactly one month later, on April 4. He was the first chief executive to die in office.

Hart, Lorenz "Larry" (1895–1943) Descended from the 19th-century German Romantic poet Heinrich Heine, Hart teamed with composer Richard Rodgers to write the lyrics of some 1,000 of the most popular and most beautifully crafted of American popular songs, including "Here in My Arms" (1926), "My Heart Stood Still" (1927), "With a Song in My Heart" (1929), "Lover" (1933), "Blue Moon" (1934), "The Lady Is a Tramp" (1937), "My Funny Valentine" (1937), "I Didn't Know What Time It Was" (1939), and "Bewitched, Bothered, and Bewildered" (1940).

Harte, Bret (1836–1902) Harte grew up in New York City. He left in 1854 to visit the California mining country and settled in San Francisco, where he became a clerk in the U.S. Mint and a magazine editor. He began writing short stories that evoked the "local color" of the California mining camps, with a sentimental turn and emphasis on remarkable incidents and characters. His 1870 collection, *The Luck of Roaring Camp and other Stories,* made him world famous—and "local color fiction" henceforth became a major American literary genre.

Harvey, Fred (1835–1901) Harvey immigrated to the United States from England in 1850 and entered the restaurant business. After the failure of his restaurant in St. Louis, he found work as a railroad freight agent. Observing the abysmal quality of railroad dining accommodations throughout the West, Harvey approached the Santa Fe Railroad with a proposal that he open a restaurant at the Topeka, Kansas, depot. This became the basis of a chain of Fred Harvey restaurants all along the Santa Fe line—the first American restaurant chain, precursor of the fast-food chains of the 20th century. Associated with the restaurants were the famous "Harvey Girls," waitresses Harvey brought out West to serve in his establishments. These women often became the wives of western bachelors.

Hauptmann, Bruno (1899–1936) Born in Germany, Hauptmann immigrated to the United States after World War I. He made his living as a carpenter and a burglar. In a sensational trial spanning January 2–February 13, 1935, he was convicted of kidnapping and murdering the 21-month-old son of American aviator hero Charles Lindbergh and his wife, Anne Morrow. Dubbed the "trial of the century," the proceedings in a Flemington, New Jersey, courthouse received intense international media scrutiny, but the conviction of Hauptmann was plagued by controversy that remains unresolved to this day. Despite the doubts and qualms of many—including New Jersey governor Harold Hoffman—Hauptmann was executed on April 3, 1936, protesting his innocence to the last.

Hawthorne, Nathaniel (1804–1864) Born and raised in New England and steeped in its history and lore, Hawthorne produced some of the greatest fiction in American literature, including his masterpiece, *The Scarlet Letter* (1850). Hawthorne was fascinated by the large themes of guilt, conscience, and community, and by his own heritage of New England Puritanism, which included an ancestor who had been a judge during the infamous Salem witchcraft trials of the seventeenth century. Hawthorne wove these themes and fascinations into richly atmospheric explorations of the human character, creating situations that made extensive use of allegory and symbolism to probe what he considered the darkest secrets of the soul.

Hay, John (1838–1905) Hay served as private secretary to Abraham Lincoln throughout his presidency (1861–1865), then held various diplomatic posts under other Republican presidents. In 1897, President William McKinley appointed him ambassador to Great Britain, then, in 1898, secretary of state. He was active in negotiating an end to the Spanish–American War (1898) and guided the nation toward becoming a major imperialist power. He advocated what he called the Open Door policy, designed to regulate relations between the Western powers and China, providing trade access to all. In 1901–1903, Hay was instrumental in clearing the way for the building of the Panama Canal.

Hayes, Mary McCauley (1753/54–1832) The wife of an artilleryman during the American Revolution, Hayes accompanied her husband in action. During the Battle of Monmouth (June 28, 1778), she carried pitchers of water to cool the guns and slake the thirst of the men. For this, she was nicknamed "Molly Pitcher." When she saw her husband fall wounded, she seized his ramrod and took his place at the gun. General Washington recognized her valor by issuing to her a warrant as a noncommissioned officer.

Hayes, Rutherford B. (1822–1893) In the election of 1876, Democrat Samuel J. Tilden outpolled Republican Rutherford B. Hayes in the popular vote and looked as if he would win an electoral majority as well; however, Republicans contested the result—charging (among other things) that the black vote had been suppressed in the South—and the election was ultimately decided by Congress in a deal that gave Hayes the presidency in exchange for his pledge to bring an immediate end to Reconstruction (including military government) in the states of the former Confederacy. Hayes was installed in office, ended Reconstruction, and, to his credit, set about cleaning out the corruption of Ulysses S. Grant's two terms. However, he was always afflicted by the stigma of the backroom deal and was universally mocked by the title, "His Fraudulency."

Hayne, Robert Y. (1791–1839) While serving as senator from South Carolina, Hayne debated Daniel Webster in 1830 on the legitimacy of nullification—the proposition that the U.S. Constitution was a compact among the individual states, and that, therefore, any state had the right to nullify a federal statute it considered in violation of the compact. The debate defined a major dispute between North and South, which would not be resolved except by the catastrophe of civil war.

Haywood, "Big Bill" (1869–1928) William D. "Big Bill" Haywood was a western miner who became active in the mine labor movement. He was a founder of the International Workers of the World (IWW) in 1905, a radical labor organization that sought to bring all workers under "one big union." Haywood was persistently harassed by federal authorities, who, after U.S. entry into World War I, arrested him and other IWW members on charges of treason and sabotage for interfering with war-related production. While on bail pending appeal, Haywood fled to Soviet Russia, where he lived the rest of his life.

Hazelwood, Joseph (1946–) On March 24, 1989, the supertanker *Exxon Valdez* ran aground 25 miles south of Valdez, Alaska, spilling 240,000 barrels of crude oil into the pristine waters of Prince William Sound. It remains the worst environmental disaster in American history. The skipper, Joseph Hazelwood of Huntington, New York, was charged with (among other things) operating a vessel while intoxicated and was found guilty of negligent discharge of oil. His conviction was overturned on appeal based on a statute that granted immunity to those reporting oil spills to the authorities. The oil spill covered some 2,600 square miles of Alaska wilderness and killed untold thousands of birds and marine animals.

Hearst, William Randolph (1863–1951) The renegade son of a California senator and gold miner, Hearst took over the ailing *San Francisco Examiner* in 1887 and transformed it into a runaway success by combining genuinely reformist investigative journalism with outright sensationalism. He repeated this success on a grander scale when he bought the moribund *New York Morning Journal* in 1895, hired the best writers and reporters to work on it, then reduced its price to a penny—thereby obtaining spectacular circulation. Hearst engaged in a circulation war with rival publisher Joseph Pulitzer and, together, the two publishers created a new brand of muckraking sensationalism dubbed "yellow journalism." Hearst went on to build a nationwide news chain and became an opinion maker of unprecedented power, typically making news as well as reporting it—as when he heightened the war fever that led to the Spanish-American War.

Hemings, Sally (c.1773–1835) Hemings was a chambermaid to Thomas Jefferson, by whom she may have had at least one child (her youngest son, Easton Hemings). DNA studies of known Hemings and Jefferson descendants and other scientific evidence have yet to resolve the controversy definitively. Jefferson, who had condemned the slave trade in his draft of Declaration of Independence, was a slave owner lifelong and, on his death, did not free Sally or any other slave.

Hemingway, Ernest (1899–1961) Many regard Hemingway as the greatest American novelist and short story writer of the 20th century. He was celebrated as much for his lean writing style—in which there seemed not a single superfluous word—as for his compelling treatment of themes of masculine identity, morality, and courage. A member of what Gertrude Stein called the "lost generation" of post-World War I writers and artists, Hemingway created fictional heroes in search of meaning in a morally and spiritually shattered world. In the process, he carved out for himself the life of a celebrity author, whose very public thirst for high-risk adventure was unquenchable. He was awarded the Nobel Prize for Literature in 1954.

Henderson, Fletcher (1898–1952) Henderson was a fine jazz pianist who created great orchestrations for large jazz ensembles and was responsible for much of the "big band" sound of the 1930s and 1940s. He was the first arranger to create fully written arrangements that did not compromise the free spirit of jazz improvisation. As Benny Goodman's principal orchestrator, Henderson was responsible for much the Goodman band's phenomenal success.

Henri, Robert (1865–1929) Henri led early 20th-century American art away from academic eclecticism—the imitation of earlier styles—toward a realism that embraced the modern urban landscape as a rich and exciting subject. Some critics derided his work and the work of the many American artists he influenced as the "Ashcan School," but he and his followers accepted the label and continued to develop this new form of unsentimental urban and industrial realism that was unique to America.

Henry, Patrick (1736–1799) A radical leader of the independence movement in Virginia, Patrick Henry was less important to the American Revolution as a political thinker than as an orator of electrifying eloquence. He is best remembered for the speech he delivered at the second Virginia Convention on March 23, 1775. After introducing uncompromising resolutions for the funding of the Virginia militia to fight the British, he concluded: "I know not what course others may take, but as for me, give me liberty or give me death."

Herbert, Victor (1859–1924) Irish born, Herbert made his reputation and fortune in the United States as the composer of innovative popular operettas that were the precursors of the musical, a uniquely American popular art form. Of his more than 40 operettas, the best-remembered are *Babes in Toyland* (1903) and *Naughty Marietta* (1910). Herbert was also a great musical businessman, who led the fight for meaningful copyright protection of music and was a founder of the American Society of Composers, Authors and Publishers (ASCAP) in 1914.

Herjolfsson, Bjarni (late 10th century) While sailing from Iceland to Greenland in 986, this Norse explorer was blown off course by a storm, which took him close enough to what is now known as Newfoundland for him to see low-lying, thickly forested hills. Eager to reach Greenland, he did not investigate—but is generally considered the first European to lay eyes on the North American mainland.

Hersh, Seymour (1937–) This investigative reporter achieved worldwide renown in 1969 by exposing the My Lai Massacre—the brutal destruction of a Vietnamese village on March 16, 1968, by a platoon of U.S. soldiers under Lieutenant William Calley—and its subsequent cover-up by the U.S. Army. Hersh was awarded the Pulitzer Prize for his My Lai stories and continued his reporting on military and security matters, which, included exposing U.S. abuse of detainees at Iraq's infamous Abu Ghraib prison (2004) and reports on U.S. military plans to employ nuclear weapons against Iran (2006).

Hickok, "Wild Bill" (1837–1876) Hickok was a radical abolitionist before and during the Civil War and worked for the Union Army as a teamster and scout. He became a deputy U.S. marshal after the war and earned a reputation as an uncompromising lawman for his work as sheriff of Hays City, Kansas, and as marshal of Abilene. He exploited his fame as star of Buffalo Bill's Wild West Show during 1872–1874, then became a drifting gambler, who met his end on March 1, 1877, at a poker table in the Number Ten Saloon in Deadwood, Dakota Territory, shot to death by Jack McCall, a total stranger.

Hill, Anita (1956–) A University of Oklahoma law professor, Hill accused Supreme Court nominee Clarence Thomas of sexual harassment and testified in sensational televised hearings during Thomas's Senate confirmation in 1991. Thomas denied the charges, which triggered long Senate debate, but failed to block his elevation to the high court. Hill was both widely praised and condemned for speaking out. She went on to become a professor of social policy, law, and women's studies at Brandeis University.

Hill, James J. (1838–1916) Hill was among the last of the titans of American rail expansion, earning the title of "Empire Builder" for his construction and consolidation of rail lines throughout the Northwest at the end of the 19th and beginning of the 20th centuries.

Hill, Joe (1879–1915) Hill was born in Sweden and immigrated to the United States in 1902. After joining the International Workers of the World (IWW) in 1910, he became an organizer, using his talent as a composer of folksongs to help drive recruitment. His most famous song, "The Preacher and the Slave," has the capitalist preacher promising workers that they "will eat, bye and bye / In that glorious land above the sky; / Work and pray, live on hay, /You'll get pie in the sky when you die." In 1914, Hill was charged with the robbery-murder of a Salt Lake City grocer and his son. Despite thin circumstantial evidence, he was convicted—undoubtedly because of his radical beliefs. He was executed on November 19, 1915, and was celebrated as a martyr to the American labor movement.

Hinckley, John (1955–) On March 30, 1981, John Hinckley, a feckless off-and-on college student, fired his Rohm RG-14 revolver six times at President Ronald Reagan as he left the Hilton Hotel in Washington, D.C., after a speaking engagement. A ricocheted bullet hit the president in the left lung.

Other shots resulted in a catastrophic head wound to Press Secretary James Brady and lesser injuries to police officer Thomas Delehanty and Secret Service agent Timothy McCarthy. Hinckley later claimed that after seeing the 1976 Martin Scorsese film *Taxi Driver*, he became obsessed with the young actress Jodie Foster and believed that he could capture her attention by killing the president. He was found not guilty by reason of insanity and was confined to Saint Elizabeth's Hospital in Washington, D.C.

Hiss, Alger (1904–1996) Alger Hiss was a distinguished State Department official and adviser to President Franklin D. Roosevelt before and during World War II. He served as temporary secretary-general of the United Nations and as president of the Carnegie Endowment for International Peace from 1946 to 1949. In 1948, Whittaker Chambers, a self-proclaimed reformed Communist, accused Hiss of passing classified documents to him for transmission to a Soviet agent. Hiss denied the charges; although he was never indicted for espionage, he was tried and convicted of perjury. He served more than three years of a five-year sentence and spent the rest of his life in an effort to prove his innocence—and was frequently cited by the American left as an example of right-wing persecution. (Soviet documents released after Hiss's death in 1996 provide strong evidence of his guilt.)

Hoffman, Abbie (1936–1989) Hoffman was a civil rights activist, who, in 1968, organized the Yippies—the Youth International Party—which protested the Vietnam War and the American "Establishment." In an era of protest, Hoffman was skilled at drawing media attention, engaging in a kind of street theater to dramatize the protest movement.

Holladay, Ben (1819–1887) Born in Kentucky, Holladay settled in Missouri, where he opened a store and hotel. During the U.S.-Mexican War (1846–1848), he made a fortune supplying the U.S. Army and used his profits to finance the purchase of army-surplus oxen and wagons, which became the basis of his freighting business between Salt Lake City, Utah, and California. Holladay steadily expanded, purchasing the Central Overland California and Pike's Peak Express, which he ultimately sold to Wells Fargo and Co. in 1866. Having pioneered big-time overland stagecoach and freight operations in the American West, he bought into steamship and railroad companies, but was wiped out in the financial panic of 1873 and retired three years later with a much-diminished fortune.

Holmes, Oliver Wendell, Jr. (1841–1935) In 1902, President Theodore Roosevelt appointed Holmes to the U.S. Supreme Court after a distinguished career as a jurist, a professor of law, and a legal philosopher. He sat on the court until he retired in 1932, when he was nearly 91 years old. Although he never served as chief justice, Holmes was the most famous jurist ever to sit on the high court. His opinions were brilliantly reasoned and eloquently written—many of them expressing the view of the dissenting minority. Holmes was a steadfast exponent of judicial restraint, who believed that law making was the business of legislators, not the courts. He was also a vigorous advocate of free speech, arguing that it could be restrained only in the event of "clear and present danger": "The most stringent protection of free speech would not protect a man in falsely shouting fire in a theatre and causing a panic."

Holmes, Oliver Wendell, Sr. (1809–1894) Holmes was a distinguished American physician, who became dean of the Harvard Medical School. He was also a tremendously popular author, whose works included gently humorous essays and genteel poems of considerable literary merit. His most beloved work was *The Autocrat of the Breakfast-Table*, a series of evocative essays of great charm. His son, Oliver Wendell Holmes, Jr., was a distinguished jurist and one of the greatest of Supreme Court justices.

Homer, Winslow (1836–1910) Homer's paintings combine a sense of drawn-from-nature spontaneity with a profound depth of psychological understanding. His best works picture human subjects against the brooding backdrop of an ultimately indifferent nature. Homer is most closely identified with the seascapes of his native New England. He added a new depth to realism, his work suggesting a wealth of emotion beneath the surface of the canvas.

Hoover, Herbert (1874–1964) Hoover came to wide public attention as President Woodrow Wilson's food administrator during World War I and, after the war, as head the American Relief Administration, which provided food to war-ravaged Europe and even Soviet Russia. ("Whatever their politics," Hoover declared, "they shall be fed.") Hoover was nominated by the Republican Party as its presidential candidate in 1928. He defeated Democrat Al Smith and was almost immediately confronted by the Stock Market crash of 1929 and the Great Depression. Hoover steadfastly resisted giving direct federal aid to the legions of the jobless, homeless, and hungry, believing that to do so would irreparably destroy individual initiative and forever change the relation of the government to the people. His administration's failure to deal effectively with the economic emergency resulted in Hoover's loss to Franklin D. Roosevelt in 1932. Unjustly, many Americans blamed

Hoover not merely for failing to alleviate the Depression, but for having caused the Depression.

Hoover, J. Edgar (1895–1972) Hoover became director of a minor federal law enforcement agency, the Bureau of Investigation, in 1924 and transformed it into the powerful Federal Bureau of Investigation, one of the most respected investigative and law-enforcement agencies in the world. He directed the bureau until his death in 1972, a tenure filled with controversy, as Hoover compiled secret dossiers on hundreds of thousands of Americans, including government officials and other high-profile figures. His power in government was unprecedented for a non-elected official, and his intentions were often shadowy and sometimes suspect.

Hopkins, Harry (1890–1946) Trained as a social worker, Harry Hopkins worked in the administration of New York governor Franklin D. Roosevelt as executive director (later chairman) of the New York State Temporary Emergency Relief Administration. When FDR entered the White House in 1933, Hopkins was named administrator of the Federal Emergency Relief Administration—in effect, czar of the New Deal. During World War II, Hopkins became the president's closest advisor and his personal emissary to the leaders of the Britain and the Soviet Union. He was among the most powerful non-elected officials in American history. A small, frail man, who suffered from cancer during his later years, Hopkins worked tirelessly through the end of the war, finally succumbing to the disease months after World War II ended.

Hopkins, Mark (1814–1878) With Collis P. Huntington (his business partner in a mercantile venture), Leland Stanford, and Charles Crocker, Hopkins formed the so-called "Big Four," who financed the Central Pacific link in the Union Pacific-Central Pacific transcontinental railroad, which was completed in 1869. Hopkins was effectively one of the financial founders of modern California.

Horney, Karen (1885–1952) Born in Germany, Horney became a physician and an apostle of Sigmund Freud's psychoanalysis. She practiced psychiatry in Germany until 1932, when she came to Chicago as director of the Institute for Psychoanalysis. She later practiced in New York City. Horney made a radical departure from Freud by arguing, in *The Neurotic Personality of Our Time* (1937), that environmental and social conditions—instinctual drives—were principal shapers of personality and causes of neurosis. It was a revolutionary philosophical, sociological, and psychological theory.

Houston, Sam (1793–1863) A Virginian by birth, Houston was sent to Texas in 1832 as President Andrew Jackson's emissary in negotiating Indian treaties there. He decided to settle in Texas in 1833 and became a leader of the rebellion against Mexico—which governed Texas—beginning in November 1835. Houston commanded the small Texas army, which, despite early reverses, triumphed at the Battle of San Jacinto on April 21, 1836 and won independence. Houston served as president of the Republic of Texas from 1836 to 1838 and from 1841 to 1844, then as one of the first two senators, after Texas was admitted to the Union in 1846. As a majority of Texans voted for secession on the eve of Civil War, Houston lost his bid for reelection to the Senate in 1858, but was elected governor in 1859. His efforts to prevent secession failed and, in 1861, he refused to swear allegiance to the

Confederacy, whereupon he was deposed and lived out the rest of his life in quiet retirement.

Howard, O. O. (1830–1909) Oliver O. Howard served with distinction during the Civil War, losing his right arm at the Battle of Fair Oaks. Despite his disability, he returned to the war. During Reconstruction, Howard, who was deeply concerned about the fate of some four million freed slaves, was named to head the Freedman's Bureau, the federal agency charged with ensuring the former slaves' welfare and integration into society. Howard's chief accomplishment was the establishment of schools and vocational training institutes under the auspices of the bureau. He was also a founder in 1867 of what became the nation's premier institution of higher education for African Americans, Howard University, which was named in his honor. Howard served as the university's third president from 1869 to 1874, when he returned to military service as a general officer in the Indian Wars of the West.

Howe, Julia Ward (1819–1910) A poet and, with her husband, publisher of the abolitionist newspaper *Commonwealth*, Howe composed the stirring "Battle Hymn of the Republic" during an 1861 visit to a military encampment near Washington, D.C. It was published in the February 1862 issue of *Atlantic Monthly* and, set to the tune of "John Brown's Body," became the quasi-official anthem of the Union Army for the rest of the Civil War.

Howells, William Dean (1837–1920) The novels of William Dean Howells are realistic chronicles of American life as it shifted from the simplicity of the early 19th century to the complexity of the turn of that century. His best work, the

1882 *A Modern Instance,* depicts the inexorable disintegration of a modern marriage, while his most popular work, *The Rise of Silas Lapham* (1885), is the story of a simple businessman's struggle to rise within Boston society. Howells was an important influence on and mentor to many of his younger contemporaries, and he was an intimate literary adviser to Mark Twain.

Hubble, Edwin (1889–1953) Hubble was the founder of extragalactic astronomy, whose observations showed that the universe was populated with many galaxies, of which our Milky Way was just one. Hubble also showed that the universe was not only expanding, but doing so at an accelerating rate. His observations and conclusions advanced astronomy in the most profound and elemental ways, and his scientific achievement must be seen as on a par with those of Copernicus and Galileo.

Hudson, Henry (ca. 1565–1611) A British sailor, Hudson made three voyages for England (1607, 1608, 1610–1611) and one for the Dutch (1609), all in an effort to discover the Northwest Passage—a water route from Europe to Asia via the Arctic Ocean. Although he failed to discover the desired route, Hudson extensively explored the northeast coast, including Hudson River and Hudson's Bay. During his last voyage, he, his son, and seven others fell victim to a mutiny and were cast adrift in Hudson's Bay on June 22, 1611. They were never heard from again.

Hughes, Charles Evans (1862–1948) Hughes was governor of New York, associate justice of the U.S. Supreme Court (1910–1919), secretary of state (1921–1919), and chief justice of the United States (1930–1941). A distinguished representative of Republican conservatism, he was defeated by Woodrow Wilson in a 1916 bid for the White House. He squared off against another Democratic president, Franklin Roosevelt in 1937, when he successfully opposed FDR's attempt to "pack" the Supreme Court by appointing new—liberal—justices to offset the conservative influence of each sitting justice over the age of 70 who refused to retire. Nevertheless, although he was a political conservative, Hughes was instrumental in Supreme Court decisions upholding important provisions of FDR's New Deal, including the right of labor unions to collective bargaining under the National Labor Relations Act of 1935 (Wagner Act) and much of the Social Security Act.

Hughes, Langston (1902–1967) Hughes briefly attended Columbia University (1921–1922), lived for a time in Harlem—center of African-American urban culture—worked as a steward on an African-bound freighter, traveled widely, then worked as a busboy in a Washington, D.C., hotel. He saw the famous white poet Vachel Lindsay in the dining room, put a copy of his poems beside Lindsay's plate, and read in the newspapers the next day that Lindsay had announced his discovery of a great "Negro busboy poet." Hughes was given a scholarship to Lincoln University, and his literary career was launched. Through numerous works of poetry and prose—especially autobiography—Hughes became widely regarded as a representative voice of black America.

Humphrey, Hubert (1911–1978) Hubert Horatio Humphrey served as Democratic senator from Minnesota from 1949 to 1965 and from 1971 to 1978. He was the representative of the liberal wing of the Democratic Party, having built his political base on a farm and labor coalition the likes of which had not been seen since early in the 20th century. From 1965 to 1969, he was vice president in the administration of Lyndon B. Johnson, and he ran against Richard M. Nixon as the candidate of a splintered Democratic Party in 1968. Conservatives found him too liberal and, at this time, liberals opposed to the Vietnam War found his continued support of that war unacceptable. Nevertheless, his loss to Nixon was by a razor-thin margin.

Hunt, E. Howard (1918–) Hunt had been an Office of Strategic Services (OSS) operative during World War II and was a CIA agent after the war. He was instrumental in the failed Bay of Pigs Invasion, the abortive attempt to overthrow Fidel Castro in 1961. In the Nixon White House, Hunt, with G. Gordon Liddy, was one of the so-called Plumbers, a secret and illegal band of operatives whose job was to plug information leaks and secure political intelligence for the Nixon administration. He and Liddy planned the burglary of Democratic National Headquarters at Washington's Watergate office complex in 1972, the exposure of which led to the downfall and resignation of the president. Convicted of burglary, conspiracy and wiretapping, Hunt served 33 months in prison. A colorful character—a prolific author of pulp spy novels—Hunt was also sinister, deemed by the Rockefeller Commission of the U.S. Congress in 1974 a suspect in the assassination of President John F. Kennedy.

Huntington, Collis P. (1821–1900) With fellow California financiers Mark Hopkins, Leland Stanford, and Charles Crocker (collectively dubbed the "Big Four"), Huntington financed and promoted construction of the Central Pacific Railroad to link up with the Union Pacific, creating the first American transcontinental railroad in 1869.

Hurston, Zora Neale (1891–1960) When she was sixteen, Hurston left her native Florida with a traveling theatrical company and lived for a time in New York's Harlem during the early part of the Harlem Renaissance, a great blossoming of African-American literary and artistic creativity. Hurston was educated at Howard University in Washington D.C. (1921–1924) and, on scholarship, studied anthropology at Barnard College in 1925–1928 under the renowned Franz Boas. She pursued graduate studies in anthropology at Columbia University and conducted groundbreaking fieldwork in folklore among African Americans in the South. Her folklore study produced major works of nonfiction and fiction based on African-American folk culture.

Hutchinson, Anne (1591–1643) In 1634, Hutchinson voyaged from England with her husband and settled in the Puritan Massachusetts Bay Colony. Here, Hutchinson conducted weekly religious meetings of Boston women. Hutchinson began giving voice to her own theological views, which included the principle that individual religious inspiration and insight trumped sermons or biblical knowledge. The Puritan establishment found this heterodoxy unacceptable, and banished her in 1637. With some followers, she settled part of Aquidneck Island in Roger Williams's Rhode Island in 1638. She moved in 1642, to Long Island, near present Pelham Bay, New York, where, in 1643 she, together with all but one of her children, was killed by Indians. Some in Puritan Massachusetts claimed this as a divine judgment against her. Modern Americans view Hutchinson as an early champion of religious liberty and even a precursor of feminism.

Ickes, Harold (1874–1952) Ickes was born on a Pennsylvania farm, received a University of Chicago education, and became a lawyer and social reformer. President Franklin D. Roosevelt tapped him to serve as secretary of the interior, and Ickes set about transforming the department with the spirit and letter of New Deal reform. He strengthened the National Parks system, he brought strict and impartial enforcement to the stewardship of America's forests and public lands—keeping real estate speculators, loggers, miners, and power interests from the unregulated exploitation of the nation's land heritage—and he ended racial segregation throughout the department, including throughout the National Parks.

Ingersoll, Robert (1833–1899) This Illinois politician commanded lordly sums for lectures on humanism, the higher criticism of the Bible, and scientific rationalism. His audiences delighted in—or were provoked by—his skewering of what he called "orthodox superstitions." Ingersoll was a representative figure of the scientific skepticism that characterized much of the late 19th century in America.

Insull, Samuel (1859–1938) A Londoner by birth, Insull worked as one of Thomas Edison's British representatives, then came to the United States in 1881 as Edison's private secretary. By 1891, he was president of the Chicago Edison Company, which furnished electrical power to the city. Insull expanded his utilities empire until, by the 1920s, his company was supplying not only all of Chicago, but most of the Midwest. The expansion was achieved through vigorous promotion of the stocks of his complex of holding companies—a practice that put him in a precarious position and caused his financial collapse during the Great Depression. Tried and acquitted on fraud and other charges, he fled to Europe.

Irving, Washington (1783–1859) Today remembered chiefly for his short stories "The Legend of Sleepy Hollow" and "Rip Van Winkle," Irving was a prolific man of letters and the first American writer to achieve a truly international reputation. His "Rip Van Winkle" is generally considered the first American short story, inaugurating a literary form in which American writers would excel.

Ives, Charles (1874–1954) Ives was the son of a bandleader who enjoyed experimenting with strange sounds and unconventional harmonies. Although Charles Ives received a formal musical education at Yale University, he soon ventured down the path his father had pointed him toward and used familiar American folk tunes, hymn tunes, and popular tunes to create harmonically and rhythmically innovative music, including piano works, symphonies and other orchestral works, chamber music, and songs. While he was certainly an avant-garde—even defiantly idiosyncratic—composer, Ives was deeply rooted in American culture and experience. He neither sought nor received much recognition in his lifetime—he made his living as an insurance executive—but his best compositions are now considered among the nation's most important "classical" music and anticipated many later developments in modern music.

Jackson, Andrew (1767–1845) Born on the frontier between North and South Carolina, Andrew Jackson lost his mother and his brother in the American Revolution, went on to become a lawyer, made and lost a fortune, killed a man in an 1806 duel in defense of his wife's honor, became a politician, was the principal victor against the Red Stick Creeks in the Creek War, and won a glorious victory at the Battle of New Orleans (1815) in the War of 1812. Defeated by John Quincy Adams in an 1824 run for the White House, he was elected four years later and introduced an unprecedented degree of egalitarian—if sometimes raucous—democracy. It was, however, Jackson, too, who promoted the Indian Removal Act of 1830, which uprooted many thousands of Indians living east of the Mississippi, exiling them to arid lands west of the river. The Cherokee called this long, often lethal march the "Trail of Tears."

Jackson, Helen Hunt (1830–1885) Jackson was a popular and prolific novelist, who was moved by the plight of the Indians, which she saw firsthand after she moved with her husband to Colorado in 1875. The result was a historical study called *A Century of Dishonor* (1881), which examined and condemned federal Indian policy. She was appointed to a federal commission to investigate conditions among Indians living on the western missions. This inspired her best-known novel, *Ramona* (1884), which was effective in raising public consciousness about the mistreatment of Native Americans.

Jackson, Jesse Louis (1941–) Born into a poor African-American family in Greenville, South Carolina, Jackson earned a scholarship to the University of Illinois during 1959–1960, completed his undergraduate degree in sociology in 1964 at the Agricultural and Technical College of North Carolina, then did postgraduate work at Chicago Theological Seminary, becoming ordained as a Baptist minister in 1968. Inspired by Martin Luther King, Jr., Jackson started Operation Breadbasket in Chicago in 1966 and, in 1971, Operation PUSH (People United to Save Humanity), an organization to promote black self-reliance. A major figure in the civil rights movement both before and after Dr.

King's assassination in 1968, Jackson led a voter registration program that helped elect Chicago's first black mayor, Harold Washington, in 1983. From this point on, Jackson earned a reputation as an influential political figure on the national as well as international scene.

Jackson, Maynard (1938–2003) Jackson was a Dallas-born lawyer and politician, whose election as mayor of Atlanta in 1973 made him the first chief executive of a large southern city. He served three terms—during 1974–1982 and 1990–1994—presiding over the spectacular growth of the South's major metropolis.

Jackson, Michael (1958–) Jackson entered show business as the youngest—and most talented—of the Jackson 5 (consisting of the five Jackson brothers), which shot to stardom in 1969 and reigned supreme on the pop charts through about 1975. Michael Jackson had his first solo hit in 1979—the album *Off the Wall*—and by the 1980s was unchallenged as the most popular entertainer in the world: the "King of Pop." His success declined in the early 1990s as his appearance and behavior became increasingly bizarre. In 1993, he was accused of child molestation by a 13-year-old boy who had been a guest at Neverland, Jackson's Los Angeles compound. In 2005, he was tried on new child molestation charges in California and, to the surprise of many, acquitted.

Jackson, Thomas "Stonewall" (1824–1863) When his bold stand at the First Battle of Bull Run turned the tide toward a Confederate victory, this Virginia general earned the sobriquet "Stonewall" and emerged in successive actions as the most innovative and skilled tactician of the Civil War. In the Shenandoah Valley, he was able to use a minimal number of men to pin down huge Union forces, and at Chancellorsville he was instrumental in achieving a crushing Union defeat. Wounded by friendly fire on May 2, 1863, he died eight days later. Robert E. Lee declared: "I have lost my right arm."

James, Frank (1843–1915) Raised with his brother on a Missouri farm, Frank James joined William Quantrill's notorious band of Confederate guerrillas during the Civil War. After the war, he and his brother formed an outlaw gang, robbing banks, stores, stagecoaches, and trains from 1866 until 1881, when Jesse was killed. Frank surrendered a few months later, but no jury would convict him. Ruthless though they were, he and his brother had attained the status of latter-day Robin Hoods. Frank retired quietly, as the legend of him and his brother continued to grow.

James, Henry (1843–1916) Henry James was the son of a theologian and the brother of philosopher-psychologist William James. He devoted his life to the writing of fiction, creating fascinating variations on a single question: What happens when the exuberant if clumsy innocence of the New World meets the sophistication and corruption of the Old? The exploration of this theme led to the creation of complex and infinitely nuanced novels examining culture, society, and human emotion. A literary craftsman of painstaking skill, his example inspired generations of American novelists after him. James lived much of his life in Europe and became a British subject shortly before his death.

James, Jesse (1847–1882) Like his older brother Frank, Jesse James joined a Confederate guerrilla gang during the Civil War. After the war, he teamed up with Frank as co-chief of what became the most notorious outlaw gang in the

American West. During its long criminal career, the James Gang chiefly robbed banks, stagecoaches, and railroads, gaining a reputation as latter-day Robin Hoods—even though, after robbing the rich, they by no means gave to the poor. The gang's career ended when Jesse, living incognito in St. Joseph, Missouri, as "Thomas Howard," was shot in the back of the head by a new gang member, Robert Ford, who betrayed him for the reward money. Ford was publicly castigated, whereas Jesse (and, to a lesser extent, Frank) was elevated to the pantheon of American folk heroes.

James, William (1842–1910) A pioneering Harvard psychologist, James emerged as the nation's leading philosopher when he published in 1907 *Pragmatism: A New Name for Old Ways of Thinking*, which proposed that the meaning as well as the truth of any idea is a function of its practical outcome. Pragmatism was born of an American culture of action and enterprise and, in turn, exerted a major intellectual influence on subsequent American thought and American ethics.

Jaworski, Leon (1905–1982) Born to Polish and Austrian immigrants, Jaworski was a prominent Texas attorney who, on November 1, 1973, was appointed to replace Archibald Cox after Cox had been fired at the behest of President Richard M. Nixon during the Watergate scandal. Jaworski pursued the Watergate investigation vigorously, engaging in a protracted constitutional battle with the White House to secure tape recordings of Oval Office conferences that implicated the president in illegal surveillance and the illegal attempt to cover up various covert White House operations.

Jay, John (1745–1829) This founding father became the first chief justice of the Supreme Court (1789–1795) and, as such,

where they lived communally in a settlement dubbed Jonestown—with Jim Jones as their absolute leader. Friends and family of some of the cult members became concerned for the welfare of their loved ones, and, in November 1978, U.S. Representative Leo Ryan led a fact-finding mission to Jonestown to investigate charges of human rights abuses there. Ryan left the compound, with 20 Temple members, after an attempt on his life. At the local airstrip, however, cultists gunned down Ryan, an NBC reporter and cameraman, a newspaper photographer, and one of the defecting cultists. Others were wounded. Immediately after this attack, on November 18, 1978, most of the Peoples Temple cultists followed Jones in committing mass suicide by drinking poison (Jones shot himself). A total of 914 died.

Jones, John Paul (1747–1792) Jones was a Scots sailor and ship's master, who, after killing a mutinous crew member, fled to America in 1775 and, at the outbreak of the revolution, joined the Continental Navy. He raided British commerce, capturing numerous ships. On September 23, 1779, he attacked a large merchant fleet under escort by the British warships *Serapis* and *Countess of Scarborough.* Outgunned, Jones fought a 3 1/2-hour battle, replying to a British surrender demand with "I have not yet begun to fight!" He captured *Serapis* and the *Countess of Scarborough,* but lost his own *Bonhomme Richard.*

Jones, Mary Harris (Mother Jones) (1830–1930) Jones was an Irish immigrant whose husband died in an 1867 epidemic in Memphis, Tennessee. Resettled in Chicago, Jones lost all that she owned in the great Chicago fire of 1871. The Knights of Labor came to her aid, and she soon became active in this early labor union. She became famous as

"Mother Jones," a dynamic labor organizer—especially for the United Mine Workers—exhorting men everywhere to "Join the union, boys." In 1898, she became a founder of the Social Democratic Party and, in 1905, of the Industrial Workers of the World (IWW).

Jones, Robert Trent "Bobby" (1902–1971) Atlanta native Bobby Jones was the first golfer to achieve the Grand Slam, winning four major tournaments in a year. His record from 1923 through 1930 was 13 championships in the four major tournaments of his era. Jones never turned pro.

Joplin, Scott (1868–1917) Joplin was an African-American pianist and composer, who was repeatedly frustrated in his efforts to be recognized as a "serious" composer, but who created classic piano rags of great beauty, including "Maple Leaf Rag" and "The Entertainer." His ragtime opera of 1911, *Treemonisha*, was not performed until 1972, long after his death. Ragtime, a highly syncopated precursor to jazz, fell out of favor until its revival in the 1970s—when Joplin's contribution to American music became widely recognized.

Joseph, Chief (ca. 1840–1904) Faced with removal from their homeland in Washington, a faction of the Nez Perce followed Chief Joseph for more than three months (June 17–October 5, 1877) in a trek of more than 1,000 miles through the rugged landscape of Oregon, Washington, Idaho, and Montana, evading—often defeating—pursuing troops who greatly outnumbered them. Joseph finally surrendered at the Battle of Bear Paw Mountain in Montana, on October 5, 1877, delivering to General Nelson A. Miles a speech that has come to symbolize the nobility of Native American resignation in the face of overwhelming force:

"Hear me, my chiefs; my heart is sick and sad. From where the Sun now stands, I will fight no more forever."

Judah, Theodore Dehone (1826–1863) Judah was born in Bridgeport, Connecticut, and was trained as an engineer. He built the Niagara Gorge Railroad and engineered eastern canals before he was hired in 1854 to survey a railroad near Sacramento, California. Believing it possible to extend the line across the Sierras, he promoted the idea to financiers, who formed the Central Pacific Railroad, with Judah as its chief engineer. When his financiers vacillated, Judah traveled to the East Coast to raise capital on his own, but succumbed en route to yellow fever. His early efforts were the beginning of the Central Pacific-Union Pacific, the transcontinental railroad finally completed in 1869.

Kahn, Louis I. (1901–1974) Louis I. Kahn was not a great financial success as an architect, but his innovative modern buildings, which featured massive forms expressive of the modern world—yet often embodying references to great historic architecture—made him one of the most talked-about architects of the 20th century. After his death, his reputation grew, and he is considered one of architecture's most important mavericks.

Karlsefni, Thorfinn (active 1002–1015) Thorfinn arrived in Greenland in 1002 and married Gudrid, widow of one of the sons of the Norse chieftain Eric the Red. About 1007, Thorfinn sailed with three vessels and 160 men to settle in Vinland, a portion of Newfoundland that had been discovered by Leif Ericsson (probably his brother) about ten years earlier. Thorfinn occupied Vinland for about two years, during which time Gudrid gave birth to the first Euro-American child, a son named Snorro. The colony was, however, abandoned, and Thorfinn returned to Greenland.

Kearny, Stephen Watts (1794–1848) Kearny was a career army officer, who first saw service in the War of 1812. At the outbreak of the U.S.- Mexican War, he led an expedition from Fort Leavenworth, Kansas, to conquer New Mexico and California. He was able to talk the Mexican defenders of Santa Fe into giving up without a fight, and he marched into the New Mexico capital without firing a shot on August 18, 1846. He then advanced to California, which he helped secure for the United States.

Keller, Helen (1880–1968) Born in Tuscumbia, Alabama, Helen Adams Keller was stricken with a scarlet fever at 19 months old, leaving her blind, deaf, and mute. Thanks to a remarkable teacher, Anne Sullivan, who remained with Keller from 1887 until Sullivan's death in 1936, Keller learned to communicate and, at 14, enrolled in the Wright Humason School for the Deaf in New York City, went on to the Cambridge (Massachusetts) School for Young Ladies, enrolled in Radcliffe College in 1900, and graduated cum laude in 1904. Having acquired skills no one so severely disabled could ever have expected to attain, Keller decided to share her experience, not only to help and to inspire other disabled persons, but to demonstrate to the sighted and hearing world that disability did not diminish intellectual capacity or humanity. She became an enormously popular author and (through an interpreter) lecturer. Her activism brought about an international revolution in the treatment of the deaf and the blind.

Kellogg, Frank (1856–1937) Kellogg was U.S. secretary of state from 1925 to 1929 in the cabinet of President Calvin Coolidge.

In 1928, he concluded with French foreign minister Aristide Briand the Kellogg-Briand Pact of 1928, a multilateral agreement to prohibit war as an instrument of national policy. The pact was signed by 62 nations, including all of those that would be the major combatants of World War II. For his effort, Kellogg received the Nobel Peace Prize in 1929.

Kellogg, W. K. (1860–1951) With his brother John Harvey Kellogg, Will Keith Kellogg founded the Battle Creek Toasted Corn Flake Company in 1906 in Battle Creek, Michigan. It subsequently became the Kellogg Company. Kellogg popularized toasted cereal—mainly in the form of cornflakes—especially for breakfast. He created a commercial food empire and changed the eating habits of virtually all Americans.

Kennan, George F. (1904–2005) A Princeton-educated diplomat, Kennan was a specialist in Soviet politics and, after World War II, while stationed in Moscow, transmitted to Washington in February 1946 the so-called "long telegram," in which he analyzed the Soviet psyche and advocated developing a policy of "containment," opposing Soviet Communist expansion wherever and whenever it appeared in the world. This policy was further articulated in a famous article published under the pseudonym "X" in the journal *Foreign Affairs* in July 1947. Containment became the cornerstone of U.S. Cold War policy for half a century.

Kennedy, Edward (1932–) U.S. senator from Massachusetts since 1963, Edward "Teddy" Kennedy is the only surviving brother of John F. Kennedy and Robert F. Kennedy, both victims of assassination. Edward Kennedy was the frontrunner for the 1972 Democratic presidential nomination until, on the night of July 18, 1969, he accidentally drove his car off a bridge on Chappaquiddick Island, Massachusetts, after a party. His passenger, 28-year-old Mary Jo Kopechne, drowned. Kennedy was convicted of leaving the scene of an accident, and although he was reelected to the Senate in 1970, his presidential aspirations were dashed.

Kennedy, John F. (1917–1963) Taking the oath of office at 43, John Fitzgerald Kennedy was the nation's youngest elected president. His assassination, on a visit to Dallas, Texas, November 22, 1963, also made him the youngest to die. Youth and the determination, idealism, and optimism of youth were at the center of the Kennedy presidency, which inspired the nation to strive toward extraordinary achievements ranging from progress in social justice to the exploration of outer space.

Kennedy, Joseph P. (1888–1969) The grandson of Irish immigrants, Joseph P. Kennedy was a Massachusetts businessman, whose enterprises included banking, ship building, motion picture production, investing, and probably Prohibition-era bootlegging. A major contributor to the Democratic Party, he secured high-level appointments in the administration of Franklin D. Roosevelt, including the ambassadorship to Britain. In this capacity, he advocated the appeasement of Adolf Hitler, whom he considered unbeatable, and encouraged FDR to steer the United States on an isolationist course. This stance ultimately ruined Kennedy's political and diplomatic career. Kennedy's ambition was then directed toward his sons, Joseph P., Jr., John F., Robert F., and Edward M. (He also had five daughters: Rosemary, Kathleen, Eunice, Patricia, and Jean). When Joseph Jr. was killed in World War II, Joseph Sr. groomed JFK for greatness, exercising all of his personal, political, and financial influence to do so.

Kennedy Robert F. (1925–1968) Brother of President John F. Kennedy, RFK served as attorney general in the Kennedy cabinet and was also the president's most trusted adviser, playing a key role in defusing the Cuban Missile Crisis, which had the potential for igniting World War III. As attorney general, Kennedy enforced federal policy and Supreme Court rulings mandating the racial integration of public facilities, schools, and universities. In 1965, he became a U.S. senator, and in 1968 began a campaign for the Democratic Party presidential nomination, running against incumbent Lyndon B. Johnson as an opponent of the Vietnam War. His presidential bid ended in his assassination after triumphing in the California primary.

Keokuk (1790?–1848?) Keokuk rose to power among the Sauk and Fox tribe along the Rock River on the Illinois-Iowa border. He opposed leaders such as Black Hawk, who urged militant resistance to white incursions into tribal lands and instead counseled accommodation with and concession to the government. As a result, the Sauk and Fox homelands were ceded to the United States and Keokuk grew wealthy, but lived in disgrace among his tribe.

Kern, Jerome (1885–1945) Although his 1912 *The Red Petticoat* was the first musical comedy containing all-Kern tunes, it was his 1927 *Show Boat* that changed the history of musical comedy, transforming the genre into serious musical drama. Kern created a whole new form of popular art—and one that was uniquely American.

Kerouac, Jack (1922–1969) Kerouac was born of French-Canadian descent in Lowell, Massachusetts, was discharged from the U.S. Navy during World War II as mentally disturbed, then made a precarious living as a merchant seaman and worked various odd jobs before publishing his first novel, *The Town and the City,* in 1950. Restless and dissatisfied with accepted literary and social conventions, he worked toward developing a new style, which was highly charged, spontaneous, and unedited, inspired by jazz improvisation and aided by drugs and liquor. In 1957, he wrote *On the Road,* a freewheeling narrative of road trips across the United States in search of fulfillment in music, literature, mysticism, sex, and life itself. The characters in *On the Road* are latter-day hoboes, who turn their backs on regular jobs, mortgages, and the ownership of things. The book became the bible of the "Beat Generation," which questioned many accepted American values, and which laid the foundation for the Hippie movement of the later 1960s.

Kerry, John (1943–) Kerry became the junior United States Senator from Massachusetts in 1985 and was the Democratic Party's nominee for president in 2004. He lost to incumbent George W. Bush, in part due to a smear campaign that called into question Kerry's military decorations earned while he served in the U.S. Navy during the Vietnam War. Kerry had first come to public attention during that war as a vocal member of Vietnam Veterans against the War during 1970–1971. The highly decorated veteran made for a passionate and compelling antiwar spokesman and earned a prominent place on President Nixon's celebrated "Enemies List."

Kesey, Ken (1935–2001) Early in the 1960s, Kesey was a paid experimental subject at a Veterans Administration hospital, who was given psychedelic drugs and reported on their effects. Combined with his work as an orderly in the hospital, this experience inspired his 1962 breakthrough novel, *One Flew over the Cuckoo's Nest* (made into a popular film in 1975). Most of Kesey's subsequent writing was autobiographical and often recounted drug-charged travels with the Merry Pranksters, a kind of commune who journeyed together in a psychedelically decorated bus during the 1960s and became symbolic of that era, its ideals, and its foibles.

Key, Francis Scott (1779–1843) Baltimore attorney Key was detained by the British aboard a warship in Baltimore Harbor during the attack on that city in the War of 1812. He passed the night anxiously observing the naval bombardment of Fort McHenry, sentinel guarding the approach to Baltimore. When the dawn's early light revealed that the star-spangled banner still waved—signifying the British failure to capture the fort—Key wrote the verses that were later set (by others) to an old English tavern tune ("To Anacreon in Heaven") and became the words of the National Anthem. ("The Star-Spangled Banner" was officially proclaimed the anthem by President Herbert Hoover in 1931.)

Kieft, Willem (1597–1647) Kieft was director-general of New Netherland (modern New York) from 1638 to 1647. During the night of February 25–26, 1643, he perpetrated a horrific massacre of Wappinger Indians—men, women, and children—at Pavonia (modern Jersey City), New Jersey for the purpose of suppressing potential Indian warfare. Instead, the Pavonia Massacre provoked massive tribal retaliation, and New Amsterdam (modern New York City) was subjected to a state of semi-siege for more than a year. War between the Indians and Dutch did not end until 1645.

Kimmel, Husband E. (1882–1968) As navy CINCPAC (Commander in Charge of the Pacific) at the outbreak of World War II, Admiral Kimmel, with his army counterpart, General Walter C. Short, took most of the blame for America's unpreparedness to resist the Japanese attack on Pearl Harbor. Unlike Short, he was never officially blamed for Pearl Harbor, but the catastrophe ended his career. Retiring from the navy, he worked for an engineering firm, then published *Admiral Kimmel's Story,* an attempt to clear his name.

King, Billie Jean (1943–) King's record, style, and character as a professional tennis player raised the status of women's professional tennis to that of a major sport. Although she won 39 major titles in her career, she may be best remembered for defeating Bobby Riggs, a loudmouth "male chauvinist" tennis player, in what was advertised in 1973 as the "Battle of the Sexes." At stake was largest tennis purse to that time.

King, Martin Luther, Jr. (1929–1968) An ordained Baptist minister, King rose to leadership of the national Civil Rights movement beginning in 1956 during the Montgomery (Alabama) Bus Boycott. He came into national prominence as founding leader of the Southern Christian Leadership Conference (SCLC), which promoted nonviolent protest to end racial segregation and discrimination throughout the nation. His stirring "I Have a Dream" speech at the Lincoln Memorial during the massive 1963 March on Washington galvanized the nonviolent Civil Rights movement and aided passage of the epochal Civil Rights Act of 1964 and the Voting Rights Act of 1965. King was awarded the Nobel Prize for Peace in 1964, and while no Civil Rights leader was more respected or influential, King found his leadership under increasing challenge from more militant black leaders, especially after (in the mid 1960s) he merged the cause of racial equality with a general drive to end poverty—regardless of race. King fell victim to an assassin's bullet on April 4, 1968, while in Memphis to aid striking sanitation workers. The night before, he had delivered his prophetic "Promised Land" speech, declaring, "I've seen the promised land. I may not get there with you. But I want you to know tonight that we, as a people, will get to the promised land."

King Philip (c. 1639– 1676) The Wampanoag sachem Metacomet—known to the colonists of New England as King Philip—was the second son of Massasoit, the chief who had befriended the Pilgrims in 1621. King Philip became chief in 1662, after the death of his brother Wamsutta, and waged war against most of white New England during 1675–1676. In proportion to the white and Indian population of New England at the time, "King Philip's War"—all but forgotten today—was the deadliest war in American history.

King, Rodney (1965–) On the night of March 3, 1991, the California Highway Patrol and Los Angeles police officers chased King—who was speeding—for eight miles before he stopped. A confrontation occurred, during which King resisted, and LAPD officers repeatedly beat King with batons. This incident (but not the resistance that had allegedly preceded it) was videotaped by a bystander, and was nationally televised on news programs. It sparked a public outcry against racist-motivated police brutality and sparked massive race riots in Los Angeles in 1992 after a jury acquitted officers on criminal charges.

Kino, Eusebio (1645–1711) This Italian-born Jesuit priest came to America as a missionary and explorer in the Spanish service and established numerous missions in the region known as Pimería Alta, which is now Sonora, Mexico, and Arizona. In contrast to many other missionaries, he opposed the Spanish enslavement of the Indians. He also aided the Pima in diversifying their agriculture.

Kirstein, Lincoln (1907–1996) Kirstein was an impresario, critic, and businessman who promoted dance by working with the famed choreographer George Balanchine to create and direct the ballet companies that were consolidated into the New York City Ballet. Committed to perpetuating American dance, Kirstein was a founder of the School of American Ballet, which he directed from 1940 to 1989.

Kissinger, Henry (1923–) No appointed official has had a more profound effect on American diplomacy than Henry A. Kissinger. Born in Germany, he fled Nazi persecution with his Jewish family in 1938 and settled in New York. Educated as a political scientist he rose through academia to become adviser for national security affairs and then secretary of state in the administrations of Richard M. Nixon and Gerald R. Ford during 1969–1976. Kissinger was a major influence on Nixon's policy of détente with the Soviet Union and, especially, with China, and was instrumental in formulating Nixon's Vietnam War policy. It was Kissinger who negotiated peace with North Vietnam's Le Duc Tho, for which he was awarded—jointly with Tho—the 1973 Nobel Prize for Peace.

Knox, Henry (1750–1806) Knox was a Boston bookstore owner who became active in the independence movement and, during the American Revolution, served as General Washington's chief artillery commander. Knox was appointed secretary of war in 1785 under the Articles of Confederation and retained this post in the cabinet of President Washington, under the newly adopted Constitution, in 1789. He served until his retirement from public life in 1795.

Koresh, David (1959–1993) Born Vernon Wayne Howell to a 14-year-old single mother in Houston, Texas, Koresh was expelled from the Seventh-day Adventist Church. He moved to Waco, Texas in 1981, where he joined the Branch Davidians, a religious community of excommunicated Seventh-day Adventists. Proclaiming himself the messiah, Koresh advocated (and practiced) polygamy, and, according to charges by former cult members, perpetrated child abuse. On February 28, 1993, responding to reports that the Branch Davidians had accumulated a stockpile of illegal weapons—and also responding to the accusations of child abuse—agents of the Bureau of Alcohol, Tobacco and Firearms (ATF) raided the Mount Carmel compound. Four ATF agents and six cultists were killed. The FBI moved in and held the compound under siege for 51 days before storming it on April 19, 1993. A fire—subsequently determined to have been started by Koresh and the cultists—consumed the compound, killing 76 people, including Koresh and 27 children. Most Americans regarded Koresh as a deranged cult leader, but some saw the assault as an example of federal tyranny against an American maverick.

Kovic, Ron (1946–) Kovic was a decorated U.S. Marine, who served two tours in Vietnam and was wounded on January 20, 1968, sustaining a spinal cord injury that left him paralyzed from the chest down. Returned to the United States, he became a vocal antiwar activist, who was arrested a dozen times for political protest. In 1974 he completed a memoir, *Born on the Fourth of July*, which (using a screenplay cowritten by Kovic) became a movie in 1989, directed by Oliver Stone and starring Tom Cruise as Kovic.

Kristol, Irving (1920–) Kristol once described himself as a "liberal mugged by reality." He was managing editor of *Commentary* (1947–1952) and was active in other liberal political journals as well as book publishing before becoming professor of social thought at the New York University Graduate School of Business (1969–1988). His political thought evolved during the 1960s into advocacy of a hawkish approach to the Cold War and a reduction of the welfare state. Most importantly, in contrast to earlier American conservatism, his neoconservative philosophy called for the active assertion of U.S. military power in foreign affairs. Neoconservatism has greatly influenced U.S. political policy, from Ronald Reagan to George W. Bush, who, in July 2002, presented Kristol with the Presidential Medal of Freedom.

Kroc, Ray (1902–1984) Kroc was a salesman and exclusive distributor for the "multimixer" milk shake blender. In 1954, he visited a multimixer client, a San Bernardino, California, hamburger joint owned by Maurice and Richard McDonald. The brothers developed an assembly-line method to make and sell a large volume of hamburgers, fries, and shakes. Impressed, Kroc licensed the McDonald format and name and, on April 15, 1955, opened the first of a planned chain of restaurants in Des Plaines, Illinois. By Kroc's death in 1984, there were 7,500 McDonald's restaurants—which had become an icon of "fast food" not only in the United States, but worldwide.

Lafayette, Marquis de (1757–1834) Eager to win glory as a soldier in a noble cause, Lafayette left his native France and arrived in Philadelphia in July 1777 to fight for American liberty. He was commissioned a major general in the Continental Army and established a close bond with General George Washington. He performed heroically at the Battle of Brandywine (September 11, 1777), returned to France and persuaded Louis XVI to send 6,000 men to fight immediately, then came back to America in April 1780 to take command of an army in Virginia. Lafayette was instrumental in bottling up Charles Cornwallis and his army on the Yorktown peninsula in late July 1780, which set Cornwallis up for the defeat that effectively ended the American Revolution.

Lafitte, Jean (1780?–1825?) Born in France, Lafitte settled in New Orleans, from which he operated as a smuggler and pirate, preying on Spanish shipping. Seeking a pardon for his illicit activities, Laffite offered the services of himself and his men to General Andrew Jackson in defense of New Orleans during the War of 1812. Lafitte fought brilliantly, and the Battle of New Orleans (December 1814–January 1815) was a great American victory. He and his men were pardoned by President James Madison.

Laffer, Arthur B. (1940–) While serving as chief economist for the U.S. Office of Management and Budget (OMB) during 1970–1972, Laffer developed the idea that lowering tax rates would actually increase tax revenues by stimulating investment. He illustrated this with the famous "Laffer Curve," a foundation of Reagan-era supply-side economics, which held that reductions in federal taxes on businesses and individuals would lead to increased economic growth. As for the reduction in social welfare programs such tax cuts might necessitate, supply-side economics held that the economic benefits to business and the wealthy would "trickle down" to the middle and lower classes as well.

La Follette, Robert M. (1855–1925) Governor of Wisconsin (1901–1906) and U.S. senator (1906–1925), La Follette led the Progressive Movement, an effort to bring about large-scale political reform. Although La Follette failed in his bid for the White House in 1924—he ran on the Progressive Party ticket—he did poll some 5,000,000 votes, nearly 17 percent of the votes cast. His Progressive philosophy was shared in varying degrees by such politicians as Theodore Roosevelt and Woodrow Wilson.

LaGuardia, Fiorello (1882–1947) La Guardia was a lawyer and reform-minded politician. He served in Congress before his election in 1933 as mayor of New York, running on the Fusion ticket, which united the Liberal and Republican parties. His object was to reform the corrupt Tammany Hall Democratic boss system. He did just that, making sweeping reforms that became the envy of the nation. Through three terms as mayor, he emerged as a beloved figure of infinite energy and great compassion, fighting corruption and organized crime, bringing new efficiency to city services, expanding municipal social-welfare services, and introducing slum-clearance and subsidized housing. Many consider him the greatest mayor of any major American city—ever.

Land, Edwin (1901–1991) While a student at Harvard, Land became interested in the phenomenon of polarized light and, in 1937, founded the Polaroid Corporation, creating polarized materials for sunglasses, 3-D movies, and military use. In 1947 he invented a single-step photographic process that enabled black-and-white pictures to be developed in 60 seconds. A color process was marketed in 1963. In an era before digital imaging, Polaroid photography was highly popular, very useful, and made Land a wealthy man.

Landers, Ann (1918–2002) Born Esther "Eppie" Pauline Friedman Lederer, she took the name Ann Landers in 1955 when she won a contest to take over what was already a popular newspaper advice column, "Ask Ann Landers." Lederer transformed it from mere popularity into a fixture of many of the nation's newspapers for the next 45 years. Ann Landers's advice was sympathetic but frank, always direct, sometimes witty, and, on occasion, stinging. Her readers asked question ranging from the trivial to the life-changing, and she faithfully engaged each of them. Landers's identical twin, Pauline Esther Friedman Phillips, was also a famous advice columnist, writing "Dear Abby" under the name Abigail Van Buren.

Landon, Alf (1887–1987) Alfred M. "Alf" Landon was Republican governor of Kansas from 1933 to 1937 and challenged Franklin D. Roosevelt for the White House in 1936. In 1912, he campaigned for Theodore Roosevelt when TR ran on the Progressive "Bull Moose" third-party ticket, and, for the rest of his political career, Landon embodied the Progressive philosophy, even after he became a Republican. Landon enjoyed tremendous popular support during the 1936 presidential election, but could not defeat the incumbent FDR. Although he never again played a major role in national politics, he remained a popular figure, a monument to the Progressive era, which had done much to reform American politics during the early 20th century.

Lange, Dorothea (1895–1965) Lange learned photography under the tutelage of the great Clarence White and worked in a San Francisco photo studio during the 1920s. It was not until the 1930s and the Great Depression that she found the subject of her lifetime: documenting the lives of the poor but proud victims of the Dust Bowl. Composed with classical elegance, her photographs convey the intense humanity of people who might otherwise have been relegated to a column of statistics. She recorded the human face of national adversity.

Lansky, Meyer (1902–1983) Born Maier Suchowljansky in Grodno, Russia, Lansky immigrated with his parents to New York's Jewish slum, the Lower East Side, where he and pal Bugsy Siegel formed a profitable street gang. With the acumen of a skilled entrepreneur and the ruthlessness of a criminal, Lansky built a powerful and multifaceted crime syndicate that became the model for organized crime in America. Grown wealthy, he bankrolled other criminals in a variety of illegal enterprises, but his specialty was always gambling. His gambling empire stretched from pre-Castro Cuba, the Bahamas, and Florida, to Las Vegas, a city his money was largely responsible for developing after World War II.

La Salle, René-Robert Cavalier, Sieur de (1643–1687) La Salle led the French exploration of the vast region watered by the Mississippi River and its many tributaries, claiming the territory for Louis XIV of France and christening it Louisiana. It was North America's most fertile land. La Salle's final expedition, dedicated to conquering part of Spanish Mexico with a handful of Frenchman and allied Indians, ended in mutiny—and his death at the hands of his own men.

Las Casas, Bartolomé de (1474–1566) A Dominican friar, Las Casas was for 12 years part of the Spanish conquest of the Americas, but was outraged by the conquistadors' inhumanity and wrote several gripping accounts of atrocities and other abuses committed against native peoples in the Caribbean and in North and South America. He was thus both an eyewitness-historian of early American exploration and settlement and a pioneering crusader for human rights.

Latrobe, Benjamin (1764–1820) Born in Britain, Latrobe studied architecture in Europe before immigrating to the United States in 1795. He established himself as the nation's first professional architect and, in effect, founded the profession of architecture in the United States. He introduced the Greek Revival style to the nation with designs for many public and government buildings. President Thomas Jefferson appointed him surveyor of public buildings in 1803 and Latrobe completed the original U.S. Capitol, among other buildings. His best-known work, however, was for the Basilica of the Assumption of the Blessed Virgin Mary, a part of Baltimore's Roman Catholic cathedral.

Lawrence, Ernest (1901–1958) As early as 1929, this brilliant and charismatic physicist drew up designs for a cyclotron, which would accelerate hydrogen ions (protons) to create nuclear disintegration—that is, to "split atoms"—thereby producing new elements. The technology was essential to advanced nuclear research, and, during World War II, it proved to be critically important to the Manhattan Project, which created the atomic bomb. Lawrence developed an electromagnetic process for separating uranium-235 to produce the fissionable material at the heart of the weapon. A man of many interests, Lawrence

also patented a picture tube for color television. He was awarded the 1939 Nobel Prize in physics, and the Lawrence Berkeley Laboratory at the University of California, Berkeley, and the Lawrence Livermore National Laboratory at Livermore, California, are named in his honor, as is element 103, lawrencium.

Lay, Kenneth (1942–2006) Lay was an American success story, rising from a poor Missouri family to build a Texas oil pipeline company into a new kind of business, an energy broker called Enron. The meteoric rise of this firm made Lay one of the nation's top-paid executives ($42.4 million earned in 1999) and an influential political figure; however, as a massive accounting scandal came to light in 2001—revealing that Enron's soaring profits were pure fiction—Lay's Enron became shorthand for corporate greed and conscienceless corruption. Lay pleaded ignorance of wrongdoing throughout his company, but was nevertheless indicted on July 7, 2004 on 11 counts of securities fraud and related charges. Convicted on 10 counts on May 25, 2006, he died—of an apparent heart attack—on July 5, 2006, somewhat more than three months before his scheduled sentencing.

Leary, Timothy (1920–1996) Leary was a Harvard University psychology professor who founded the Harvard Psychedelic Drug Research Program and administered psilocybin ("magic mushrooms") to graduate students. Dismissed from Harvard in 1963, he moved into a mansion in Millbrook, New York, where he presided over a small community of experimenter with the psychedelic drug LSD. He claimed that the dr enabled a spiritual "mind-expanding" state superior to a thing contemporary conventional American society ha offer, and he advised his large lecture audiences to "tur

tune in, and drop out." The phrase became a slogan of the 1960s counterculture movement.

Ledbetter, Huddie "Leadbelly" (1885?–1949) Leadbelly was born and raised in Louisiana and became an itinerant blues performer. He was a blues guitar genius and a composer who absorbed folk traditions then synthesized them into a vast repertoire of original "folk-blues" songs. His life, however, was marked by intense violence. Imprisoned for murder in 1918, he was released after six years, having been pardoned by the governor of Texas after he heard him sing. Imprisoned at Angola, Louisiana, for attempted murder in 1930, he was released in 1934 thanks to the efforts of father-and-son folklorists John and Alan Lomax. Leadbelly embarked on a performing career, but nevertheless died in poverty. Of his many songs, "Goodnight, Irene," "The Midnight Special," and "Rock Island Line" have become not only enduring classics but lucrative bestsellers—for performers other than the composer.

Lee, Henry "Light-horse Harry" (1756–1818) Lee was the rarest of American officers during the revolution: a skilled cavalry commander. He earned his nickname, "Light-horse Harry," as commander of dragoons—swift-moving, elite troops who rode into battle then fought, dismounted, as infantry. On the death of George Washington in 1799, Lee wrote the resolution passed by Congress, which called the first president "first in war, first in peace, and first in the hearts of his countrymen." Light-horse Harry was the grandfather of Robert E. Lee.

Lee, Richard Henry (1732–1794) Although less famous today than John Adams, Thomas Jefferson, and the like, Lee was a crucial player in the American independence movement. Prominent in Virginia life and politics, he served in the House of Burgesses from 1758 to 1775 and was instrumental in mounting opposition to the Stamp Act and the Townshend Acts, the onerous British taxation policies that provoked the American Revolution. During the revolution, he worked with Patrick Henry and Thomas Jefferson to create the committees of correspondence, which coordinated policies and military campaigns among the colonies. After the revolution, Lee opposed replacing the Articles of Confederation with the Constitution because he distrusted strong central government. Yet, after ratification, he faithfully served his nation and state as senator from Virginia in the first Congress under the Constitution, from 1789 to 1792.

Lee, Robert E. (1807–1870) One of the illustrious Lees of Virginia, Robert E. Lee graduated from West Point in 1829, second in his class. Since the most promising graduates were customarily assigned to the Corps of Engineers, Lee became an engineering officer—and a brilliant one. It was, however, his heroic performance in the U.S.-Mexican War (1846–1848) that gained him his first fame. General Winfield Scott called him "the very best soldier I ever saw in the field." With the outbreak of the Civil War, Abraham Lincoln offered Lee command of the Union armies. He refused, because he could not bring himself to take up arms against his "native country"—by which he meant Virginia—and, resigning his U.S. Army commission, joined the army of the Confederacy. Initially serving as military adviser to Jefferson Davis, he rose to become commander of the Army of Northern Virginia, principal force of the Confederate army. Typically outnumbered and outgunned, he nevertheless compiled a remarkable record of victory, produced by his uncanny tactical skill and his charismatic leadership. His defeat at the Battle of Gettysburg in July 1863 was the turning point of the war, and his surrender at Appomattox Courthouse April 9, 1865, was the symbolic end of the Civil War. Despite the bitterness of the conflict, Lee emerged from the Civil War as the nation's most respected—even most beloved—military commander.

Leisler, Jacob (1640–1691) German-born militia commander Jacob Leisler rallied and led New York farmers and merchants in an uprising against Catholics and suspected Catholics in the English colonial administration. The rebellion was suppressed, and Leisler was hanged as a traitor on May 16, 1691, but the movement he began persisted for years as a powerful anti-Catholic—and anti-aristocratic—force in the New York colony. It was an early challenge to royal British authority in America and may be seen as a distant precursor of the American Revolution.

LeMay, Curtis E. (1906–1990) A career military aviator, LeMay was one of the architects of strategic bombing doctrine during World War II and was especially effective as commander of the Twentieth Air Force, which conducted the strategic bombing of Japan, culminating in the dropping of atomic bombs on Hiroshima and Nagasaki on August 6 and 9, 1945, which brought the war to an end. In the postwar era, LeMay assembled and commanded the Strategic Air Command, a major component of the U.S. "nuclear deterrent," which simultaneously threatened and prevented World War III. Conservative and irascible, LeMay was uncompromising in his military and political views. He retired from the U.S. Air Force in 1965 and, three years later, was running mate to segregationist candidate George C. Wallace on a third-party presidential ticket.

L'Enfant, Pierre (1754–1825) Born in France, Pierre L'Enfant came to the United States with Major General Lafayette as a military engineer in the service of the American Revolution. After the war, he designed in 1791 the street plan of the "Federal City in the United States," subsequently named Washington, D.C. In addition to laying out the United States capital city—establishing its famous wheel-and-spoke pattern that exists to this day—L'Enfant redesigned New York's Federal Hall and produced designs for houses, coins, medals, and furniture.

Leopold, Nathan (1904–1971) On May 21, 1924, with college friend Richard A. Loeb, Nathan Leopold kidnapped and murdered 14-year-old Robert ("Bobbie") Franks for no other purpose than to commit the "perfect crime" that demonstrated (as Leopold saw it) intellectual superiority. At trial, the pair was defended by Clarence Darrow, who did not claim the innocence of his clients, but successfully mitigated their sentence from death to life imprisonment, arguing for the first time in American legal history that they were psychopaths—sane, yet constitutionally incapable of moral judgment. Leopold was paroled in 1958 and worked among the poor of Puerto Rico as a hospital technician.

Leslie, Frank (1821–1880) Henry Carter was born in England and learned the engraver's trade while working for the *Illustrated London News.* He came to New York City in 1848 and, in 1855, under the pseudonym "Frank Leslie," began publishing *Frank Leslie's Illustrated Newspaper*, which featured superbly engraved illustrations and became the most popular and influential weekly in the nation. He introduced the technique of dividing drawings into modular blocks that could be given to several engravers, then reassembled for

reproduction. This greatly speeded the work and enabled the illustration of fast-breaking news events. He made his fortune providing illustrated coverage of the Civil War.

Lewinsky, Monica (1973–) Lewinsky began working as an intern in the Clinton White House in 1995, but it was while she was employed as a paid Pentagon staffer that she had a short-term sexual relationship with Clinton. The scandal was detailed in a report written under the direction of Kenneth Starr, an independent counsel appointed to investigate allegations of possibly impeachable offenses committed by the president. The report concluded that Clinton had violated his oath of office by perjuring himself in a sworn deposition he had given in an earlier sex scandal. Motivated in part by the Lewinsky affair and based on the Starr Report, Congress voted, along party lines, to impeach President Clinton, who was nevertheless acquitted on February 12, 1999. After the scandal, Lewinsky used her dubious celebrity to start a designer handbag business (closed in 2004) and to host a short-lived "reality TV" series, *Mr. Personality* (2003). She then enrolled in graduate school, studying social psychology.

Lewis, John L. (1880–1969) With his bulldog chin and dramatically heavy eyebrows, Lewis was a formidable-looking figure who came to symbolize the labor movement in America from roughly 1920 to 1960. He was president of the United Mine Workers of America (1920–1960) and principal founder of the Congress of Industrial Organizations (CIO), serving as its president from 1936 to 1940. With genius and determination, Lewis exploited President Franklin D. Roosevelt's New Deal to carve out a strong position for labor even in the depths of the Great Depression.

Lewis, Meriwether (1774–1809) Lewis was a U.S. Army officer of great promise when he became personal secretary to President Thomas Jefferson, who knew the young man's family and regarded Lewis as a protégé. Together, Lewis and the president planned a great expedition through the Far West, and when the Louisiana Purchase was approved, Congress financed the first overland expedition to the Pacific Northwest. With his handpicked co-captain, William Clark, Lewis led a small band from St. Louis to the Pacific and back—a journey that spanned 1804 to 1806. Lewis and Clark returned with a great narrative journal of the expedition, a wealth of scientific and geographical data, and the foundation of good relations with several Indian tribes. It was the opening of the American West.

Lewis, Sinclair (1885–1951) Lewis's fiction combined realism with broadly drawn satire to skewer complacent and obtuse aspects of American society. His masterpiece is the 1920 *Main Street,* which presents a full-length portrait of mid-American society. *Babbitt,* which followed in 1922, is a story of American complacency—so persuasive that the word "Babbittry" entered the lexicon of American social criticism. In 1930, Lewis became the first American to win the Nobel Prize for Literature.

Lichtenstein, Roy (1923–1997) Trained under the gritty American painter Reginald Marsh, Lichtenstein began his art career painting western American subjects and venturing into Abstract Impressionism, the dominant style of the early 1950s. In 1960, however, he began to incorporate aspects of Abstract Expressionism with pop culture images, including cartoon figures. Increasingly, he exploited the look of comic-strip art, often magnifying the dot pattern used in four-color pulp-press printing. The work struck a

chord and became an icon of American art in the 1960s, launching the "Pop art" movement.

Liddy, G. Gordon (1930) Liddy was a former FBI special agent who worked for the Nixon reelection campaign's Committee to Re-Elect the President (CREEP), bringing to CREEP his expertise as the chief of the "Plumbers," the illegal covert unit the president used to stop information leaks. With E. Howard Hunt, Liddy planned the break-in of Democratic National Committee headquarters in Washington's Watergate complex in 1972. The object was to sabotage the Democratic presidential campaign. The operation was bungled, Liddy and the other "Watergate burglars" were arrested, and Liddy was ultimately convicted of conspiracy, burglary, and illegal wiretapping. He served four and a half years of a twenty-year sentence before President Jimmy Carter's commutation freed him.

Liliuokalani (1838–1917) Lydia Kamakaeha was the sister of David Kalakaua, who was chosen king of Hawaii in 1874. When the heir apparent, Kalakaua's brother, W.P. Leleiohoku, died in 1877, Lydia became heir presumptive and received her royal name, Liliuokalani. She ascended the Hawaiian throne in January 1891, when King Kalakaua died. The first woman to reign over Hawaii, she was also the last Hawaiian sovereign. Sanford Dole, the American-born head of the Missionary Party, asked her to abdicate in January 1893. When she refused, he simply declared her deposed, created a provisional government, and sought annexation by the United States. To avoid a civil war, Liliuokalani stepped down, but appealed to President Grover Cleveland to restore her. Cleveland gave the order, but Dole refused to obey it. A royalist insurrection erupted but was quickly suppressed, and on January 24, 1895, in exchange for pardons for her jailed partisans, the queen formally abdicated. She continued to fight U.S. annexation, which came nevertheless in July 1898—the very year in which she composed "Aloha Oe," the most familiar of all Hawaiian songs.

Limbaugh, Rush (1951–) Since 1988, Limbaugh has hosted a nationally syndicated conservative radio talk show, heard by an estimated 13.5 million listeners per week (as of 2005). Not only has Limbaugh been credited with articulating the conservative point of view for the masses, he was identified as a motivating force behind the 1994 Republican sweep of Congress. Media experts have even attributed the revival of AM radio—moribund by the 1970s—to Limbaugh's tremendous popularity. In 2003, Limbaugh received unwanted publicity when his addiction to prescription pain relievers came to light.

Lincoln, Abraham (1809–1865) Almost universally regarded as the greatest of American presidents, Lincoln presided over a nation torn by the Civil War. He prosecuted that war to restore the Union, and, in the process, he set in place the legal machinery by which slavery in the United States was abolished. Lincoln was a leader of extraordinary courage, wisdom, eloquence, and compassion. Although he fought the war without compromise, he advocated amnesty and forgiveness for the breakaway Confederate states. Lincoln was assassinated by John Wilkes Booth, a Confederate sympathizer, on April 14, 1865. The president died the following morning.

Lincoln, Mary Todd (1818–1882) The wife of Abraham Lincoln (married on November 4, 1842), Mary Todd Lincoln endured the deaths of two of her sons in childhood (and a

third as a young man), the emotional devastation of the Civil War (in which her half-brothers fought for the Confederacy), and the assassination of her husband. She was an unpopular First Lady, in part because of her Southern birth and in part because of her extravagant spending on clothing and furnishings. Like her husband, she suffered from bouts of severe depression. Her only surviving son, Robert Todd Lincoln, caused her commitment to an asylum in 1875. She was released after a court hearing in 1876, but believed herself to have been publicly humiliated. She fled to Europe, returning to Springfield, Illinois, in 1880, where she died three years later.

Lindbergh, Anne Morrow (1906–2001) When Anne Morrow married him on May 27, 1929, Charles A. Lindbergh was the most famous man in America—perhaps in the world. Anne immediately took up flying and became the first American woman to earn a first-class glider pilot's license. With her husband, she flew and charted air routes between continents throughout the 1930s. Together, the Lindberghs were the first pilots to fly from Africa to South America. Anne endured the loss of her firstborn, Charles Augustus Lindbergh III, who was kidnapped and murdered in 1932. She earned fame in her own right as an author, especially of autobiography, including her 1955 *Gift from the Sea*, a meditation on womanhood, and her most significant work of autobiography, *Hour of Gold, Hour of Lead* (1973).

Lindbergh, Charles A. (1902–1974) The maverick son of a U.S. Congressman from Minnesota, Lindbergh had a passion for flying, and on May 20–21, 1927, made the first nonstop solo flight across the Atlantic, from New York to Paris. The feat catapulted the tall, handsome, shy aviator to global fame. He was the most lauded non-military hero in

American history. Lindbergh devoted much of the rest of his life to pioneering commercial aviation. With his wife, Anne Morrow Lindbergh, he endured the tragic kidnapping and murder of his infant son in 1932, an episode that drew the heartfelt sympathy of the nation. He fell from grace, however, later in the 1930s for accepting a decoration from the Nazi government of Germany and, in 1940–1941, for his advocacy of American isolationism. In his later years, Lindbergh became a passionate environmentalist.

Lippmann, Walter (1889–1974) Through a career spanning 60 eventful years, Walter Lippmann earned a reputation as America's most respected political columnist and opinion maker. In 1914, he was a founder of *The New Republic* and a key advisor to President Woodrow Wilson. A true political philosopher, he speculated in his most provocative book, *Public Opinion* (1922), that democracy suffered in an era of mass communication, in which citizens were given slogans rather than genuine ideas. Despite his ongoing doubts about democratic government, he never abandoned the ideal of government by the people and remained a spokesman for the liberal point of view.

Lisa, Manuel (1772–1820) Born in New Orleans of Spanish parents, Lisa became a U.S. citizen following the Louisiana Purchase of 1803. In 1807, he built a trading post fort at the mouth of the Bighorn River (in modern Montana), which developed into a center of the great American fur trade—the first important industry of the American West, which opened up commerce with the Indians of the region and generally spurred exploration and settlement of the Far West. Lisa's establishment became the headquarters from which a generation of "mountain men"—fur traders and trappers—explored the remotest reaches of the North American continent.

Lodge, Henry Cabot (1850–1924) Like his chief rival, Woodrow Wilson, Lodge held a Ph.D. in political science and had been a college professor. In 1893, he was elected senator from Massachusetts and served until his death in 1924. An advocate of isolationism, he successfully opposed Wilson's attempt to bring the United States into the League of Nations after World War I. Lodge's opposition ushered in a Republican-dominated period of U.S. withdrawal from world affairs.

Lodge, Henry Cabot (1902–1985) Grandson and namesake of Henry Cabot Lodge (1850–1924), Lodge had a distinguished career in Republican politics, including service in the U.S. Senate (1937–1944, 1947–1952) and, most fatefully, as ambassador to South Vietnam during (1963–1964 and 1965–1967), the years of the expanding Vietnam War—an expansion Lodge advocated. In 1969, Lodge also served as chief negotiator in the Paris Peace talks between the United States and North Vietnam.

Loeb, Richard (1905–1936) On May 21, 1924, with college friend Nathan Leopold, Loeb kidnapped and murdered 14-year-old Robert ("Bobbie") Franks for no other purpose than to commit the "perfect crime." At trial, the pair was defended by Clarence Darrow, who did not claim the innocence of his clients, but successfully mitigated their sentence from death to life imprisonment, arguing for the first time in American legal history that they were psychopaths—sane, yet incapable of moral judgment. In contrast to Leopold, who, after parole in 1958, dedicated himself to working among the poor of Puerto

Rico as a hospital technician, Loeb, the more ruthless of the two, was murdered by a fellow inmate, toward whom he had made sadistic homosexual overtures.

London, Jack (1876–1916) London was born John Griffith Chaney in San Francisco and led a life as an adventurous hobo-drifter, educating himself in public libraries. Inspired by the "superman" philosophy of Friedrich Nietzsche, he began to write stories of man against the elements, each tale suffused with his romantic interpretation of Nietzsche's amoral will to survive and dominate. London wrote rapidly and became the most highly paid author in America. His most memorable works include *Call of the Wild* (1903) and *White Fang* (1906)—both set in Alaska—and *The Sea Wolf* (1904), his fullest portrait of the hero as a Nietzschean superman. No American writer has been more widely translated.

Long, Huey (1893–1935) Long rose from backwoods Louisiana poverty to become governor of the state and a U.S. senator. He was a charismatic demagogue, not above shameful displays of emotion and even buffoonery, which earned him the sobriquet "Kingfish." Campaigning on the slogan "every man a king," he developed a Share-the-Wealth program in which increased inheritance and income taxes, plus a severance tax on oil, were intended to redistribute wealth to the poor. He was also, however, a corrupt political boss, whose tenure in office amounted to a dictatorship. He paid a dictator's price on September 10, 1935, when Carl Austin Weiss—whose father Long had publicly vilified—shot him down in the Louisiana state house.

Longfellow, Henry Wadsworth (1807–1882) Born in Portland, Maine (at the time a part of Massachusetts), Longfellow graduated from Bowdoin College, where he read widely and began publishing verses of his own. He became a professor first at Bowdoin then at Harvard. After the death of his wife in 1835, he began writing poetry in earnest—and in great abundance—colored by a lush romanticism. In addition to such popular lyrics as "The Village Blacksmith" (perhaps the best-known poem in American literature), he wrote American epic narratives, inspired by the long narratives of the ancient poets. The most important of these were *Evangeline* (1847)—the story of lovers separated when the British expelled the Acadians from Nova Scotia—and *The Song of Hiawatha* (1855), an evocation of an American Indian hero, inspired by the Finnish epic *Kalevala*.

Longstreet, James (1821–1904) A South Carolinian, Longstreet fought as a Confederate officer in many of the major battles of the Civil War. He was Robert E. Lee's second in command at Gettysburg, and his reluctance to organize the celebrated "Pickett's Charge" has often been cited as the reason for Lee's defeat in this turning-point battle. (Many others, however, place the blame on Lee himself.) After Gettysburg, Longstreet performed brilliantly at Chickamauga in September 1863 and in the Wilderness Campaign. He was with Lee when the general surrendered the Army of Northern Virginia at Appomattox Courthouse in April 1865.

Lopez, Barry Holstun (1945–) Lopez emerged in the 1970s as one of the nation's most compelling writers on nature and the environment. Although works such as *Of Wolves and Men* (1978) and *Arctic Dreams: Imagination and Desire in a Northern Landscape* (1986) confront the natural world on its own terms, they also develop natural history as an extended metaphor to illuminate human moral issues, including humankind's role in the system of nature.

Louis, Joe (1914–1981) Joe Louis became world heavyweight champion on June 22, 1937, when he knocked out James J. Braddock, and he held the title until his first retirement on March 1, 1949. He held the title longer than any other heavyweight in history, successfully defending it 25 times (21 times by knockouts). A hero to the African-American community, Louis appealed to fight fans of all races. His 1938 victory over German champion Max Schmelling—who had the personal endorsement of Adolf Hitler—was widely hailed as a victory over Nazi claims of racial superiority.

Lowell, James Russell (1819–1891) In his day, Lowell was one of America's most popular poets and essayists. His reputation declined in the 20th century, during which critics condemned him as excessively genteel and imitative. Nevertheless, his lasting impact on American literature was profound: as a critic, he educated the literary taste of the American public and created a popular interest in and respect for American literature.

Lowell, Robert, Jr. (1917–1977) Great grand-nephew of James Russell Lowell, Robert Lowell earned an international reputation for his complex and emotionally compelling autobiographical poems. He was honored by an appointment as poetry consultant to the Library of Congress and by two Pulitzer Prizes. In the 1960s, the ferment of the Civil Rights movement and the Vietnam War drew him out of his autobiographical introspection and engendered three masterpiece volumes: *For the Union Dead* (1964), *Near the Ocean* (1967), and *Notebook 1967–68* (1969).

Lucas, George (1944–) Lucas combined a passion for science fiction with a passion for film to create some of the most spectacularly popular American movies in history. His first feature was *THX 1138* (1971), a robotic science fiction tale, which instantly commanded a cult following. He stepped into the cultural mainstream in 1973 with *American Graffiti*, a richly nostalgic look at teenage life in the early 1960s. Despite the commercial success of this film, Lucas's next movie did not appear until 1977. It was a return to science fiction with *Star Wars*, a highly imaginative feature that combined advanced special effects with the excitement and innocence of the matinee serials familiar to an earlier age of moviegoers. *Star Wars* proved a durable franchise, spawning various sequels and entering the pantheon of modern American pop culture.

Luce, Henry (1898–1967) Luce launched *Time* magazine with his Yale University chum Briton Haden in 1923 and took it over completely after Haden's death in 1929. That same year, Luce introduced *Fortune*, a unique magazine devoted to business. *Time* was aimed at presenting news with a point of view; *Fortune* was intended to be indispensable to the person of business; and in 1936, *Life* was introduced as a popular picture magazine. With this triumvirate, Luce had created the first great American magazine empire and became one of the most influential opinion makers in the world.

Luciano, Lucky (1896–1962) From the day Luciano (born Salvatore Lucania) emigrated from Italy with his parents at age ten, he embraced criminal activity, beginning with strong-arm robbery, shoplifting, and extortion, and soon graduating to drug dealing before entering the organized underworld of New York City and rising to the top of the various rackets. By the early 1930s, Luciano had become *capo di tutti capi* ("boss of all the bosses") and in 1934 succeeded in organizing criminal enterprises nationwide into a kind of cartel or syndicate of unprecedented power and influence. Successfully prosecuted by New York's Thomas E. Dewey in 1936, Luciano was given a 30– to 50–year sentence, ruling his criminal empire from his cell. In 1946, his sentence was commuted to deportation. He then continued to influence American criminal enterprise even from abroad.

Luks, George (1867–1933) Luks made his early living in art as a newspaper correspondent-artist and then as a newspaper cartoonist. He earned enough money to finance study in Paris during 1902–1903, where he was not only exposed to modern art, but to the rich life of the city. It was this latter interest that he brought back with him when he returned to New York. With like-minded artists, Luks founded a group called simply The Eight, which soon became associated with a larger movement in American urban realism. The press dubbed it the "Ashcan School," and Luks was one of the leading practitioners of this distinctly modern, distinctly American style.

MacArthur, Douglas (1880–1964) The son of Medal of Honor winner General Arthur MacArthur, Douglas MacArthur was a star cadet at West Point and served valiantly in World War I. At the outbreak of World War II, he was in command of the Philippines and fought a gallant but doomed defense against the Japanese invasion until he was ordered by President Franklin D. Roosevelt to evacuate to Australia. He then assumed overall command of the Southwest Pacific Theater and was a prime architect of the U.S. victory over Japan. He was appointed to head the U.S. occupation government of Japan after the war and proved to be an enlightened administrator who was tremendously popular with the Japanese and who brought genuine democracy into Japanese government—for the first time in that nation's history. In 1950, MacArthur took command of U.S.-led United Nations forces at the outbreak of the Korean War. The conflict occasioned both his greatest military exploit—the daring and brilliant Inchon Landing (which temporarily turned the tide of the war)—and his dismissal by President Harry S. Truman for insubordination when he refused to fight the "limited" war national policy dictated. MacArthur's best modern biographer, William Manchester, aptly dubbed him the "American Caesar."

Macdonald, Dwight (1906–1982) During the 1940s, Macdonald made his debut as a man of letters by founding the magazine *Politics*, which published work by the most important literary, philosophical, and political thinkers of the day. He earned widespread notoriety as an extraordinarily perceptive film critic and staff writer for *The New Yorker* (1951–1971) and *Esquire* magazine (1960–1966), but his most important contribution to American intellectual life was his analysis of what he called "middlebrow" (as opposed to "highbrow" and "lowbrow") culture, which included most of mass or popular American culture. He was one of the first genuinely perceptive critics to take popular culture seriously and to write about it in ways that illuminate American values and the American character.

Madison, Dolley (1768–1849) Dolley Payne married James Madison on September 15, 1794, and, when he became president of the United States in 1809, she took up what she saw as the duty of the chief executive's wife: managing the social aspects of life at the White House. She was a valuable political asset to the Madison presidency, creating an atmosphere of great charm and warmth. She is also widely credited with introducing ice cream to America.

Madison, James (1751–1836) Madison may be the least well-known of the founding fathers of the United States. He was, however, a key creator of the Constitution and, with Alexander Hamilton and John Jay, wrote *The Federalist Papers*, which were indispensable in securing ratification of the document. In the House of Representatives (under that new Constitution), Madison sponsored the Bill of Rights. A junior colleague of Thomas Jefferson, he served as his secretary of state and was instrumental in the Louisiana Purchase. His presidency (1809–1817) was marred by the War of 1812, during which Washington, D.C. was burned by the British, forcing Madison and his wife, Dolley, to flee.

Madonna (1958–) Madonna—original name Madonna Louise Ciccone—began her entertainment career as a dancer, but by the beginning of the 1980s was singing elaborately produced pop songs focused on love and sex. She exploited her sexuality to fashion herself into a cultural and commercial icon who, for more than a decade, was unchallenged as the reigning queen of pop music. As skilled a businesswoman as she was an entertainer, Madonna gained extraordinary power and influence in the entertainment industry.

Mahan, Alfred Thayer (1840–1914) Although he was the son of a West Point professor, Mahan graduated from the U.S. Naval Academy at Annapolis (1859) and served as a naval officer for some 40 years. From 1886 to 1889, he was president of the Naval War College at Newport, Rhode Island, and lectured on sea power. His 1890 collection of lectures, *The Influence of Sea Power upon History, 1660–1783*, postulated that sea power was crucial throughout history in the attainment of national supremacy. This and his next book, *The Influence of Sea Power upon the French Revolution and Empire, 1793–1812* (1892), guided U.S. global military strategy during both world wars and helped to transform the nation into a major naval power.

Mailer, Norman (1923–) Mailer burst onto the literary scene with his 1948 World War II novel *The Naked and the Dead*, for which he was hailed as "the next" Ernest Hemingway. Mailer produced a series of distinguished (if controversial) works of fiction following this debut, but his most important contribution to American literature and culture was his unique synthesis of journalism and fiction called the "New Journalism." This journalistic/literary form used the aesthetic techniques of fiction to report on key events and personalities. His 1968 *The Armies of the Night*, which grew out of the Vietnam-era antiwar movement, was a breakthrough in this uniquely American genre.

Malamud, Bernard (1914–1986) Born in New York, Malamud was the son of Russian Jews and developed his writing career by creating parable-like chronicles of the Jewish immigrant experience. Although he was very successful as a novelist (especially with *The Natural* in 1952 and *The Assistant* in 1957), his masterpieces are his short stories, which employ an elegantly terse style to evoke great depth of character and meaning.

Malcolm X (1925–1965) Malcolm X was born Malcolm Little in Omaha and grew up in Lansing, Michigan, where white supremacists burned his house down and, later, murdered his father. Malcolm Little embarked on a career as a petty criminal, was sentenced to prison for burglary, and, while in prison, became a convert to the Nation of Islam ("Black Muslim"). Rejecting his "slave name," he called himself Malcolm X. He became a Black Muslim preacher, but, even more, emerged as a charismatic and electrifyingly eloquent speaker on black pride and black nationalism during the early 1960s. His rhetoric was angry, and he presented a dramatic contrast to the non-violent approach of Martin Luther King, Jr. At first unwilling to reconcile with white society, he became increasingly amenable to the coexistence of the races as he matured in his Muslim faith. He was, however, gunned down by Black Muslim assassins on February 21, 1965—but not before he had written (with Alex Haley) *The Autobiography of Malcolm X* (1965), a book that made him a role model and hero to a generation of African-American youth.

Mann, Horace (1796–1859) Raised in poverty and largely self-educated, Mann believed that the prosperity of a democratic society required free universal public education carried out by highly trained professional teachers. He was the nation's first important advocate of public education.

Manson, Charles (1934–) Charles Manson was a career criminal, who, in the 1960s—an era in which communes and non-conventional living arrangements were common—led a group he called "the Family" and also known as the "Manson Family." On August 8, 1969, Manson masterminded the singularly bloody murders of Sharon Tate (pregnant actress wife of movie director Roman Polanski) and four others in the Tate-Polanski Beverly Hills home. On August 9, the Manson Family similarly slaughtered Leno and Rosemary La Bianca in their Los Angeles home. Manson and his "family" were soon captured. Identified as the instigator and planner of the murders, Manson was sentenced to life imprisonment. He came to symbolize the darkest aspects of freewheeling 1960s counterculture and entered the pantheon of American pop culture as the incarnation of senseless but elemental evil.

Marcy, William L. (1786–1857) Marcy was a leading New York state Democrat who, while serving in the Senate, defended and sought to justify the so-called "spoils system" (by which those elected to office enjoyed the privilege of making lucrative political patronage appointments, regardless of an appointee's qualifications for the position), declaring simply "to the victor belongs the spoils."

Marion, Francis (1732–1795) A commander of South Carolina forces during the American Revolution, Marion led a band of guerrillas in bold actions that often defeated British military formations of superior strength. His comrades dubbed him the "Swamp Fox," and his fame was sufficient to propel him into the Senate after the war (1782–90).

Marquette, Jacques (1637–1675) With Louis Jolliet, this French Jesuit missionary explored the Mississippi River and charted its course. The explorations of Jolliett and Marquette were the basis for French claims to the vast territory dubbed Louisiana.

Marshall, George C. (1880–1959) During World War II, Marshall was chief of staff of the U.S. Army—the senior officer of the army. After the war, he served Harry S. Truman as secretary of state (1947–1949) and then as secretary of defense (1950–1951). While he was secretary of state, Marshall collaborated on and championed the European Recovery Program—a massive U.S. funding of postwar recovery—which was popularly known as the Marshall Plan. He was recognized in 1953 with the Nobel Prize for Peace—the first former professional soldier to be awarded the prize.

Marshall, John (1755–1835) Marshall was the fourth chief justice of the United States and perhaps the Supreme Court's single most important figure. He was the architect of American system of constitutional law, and he raised the judicial branch to equal status with the executive and legislative branches of the U.S. government by introducing the doctrine of judicial review, whereby the Supreme Court has the authority to determine the constitutionality of any law that meets with legal challenge. In thirty years as chief justice, Marshall wrote 519 of the more than 1,000 decisions in which he participated.

Marshall, Thurgood (1908–1993) Marshall earned fame as an attorney for the National Association for the Advancement of Colored People (NAACP), who argued the case of *Brown v. Board of Education of Topeka* (1954) before the U.S. Supreme Court and won an epoch-making decision that declared racial segregation in public schools unconstitutional. In 1961, President John F. Kennedy nominated Marshall to the U.S. Court of Appeals for the Second Circuit. Southern senators delayed confirmation, but he was ultimately seated. In 1965, Lyndon Johnson named Marshall U.S. solicitor general, then nominated him to the Supreme Court in June 1967. He served as one of the high court's great liberal voices.

Marx Brothers (Chico [Leonard, 1887–1961], Harpo [Adolph or Arthur, 1888–1964], Groucho [Julius Henry, 1890–1977], Gummo [Milton, 1892–1977], Zeppo [Herbert, 1901–1979]) The Marx Brothers—in varying combinations—began performing onstage in 1904, earned a reputation on Broadway (for their 1924 musical-comedy revue *I'll Say She Is*, which was followed by other stage hits), but claimed an international reputation for their films, beginning in 1929 with *The Cocoanuts* and continuing through the 1930s with *Monkey Business* (1931), *Horse Feathers* (1932), *Duck Soup* (1933) *A Night at the Opera* (1935), and *A Day at the Races* (1937). Their exuberantly absurdist humor skewered all that was socially respectable—with hilarious results.

Mason, George (1725–1792) Mason was a Virginia revolutionary leader who, in 1776, drafted his state's constitution, which included a declaration of rights that inspired Thomas Jefferson to include the concept of "unalienable rights" in the Declaration of Independence. Mason's constitution and declaration of rights served as models for most of the other states and were the basis for the Bill of Rights—the first ten amendments to the U.S. Constitution.

Massasoit (ca. 1590–1661) Sachem of the Wampanoag Indians of New England, Massasoit befriended the Pilgrims who landed at Plymouth in 1620 and, by showing them how to plant successfully in the region's flinty soil, was instrumental in their survival. Massasoit maintained friendly relations with the settlers throughout his life, establishing a profitable trading relationship with them.

Mather, Cotton (1663–1728) Mather was a Puritan conservative who tried desperately to maintain the old order in which the clergy served as the government of Massachusetts. A man of remarkable learning and industry, he was superstitious (a believer in witchcraft), yet also scientific (he was a pioneer in advocating smallpox inoculation). The most famous of New England's Puritans, he was one of the most prolific writers who ever lived, the author of about 400 works, including the monumental *Magnalia Christi Americana* (1702), a church history of America from the founding of New England to his own day.

Mather, Increase (1639–1723) Increase Mather led the Puritans of New England as the torch passed from the first-generation settlers of Plymouth to the second—those actually born in America. Among his many books was *An Essay for the Recording of Illustrious Providences* (1684), which (some historians believe) set the stage for the Salem witch trials of 1692. Increase Mather's most famous son was Cotton Mather, the most celebrated of all Puritan leaders and thinkers.

Mauchly, John W. (1907–1980) With his student J. Presper Eckert, this University of Pennsylvania professor created in 1946 ENIAC (Electronic Numerical Integrator and Computer), the first all-electronic digital computer. Previous computers had been electromechanical. ENIAC was commissioned by the U.S. government primarily for military applications. It incorporated in rudimentary form all of the circuitry employed in modern computers.

Mayer, Louis B. (1885– 1957) Born Eliezer Mayer in Minsk, Russia, Mayer immigrated to the United States with his family when he was a boy. He opened his first nickelodeon in Haverhill, Massachusetts, in 1907 and within little more than a decade owned and operated New England's biggest movie theater chain. In need of movies for his theaters, Mayer started Louis B. Mayer Pictures and Metro Pictures Corporation in 1918. He merged these companies with the Goldwyn Pictures Corporation in 1924 to form Metro-Goldwyn-Mayer—MGM—and for the next thirty years Mayer reigned as the most powerful movie producer in Hollywood. The heart of his operation was the "star system," which he created during the late 1920s and early 1930s, putting under exclusive contract a galaxy of motion picture actors certain to attract large audiences.

Mays, Willie (1931–) Mays started playing baseball in the Negro National League in 1948. At about this time, Jackie Robinson crossed the "color line," and major league baseball was integrated. Mays was recruited by the New York (later San Francisco) Giants for the minors in 1950 and entered the major league team in 1951. By 1966, he was earning the highest salary of any baseball player of the time. In 1972, he was traded to the New York Mets and retired the following year. His home run career total was 660 and his batting average .302. He had 3,283 hits to his credit. Many fans consider him baseball's best all-around player.

McAuliffe, Christa (1948–1986) Born Sharon Christa Corrigan, McAuliffe was a Maryland schoolteacher chosen in 1984 out of some 10,000 applicants as the first ordinary citizen (non-pilot, non-scientist) in space. Her enthusiastic participation in the mission of the space shuttle *Challenger* drew much public interest and focused more public attention on the January 28, 1986, launch than usual. Seventy-four seconds after liftoff, *Challenger* exploded, killing all seven on board. Subsequent investigation revealed that the accident resulted from the failure of a seal on a solid-fuel booster rocket, a failure NASA knew was possible, but, to avoid further delays of an already repeatedly delayed launch, downplayed. McCauliffe was hailed as a hero, but public support for the space program diminished.

McCarthy, Eugene (1916–2006) Democrat Eugene McCarthy was elected to the Senate from Minnesota in 1958 and served in relative obscurity until, on November 30, 1967, he announced that he would challenge incumbent president Lyndon B. Johnson in the Democratic primaries. McCarthy became the principal anti-Vietnam War candidate, a figure around whom the antiwar movement rallied. His candidacy encouraged Robert F. Kennedy to declare his candidacy as well, also on an antiwar platform. McCarthy's performance in the primaries was among the factors that prompted President Johnson to withdraw as a candidate for reelection in 1968.

McCarthy, Joseph R. (1908–1957) Elected to the Senate from Wisconsin in 1946, McCarthy had an undistinguished career until he announced in a February 1950 speech to a Republican women's organization in Wheeling, West Virginia, that he possessed the names of 205 Communists who had infiltrated the State Department. Although McCarthy was never able to substantiate the charges, he fueled a red scare that propelled his reelection in 1952 and his chairmanship of the Government Committee on Operations of the Senate and of its permanent subcommittee on investigations. This gave him a forum to air his sensational allegations of Communist subversion in government, industry, Hollywood, and the U.S. Army. Although McCarthy never succeeded in actually identifying a single subversive, the anti-Communist hysteria he generated dominated much of the national life for the next two years. His innuendo was sufficient to ruin many careers, and McCarthy became an intensely polarizing figure: reviled by many, and regarded as a patriot-hero by many others. Most politicians were afraid to challenge him, but as his allegations became increasingly reckless the challenges began to come. When he turned against fellow Republicans, including President Dwight D. Eisenhower, and also alleged that the army had been infiltrated by Communists, the Senate held 36 days of nationally televised hearings on his charges. This proved to be his downfall, as the American public saw in McCarthy a desperate, reckless bully. On December 2, 1954, McCarthy's Senate colleagues censured him for conduct unbecoming a senator. The era of McCarthyism was at an end.

McCormick, Cyrus (1809–1884) McCormick was raised in rural Virginia, where his father was a farmer, blacksmith, and sometime inventor. Cyrus McCormick had little formal education, but spent most of his time in his father's workshop. In 1831, he began working on a mechanical reaper, and by 1834 had sufficiently perfected the horse-drawn device to secure a patent. The McCormick reaper revolutionized agriculture, accomplishing in a single hour what took 20 hours by hand labor. It made possible large-scale farming—and without slave labor. With John Deere's "Grad Detour" plow, the reaper was instrumental in opening up the American West to agricultural settlement on a vast scale.

McClellan, George B. (1826–1885) When President Lincoln appointed George B. McClellan to command the Army of the Potomac in May 1861, the Union press hailed the dashing officer as the "Young Napoleon." With great skill, McClellan transformed a blue-uniformed rabble into a disciplined army, yet he repeatedly avoided decisive combat.

McClellan's overly cautious approach prompted Lincoln to diagnose him as having a "case of the slows," and the president relieved him of major command. McClellan's lack of aggressiveness prolonged the bloody Civil War.

McGillivray, Alexander (ca. 1759–1793) Of mixed European and Indian blood, McGillvray was chief of the Creek Indians and successfully resisted white invasion of Creek tribal lands for years. To achieve this, he fought alongside the British during the American Revolution, then, after the war, negotiated an alliance with Spanish interests in America. In 1789, he was finally able to negotiate a favorable treaty with President George Washington's secretary of war, Henry Knox, which set a limit to white American settlement. McGillivray was one of very few Native American leaders who enjoyed significant success in retaining for his tribe both its tribal identity and its lands in the face of white American expansion—at least for the span of a generation.

McGovern, George (1922–) Democratic U.S. senator from South Dakota, McGovern emerged as an anti-Vietnam War presidential candidate, challenging Republican incumbent Richard M. Nixon in 1972. McGovern not only advocated an immediate end to the war in Vietnam, he called for a broad agenda of social and economic reforms that recalled Lyndon Johnson's "Great Society" program of the 1960s. McGovern's liberal stance failed to unify the Democratic Party, and he lost to Nixon by a landslide.

McGuffey, William Holmes (1800–1873) A professor at Miami University of Ohio, William McGuffey wrote and published his first reading and spelling elementary instruction text in 1836. Over the years—and into the 20th century—

the *McGuffey Readers* would not only teach generations of Americans to read and to spell, but would also impart instruction in religion, morality, ethics, and patriotism, helping to create many aspects of a common American cultural heritage.

McKinley, William (1843–1901) Republican William McKinley entered the White House in 1897. Amid a political and popular clamor for war with Spain—for the purpose of "liberating" Cuba—McKinley ultimately acquiesced, and the brief Spanish-American War (1898) transformed Cuba from a Spanish colony into an American client state. The war also resulted in U.S. annexation of the Philippines, Puerto Rico, and Guam (and it also helped to propel the annexation of Hawaii). Thus McKinley presided over an intense period of U.S. global expansion, which transformed the nation into a major world power and an imperialist force. McKinley's post-war popularity was such that he was reelected in 1900; however, while attending the Pan-American Exhibition in Buffalo, New York, he was shot at pointblank range on September 6, 1901 by a self-proclaimed anarchist, Leon Czolgosz. He died on September 14 and was succeeded by his vice president, Theodore Roosevelt.

McKissick, Floyd (1922–1991) Born in Asheville, North Carolina, McKissick was the first African American to study at the University of North Carolina Law School. He became active in the NAACP and the Congress of Racial Equality (CORE) and participated in every major aspect of the Civil Rights movement during the 1950s and 1960s. He became CORE's national director in 1966, and began to turn the attention of the organization from the rural South to the problems of the northern urban ghettos. Beginning in 1968,

McKissick developed Soul City, North Carolina, intended as model town and industrial project.

McLuhan, Marshall (1911–1980) Although Marshall McLuhan was a Canadian, his major impact was on American popular culture, which he helped to shape in the 1960s with his analysis of the extraordinarily pervasive influence of television and computers on all modes of information and thought in virtually every cultural field. He declared that "the medium is the message" and predicted the obsolescence of the printed book, which would yield to electronic media destined to transform a diverse world into a "global village."

McNamara, Robert (1916–) McNamara was president of the Ford Motor Company when President John F. Kennedy appointed him secretary of defense in 1961. McNamara revolutionized the Pentagon by revamping the military bureaucracy, cutting costs, and refocusing the thrust of defense policy from its strategic (nuclear) emphasis to the doctrine of flexible response, enhancing the military's ability to fight smaller conventional wars. During the Kennedy administration, McNamara played a major role in successfully resolving the Cuban Missile Crisis, but he was also instrumental in greatly expanding America's involvement in the Vietnam War, especially during the administration of JFK's successor, Lyndon B. Johnson.

McPhee, John (1931–) McPhee is a journalist who has written a series of popular books focusing on the environment and key aspects of technology and current events. Many of his works first appeared, at least in part, in *The New Yorker.* His first major book was a study of New Jersey's surprisingly remote semi-wilderness, *The Pine Barrens* (1968). Alaska was profiled in *Coming into the Country* (1977), the citrus industry was the focus of *Oranges* (1967), aeronautics in *The Deltoid Pumpkin Seed* (1973), and nuclear terrorism in *The Curve of Binding Energy* (1974). During the 1980s he wrote a series of books on the geology of the American West.

McVeigh, Timothy (1968–2001) A decorated veteran of the Persian Gulf War (1991), McVeigh left the army after he failed to qualify for a Special Forces assignment. Disaffected with the federal government, he packed a rented Ryder truck with explosive material made from nitrate fertilizer and detonated it beside the Alfred P. Murrah Federal Building in Oklahoma City on August 19, 1995. In the deadliest incident of domestic terrorism in American history, 167 persons were killed (including many children in the building's daycare center), and many more were injured. Apprehended, tried, and convicted, McVeigh was sentenced to death and was executed on June 11, 2001.

Mead, Margaret (1901–1978) Mead was a student of pioneering anthropologists Franz Boas and Ruth Benedict, earning her Ph.D. in 1929. She wrote 23 books during her long career, beginning in 1928 with *Coming of Age in Samoa*, a bestseller and a classic study of adolescence in an "undeveloped" region. Mead popularized anthropology's relativistic approach to culture, enabling many of her readers and lecture audiences to overcome ethnocentrism and appreciate our common humanity. Although many scientists questioned Mead's reliance on observation over statistics and her absolute belief in cultural determinism, the force of her charismatic personality could not be denied, and she surely advanced popular interest in the human sciences.

Meade, George G. (1815–1872) Meade was a Union cavalry officer not noted for his brilliance, but respected for his careful competence. He was in command of the Army of Potomac when it engaged Robert E. Lee's Army of Northern Virginia at a Pennsylvania crossroads town called Gettysburg during July 1–3, 1863. After a bad start, Meade prevailed over Lee, thereby turning the tide of the war. His failure to pursue the defeated Army of Northern Virginia, however, almost certainly prolonged the conflict.

Mellon, Andrew W. (1855–1937) A financier—his fortune was built on steel—Andrew Mellon was appointed secretary of the Treasury by Warren G. Harding. He served under Harding, Calvin Coolidge, and Herbert Hoover, from 1921 to 1932, and reduced the national debt from $24 billion in 1920 to $17,604,000,000 by reforming taxation, generally reducing tax rates. The reductions stimulated the economy and were credited with the 1920s economic boom. Mellon fell from favor, however, after the onset of the Great Depression in 1929. Among As for Mellon's philanthropy, it built the National Gallery of Art in Washington, D.C.

Melville, Herman (1819–1891) Herman Melville went to sea as a young man and used his experiences as the basis for his first two novels, *Typee* (1846) and *Omoo* (1847), South Seas adventure tales that were popular successes. His next work, *Mardi* (1849), was far more experimental and failed to find a public. He returned to simpler, more popular fare with *Redburn* (1849) and *White-Jacket* (1850), then embarked upon his masterpiece, *Moby-Dick* (1851), an epic story woven around a sea captain's obsessive quest for vengeance against the white whale—Moby-Dick—that had severed his leg. Filled with brilliant philosophical digression, the book is a mighty allegory of humanity's relation to nature and, indeed, the universe itself. The book was a popular and critical failure, as was most of the rest of Melville's literary output. Although he continued to write sporadically, he supported himself and his family as a custom's inspector. His literary reputation came posthumously, with the rediscovery of his work in the late 1920s. Since then, he has come to be widely regarded as the greatest of all American novelists.

Mencken, H. L. (1880–1956) Henry Louis Mencken was a brilliant journalist and social critic, who—with great high spirits—lampooned organized religion, business, and especially the American middle class, which he dubbed the "boobocracy" or "booboisie." Mencken made controversy fun. A penetrating literary critic, his influence on American literature—especially fiction—during the 1920s was profound. He was also a serious student of linguistics, and his massive study, *The American Language* (1919), is a monument of linguistics and also a delight to read.

Mercer, Hugh (1726–1777) Mercer was born in Scotland and fought at the bloody Battle of Culloden Moor (1746), then fled to America, where he practiced as a physician. Mercer fought in the French and Indian War and belonged to the same Masonic lodge as George Washington. The two became friends, and, at the outbreak of the American Revolution, Mercer first served in the militia and then in the Continental Army. He was Washington's close comrade and distinguished himself particularly during the crossing of the Delaware and Battle of Trenton on December 26, 1776. His death at the Battle of Princeton, which followed the triumph at Trenton, made Mercer a martyr of the revolution and a symbol of heroic sacrifice for liberty.

Mercer, Johnny (1909–1976) Born John Herndon Mercer in Savannah, Johnny Mercer was a lyricist of great wit and charm, ranging from breezy to wistfully romantic. His most popular songs include "Lazy Bones," "Jeepers Creepers," "Blues in the Night," "That Old Black Magic," "Laura," "Accent-tchu-ate the Positive," "Autumn Leaves," "Moon River," and "Days of Wine and Roses." An astute businessman, Mercer in 1942 cofounded Capitol Records and served as the company's president and chief talent scout.

Michelson, A. A. (1852–1931) Born in Prussia, Michelson immigrated to the United States with his parents when he was two years old. He determined the speed of light with great accuracy and established it as a fundamental constant. His experiments with the American physicist Edward Williams Morely provided the foundation on which Albert Einstein would formulate his Special Theory of Relativity in 1905. Michelson was awarded the 1907 Nobel Prize for Physics.

Mifflin, Thomas (1744–1800) Like so many other participants in the American Revolution, Mifflin was a prosperous merchant. He held numerous offices in the colonial and revolutionary government of Pennsylvania and fought in the American Revolution as a major general. Although he preferred action in the front lines of combat, he accepted the thankless task of quartermaster—the officer responsible for supply and logistics—and absorbed much criticism during his tenure in this post.

Miles, Nelson A. (1839–1925) Miles was a brilliant—and temperamental—officer who received the Medal of Honor for his gallantry at Chancellorsville during the Civil War and went on to become an important commander in the Indian Wars.

He was in overall command during the infamous Massacre at Wounded Knee (December 29, 1890)—which he condemned—and it was he who accepted the final surrender of Sioux, thereby ending the era of the Indian Wars. Miles fought in the Spanish-American War—he was, at the time, commanding general of the U.S. Army—and led the invasion of Puerto Rico, then served as the first head of the military government of that island after the war. He retired from the army in 1903, but, when he was in his late seventies, asked to serve in World War I. President Woodrow Wilson turned him down.

Milken, Michael (1946–) Head of the bond-trading department of Drexel Burnham Lambert, Milken began in the early 1980s exploiting "junk bonds"—hitherto neglected non-investment-grade bonds issued by new companies or companies in trouble. Because of the great risk they carried, junk bonds earned high rates of return—as long as the issuers remained solvent. Milken persuaded savings and loan associations, pension funds, insurance companies, mutual funds, and other institutions to invest in junk bonds, creating a massive influx of capital that fueled an emerging class of entrepreneur called corporate raiders. These individuals specialized in acquiring companies then dismantling or merging them. Such activity came to characterize the frenetic economy of the 1980s. Milken was the king of junk bonds until he was implicated with one of his clients, Ivan Boesky, in an insider trading scheme. He was forced out of Drexel in 1989, and, without him, the junk-bond market imploded. Convicted of securities fraud, Milken was sentenced to 10 years in prison and ordered to pay $600 million in fines.

Miller, Arthur (1915–2005) Miller came of age during the Great Depression and was moved by this background to write plays that combined an acute social consciousness with penetrating and compassionate insight into individual humanity. In his most famous play, *Death of a Salesman* (1949), Miller created an Everyman character—an embodiment of aspiration and disappointment—who also emerges as one of the great portraits of personality in all drama.

Miller, Glenn (1904–1944) During the 1920s and 1930s, Miller was a successful freelance trombonist and arranger, who repeatedly attempted to make a go with a band of his own, but succeeded only after he had formulated a unique sound that was not only an unmistakable individual signature, but came to be identified with the World War II era of swing. During the war, Miller put his career on hold to lead a U.S. Army Air Forces band, bringing "the sound of home" to GIs stationed overseas. On December 16, 1944, while flying from England to Paris, his plane was lost over the English Channel. Neither the aircraft wreckage nor any sign of Miller was ever recovered.

Minuit, Peter (1580?–1638) Minuit was a Dutch settler who sailed to North America and arrived at the mouth of the Hudson River on May 4, 1626. He was subsequently appointed by the Dutch West India Company director general of the colony on Manhattan. Wanting to legitimate the Dutch claim to the island, he gathered the local Indian leaders and "purchased" Manhattan for goods valued at 60 guilders on August 10, 1626. Historians calculated this as $24. Minuit then founded the town of New Amsterdam at the southern tip of Manhattan. It was renamed New York when the British took it over in 1664.

Miranda, Ernesto (1941–1976) Ernesto Miranda was a career criminal who, in 1963, was arrested for a series of rapes in

Phoenix, Arizona. On the basis of his confession, he was convicted; however, the U.S. Supreme Court on June 13, 1966, overturned the conviction because the police had failed to inform Miranda of his Fifth Amendment right to avoid self-incrimination by refusing to answer police questions without the presence of legal counsel. As a result of this decision, arresting officers now read suspects their "Miranda rights," informing them that they have the right to remain silent and to have an attorney present before any questioning is conducted. (Miranda was later retried and convicted on new evidence.)

Mitchell, Margaret (1900–1949) In 1926, Atlanta journalist Margaret Mitchell began writing an epic Civil War novel told from the Southern point of view. It took her a decade to complete, but when *Gone with the Wind* was published in 1936, it became a runaway bestseller—a million copies flying off the shelves within six months of publication and its heroine and hero, Scarlett O'Hara and Rhett Butler, becoming household names. It was made into a movie in 1939, starring Clark Gable and Vivien Leigh, which, for twenty years after its release was the top-earning movie in cinema history.

Mitchell, John (1913–1988) Richard M. Nixon appointed Mitchell attorney general in 1969. He made himself controversial—even widely despised—for endorsing two Supreme Court nominees rejected by the Senate as unqualified, for approving wiretaps not authorized by any court, for vigorously prosecuting anti-Vietnam War protesters, and for attempting to block publication of the "Pentagon Papers." In March 1972, Mitchell stepped down as attorney general to become head of Nixon's reelection committee but resigned in July during the early phases of the Watergate scandal. Convicted in 1975 of conspiring in the Watergate break-in, obstructing justice, and perjury, he entered prison in 1977 and was paroled in 1979.

Monk, Thelonious (1917–1982) Thelonious Monk was a jazz pianist at Minton's Play House, a major modern jazz venue in New York City during the early 1940s. He was a prime mover of bebop, which took the era's "swing" style in new and adventurous directions. An enormously prolific composer, he created works of jagged, angular complexity, full of odd harmonies and "wrong" notes, with strangely accented rhythms, and always supremely inventive and intriguing. His best-known compositions—including "Well, You Needn't," "Straight, No Chaser," "Mysterioso," "Epistrophy," "Blue Monk," and " 'Round Midnight"—are considered monuments of modern jazz.

Monroe, James (1758–1831) Monroe fought alongside General George Washington during the American Revolution and, afterward, studied law with Thomas Jefferson. He was elected the fifth president of the United States in 1816 and served from 1817 to 1825. Despite economic hardship during this period, Monroe's administration was dubbed the "Era of Good Feelings." Monroe's most famous contribution to American history was his promulgation on December 2, 1823, of the so-called "Monroe Doctrine, " which put European powers on notice that the United States would resist any attempt to establish colonies in the Western Hemisphere or otherwise interfere in the affairs of the region. The doctrine further stated the intention of the United States to hold itself aloof from European affairs. The Monroe Doctrine has exerted a powerful influence on U.S. foreign policy ever since.

Monroe, Marilyn (1926–1962) Born Norma Jean Mortenson in Los Angeles, she later took her mother's name, Baker, but became known to world by her screen name, Marilyn Monroe. She struggled in bit parts until one of these—an uncredited appearance in *The Asphalt Jungle* (1950)—elicited an avalanche of fan mail, and she soon climbed to top billing when studios promoted her as a "love goddess." Monroe was more than a movie idol; she became, through some 23 movies, the central sex symbol of the 1950s and entered the pantheon of American popular culture. She died mysteriously on August 5, 1962, of an overdose of sleeping pills. The coroner's verdict was suicide, but rumors of murder continue to circulate—including an unsubstantiated theory that she was killed at the behest of the Kennedy family (she almost certainly had a romantic affair with President Kennedy and may have been involved with Robert F. Kennedy as well).

Morgan, Daniel (1736–1802) Morgan was a frontiersman who led a unit of handpicked Virginia riflemen during the revolution. A master of guerilla warfare, he played major roles in the U.S. invasion of Canada early in the war and in the battles at Saratoga in 1777, but his most important victory was at the Battle of Cowpens, South Carolina (January 17, 1781), which helped turn the tide of the war in the South.

Morgan, J. Pierpont (1837–1913) The son of a financier, J. P. Morgan made his fortune—and fortunes for others—by reorganizing a number of major railroads and consolidating United States Steel, International Harvester, and General Electric. For a long time, Morgan was the single most powerful figure on Wall Street.

Morgenthau, Henry, Jr. (1891–1967) A brilliant manager of money, Morgenthau served as secretary of the Treasury through President Franklin D. Roosevelt's dozen years in office (1934–1945), During this period, which saw both the massive expenditures of the Depression-era New Deal and World War II, Morgenthau was in charge of some $370 billion in spending—three times the funds than were managed by his 50 predecessors combined. Morgenthau's uncompromising proposal after World War II that Germany be permanently reduced to a pre-industrial agricultural economy was rejected by President Harry S. Truman and prompted Morgenthau's resignation.

Morris, Gouverneur (1752–1816) Morris was a man of contradictions. Highly conservative (he was an extreme Federalist, who believed in the strongest possible central government, including presidential tenure for life and presidential appointment of senators), he was nevertheless a zealous champion of independence during the American Revolution and a strong advocate of unlimited religious freedom. Under the Articles of Confederation, Morris formulated the decimal coinage system that became the basis of the U.S. monetary system. A key delegate to the Constitutional Convention, he was a principal drafter of the document.

Morris, Robert (1734–1806) Born in England, Morris immigrated to Maryland in 1747 then moved to Philadelphia, where he became a prominent merchant. Active in the American Revolution as vice president of the Pennsylvania Committee of Safety (1775–1776) and a delegate to the Continental Congress (1775–1778) and the Pennsylvania legislature (1778–1779, 1780–1781, 1785–1786), Morris was the primary manager of finance for the war effort from 1776 to 1778. Later, he worked as a fund raiser, requisitioning cash from the states and borrowing from the French. In 1781, he founded the Bank of North America and was superintendent of finance under the Articles of Confederation from 1781 to 1784. Ironically, his personal finances suffered toward the end of his life, and from 1799 to 1801 he was incarcerated in debtors' prison.

Morrison, Toni (1931–) Morrison was born Chloe Anthony Wofford in Ohio and created a career in fiction by writing of the African-American experience, often from the female point of view. Her works span slave times to the present. She burst onto the literary scene with her 1977 *Song of Solomon,* and her 1987 *Beloved* won the Pulitzer Prize for fiction. She was awarded the Nobel Prize for Literature in 1993.

Morse, Samuel F. B. (1791–1872) Samuel Finley Breese Morse embarked on a career as a painter and received acclaim in this field, but little monetary reward. He turned to invention, and in the 1830s designed the first truly practical telegraph. He successfully commercialized the invention beginning on May 24, 1844, with a spectacular demonstration in which he sent the question "What hath God wrought?" over some 40 miles of wire from the main chamber of the U.S. Supreme Court in Washington to Alfred Vail in Baltimore. Morse also invented the Morse Code (in 1838), which was for well over a century a major means of communication both by wired and wireless systems.

Moses, Grandma (1860–1961) Anna Mary Robertson Moses was popularly known as Grandma Moses because of her long life. She was born in rural New York and farmed there and in

Shenandoah Valley of Virginia. She began painting the landscapes familiar to her, partly in imitation of Currier & Ives prints, but also in a manner true to her charmingly naïve vision. A collector exhibited her work in New York City in 1939–1940, and it met with instant national acclaim. She became the most celebrated of American folk artists.

Moses, Robert (1888–1981) Robert Moses was an urban planning commissioner of boundless ambition, who created public works that profoundly transformed the cityscape of New York and served as a model—and sometimes a cautionary example—for the nation as a whole. Moses was wholly or partly responsible for some 35 new highways, a dozen bridges, many city parks, the Lincoln Center for the Performing Arts, Shea Stadium, numerous housing projects, two hydroelectric dams, and the entire 1964 New York World's Fair. He was also a moving force behind the construction of the United Nations headquarters buildings in New York. Widely admired, Moses was also condemned as a megalomaniacal empire builder, who did not scruple at tearing down buildings of historical importance and even entire neighborhoods.

Mott, Lucretia (1793–1880) Born Lucretia Coffin in Nantucket, Massachusetts, Mott was a liberal reformer active in the abolition movement. With Elizabeth Cady Stanton, she founded the American Equal Rights Association and other activities of the first organized women's rights movement in the country.

Mudd, Samuel (1833–1883) Mudd was a Maryland physician and Confederate sympathizer who met John Wilkes Booth through a mutual acquaintance. After Booth assassinated

President Abraham Lincoln and made his escape, he stopped at Mudd's home around four o'clock in the morning on April 15 to seek the doctor's aid in setting his leg, which he had broken when he leaped from the presidential box to the stage of Ford's Theatre after shooting the president. Mudd was subsequently convicted of conspiracy to murder Lincoln. Sentenced to life imprisonment, he was incarcerated at Fort Jefferson in the Dry Tortugas, some 70 miles west of Key West, Florida. He protested innocence of the conspiracy and claimed that he had merely aided an injured man. Mudd's heroic medical work during a yellow fever outbreak at the fort in 1867 earned him a presidential pardon in 1869.

Muhammad, Elijah (1897–1975) Elijah Muhammad was born Elijah Poole in Georgia and took his Muslim name after he became assistant minister to Wallace D. Fard, founder of the Nation of Islam, popularly called the Black Muslims. Elijah Muhammad became head of the Muslims after Fard disappeared in 1934. Under his leadership, the Black Muslims expanded into a major black nationalist movement.

Muir, John (1838–1914) Muir was born in Scotland and immigrated to the United States in 1849. He embarked on a career as an inventor, but, after suffering an industrial accident in 1867, turned to the natural world. He wrote eloquently of the beauties of North America and of the vital importance of the wilderness, especially in modern life. He became a passionate advocate of forest conservation. A charismatic organizer, he was in large part responsible for the creation of California's Sequoia and Yosemite national parks.

Murrow, Edward R. (1908–1965) Murrow was a radio and television broadcaster-journalist, whose radio reports of key

European events preceding World War II and of World War II itself (especially the Battle of Britain) were not only broadcasting landmarks, but helped shape America's attitude toward the Axis and the Allies. Murrow became a pioneer of television news during the infancy of the medium, inaugurating a highly respected weekly news digest called *See it Now.* During the early 1950s, Murrow's television broadcasts were instrumental in exposing the reckless demagoguery of anti-Communist witch hunter Senator Joseph McCarthy and did much to bring about the end of the infamous McCarthy era. Murrow became an enduring model for journalists in the age of electronic media.

Murtha, John (1932–) Murtha joined the U.S. Marine Corps in 1952, served as a drill instructor, and was subsequently commissioned an officer. A member of the Marine Corps Reserve during the Vietnam War, Murtha volunteered to serve in Vietnam from 1966 to 1967 and was highly decorated. Elected to Congress from Pennsylvania's 12th congressional district in 1974, he earned a reputation as a populist Democrat. He came to national prominence on November 17, 2005 when he called for U.S. withdrawal from the Iraq war, which President George W. Bush had begun in 2003. Within a short time, Murtha became the most vocal and visible critic of the war in Congress.

Muybridge, Eadweard (1830–1904) Born in England, Muybridge immigrated to the United States in his youth and came to international attention in 1868 with a spectacular large-scale portfolio of photographs of Yosemite Valley, California; however, it is on his experiments with photographing motion that Muybridge's enduring reputation rests. In 1872, financier Leland Stanford commissioned him to settle a wager by proving that, at a given moment, all four legs of a trotting horse leave the ground simultaneously. By 1877, Muybridge created an array of cameras that captured the horse's motion. Not only did this prove Stanford correct, it was the rudimentary beginning of the art and science of photographing motion. Muybridge later invented the zoopraxiscope, a device that projected images in rapid succession, thereby producing the illusion of live movement. The device was a precursor of cinema.

Nabokov, Vladimir (1899–1977) Vladimir Vladimirovich Nabokov was born in Russia and immigrated to England in 1919, lived variously in Europe, then came to the United States, becoming a citizen in 1945. A prolific author in Russian as well as English, his most famous novel is *Lolita* (1955), the narrative of a middle-aged man's obsession with a seductively nubile young girl. A controversial bestseller, the novel treated sensational and provocative material with extraordinarily elegant word play and intricate, bravura literary effects. The character of Lolita became an icon of popular culture.

Nader, Ralph (1934–) Nader earned his law degree from Harvard in 1958 and, while working as a consultant to the U.S. Department of Labor, published in 1965 *Unsafe at Any Speed*, which assaulted the U.S. auto industry for sacrificing safety to profits. The book made Nader a household name and prompted passage in 1966 of the National Traffic and Motor Vehicle Safety Act, which gave the federal government substantial authority in promulgating automobile safety standards. Nader went on to lead a band of dedicated consumer and social activists ("Nader's Raiders"), who attacked a wide range of public policy issues. He also founded Public Citizen, a major advocacy group. Nader ran for president as Green Party candidate in 1996 and 2000.

Naismith, James (1861–1939) In 1891, Canadian-born Naismith was an instructor at the YMCA International Training School in Springfield, Massachusetts. In search of way to increase YMCA attendance during the winter, he invented an entirely new indoor game, which he called basketball. It used a ball and two peach baskets as goals, and because it was intended for indoor play, players were not allowed to tackle or otherwise make contact with one another, nor were they permitted to run with the ball. Basketball quickly developed into one of the most popular games in the United States.

Nast, Thomas (1840–1902) Born in Bavaria, Nast immigrated to the United States as boy of 6 and, at 15, became an artist for *Frank Leslie's Illustrated Newspaper.* He depicted stirring action scenes in the Civil War (Lincoln called him "our best recruiting sergeant"), but was best known for his scathing political cartoons attacking William M. "Boss" Tweed, the corrupt political leader of New York's Tammany Hall in the 1870s. Thanks largely to Nast, Tammany collapsed. Nast also created the donkey and elephant that became the enduring emblems of the Democratic and Republican parties.

Ness, Eliot (1903–1957) In 1929 Ness was hired as a Department of Justice agent to lead the Chicago branch of the Prohibition Bureau for the purpose of investigating and prosecuting the infamous Al Capone. His force of nine investigators, regarded as immune to corruption, were dubbed the Untouchables. Information gathered by the Untouchables eventually resulted in Capone's conviction for income tax evasion.

Nevelson, Louise (1899/1900–1988) Born Louise Berliawsky in Kiev, Ukraine, she immigrated to the United States with her family in 1905 and in 1920 married businessman Charles Nevelson, whom she subsequently left in order to pursue her artistic career. Nevelson created unique abstract sculptures, typically monochromatic, and almost always interlocking assemblages of found objects. Although she exhibited as early as 1941, it was not until the 1950s that she received wide recognition.

Newton, Huey P. (1942–1989) Newton was an African-American political activist who co-founded (with Bobby Seale) the Black Panther Party in Oakland, California, in 1966, to defend the black community against police brutality. Many in the white community considered the Black Panthers a street gang and Newton an example of dangerous black militancy; however, Newton saw the Panthers as a means of providing social services to the black community. Accused of murder in 1974 (he had previously served time for manslaughter), Newton fled to Cuba, but returned to face charges. Two trials ended in hung juries. Newton earned a Ph.D. in social philosophy from the University of California at Santa Cruz in 1980. He was found, shot to death, on an Oakland street in 1989.

Niebuhr, Reinhold (1892–1971) Niebuhr's critique of theological liberalism during the 1920s profoundly shaped modern American Protestantism. For many intellectual Protestants, it was Niebuhr's philosophy that helped them to maintain their faith. During World War II, this former pacifist played an important role in persuading American Christians to support the struggle against Hitler and Nazism.

Nimitz, Chester W. (1885–1966) A brilliant administrator, strategist, and naval leader, Nimitz was the principal architect of the U.S. naval victory against Japan in the Pacific during World War II. He had overall command of all naval and land forces and, in conjunction with General Douglas MacArthur, formulated the "island-hopping" strategy that closed in on the Japanese home islands, leading to the defeat of the enemy and the end of the war.

Nixon, Richard M. (1913–1994) A California Republican, Nixon rose to national prominence as a red-baiting U.S. representative (1948–1951) and senator (1951–1953), earning the epithet "Tricky Dick" for his ruthless campaign tactics. Tapped as Dwight Eisenhower's running mate in 1952, he served two terms as vice-president (1953–1961), then was defeated by John F. Kennedy in the presidential elections of 1960 and also lost the California gubernatorial race in 1962. Although many wrote off his political career, he reemerged as the Republican presidential candidate in 1968 and defeated Democrat Hubert Humphrey. Nixon promised to end the war in Vietnam, and although he did withdraw large numbers of U.S. troops, he expanded the air war with massive bomb strikes and invaded Vietnam's neighbor, Cambodia. His Vietnam policy increased the tempo and severity of antiwar demonstrations in the U.S. Conservative though it was, the Nixon administration also saw great strides in environmental legislation and in progress toward the end of the Cold War, as this hardline "Cold Warrior" reached out to the Soviet Union and, more successfully, to China. "Tricky Dick" reemerged, however, miring his second term in the Watergate scandal, a complex of illegal activities to sabotage the Democrats in 1972 and to cover up afterward. At 11:35 a.m. on August 9, 1974, Nixon became the first U.S. president to resign his office.

Noguchi, Isamu (1904–1988) Although born in Los Angeles, Noguchi grew up in Japan, then studied sculpture in

New York and worked as Constantin Brancusi's assistant in Paris. In that city, he fell under the influence of the great modern sculptors Alberto Giacometti and Alexander Calder as well as the painters Picasso and Miró. Propelled by these influences, he went on to develop a sculptural style all his own, abstractions built on organic shapes, suggesting a harmonious relation to nature. His work was often integrated into modern buildings, and he designed entire sculptural gardens, bringing nature into the often relentlessly mechanical modern scene.

Norris, Frank (1870–1902) A West Coast journalist, Norris created a new kind of American novel, which embodied a "naturalist" vision, suggesting that human events were driven by essentially natural forces, amoral and beyond the individual's will or control. *McTeague* (1899) presented an almost surreal vision in this vein, telling the story of brutish dentist who kills his wife then dies as he flees through Death Valley. His subsequent work was more realistic, culminating in *The Octopus* (1901), which depicted the amoral forces of economics in society. Norris's life was cut short by a failed appendicitis operation.

North, Oliver (1943–) North was a U.S. Marine lieutenant colonel assigned as chief aide to Vice Admiral John M. Poindexter, national security advisor to President Ronald Reagan. In the 1980s, the Reagan administration wanted to support the "contras," a right-wing military group opposed to the Marxist Sandinista government of Nicaragua. When Congress barred such aid, North, with Poindexter, formulated a secret plan by which the United States would sell arms to Iran (a terrorist nation and sworn enemy of America) in order to persuade it to help secure the liberation of U.S. hostages held in Lebanon. Additionally, the proceeds from the arms sale would be funneled to the contras, without the knowledge of Congress. Exposure of "Iran scam" or "Iran-gate"—as the press called the affair—in 1986 threatened to topple the Reagan administration and resulted in the prosecution of North (convictions were later dismissed).

Novak, Robert (1931–) Novak built his journalistic career on political reporting and commentary with an insider's view. He had access to so many highly placed sources that colleagues and politicians dubbed him the "Prince of Darkness." In 2003, he "outed" in his column undercover CIA operative Valerie Plame, wife of an opponent of George W. Bush's decision to invade Iraq. The subsequent investigation of deliberate leaks from high-level Bush administration sources shook the administration and resulted in the prosecution of Lewis "Scooter" Libby, top aide to Vice President Dick Cheney. Novak's motives and ethics came under sharp scrutiny, as did the political agendas of a number of journalists on the left as well as the right.

O'Connor, Flannery (1925–1964) Born and raised in Georgia, O'Connor wrote highly imaginative novels and short stories set in the rural South and peopled by dark characters who are both deeply alienated from humanity and obsessed with God and religion. Her fiction is idiosyncratic in the extreme, yet firmly based in southern regionalism and always philosophically provocative.

O'Connor, Sandra Day (1930–) Raised on an Arizona ranch, O'Connor practiced as an attorney, served in the Arizona Senate, then as a superior court judge (1974–1979) and an appeals judge (1979–1981). Nominated for the U.S.

Supreme Court by President Ronald Reagan, she was sworn in on September 25, 1981. O'Connor served until she retired in 2006 (when she was succeeded by Samuel Alito) and was known for her moderate conservative orientation.

Odets, Clifford (1906–1963) Born in Philadelphia, Odets was a stage actor during most of the 1920s and began writing plays in the 1930s, during the Great Depression. Leftist, even socialist in orientation, Odets's plays made for high drama while appealing to the social consciousness of the audience. Their great strength was that their political orientation never overshadowed their humanity, as in his masterpiece, *Awake and Sing* (1935), which endures as a moving portrait of a family.

Ogelthorpe, James (1691–1785) A professional British soldier, Ogelthorpe entered Parliament in 1722 and, in 1729, chaired a committee on prison reform. This inspired him to found a North American colony that would offer the poor a new start and an alternative to debtor's prison. It would also serve as a haven for persecuted Protestant sects and would be founded on generally utopian principles, including relative equality of wealth (no one would be permitted to own more than 100 acres) and the prohibition of rum as well as slavery. Georgia (as he called his utopia) was chartered in 1732 and founded the following year. The utopian provisions were quickly renounced by settlers, however, and Oglethorpe, disillusioned, returned to England in 1734.

Oglivy, David (1911–1999) Dubbed in the 1970s "the Father of Advertising," Oglivy was certainly among the most influential and creative practitioners of the art and business of commercial persuasion. He had been born in England, falling into advertising through an early career in sales. He came to the United States just before World War II and, in 1949, founded his own agency. His early campaigns—especially those for Hathaway shirts and Schweppes beverages—made a permanent impression on American popular culture and changed the advertising industry forever.

O'Keeffe, Georgia (1887–1886) During her long career, O'Keefe combined bold abstraction with images from nature to produce powerfully expressive paintings of great beauty, suggestive of erotic and emotional depths. She is most closely associated with imagery drawn from the desert of the American Southwest, but her works are universal rather than regional in appeal, a fusion of an organic vision with a modernist aesthetic.

Oliver, Joseph "King" (1885–1938) Oliver grew up on a Louisiana plantation and began playing cornet in New Orleans in 1907. He was a bandleader by 1915 and moved to Chicago in 1916. The music he played was the earliest style of jazz, and in 1920 he hired young Louis Armstrong, who grew to his early maturity as a cornetist with Oliver. Oliver and his band are considered the foundation on which jazz was subsequently built by Armstrong and others.

Olmsted, Frederick Law (1822–1903) Olmsted was trained as an engineer, but earned his fame as a landscape architect with his design for New York's Central Park in 1857. Universally acclaimed for this work—which combined an unerring urban aesthetic with the preservation of a genuinely wild element—Olmsted was hired to design city parks throughout the United States. His work gave rise to the "city beautiful" movement and was a welcome antidote to the blight of industrialization and urban sprawl that threatened the nation during the second half of the 19th century.

Oñate, Don Juan de (1550?–1630) A conquistador, Oñate established the Spanish colony of New Mexico in 1598 and served as its royal governor. He was a despot, obsessed (as many early Spanish explorers and settlers were) with finding the legendary Seven Cities of Gold in the New World. His explorations failed to find gold, but did chart vast regions of the American Southwest. Onate's harsh treatment of Indians and Spanish settlers alike resulted in his expulsion from his own colony. His sentence was subsequently reversed, but he was never restored to the office of governor.

O'Neill, Eugene (1888–1953) O'Neill was the son of an actor and a frail, opium-addicted mother. His unstable but emotionally rich upbringing would prove a rich source of dramatic material when he started to write for the stage, beginning with an early masterpiece of 1916, *Bound East for Cardiff*. By the time of his death in 1953, O'Neill had created some of the greatest plays of the 20th century, including *Beyond the Horizon* (1920), *Anna Christie* (1922), *Strange Interlude* (1928), *Ah! Wilderness* (1933), *The Iceman Cometh* (1946), and epic *Long Day's Journey into Night* (produced posthumously 1956). His work is characterized by a lyrical, intensely personal vision that is nevertheless universal in application, dealing with remorse, forgiveness, betrayal, and faith. O'Neill was awarded the Nobel Prize for Literature in 1936.

Oppenheimer, J. Robert (1904–1967) A brilliant and charismatic theoretical physicist, Oppenheimer was tapped as director of the Los Alamos laboratory during World War II. His mission was to lead a large team of scientists in the Manhattan Project, which built the atomic bomb. The effort was a success—two bombs dropped on Japan ended the war—and Oppenheimer went on to direct the Institute for Advanced Study at Princeton from 1947 to 1966. His opposition to the development of the hydrogen bomb (much more powerful than the atomic bomb) after the war led to accusations of disloyalty and his removal as adviser to the highest levels of government.

Osceola (1804–1838) Osceola was a Seminole chief and war leader who led the resistance to the removal of the Seminoles and closely allied Creeks from the Southeast to "Indian Territory" west of the Mississippi. His unifying leadership during the early part of the Second Seminole War (1835–1842) was both brilliant and highly effective. Despite a flag of truce, he was seized and imprisoned in 1837 and died in captivity.

O'Sullivan, John L. (1813–1895) In May 1845, *New York Post* editor O'Sullivan wrote an article in the *United States Magazine and Democratic Review* proposing annexation of the Republic of Texas. He declared: "It is our manifest destiny to overspread and possess the whole of the continent which Providence has given us for the development of the great experiment of liberty and federated self-government entrusted to us." The phrase "manifest destiny" electrified the nation and was instantly seized upon as a justification for United States' possession of territory from the Atlantic to the Pacific—even if acquiring the land meant war. Most immediately, "manifest destiny" became a justification for the U.S.-Mexican War of 1846–1848.

Oswald, Lee Harvey (1939–1963) A disaffected U.S. Marine Corps veteran, Soviet sympathizer, and pro-Castro activist, Oswald was employed by the Texas School Book Depository in Dallas. From the sixth floor of the depository on November 22, 1963, at 12:30 p.m., he shot President Kennedy and Texas governor John Connally as their motorcade passed below his window. The president died with a half hour; the governor recovered. In an escape attempt, Oswald shot and killed Dallas police officer J. D. Tippett and was himself shot to death on November 24, while in police custody, by Dallas nightclub owner Jack Ruby. Both Oswald's role in the assassination and Ruby's killing of Oswald instantly drew the speculation of conspiracy and remain controversial to this day.

Otis, Elisha Graves (1811–1861) In 1852, this mechanic and inventor designed a "safety hoist" to aid in the installation of heavy machinery. The hoist had an automatic brake, which would prevent the load from falling if a cable broke. In 1853, he adapted this to passenger elevators, which he began manufacturing. The Otis elevator made practical the skyscraper, which, later in the century, would become the iconic feature of the American urban landscape.

Otis, James (1725–1783) A Massachusetts attorney and early advocate of American independence, Otis resigned as Boston's chief enforcer of British taxes and duties, explaining his resignation in a speech of February 24, 1761, by declaring that "Taxation without representation is tyranny." This phrase electrified and defined the American independence movement.

Outcault, Richard (1863–1928) Outcault was a popular illustrator who contributed to humor magazines in the late

19th century. When Joseph Pulitzer's *New York World* debuted its color-reproduction press, Outcault's drawing of a street urchin clad in a nightshirt was selected as the first color subject on February 16, 1896. The bright yellow nightshirt made such a sensation that the character was dubbed the "Yellow Kid" and became the basis of the first comic strip—soon a staple feature of American newspapers. Pulitzer's rival, William Randolph Hearst, hired Outcault away from the *World,* initiating a bidding war for the cartoonist's services. This highly publicized contest gave rise to the phrase "yellow journalism" to describe the sensational publishing practices of great rival papers vying for subscribers.

Owen, Robert Dale (1801–1877) The son of the English Utopian reformer and philosopher Robert Owen, Robert Dale Owen grew up in New Lanark, Scotland, his father's model industrial/utopian community. In 1825, he immigrated to the United States with his father and was instrumental in founding New Harmony, Indiana, the nation's most famous experiment in utopian living.

Owens, Jesse (1913–1980) Owen set a world record in the running broad jump that remained unbroken for a quarter century. An African American, he won four gold medals at the 1936 Olympic Games in Berlin, each victory a stunning blow to Adolf Hitler's contention of the superiority of the "Aryan race."

Paine, Thomas (1737–1809) Born in England, Paine was apprenticed to his father, a corset maker, and also tried other occupations—all without success. On the recommendation of Benjamin Franklin (whom he met in London), Paine immigrated to America in 1774, became a writer in Philadelphia, and was prompted by the revolutionary physician Dr. Benjamin Rush to write a pamphlet in support of independence from England during the intense colonial debate on the subject. Paine's *Common Sense* was published on January 10, 1776, and became a runaway bestseller, swinging the debate in favor of independence. Paine became an ardent revolutionary and, between 1776 and 1783, wrote the so-called "Crisis" papers, which were invaluable in keeping the Patriot cause alive during the war.

Paley, William S. (1901–1990) Vice president of his father's cigar business, Paley discovered the power of radio advertising, became a major advertiser, and, in 1927, invested in the Columbia Broadcasting System (CBS), then a fledgling radio network. The following year, he became president of CBS and, over the next half century, directed its growth into a mass media powerhouse. Paley is regarded as one of the fathers of American radio and television broadcasting.

Palmer, A. Mitchell (1872–1936) As U.S. attorney general, Palmer, on January 2, 1920, sent federal agents to round up suspected Communist sympathizers in massive raids carried out simultaneously in 33 cities. Six thousand persons, including American citizens and recent immigrants, were arrested. Palmer's raids created the nation's first "Red Scare," or anti-Communist witch hunt. Although 556 of those arrested were deported, most convictions arising from the raids were overturned and Palmer was ultimately discredited. His young protégé, J. Edgar Hoover, not only escaped censure, but went on to lead the agency that became the FBI.

Parker, Bonnie, and Clyde Barrow (1910–1934; 1909–1934) Barrow was a career criminal when he met Bonnie Parker in January 1930. After serving a 20-month prison term, he teamed up with her and embarked on a nearly two-year bank robbery spree through in Texas, Oklahoma, New Mexico, and Missouri that commanded sensational national attention. Portrayed as a romantic heroine and hero, who robbed the banks that foreclosed on many hard-working people ruined by the Great Depression, "Bonnie and Clyde" were, in fact, murderers, who killed three police officers. They themselves were gunned down at a roadblock in Gibsland, Louisiana, on May 23, 1934. Their violent deaths together added to their popular legend, and they became the subject of books and a notable 1967 film by director Arthur Penn.

Parker, Charlie "Bird" (1920–1955) Charles Parker, Jr.—called Charlie Parker or, simply, "Bird"—was a jazz alto saxophonist whose bebop virtuosity and extraordinary improvisatorial imagination made him a legend. As a performer, composer, and bandleader, Parker was the single most important exponent of the bebop style of the 1940s and 1950s. If his career was legendary for its genius, his fate as a doomed heroin addict was also an icon of the world of jazz. He is widely regarded as the greatest jazz instrumentalist of all time.

Parker, Dorothy (1893–1967) Born Dorothy Rothschild, Parker was a writer for *Vogue* and a drama critic for *Vanity Fair,* which fired her in 1920 because her reviews were too caustic. Working as a freelance writer, she produced short stories and verse, which were notable for their cynicism, acerbic wit, and quotability. In the 1920s, she was the nucleus of the Algonquin Round Table, an assemblage of the "smartest" literary figures of the day—including Robert Benchley, Robert

E. Sherwood, and James Thurber, among others—who gathered in the dining room of Manhattan's Algonquin Hotel, generating wit that was often retailed to the public in the pages of the *New Yorker.* Parker was an icon of 1920s cynical intellectualism and of female liberation.

Parker, Theodore (1810–1860) A Unitarian pastor and theologian, Parker was active in the abolition movement but exerted his most lasting influence on American religion by repudiating a great deal of Christian dogma and emphasizing instead a personal relationship with God derived from an intimate experience of nature and introspection.

Parkman, Francis (1823–1893) A prolific historical writer, Parkman is best remembered for his seven-volume history of France and England in colonial North America, covering the period through the French and Indian War. Parkman portrayed colonial American history with an epic sweep as a contest among competing civilizations: English, French, and Native America. While modern historians reject some of his interpretations, all acknowledge that he brought to the study of history an awareness of its great drama, which he skillfully conveyed to generations of readers.

Parks, Rosa (1913–2005) An African-American seamstress and early civil rights activist, Rosa Parks purposely violated a Montgomery, Alabama, city ordinance by refusing to relinquish her bus seat to a white man. Her arrest triggered the Montgomery Bus Boycott, which lasted more than a year and forced the integration of the city's buses. The boycott became the framework within which the early national civil rights movement was organized in large part under the leadership of the young Martin Luther King Jr.

Parris, Betty (1682–1760) Elizabeth "Betty" Parris was nine years old when she fell ill with convulsions, grotesque contortions, and outbursts of nonsensical speech in 1692. She was diagnosed as having been "bewitched," and her case triggered the infamous Salem witchcraft trials that year.

Parris, Samuel (1653–1720) The Puritan minister of Salem Village (modern Danvers), Massachusetts, Parris was the father of Betty Parris and the uncle of Abigail Williams, two young girls diagnosed as having been bewitched. Parris accused a slave, Tituba, of witchcraft and beat out a confession from her that led to general hysteria in the Salem region with many accusations of witchcraft. The affair culminated in the infamous Salem witch trials of 1692.

Pastor, Tony (1837–1908) Pastor debuted at P. T. Barnum's American Museum in New York City when he was six and was a stage entertainer until he opened his own variety theater in New York City in 1865. In 1881, he opened a second venue, the Fourteenth Street Theatre, and advertised a new kind of popular entertainment—vaudeville—which catered to ladies and family audiences, in contrast to the vulgar fare presented in other popular variety houses. Pastor's version of vaudeville developed into the most important form of American popular entertainment before the proliferation of film and electronic media.

Patton, George Smith, Jr. (1885–1945) Patton graduated from West Point in 1909 and, during World War I, pioneered the use of the tank in the American army. During World War II, he helped to fashion the U.S. Army into a victorious force in North Africa, became the conqueror of Sicily, then went on to lead his Third Army in a spectacular drive across

France and Germany unparalleled in U.S. military history, liberating thousands of towns and villages and capturing more than a million enemy soldiers. Patton was a legendary leader, whose difficult temperament often took him to the verge of being relieved of command—his outstanding combat record notwithstanding. His men memorialized him as "Old Blood-and-Guts."

Paul, Alice (1885–1977) A radical suffragist, Paul was jailed three times for her activities on behalf of woman suffrage. In 1923 she drafted and presented to Congress an equal rights amendment to the Constitution, intended to ensure legal equality for women. Her campaign for passage and ratification of the amendment failed, as did subsequent attempts long after her death.

Peale, Charles Willson (1741–1827) Peale was born in Maryland, became a much sought-after portrait painter, then studied in England, returning to America at the outbreak of the revolution. Active in the independence movement, he painted portraits of the most important figures of the revolution and in 1782 opened in Philadelphia a public portrait gallery of revolutionary heroes. Four years later, he founded a museum of natural history. Peale's Museum (later called the Philadelphia Museum) was the first major museum in the United States.

Peckinpah, Sam (1925–1984) Born David Samuel Peckinpah in Fresno, California, Peckinpah directed his first great western, *Ride the High Country*, in 1962. A literate take on the popular western film genre, the film featured characters in search of fortune or redemption of honor, playing out their violent stories against the backdrop of the majestic

American West. These themes were developed with even greater complexity in Peckinpah's masterpiece, *The Wild Bunch* (1969), which also featured intricately choreographed, beautifully filmed, and masterfully edited sequences of intense yet poetic violence—for which the director was both praised and condemned.

Pei, I. M. (1917–) Pei immigrated to the United States in 1935 and studied architecture at the University of Pennsylvania and the Massachusetts Institute of Technology. He rose to fame beginning in the 1950s with his magnificent, even exuberant elaboration of the austere "International Style" in such buildings as the National Center for Atmospheric Research (Boulder, Colorado), John F. Kennedy Memorial Library (Harvard University), the East Building of the National Gallery of Art (Washington, D.C.), and the New York City Convention Center.

Peirce, Charles Sanders (1839–1914) Peirce possessed an intellect of tremendous scope but is best known for his work in logic and philosophy. He was a metaphysician, who evolved a theory of basic reality; he was a theoretician of the nature of chance and continuity; he was a mathematician, who contributed to the development of linear algebra; he was a logician, who was among the creators of the algebra of logic and other systems basic to modern logic; he was a psychologist, who speculated on many of the bases of human motivation; and he was a pioneering semiotician, who investigated the nature of language and meaning. Peirce even made early contributions to computer theory. Many students of intellectual history consider Pierce the single most original thinker the nation ever produced.

Penn, William (1644–1718) An English Quaker, Penn secured a charter in 1681 to found a new proprietary colony in America. Called Pennsylvania (in honor of his father), the colony offered religious toleration (including refuge for the universally persecuted Quakers), a significant degree of democracy, and a commitment to fair and peaceful relations with the local Indians. The "Frame of Government" Penn drew up for the colony is considered a precursor of the U.S. Constitution and Bill of Rights.

Perot, H. Ross (1930–) Perot made a fortune in the computer and data-processing business and used part of his wealth in 1992 to finance his independent run for the White House. He attracted an extraordinarily large following, which demonstrated the widespread dissatisfaction of the American electorate with both the Republican and Democratic parties. Even though Perot dropped out of the race from July to October, he captured 19 percent of the popular vote in November—the best performance by any independent candidate in U.S. history. Running again in 1996 as the candidate of the Reform Party (which he founded in 1995), Perot captured a diminished but still respectable 8 percent of the popular vote.

Perry, Matthew C. (1794–1858) President Millard Fillmore commissioned Perry in 1852 to lead a naval expedition to persuade Japan to open diplomatic relations with the United States. Perry concluded that the only way to end Japanese isolationism was to intimidate the government with a display of naval force. Accordingly, he boldly sailed into fortified Uraga harbor on July 8, 1853, and effectively extorted a treaty. This ushered the United States onto an equal footing with Britain, France, and Russia in the economic exploitation of Asia.

Perry, Oliver Hazard (1785–1819) During a critical phase of the War of 1812, Oliver Hazard Perry quickly constructed an inland U.S. naval fleet and, on September 10, 1813, used it to defeat the Royal Navy flotilla in the Battle of Lake Erie. The victory cut off the British army's waterborne supply route and enabled General William Henry Harrison to win, on land, the crucial Battle of the Thames (in Ontario, Canada). Having triumphed on Lake Erie, Perry sent a famous dispatch to Harrison: "We have met the enemy, and they are ours."

Pershing, John J. (1860–1948) In 1906, John J. "Black Jack" Pershing (his nickname was conferred when he commanded a regiment of black cavalrymen) was personally promoted in one leap from captain to brigadier general by President Theodore Roosevelt. When the U.S. entered World War I in 1917, Pershing was chosen to command the AEF, all of the land forces sent overseas to fight the war. Pershing virtually created the AEF, and he successfully resisted French and British attempts to preempt command of the force. Emerging victorious from the war, he was promoted to the specially created rank of general of the armies (six stars), the highest military rank ever conferred on an American officer.

Phillips, Wendell (1811–1884) A prominent attorney, Phillips became the most popular and persuasive anti-slavery lecturer in the years leading up to the Civil War. His oratory electrified audiences and galvanized the abolition movement, earning him a national reputation as the greatest orator of the era.

Pierce, Franklin (1804–1869) Pierce was elected president in 1852 on the Democratic ticket and served through 1857. He proved a weak chief executive, who evaded the difficult issues surrounding slavery. This contributed to the nation's inexorable drift toward civil war.

Pike, Zebulon (1779–1813) During 1805–1807 Lieutenant Zebulon Pike led important explorations into the American West. His report on the military weakness of Spanish-held Santa Fe whetted the appetite of U.S. expansionists and helped pave the way to the U.S.-Mexican War years later. Pike was killed in action during the War of 1812. Pikes Peak (in Colorado) was named in his honor.

Pinchot, Gifford (1865–1946) Pinchot was an American naturalist trained in France, Switzerland, Germany, and Austria in forestry techniques. His work at Biltmore, the North Carolina estate of George W. Vanderbilt, in the 1890s was the first application of scientific forestry in the United States. In 1898, Pinchot was named the first chief of the federal agency that became the U.S. Forest Service. Under Presidents William McKinley, Theodore Roosevelt, and William Howard Taft, Pinchot instituted scientific forest development and conservation. He was one of the nation's major environmental scientists.

Pinckney, Charles (1757–1824) A South Carolina delegate to the 1787 Constitutional Convention at Philadelphia, Pinckney presented a thorough plan of the federal government, which significantly influenced the Constitution. It is believed that Pinckney played a major role in shaping the style and form as well as the content of the Constitution.

Pinckney, Charles Cotesworth (1746–1825) The cousin of Charles Pinckney, C. C. Pinckney fought in the American Revolution and, in 1796, was appointed U.S. minister to

France. Refused recognition by the Directory (the French revolutionary government), he was joined in 1797 by John Marshall and Elbridge Gerry in an effort to establish diplomatic relations with the new government. French negotiators (in Pinckney's correspondence called "X,Y, and Z") solicited a bribe in return for official recognition. Pinckney indignantly refused, and the resulting "X, Y, Z Affair" triggered an undeclared naval war with France to protect U.S. neutrality rights and rights of navigation on the high seas. Pinckney's steadfastness was a key to the defense of U.S. sovereignty in the earliest days of the republic.

Plath, Sylvia (1932–1963) Plath enjoyed early academic and literary success, but was plagued by suicidal depression. Her most characteristic mature work—confessional poems focusing on alienation, death, and suicide, with strong feminist undertones—were little appreciated in her lifetime, but were increasingly widely read within years after her suicide and came to be regarded as milestones in modern women's literature.

Pocahontas (1595–1617) Pocahontas was the pet name (it meant "frolicsome") of Matoaka, daughter of the important sachem Powhatan (Wahunsonacock), leader of some 30 tribes that lived near the Jamestown (Virginia) settlement of the English. Pocahontas was a young girl in 1607 when she saved the life of the colony's military leader, Captain John Smith—reportedly laying her head atop the captive Smith's to prevent him from being brained. Based on this incident, Pocahontas entered into romantic American folklore, literature, visual art, and even opera. She was an informal goodwill ambassador between the Indians and the colonists. She married colonist John Rolfe, with whom she traveled to

England, where she was presented at the court of James I. She died in England of smallpox.

Poe, Edgar Allan (1809–1849) Long regarded as one of the nation's most important writers, Poe struggled with poverty lifelong. His dark-hued, melodic lyrics earned him little money or recognition—although his best-known poem, "The Raven" (1845) did win a literary prize—and his short fiction, ranging from tales of terror to the first detective story ("The Murders in the Rue Morgue," 1841)—did not receive wide recognition until after his death. In addition to his poetry and fiction, Poe was a major literary critic—although his criticism was frequently colored by personal prejudice.

Polk, James K. (1795–1849) Polk was elected on the Democratic ticket in 1844 and served as president from 1845 to 1849. With the party torn among Martin Van Buren, Lewis Cass, and James Buchanan, Polk emerged as a compromise candidate. Because he was relatively obscure, he was referred to as a "dark horse." During the Polk administration, Texas was annexed, and the United States fought the U.S.-Mexican War—referred to by those who opposed it as "Mr. Polk's War." As a result of victory in the war, the United States acquired the Southwest, including California.

Pollock, Jackson (1912–1956) Paul Jackson Pollock—known as Jackson Pollock—made a radical break with accepted conventions of painting by developing "action" techniques, creating painting through free-associative gestures, typically using his brushes as sticks, from which the paint was dripped onto the canvas rather than applied with the bristles. Pollock's action paintings impress the viewer as transcriptions of pure energy, and his work is considered some of the most important in 20th-century art.

Ponce de León, Juan (1460–1521) This Spanish conquistador and explorer founded Caparra, the oldest settlement in Puerto Rico, and in 1513 discovered and explored Florida. His explorations were propelled in large part by a quest for a miraculous rejuvenating natural spring, known as the fountain of youth.

Pontiac (ca. 1720–1769) An Ottawa chief, Pontiac became a major intertribal leader when he organized Indians in the region of the Great Lakes to resist the encroachment of white settlers at the end of the French and Indian War. Pontiac's Rebellion began on May 7, 1763, when he led a raid on Fort Detroit. It continued until 1766, when the intertribal alliances fell apart.

Popé (died 1692) On August 10, 1680, this medicine man from the Tewa pueblo led a meticulously planned and coordinated revolt by Native American pueblos against the Spanish overlords. The rebellion culminated in the invasion of Santa Fe (New Mexico) on August 15. The Spanish did not regain control of Santa Fe until 1692 and of all the pueblos until 1696.

Porter, Cole (1891–1964) Porter composed for the musical stage, creating tunes and lyrics of consummate wit and worldly sophistication. Many of his songs became standards, including "Night and Day," "I Get a Kick Out of You," "Begin the Beguine," "I've Got You Under My Skin," "In the Still of the Night," "Just One of Those Things," "Let's Do It," and "I Love Paris."

Porter, Edwin S. (1869/70–1941) Born in Scotland, Porter immigrated to the United States and worked in Thomas Edison's workshop-laboratory from 1895 to 1911. Edison, who invented all of the basic technical elements of filmmaking, chose Porter to exploit his inventions by creating films. With considerable artistic instinct and skill, Porter brought narrative drama to film and was especially adept at exploiting point of view and dramatic editing. Porter's two major pioneering productions were the first U.S. documentary, the 1903 *Life of an American Fireman,* and the first true narrative film, *The Great Train Robbery,* also produced in 1903.

Porter, Katherine Anne (1890–1980) Texas-born Porter specialized in creating beautifully wrought, richly textured, emotionally insightful long short stories that are, in effect, miniature novels. From the 1930s on, she enjoyed great critical acclaim, but did not command a large popular audience until the publication of her long-anticipated full-length novel, *Ship of Fools,* in 1962. A bestseller, it was made into a major film in 1965.

Post, Emily (1872–1960) Post was a regular contributor to magazines in the early 20th century and also wrote light fiction. In 1922, her publisher asked her to write a guide to etiquette. She produced that year *Etiquette in Society, in Business, in Politics, and at Home,* which was an immediate bestseller and was frequently updated. Post became an etiquette columnist and radio commentator, and she was unchallenged through much of the 20th century as the arbiter of good manners in America.

Pound, Ezra (1885–1972) Pound was a challenging modern poet who promoted the work of other modernists, including

William Butler Yeats, James Joyce, Ernest Hemingway, Robert Frost, D.H. Lawrence, and T.S. Eliot. His influence on modern literature—including modern American literature—was therefore profound. During World War II, this Idaho-born poet lived in Italy and made pro-fascist broadcasts. He was arrested after the war on charges of treason and confined to a Washington, D.C.-area asylum until 1958.

Powell, Adam Clayton, Jr. (1908–1972) The son of a pastor and a pastor himself, Powell became the first black man to serve on the New York City Council in 1941. He went on in 1945 to become the U.S. representative from Harlem and served 11 terms in Congress as a champion of civil rights legislation. Powell was sued in the early 1960s by a woman who claimed he had wrongly accused her of collecting police graft. He was cited for contempt of court in 1966 for refusing to pay damages, and the following year the House voted to deprive him of his seat. Reelected nevertheless in 1968, he lost his House seniority and, after defeat in the 1970 Democratic primary, retired.

Powell, Colin (1937–) Powell was the son of Jamaican immigrants and grew up in Harlem and the Bronx. He joined the army after graduating from the City College of New York in 1958, served two tours in Vietnam, then had a series of political positions in the White House and Pentagon. President Ronald Reagan appointed Powell deputy director of the Office of Management and Budget in 1987, and in 1989 President George H. W. Bush nominated him as chairman of the Joint Chiefs of Staff. He came to public attention for his leading role in the Persian Gulf War (1990–1991). George W. Bush appointed him secretary of state in 2001. In 2003, Powell presented to the United Nations the American case for going to war with Iraq. He resigned at the conclusion of Bush's first term.

Powell, John Wesley (1834–1902) Despite having lost an arm in the Civil War, Powell was an intrepid explorer of the American Southwest, especially the Grand Canyon and the Colorado River. From 1871 to 1879, he led a federal geologic and geographic survey of western lands, in the process establishing many of the fundamental practices of geology. As an ethnologist, Powell published the first classification of American Indian languages. Appointed the first director of the U.S. Bureau of Ethnology (1879) and director of the U.S. Geological Survey (1881–1892), Powell was also author of *Report on the Lands of the Arid Region of the United States* (1878), a major landmark in the study of ecology.

Powers, Francis Gary (1929–1977) Employed by the CIA as a pilot, Powers was captured on May 1, 1960, when his U-2 spy plane was shot down over the Soviet Union. The resulting "U-2 Affair" exacerbated the Cold War between the U.S. and the USSR, prompting the cancellation of a major summit meeting between President Dwight D. Eisenhower and Soviet premier Nikita Khrushchev. Tried and convicted of espionage, Powers was sentenced to 10 years in prison, but was exchanged in 1962 for Soviet spy Rudolf Abel.

Powhatan (died 1618) Wahunsonacock, called Powhatan by the English, was the sachem of more than 30 tribes, representing 128 villages with some 9,000 inhabitants living in territory from the Potomac River to the Great Dismal Swamp. Although this powerful chief initially opposed the settlement of the English colony at Jamestown in 1607, he soon established a friendly trading relationship with it. Possibly credible legend has it that his change of heart was due to the intercession of his daughter Pocahontas. Whatever his motives, his cordial treatment of the English was critical to the survival of the struggling settlement.

Prescott, William Hickling (1796–1859) Prescott is best remembered for his monumental *History of the Conquest of Mexico* (1843) and *History of the Conquest of Peru* (1847). He based his work on careful reading of original documents and strict analysis of evidence. His great gift as a historian was to combine this "scientific" approach with a major literary talent to produce histories that have endured both as history and literature for more than 150 years.

Presley, Elvis (1935–1977) Presley was born to a poor family in Tupelo, Mississippi, and moved with them to Memphis when he was in his teens. He auditioned for local record producer Sam Phillips, who, in 1954, issued Presley's version of the blues classic "That's All Right Mama." It was the birth of "rockabilly"—a fusion of rock and roll and country and western with the African-American blues tradition—and soon took the country by storm. On September 9, 1956, Presley sang on the *Ed Sullivan Show*, the most influential variety TV program of the 1950s. From that point until his death (except for an interval of military service), Presley was the most popular of rock and roll performers, achieving status as a pop culture icon—feared by parents and adored by young fans.

Pulitzer, Joseph (1847–1911) Born in Hungary, Pulitzer immigrated to the United States in 1864 to fight in the Civil War. He became a German-language reporter after the war, bought into the St. Louis paper for which he worked, sold his share at a profit, and repeated the process with another paper. By 1878, he was publishing the city's most important (English-language) daily, and in 1883 he moved to New York, where he purchased the *World* and transformed it into the city's leading paper. Pulitzer engaged in a fierce circulation war with rival William Randolph Hearst in the late 1890s, giving rise to the era of "yellow journalism." Pulitzer established many of the practices of modern journalism. He posthumously endowed the Columbia University School of Journalism and the Pulitzer Prize for excellence in journalism and other creative fields.

Pullman George Mortimer (1831–1897) Pullman's "Pioneer" sleeping car appeared in 1865 and transformed long-distance rail travel, creating great profit for the railroads and making Pullman a vast fortune. He became a major industrialist, who attempted to control every aspect of his employees' lives, building the quasi-utopian town of Pullman (now a neighborhood on Chicago's South Side), in which his employees were obliged to live. Pullman's extreme paternalism became a subject of great controversy and conflict between the forces of capital and labor.

Pynchon, Thomas (1937–) Pynchon created novels with a strong element of science fiction and fantasy that explore the alienated human condition in modern post-industrial society. His favorite metaphors are drawn from modern physics and often center on the concept of entropy, the inevitable approach of universal chaos. His masterpiece, the 1973 *Gravity's Rainbow*, set in Germany after World War II, is a strange, darkly humorous vision of a modern apocalypse. Widely acclaimed, Pynchon has remained personally aloof, as enigmatic as his novels.

Quantrill, William (1837–1865) Quantrill was a career criminal who, at the outbreak of the Civil War, organized a cutthroat band of guerrillas loosely attached to the Confederate Army. On August 21, 1863, his guerrillas raided Lawrence, Kansas, killing at least 150 residents and burning much of the town. In October of the same year, they put on Union uniforms and ambushed a Union detachment at Baxter Springs, Kansas, killing 90 soldiers. Quantrill was finally gunned down on June 6, 1865, during a Kentucky raid.

Quayle, Dan (1947–) James Danforth Quayle was the scion of a prominent Indianapolis family who served two terms in the House of Representatives (1977–1981) and was twice elected to the Senate (in 1980 and 1986). Tapped by George H. W. Bush as his running mate in 1988, Quayle was inaugurated as vice president in 1989. Despite his political experience, Quayle was seen as an intellectual lightweight, a reputation that he was never able to live down.

Raleigh, Sir Walter (1554?–1618) A colorful courtier in the court if Elizabeth I, Sir Walter Raleigh organized and sponsored an English colony on Roanoke Island, in what is today North Carolina's Outer Banks. The colony was established in August 1585, but was quickly abandoned. In July 1587, another contingent of 150 colonists arrived to reestablish the settlement, only to vanish, leaving the word *Croatoan* carved into a tree as their only trace. Raleigh never visited the colony himself.

Randolph, A. Philip (1889–1979) Randolph was an early civil rights leader who sought racial equality primarily through organizing black labor, beginning with the

Brotherhood of Sleeping Car Porters, of which he became president in 1925. Against much white opposition, Randolph fashioned the Brotherhood into the first successful black trade union. Shortly before U.S. entry into World War II, he persuaded President Franklin D. Roosevelt to issue an executive order (June 25, 1941) barring discrimination in defense industries and federal bureaus. After the war, Randolph founded the League for Nonviolent Civil Disobedience against Military Segregation and persuaded President Harry S. Truman to desegregate the armed forces (July 26, 1948).

Randolph, Edmund (1753–1813) Randolph was a prominent Virginia lawyer and pro-independence politician. In 1787, he was a delegate to the Constitutional Convention, at which he proposed the "Virginia Plan" (the basis for the bicameral Congress) and was a member of the committee that drafted the document. He withheld his own signature from the finished Constitution because he believed it provided insufficient protection of the rights of states and individuals; nevertheless, he exercised his powerful influence to persuade Virginia to ratify it. Randolph served in George Washington's cabinet, first as attorney general and then as secretary of state.

Rankin, Jeannette (1880–1973) Rankin was elected the first woman member of Congress, serving as a representative from Montana from 1917 to 1919 and from 1941 to 1943. She was a feminist crusader and an absolute pacifist. In 1917, she was one of only 49 members to vote against the declaration of war against Germany (World War I) and in 1941 was the only member not to vote "yea" on the declaration against Japan (World War II).

Rauschenberg, Robert (1925–) Rauschenberg burst onto the modern art scene with radical all-white paintings—essentially blank surfaces—in 1951, which were followed by a series of "Black Paintings" and "Red Paintings," which incorporated found objects attached to the canvas. Increasingly, Rauschenberg added three-dimensional found objects to his paintings, completely obliterating the distinction between painting and sculpture. Because Rauschenberg's assemblages often featured the detritus of popular culture, he is credited as a forerunner of Pop Art. As his work challenges the traditional distinction between sculpture and painting, so it raises questions of just what it is that constitutes art.

Rayburn, Sam (1882–1961) Texas Democrat Rayburn served in the U.S. House of Representatives from 1913 to 1961, 17 of those years as speaker. A champion of Franklin Roosevelt's New Deal, he was a mentor to generations of young members of Congress and was valued by four presidents—FDR, Truman, Eisenhower, and Kennedy—as a blunt and knowledgeable adviser.

Reagan, Ronald W. (1911–2004) Ronald Reagan grew up in small-town Illinois. After fulfilling his initial ambition to be a radio sports announcer, he went to Hollywood and became a popular B-level actor. When his film career waned, he worked on television. Reagan's presidency of the Screen Actors Guild piqued his interest in politics, and although he had been a Democrat for much of his life, his increasing attraction to a conservative orientation during the 1950s drew him to the Republican Party and, in particular, to its Conservative wing. In 1966, he defeated the popular Democratic incumbent Pat Brown for the governorship of California and served two terms. He was nominated as the

Republican presidential candidate in 1980, then easily defeated incumbent Jimmy Carter. Reagan's was an affable, optimistic White House presence, which exuded a confidence reminiscent of Franklin Roosevelt. He introduced a new patriotism and a new approach to the economy, which favored business, cut taxes, and diminished the welfare state. In foreign policy, Reagan was widely credited with bringing about the downfall of Soviet communism.

Red Cloud (1822–1909) Chief of the Oglala Teton Sioux, Red Cloud led, during 1865–1867, a highly successful resistance to the federal government's attempt to develop the Bozeman Trail as a through route to the goldfields of Montana. Thanks to Red Cloud's efforts, the government concluded the Treaty of Fort Laramie (1868), which closed the trail and recognized various Indian rights. It was a rare triumph for Native Americans.

Reeb, James (1927–1965) Born in Wichita, Kansas, Reeb was a white minister of the Unitarian church, who participated in a Southern Christian Leadership Conference (SCLC) demonstration in Selma, Alabama, in 1965. He was among the demonstrators attacked by a white mob on March 8, a date known as Bloody Sunday. Savagely beaten and clubbed, Reeb sustained severe head trauma and died in the hospital on March 10. His grisly death reverberated through the nation, raised the northern white consciousness, and increased the volume of condemnation against the racism of the South.

Reed, John (1887–1920) Reed grew up in a privileged Portland (Oregon) family and became active as a journalist covering leftwing politics. He increasingly made the transition from reportage to active participation, and, becoming a personal friend of V. I. Lenin, lived in Russia during the Bolshevik Revolution of 1917. He returned to the United States and reported on the revolution in his most celebrated work, *Ten Days That Shook the World* (1919). When the U.S. government indicted him for treason, Reed fled to the Soviet Union, where he succumbed to typhus. The Soviets buried him in a place of honor beside the Kremlin wall.

Rehnquist, William (1924–2005) Rehnquist was a Phoenix, Arizona, attorney from 1953 to 1969, active in conservative Republican politics. President Richard M. Nixon appointed him an assistant attorney general in 1969 and nominated him to the U.S. Supreme Court in 1971. Citing his hostility toward civil rights, Senate liberals tried unsuccessfully to defeat the nomination. His steadfast conservatism on the court prompted President Ronald W. Reagan to nominate him as chief justice in 1986. Rehnquist dissented from the high court's reaffirmation of abortion rights and its protection of gay rights.

Remington, Eliphalet (1793–1861) Born in England, Remington immigrated to the Utica, New York, area with his family in 1800. In 1816, young Remington fashioned his first flintlock at his blacksmith father's forge. The gun greatly impressed neighbors, who ordered copies—and thus Remington found himself in the firearms business. He built his first factory in 1828, and the Remington company went on to become the principal firearms supplier to the U.S. military, through the Civil War in the 19th century and the two world wars of the 20th.

Remington, Frederic (1861–1909) Trained in eastern art schools, Remington traveled throughout the American West, painting and sculpting the familiar figures of the region:

Indians, cowboys, soldiers, and horses—always in action, often in combat.

Revere, Paul (1735–1818) Paul Revere learned the art of silversmithing from his father, a Huguenot refugee who had settled in Boston. Widely praised as a great artisan, Revere prospered—his work is much prized today—but it was for his daring performance as a courier for Boston's revolutionary Committee of Public Safety that he is even better remembered. On the night of April 18, 1775, he rode through Boston and environs to warn residents that the British, en route to Lexington and Concord, were coming. Thus roused, the Patriot militia was able to offer stiff resistance—and the American Revolution began. Revere's deed entered into American historical consciousness largely through the 1863 ballad, "Paul Revere's Ride," by Henry Wadsworth Longfellow.

Rice, Condoleezza (1954–) On January 26, 2005, when she replaced Colin Powell, Condoleezza Rice became the first African-American woman to serve as secretary of state. She came to the office after a distinguished career as a political scientist and after having served as President George W. Bush's national security adviser. Earlier, she had served President George H. W. Bush as an expert on Soviet affairs. As secretary of state, Rice proved controversial because of her role in the U.S. war in Iraq (2003–).

Richardson, Elliot (1920–1999) A prominent attorney and politician, Richardson had the distinction of being the only person to serve in four Cabinet posts in U.S. history: as Secretary of Health, Education, and Welfare (1970–1973), Secretary of Defense (January–May 1973), Attorney General (May 24–October 1973), and Secretary of Commerce

(1976–1977), but it is for his role in the Watergate affair that he is best remembered. On October 20, 1973, President Nixon ordered Attorney General Richardson to fire Watergate Special Prosecutor Archibald Cox (who demanded that President Nixon turn over tape recordings of Oval Office conversations). Richardson resigned rather than obey the order. Richardson's second-in-command, Deputy Attorney General William Ruckelshaus, also refused to fire Cox, and resigned, whereupon the president called on U.S. Solicitor General Robert Bork (a staunch conservative) to fire Cox. The sequence of resignations and firings was dubbed the "Saturday Night Massacre" and ensured Nixon's downfall.

Rickey, Branch (1881–1885) In 1947, as president and general manager of the Brooklyn Dodgers baseball team, Branch Rickey concluded a contract with Jackie Robinson, who thus became the first African American to play on a modern major league team. Before this, professional ball had been strictly segregated, with black players restricted to the Negro Leagues. By "crossing the color line" in professional baseball, Rickey and Robinson provided a spark that helped ignite a movement toward racial integration on a national scale.

Rickover, Hyman G. (1900–1986) Hyman Rickover was a U.S. Navy officer who championed and directed the development of the world's first nuclear-powered ship's engines and the first nuclear-powered submarine, the *USS Nautilus*, which was launched in 1954. In addition to fathering the nuclear navy, Rickover was a major advocate of harnessing atomic energy for peaceful purposes.

Ridgway, Matthew B. (1895–1993) Matthew Bunker Ridgway commanded the 82nd Airborne Division during World War

II and, with it, planned and executed the first major airborne (paratroop) assault in U.S. military history during the Sicily campaign in July 1943. Airborne assault became a major tactic in World War II and subsequent conflicts. Ridgway also served as commander of the Eighth Army in the Korean War and in 1951 succeeded Douglas MacArthur as overall commander of U.S. and United Nations forces in Korea.

Riesman, David (1909–2002) Riesman's *The Lonely Crowd: A Study of the Changing American Character* (1950) was a groundbreaking, provocative, and highly influential study of the urban middle class of postwar America. Riesman analyzed and defined the sense of individual alienation among the dominant class in America, which (as he saw it) emphasized conformity at the expense of self-fulfillment and the development of deep interpersonal relationships.

Riis, Jacob A. (1849–1914) After immigrating from Denmark, Riis became a journalist in New York. He explored the slums of the city's Lower East Side and published, in 1890, *How the Other Half Lives*, a dramatic combination of text and photographs documenting life in those slums—a life virtually unknown to the city's (and the nation's) prosperous middle class. His book stirred the American conscience and spurred legislation aimed at slum clearance and general urban social reform.

Robbins, Jerome (1918–1998) Robbins was born Jerome Rabinowitz in New York City. After briefly studying chemistry at New York University, he followed his true passion, the dance, and joined what is now the American Ballet Theater in 1940. He debuted as a choreographer in 1944 with Leonard Bernstein's ballet *Fancy Free*, which was a tremendous popular and critical success. Robbins went on to choreograph many modern ballets, Broadway musicals, and Hollywood movies. His genius was in his integration of colloquial and popular American dance into ballet.

Robertson, Pat (1930–) Pat Robertson emerged in the 1960s and 1970s as a leading evangelical Christian broadcaster and a prime mover of the so-called Christian Right, a movement that promotes conservative Christian "values" in American politics and that is criticized by some for violating the Constitutional separation of church and state. In addition to having founded and operated many Christian/political organizations and corporations, Robertson hosts *The 700 Club,* a very successful Christian television talk show. Robertson ran unsuccessfully in the 1988 presidential primaries and is a major supporter of the Republican Party. He is a vocal and controversial opponent of abortion and gay rights.

Robeson, Paul (1898–1976) Robeson earned a law degree from Columbia University in 1923, but, as a black man, found little opportunity to practice and became an actor. He was closely associated with the playwright Eugene O'Neill, appearing in O'Neill's *All God's Chillun Got Wings* (1924) and *The Emperor Jones* (1924), which made him a star. Robeson was also one of the great baritones of the 20th century. He brought the Negro spiritual to white audiences and became internationally famous in the role of Joe, singing "Ol' Man River" in Jerome Kern's epoch-making musical *Show Boat.* Beginning in the 1930s, Robeson became a left-wing political activist, for which his career suffered.

Robinson, Jackie (1919–1972) On April 15, 1947, Jackie Robinson walked onto Ebbets Field as a Brooklyn Dodger, the first black man to play in Major League baseball. He had been signed by Dodgers president and manager Branch Rickey and endured racial slurs and threats of violence to compile an extraordinary record as an infielder and outfielder from 1947 through 1956. Playing offense, he led the National League in stolen bases and won the 1949 batting championship with a .342 average.

Rockefeller, John D. (1839–1937) Rockefeller got into the oil business in 1863 and founded Standard Oil in 1870. He rapidly built the company into the first great U.S. business "trust" by buying out all competitors and vertically integrating all aspects of the oil business, from drilling, to refining, to transporting, to marketing. Rockefeller's aggressive business practices provoked a federal response in the form of the Sherman Antitrust Act (1890). Ruthless as a capitalist, Rockefeller was also one of the world's great philanthropists, contributing some $500 million to create the University of Chicago, the Rockefeller Foundation, and other charitable institutions.

Rockefeller, Nelson (1908–1979) From the late 1950s through much of the 1970s, Rockefeller was the embodiment of the liberal wing of the Republican Party and tried to be a moderating and unifying force in the nation's often divisive politics. He failed in three bids to secure the Republican presidential nomination, and by 1976 was sidelined, as the Republican Party became increasingly the party of conservatism. Rockefeller served four terms as New York governor (1959–1973) and was appointed vice president in the administration of President Gerald Ford (1974–1977).

Rockwell, Norman (1894–1978) During nearly a half-century, Norman Rockwell created 317 covers for *The Saturday Evening Post,* most depicting homely scenes embodying "traditional" American values—mom and apple pie—yet without excessive sentimentality and always with wry humor and consummate skill.

Rodgers, Richard (1902–1979) From the 1920s through the end of the 1950s, Richard Rodgers was one of the leading composers of the American musical, producing with lyricists Lorenz Hart and Oscar Hammerstein II some of the most popular and best Broadway shows of all time, including *Oklahoma!* (1943), *Carousel* (1945), *South Pacific* (1949), *The King and I* (1951), *The Flower Drum Song* (1958), and *The Sound of Music* (1959).

Roebling, John Augustus (1806–1869) Born in Germany, Roebling immigrated to the United States when he was 25 and made a fortune as a manufacturer of wire and cable. He used the cable in the design of suspension bridges, including two in Pittsburgh, one at Niagara Falls, and one across the Ohio River between Cincinnati, Ohio, and Covington, Kentucky. His masterpiece design was the Brooklyn Bridge. Injured during the earliest phase of construction, he succumbed to tetanus, and his work was carried through to completion by his son, Washington Augustus Roebling.

Roebling, Washington Augustus (1837–1926) A German-born American civil engineer, Roebling directed construction of the Brooklyn Bridge, an engineering masterpiece of great beauty, which he had designed with his father, John Augustus Roebling, who was killed in an early phase of construction. Washington Roebling labored 13 years, from

1869 to 1883, to complete the bridge. Stricken with "the bends" (decompression sickness) after working too long in an underwater caisson, he became a semi-invalid for the rest of his long life.

Rolfe, John (1585–1622?) Rolfe sailed from England to Virginia in 1609, but, because of a shipwreck, did not arrive until 1610. He was the first planter to profit from the cultivation of tobacco, which became Virginia's principal export, but he is most famous for marrying Pocahontas, daughter of the powerful Indian chief Powhatan, on April 5, 1614. The marriage helped to ensure peace between Jamestown and the Indians. Rolfe returned with Pocahontas to England, where he presented her at the court of James I. She was warmly greeted, but, tragically, succumbed to smallpox in March 1617.

Roosevelt, Eleanor (1884–1962) Eleanor Roosevelt married her distant cousin, Franklin Roosevelt, on March 17, 1905, and gave birth to six children (one died in infancy). She was her husband's political partner and, after he was stricken with polio in 1921, was indispensable to his recovery. Throughout FDR's political career, Eleanor Roosevelt was an activist in social and humanitarian causes. After her husband's death in 1945, she served as a United Nations delegate. Eleanor Roosevelt was a woman of great influence, who was internationally admired.

Roosevelt, Franklin D. (1882–1945) Roosevelt was the scion of a prominent New York family who overcame the paralytic effects of polio (contracted in 1921) to become governor of New York and president of the United States for an unprecedented four terms, from 1933 to 1945. Not since Abraham Lincoln had a president faced more or more serious crises in office, beginning with the Great Depression (which he addressed with the New Deal and other social legislation and programs) and World War II (in which he emerged as a great wartime leader). FDR extensively expanded the role and powers of the federal government and was held in great esteem and affection by a majority of the American people. Most historians judge him to be the greatest president of the 20th century.

Roosevelt, Theodore (1858–1919) One of the American giants of the early 20th century, Roosevelt was an author, a rancher, a naturalist, a big game hunter, a soldier, New York City police commissioner, navy secretary, governor of New York, political reformer, vice president, and, from 1901 to 1909, president of the United States. When he entered the Oval Office in 1901 upon the assassination of William McKinley, he expanded the powers of the chief executive and the federal government, championed government intervention for the public interest, favored the rights of labor over big business, fought the "trusts" (monopolistic business practices), championed the Pure Food and Drug Act of 1903, and transformed the nation into a major world power. An ardent conservationist, TR created the National Park system. He initiated construction of the Panama Canal, and was awarded the Nobel Prize for Peace in 1906 for his role in mediating an end to the Russo-Japanese War.

Root, Elihu (1845–1937) Root was secretary of war under William McKinley and Theodore Roosevelt from 1899 to 1903, responsible for creating governments for the territory ceded by Spain to the U.S. as a result of the Spanish-American War (1898) and for reorganizing and reforming the U.S. Army. As Roosevelt's secretary of state from 1905 to 1909, he concluded agreements by which Japan pledged to respect the Open Door Policy in China, and he negotiated arbitration treaties with more than 20 nations. For his contributions to peace and "general world harmony," Root was awarded the Nobel Prize for Peace in 1912.

Roper, Elmo (1900–1971) Roper developed a scientific poll for political and public opinion forecasting.

Rose, Pete (1941–) Nicknamed Charlie Hustle, Rose broke Ty Cobb's record for career hits (4,191) in 1985 and was recognized as well for his all-around skill and enthusiasm at play. Rose's career total of hits was an astronomical 4,256, and he set records for most games played (3,562), most times at bat (14,053), and most seasons with 200 hits or more (10). He was denied a place in the Baseball Hall of Fame as a result of a 1989 baseball commission decision banning him from the game for life because of illegal gambling on the sport.

Rosenberg, Julius (1918–1953), and Ethel Greenglass Rosenberg (1915–1953) On June 19, 1953, Julius Rosenberg and his wife, Ethel, became the first American civilians to be executed for espionage. Julius, a member of the Communist party, had been employed as an engineer by the U.S. Army Signal Corps during World War II. Largely on the basis of testimony by Ethel's brother, David Greenglass, who had worked on the "A-bomb" project at Los Alamos, New Mexico, he and Ethel were found guilty of supplying Soviet agents with nuclear secrets. Deep in the Cold War, their death sentences provoked international protest and polarized American public opinion, but President Eisenhower, convinced of the couple's guilt, refused to commute the sentences. (Soviet documents released in the 1990s suggest that Julius was in fact a spy, but that his wife was substantially innocent. Experts continue to debate the actual value of the secrets leaked.)

Rostow, Walt (1916–2003) As adviser to Presidents Kennedy and Johnson, Rostow argued persuasively for the expansion of the U.S. role in the Vietnam War, continuing to hold this position long after most other highly placed government officials had concluded that the war was unwinnable and advised withdrawal rather than escalation.

Rothko, Mark (1903–1970) Born Marcus Rothkovitch in Russia, Rothko immigrated to the U.S. with his family in 1913. He began painting in 1925, at first in a realistic style, but gradually developed a new, intensely introspective non-objective style, which evolved into color-field painting. Rothko's mature canvases juxtapose large areas of soft, almost contourless colors that appear to hover and gently vibrate in space above the painting. The effect is serene, contemplative, and quietly spiritual, a marked contrast to the prevailing freneticism of Abstract Expressionism.

Rothstein, Arthur (1882/1883–1928) Rothstein straddled the worlds of powerful politicians and powerful crime lords as a Prohibition-era bootlegger and gambler who specialized in influence peddling. It is generally believed that Rothstein arranged the bribery scheme that "fixed" (corrupted) the 1919 World Series in the so-called Black Sox baseball scandal. He was mortally wounded by a gunshot in a poker game on November 4, 1928, and died two days later—without revealing the identity of his assailant.

Rowlandson, Mary (ca. 1637–1710/11) A New England colonist, Rowlandson and her three children were captured by Indians in February 1676 during King Philip's War. Rowlandson and two of her children survived; she was ransomed in May 1676 and the children a little later. Rowlandson wrote an account of her captivity, which was published in 1682 and republished many times. The vivid narrative was avidly and widely read and is today regarded as a valuable account of survival and of Indian life.

Rubin, Jerry (1938–1994) Rubin was a sometime journalist who became a social activist in 1964 when he participated in a protest in Berkeley, California, against a local grocer who refused to hire African Americans. Soon Rubin was leading protests of his own. He became a high-profile protest organizer during the Vietnam War and, with Abbie Hoffman, founded the Yippies (Youth International Party), who offered Pigasus, a pig, as their presidential candidate. Rubin developed protest into a kind of street theater and was tried (as one of the "Chicago 7") for his role in the disruption of 1968 Democratic National Convention.

Ruby, Jack (1911–1967) Born Jacob Rubenstein in Chicago, he changed his name to Jack Ruby in 1947. A small-time mobster, Ruby owned or managed Dallas nightclubs and strip clubs. On November 24, 1963, two days after Lee Harvey Oswald was arrested for the assassination of President John F. Kennedy, Ruby shot Oswald at point-blank range as he was being transferred from police headquarters to a jail. The shooting was televised. Ruby was convicted of murder on March 14, 1964, and sentenced to death, but was subsequently granted a new trial. He died of a pulmonary embolism before the new proceedings began. Ruby's motive has never been determined. Some believe he was hired (perhaps by the Mafia) to silence Oswald, who was part of a conspiracy to assassinate Kennedy. Others believe he sought vengeance on the killer of the president he greatly admired.

Rush, Benjamin (1746–1813) Rush was a pioneering American medical researcher and respected teacher of medicine. He was a pioneer in the field of psychiatry and a crusader for the humane treatment of asylum inmates. He was also a prime mover of the independence movement, a member of the Continental Congress, and a signer of the Declaration of Independence. It was at his instigation that Thomas Paine wrote *Common Sense* (1776), which was an important catalyst for independence.

Rusk, Dean (1909–1994) As secretary of state in the Kennedy and Johnson administrations, Rusk was a committed "cold warrior" (hardline anti-Communist) who supported the Vietnam War and its escalation. Rusk became the lightning rod for much antiwar protest.

Rustin, Bayard (1910–1987) Rustin combined opposition to racial segregation with a commitment to nonviolence and pacifism. He was the principal organizer of the 1963 March on Washington, which was a high point of the Civil Rights movement and occasioned Martin Luther King's great "I Have a Dream" speech.

Ruth, Babe (1895–1948) George Herman "Babe" Ruth started his career in 1914 as a minor league pitcher and was sold to the Boston Red Sox later that first season. He was sold to the New York Yankees in 1920—the team with which he played through 1934. Known as the "Sultan of Swat," his record of 60 home runs in a major-league season (1927) was unbroken until Roger Maris's disputed 1961 record (or Mark McGwire's undisputed 1998 record). He was the first superstar sports celebrity, as famous for his high-living extravagance off the field as for his performance on it. Ruth was an icon of baseball and one of America's most beloved sports figures.

Ryder, Albert Pinkham (1847–1917) In an era of realism, Ryder was a maverick who created dark, mysterious, profoundly spiritual seascapes and landscapes. A recluse, he produced no more than 150 paintings, which became known mostly after his death. He was an American mystic and romantic, his work entirely original and unrelated to any European (or, for that matter, American) predecessors.

Saarinen, Eero (1910–1961) Finnish-born Saarinen was the son of famed architect Eliel Saarinen and immigrated to the United States with his family in 1923. Eero began as a student of sculpture; this profoundly influenced his architecture, which broke with the severe rectilinear lines of the prevailing International School and introduced sweeping curves and a sense of dynamic, organic motion. His masterpiece may well be the controversial Trans World Airlines (TWA) terminal at John F. Kennedy International Airport, New York City (1956–1962).

Sabin, Albert (1906–1993) Born in Bialystock (at the time in Russia, now in Poland), Sabin immigrated to the United States with his parents in 1921. In 1957, he developed an alternative to Jonas Salk's polio vaccine, using a live but weakened virus rather than a killed virus. Administered orally rather than by injection, the new vaccine provided immunity over a longer period than the Salk vaccine.

Sacco, Nicola (1891–1927) Sacco was born in Italy and immigrated to the United States when he was seventeen. He worked in a Massachusetts shoe factory and became a left-wing political activist. On May 5, 1920, Sacco and his friend and fellow leftist Bartolomeo Vanzetti were arrested for the robbery-murders of a shoe factory paymaster and a guard. On flimsy circumstantial evidence, they were convicted in 1921. The case became an international cause célèbre as prominent intellectuals the world over protested that the men had been convicted for their political beliefs. On August 23, 1927, after seven years of appeals and incarceration, Sacco and Vanzetti were executed. Riots broke out in England and Germany, and protestors in Paris bombed the U.S. embassy.

Sage, Russell (1816–1906) Sage worked his way up from grocery store errand boy to a major investor in the nation's developing railroad and telegraph systems, whose growth his management greatly spurred. Sage introduced a key innovation into the U.S. stock market in 1872, "puts and calls"—options to sell or buy a set amount of stock at a set price and within a specified time limit. Working with financier Jay Gould, he used this in his manipulation of stocks. Sage's fortune became the basis of the Russell Sage Foundation, devoted to social research.

Salinger, J. D. (1919–) Salinger created a literary sensation with his 1951 novel *The Catcher in the Rye,* whose troubled adolescent hero, Holden Caulfield, was hailed as a 20th-century Huckleberry Finn, an innocent lost in a corrupt society. The novel struck a chord in the American consciousness that has yet to cease reverberating. Salinger shied away from the celebrity that followed the publication of the novel, wrote only 13 short stories in addition to it, and has lived a secretive life ever since.

Salk, Jonas (1914–1995) The public release of Jonas Salk's polio vaccine on April 12, 1955, ended the scourge of one of the cruelest diseases, which brought death or paralysis to millions—especially children. Celebrated as a medical hero, Salk went on to become director of the Institute for Biological Studies in San Diego, California, which was later named for him: the Salk Institute.

Samoset (ca. 1590 – 1653) Samoset greeted the Pilgrims at Plymouth Colony on March 16, 1621. He spoke English and reportedly said, "Greetings, Englishmen. Do you have any beer?" An Abenaki sagamore (subchief), he introduced the Pilgrims to Squanto, who served as an emissary between the newcomers and the local Indians.

Sandburg, Carl (1878–1967) As a young man, Sandburg worked a variety of odd jobs, including as a newspaper reporter. He burst onto the literary scene in 1914 with his *Chicago Poems,* verses dedicated to urban America and the men and women who built it and worked in it. Sandburg's choice of subject and his muscular free verse drew comparisons with Walt Whitman. Sandburg was also a passionate folklorist, who issued two great folksong collections, *The American Songbag* (1927) and *New American Songbag* (1950). His multivolume biography of Abraham Lincoln (1926–1940) earned the 1940 Pulitzer Prize in history.

Sanger, Margaret (1879–1966) A feminist and nurse, Sanger (who was born Margaret Louisa Higgins) challenged prevailing statutes and morality to found the birth-control movement in the United States. She is generally credited as the originator of the term "birth control" and the concepts associated with it.

Sargent, John Singer (1856–1925) Sargent was born in Italy of American parents and did not come to the United States until 1876. Influenced by the French Impressionists, he created a lush bravura style, which he used to paint elegant portraits of wealth and privilege in America and Europe. His work is a vivid and beautiful evocation of the exuberant Edwardian age on both sides of the Atlantic.

Sarony, Napoleon (1821–1896) Born in Quebec, Canada, Sarony settled in New York City about 1836. He started his career as an illustrator for Currier & Ives, then became a lithographer. By the mid 1860s, he opened a photographic portrait studio and built his career photographing the celebrities of his day, paying them for the privilege and making his money selling the pictures.

Schiavo, Terri (1978–2005) On March 31, 2005, Terri Schiavo died, after her husband, Michael Schiavo, won the right to remove the feeding tube that had sustained her life since she slipped into a coma on February 25, 1990. The Schiavo case had been argued in the courts beginning in 1993. During 2003, Florida governor Jeb Bush, brother of President George W. Bush, intervened against Michael Schiavo, and as state and federal courts repeatedly upheld Michael Schiavo's right as his wife's guardian to remove her feeding tube, Congress, shortly after 12:30 a.m. on March 21, 2005, passed a private bill granting Schiavo's parents the right to continue suing for the maintenance of the feeding tube and to order reinsertion of the feeding tube while the suit was pending. President Bush signed the measure at 1:11 a.m., but a federal district court refused to order the tube reinserted, and the U.S. Supreme Court refused to hear the parents' appeal.

Schine, G. David (1927–1996) Schine was hired by Senator Joseph McCarthy and his special counsel Roy Cohn as an investigative staff member. McCarthy and Cohn's illegal efforts to secure Schine preferential treatment after he was drafted into the army became a focus of the Army-McCarthy Hearings (1954), which were seen by some 20 million television viewers. Schine became a household name in a scandal intensified by a rumored homosexual relationship between him and Cohn.

Schlesinger, Arthur M., Jr. (1917–) Schlesinger was a Harvard history professor, whose Pulitzer Prize-winning *The Age of Jackson* (1946) and *The Age of Roosevelt* (1957–1960) are masterpieces of American history. Schlesinger was no ivory-tower academic, but served as an adviser to Adlai Stevenson and John F. Kennedy. Schlesinger's history of the Kennedy administration, *A Thousand Days: John F. Kennedy in the White House* (1965), also won a Pulitzer Prize.

Schurz, Carl (1829–1906) Schurz was born, raised, and educated in Germany. A participant in the failed German revolution of 1848, he was imprisoned, but escaped and immigrated to the United States (1852). He was an abolitionist and served as a brigadier general of volunteers during the Civil War. After the war, he was an advocate for the rights of liberated slaves. He was a journalist for a time, then served as a U.S. senator from 1869 to 1875. He was secretary of the interior (1877–1881) under Rutherford B. Hayes and pushed for civil-service reform and a more humane Indian policy. In the 1880s, Schurz returned to journalism and the crusade for honest politics.

Schwerner, Michael (1939–1964) With fellow Congress of Racial Equality (CORE) activists James Earl Chaney and Andrew Goodman, Schwerner was murdered by Ku Klux Klan members on June 21, 1964, while working to register black voters in Mississippi. Schwerner was a white New Yorker dedicated to social justice.

Scopes, John T. (1900–1970) A high school teacher, Scopes deliberately violated a Tennessee state law forbidding the teaching of Darwin's Theory of Evolution. In a sensational July 1925 trial that riveted the nation, Scopes was tried. He was defended by an attorney hired by the American Civil Liberties Union, the great Clarence Darrow. Assisting the prosecution was William Jennings Bryan, perennial populist presidential candidate and a committed religious fundamentalist. Found guilty, Scopes was fined an inconsequential sum, but, on appeal, his conviction was reversed on technical grounds.

Scorsese, Martin (1942–) Scorsese emerged in the 1970s as a major American film maker with movies that focused on the violent aspects of American culture. His early masterpiece, *Taxi Driver* (1976), depicted an alienated New York cabbie who sees political assassination as the only alternative to accepting the corruption of modern life.

Scott, Dred (1795–1858) Dred Scott was a slave whose owner had taken him from the slave state of Missouri to the free state of Illinois; Scott therefore sued for his freedom in 1846 on the grounds that his sojourn in free territory had made him free. The case worked its way up to the Supreme Court, whose chief justice, Roger B. Taney, handed down a decision on March 6, 1857, holding that neither slaves nor free blacks were citizens so therefore could not sue in federal court; further, Taney held that the Missouri Compromise (under which suit was brought) was unconstitutional because Congress had no authority to prohibit slavery in territories. By affirming constitutional protection of slavery in all circumstances, the Dred Scott decision made civil war virtually inevitable, since only a constitutional amendment could end slavery—and the slaveholding South would never voluntarily ratify such an amendment.

Scott, Winfield (1876–1866) Scott became a captain of artillery in 1808 and fought heroically in the War of 1812, in the wars associated with the Indian Removal Act (during the 1830s), and in the U.S.-Mexican War (1846–1848). Named commanding general of the U.S. Army in 1841, he served as such until 1861, through the first months of the Civil War. He was the leading American military officer between the Revolution and the Civil War.

Scripps, Edward W. (1854–1926) Scripps founded his first newspaper, the *Penny Press* in Cleveland, Ohio, in 1878, then assembled the first major chain of newspapers in the United States in 1894. By 1909, he owned 34 newspapers in 15 states. In 1902, Scripps also founded the first news syndicate, the Newspaper Enterprise Association, which supplied features, illustrations, and cartoons to newspapers. This evolved into the United Press, which later became United Press International.

Seale, Bobby (1936–) A Dallas-born African-American political activist, Seale broke away from the non-violent civil rights movement led by Martin Luther King, Jr. and advocated militant black empowerment, including the Black

Panther Party, founded in Oakland, California, in 1966. In 1969, Seale was one of the "Chicago 7," seven political activists tried for conspiracy to incite riots during the Democratic national convention of 1968.

Sears, Richard W. (1863–1914) In 1889, R. W. Sears, engaged in the mail-order watch business, founded with A. C. Roebuck a catalog-based general mail-order business, which rapidly grew into the giant of the industry and transformed American retail commerce.

Seeger, Pete (1919–) In the 1940s, Seeger worked as an itinerant folk singer and in 1948 organized the Weavers, a popular folk-singing group that inspired the folk revival of the 1960s, which, in turn, was associated with the counterculture of that era.

Sequoyah (1760?– 1843) Convinced that the secret of the dominance of the white race was their written language, Sequoyah, son of a white trader and a Cherokee woman, created the first written Indian alphabet and language in 1824, effectively committing the Cherokee tongue to writing.

Serra, Junípero (1713–1784) A Spanish Franciscan missionary, Serra founded Mission San Diego, the first California mission, on July 16, 1769. Through 1782, he founded eight more California missions extending the length of Alta (Upper) California and ensuring Spanish control of the region.

Sewall, Samuel (1652–1730) Born in England, Sewall settled in Massachusetts and became a prosperous merchant. He was one of the judges in the infamous Salem witchcraft trials of 1692 and the only judge to admit the error of the 19 executions. Sewall kept a remarkable diary, which provides a window into the life, mind, and aspirations of Puritan New England.

Seward, William H. (1801–1872) Seward was an attorney, politician, and abolitionist who served in the cabinet of Abraham Lincoln as secretary of state. He survived an assassination attempt by one of John Wilkes Booth's co-conspirators and, in 1867, during the administration of Andrew Johnson, negotiated the purchase of Alaska from the czar of Russia. The acquisition was widely mocked as "Seward's folly" by Americans who could see no value in a "frozen wasteland."

Shahn, Ben (1898–1969) Shahn was born in Kaunas, Russia, which is now a part of Lithuania, and immigrated with his family to New York City in 1906. He learned the lithographer's trade and became an artist specializing in strong graphic works that combined elements of realism and abstraction, typically to convey leftist political themes. His later work became more introspective and reflective of his Russian-Jewish heritage.

Shaw, Anna Howard (1847–1919) Born in England, Shaw immigrated with her parents to the United States in 1851. She became a licensed Methodist preacher in 1871 and the first woman minister of the Methodist Protestant Church in 1880. She resigned in 1885 to devote herself full-time to the National American Woman Suffrage Association and the struggle to obtain for women the right to vote.

Shays, Daniel (1747–1825) Responding to economic depression, high taxes, and a wave of frontier property foreclosures, western Massachusetts farmer and American Revolution veteran Daniel Shays led what became known as "Shays's Rebellion" in an effort to prevent western Massachusetts courts and other officials from executing foreclosures. Because the federal government had no army under the Articles of Confederation, Massachusetts governor James Bowdoin appealed to Boston merchants to finance a force of 4,400 volunteers to quell the uprising. Fear of future rebellions spurred Congress to call a convention to draw up new constitution to create a stronger central government.

Shepard, Alan B., Jr. (1923–1998) A naval aviator, Shepard became one of the seven original Mercury astronauts in 1959 and was the first American in space. He was launched on a 15-minute suborbital flight in the *Freedom 7* space capsule on May 5, 1961.

Sheridan, Philip (1831–1888) Sheridan's aggressive leadership under Ulysses S. Grant during the closing year of the Civil War accelerated the Confederate defeat. After the Civil War, he was William Tecumseh Sherman's second in command during the Indian Wars in the American West. He became infamous for allegedly quipping, "The only good Indian is a dead Indian."

Sherman, Roger (1721–1793) Sherman was a Connecticut delegate to the 1787 Constitutional Convention in Philadelphia. When the convention deadlocked over the Virginia Plan (calling for Congressional representation proportionate to state population) versus the New Jersey Plan (calling for equal representation among the states). Sherman's "Great Compromise" proposed equal representation in the Senate and proportional representation in the House of Representatives. With this, the convention moved forward, and the Constitution was offered for ratification.

Sherman, William Tecumseh (1820–1891) During the last year of the Civil War, Sherman was Ulysses S. Grant's top lieutenant. His "March to the Sea" from Atlanta to Savannah in 1864–1865 brought the war to the Confederate civilian population by cutting a wide swath of total ruin. Sherman was a brutal realist who believed the object of war was to create maximum devastation to achieve total victory as rapidly as possible. After the Civil War, he applied this approach to the Indian Wars, often with tragic results.

Short, Walter C. (1880–1949) With his naval counterpart, Admiral Husband E. Kimmel, Lieutenant General Walter Short absorbed most of the blame for unpreparedness during the Japanese attack on Pearl Harbor, December 7, 1941. The attack ended Short's career.

Siegel, Bugsy (1906–1947) Benjamin "Bugsy" Siegel was a major figure in organized crime when, in 1945, using crime syndicate money, he began developing Las Vegas, Nevada, as a gambler's paradise. When cost overruns became excessive, Siegel's backers suspected that he was skimming syndicate money. On June 20, 1947, he was gunned down in his Beverly Hills, California, home.

Simpson, O. J. (1947–) Orenthal James Simpson was a star of the University of Southern California football team (named All-American, 1967–1968) and went on to a stellar professional career as a great running back. After retiring from football, he went on to a sportscasting and acting career. On June 12, 1994, his ex-wife, Nicole Brown Simpson, and her friend Ronald Goldman were brutally stabbed to death. Simpson was accused of the crime and, after a sensational, televised 266-day trial, was found not guilty, despite what the prosecution characterized as a "mountain of evidence" against him. Most African Americans, including those on the jury, believed his defense, that he was the innocent victim of racist Los Angeles police officers determined to frame him for the murder of his white ex-wife and her white friend. The verdict and the public response to it were themselves dramatic evidence of the deep racial divides in American society.

Sinatra, Frank (1915–1998) Francis Albert Sinatra achieved his breakthrough fame in the 1940s, when he became the most popular singer in America and an idol to millions of teenage girl fans known as "bobby soxers." His popularity was somewhat eclipsed in the 1950s by the emergence of rock and roll, but he emerged as a notable screen actor during this period. Toward the end of the decade, he was the nucleus of the Las Vegas "Rat Pack" (with Sammy Davis Jr., Dean Martin, and Joey Bishop), which was considered the height of bon vivant sophistication. Sinatra's artistic career was sometimes overshadowed by his very public personal life, which included ties to the Mafia, yet his enduring legacy is his body of recorded work, and many consider him the greatest American singer of 20th-century popular music.

Sinclair, Harry F. (1876–1956) The founder of Sinclair Oil Corporation (now merged into Atlantic Richfield Company), Sinclair was at the heart of the infamous Teapot Dome scandal of the 1920s, in which Secretary of the Interior Albert Fall gave Sinclair a no-bid lease on a naval oil reserve known as the Teapot Dome in return for a bribe. Sinclair was acquitted on bribery and conspiracy charges, but served 6 1/2 months for contempt of court and contempt of the U.S. Senate.

Sinclair, Upton (1878–1968) Sinclair burst onto the literary scene in 1906 with *The Jungle*, a novel set in the stockyards of Chicago and exposing, in vividly nauseating detail, the sordid practices of the meat-packing industry, which greedily purveyed tainted meat to the American masses. The novel presented the meatpackers as a melodramatic metaphor for the worst of American big business: a heartless monolith willing to sicken or even kill the public for the sake of profit. The book spurred Congress to pass the Pure Food and Drug Act and Meat Inspection Act.

Singer, Isaac Bashevis (1904–1991) Born in Poland, Singer immigrated to the United States in 1935, becoming a citizen in 1943. He wrote novels and short stories in Yiddish (though they became best known to American readers through English translation) and evoked the world of Jewish life in pre-Holocaust Poland as well as the immigrant experience in the United States. Singer received the 1978 Nobel Prize for Literature.

Sirica, John (1904–1992) The undistinguished chief judge of the U.S. District Court for the District of Columbia, Sirica was thrust into the national spotlight when he presided over the trial of the Watergate burglars (Nixon's "Plumbers") in 1973. His demand that President Nixon turn over his tape recordings of White House conversations triggered the Constitutional crisis that precipitated Nixon's downfall and resignation.

Sitting Bull (Tatanka Iyotake, 1831–1890) In youth, Sitting Bull earned a reputation as a fierce warrior and was revered for his bravery, strength, generosity, and wisdom. His fame and influence spread far beyond his own Hunkpapa Sioux tribe, and he became a living legend in both white and red America. With chiefs Crazy Horse and Gall, Sitting Bull led the resistance against the white invasion of the sacred Black Hills after gold was discovered there in 1874. Following the annihilation of Custer's command at the Little Bighorn in 1876, Sitting Bull and his closest followers fled to Canada. Upon his return to the United States in 1881, he was imprisoned for two years and then sent to Standing Rock Reservation. In 1883, he traveled as a performer with Buffalo Bill Cody's Wild West Show. In 1890, Sitting Bull became identified with a Native religious movement known as the Ghost Dance, which whites greatly feared. He was killed during an attempt to arrest him.

Skinner, B. F. (1904–1990) Psycholigist Burrhus Frederic Skinner built on the work of Russian physiologist Ivan Pavlov and American psychologist John B. Watson to create a human psychology based on behaviorism—a system of physiological responses to stimuli in the environment. Praised by some for bringing scientific clarity and rigor to psychology, he was condemned by others for oversimplifying human behavior. In either view, his was undeniably a profound influence on modern psychology and sociology.

Sloan, Alfred P., Jr. (1875–1966) In 1920, when he was vice-president of General Motors (he later became chairman), Sloan introduced a new concept in the marketing of technological goods: planned obsolescence. With the automobile market stagnant by the end of the nineteen-tens and the pace of genuine technological innovation insufficiently rapid to grow the market, Sloan proposed a program of annual stylistic alterations, which (he believed) would give consumers the feeling that the automobile they owned was obsolete and would therefore motivate the purchase of a new model. Planned obsolescence stimulated GM growth, but it also diverted corporate research from significant technological innovation to mere cosmetic change. Later in the century, this would have a profoundly negative effect on the American auto industry.

Sloan, John (1871–1951) Sloan specialized in urban subjects—everyday life in New York—and became identified with painters who engaged similar subjects, collectively called the Ashcan School. It was a reference to the nitty-gritty reality of their work, which was some of the most original in American art.

Smith, Al (1873–1944) Smith worked his way up through city and state politics, gaining election to New York governor four times. He was nominated as the Democratic candidate for president in 1928—the first Roman Catholic ever to run for the office. Although urban America favored him, the rural districts sent Republican Herbert Hoover to the White House.

Smith, Bessie (1898?–1937) Elizabeth—Bessie—Smith was born and raised in the South, which she toured as a singer. In the 1920s, she settled in Philadelphia and made her first blues recordings, which, although intended for the "race market" (black audiences), crossed over into the white mainstream and were big hits. Smith took her blues style into various jazz sessions with most of the great musicians of the 1930s before she succumbed to alcoholism.

Smith, Henry Nash (1906–1986) Born in Texas, Smith became a professor of American literature, but branched out to take an interdisciplinary approach, encompassing literature, history, folklore, cultural studies, art, and psychology to create a new academic field, American Studies. His 1950 book, *Virgin Land: The American West as Symbol and Myth*, catapulted Smith to national recognition and is considered the first American Studies text.

Smith, Jedediah Strong (1798–1831) Smith was a mountain man—a fur trader—who, in 1826, became the first American to enter California from the east and return overland.

Smith, John (1580–1631) Smith was a soldier of fortune who served as military leader of the English settlers who founded Jamestown, Virginia, on May 14, 1607. His efforts were critical to the struggling colony's survival, and he assured himself a place in history through his writings, including the 1624 *Generall Historie of Virginia, New England, and the Summer Isles*, which contains the first account of how Pocahontas, daughter of the powerful Indian sachem Powhatan, saved Smith's life—a tale (perhaps true) that entered American folklore, legend, and literature.

Smith, Joseph (1805–1844) On April 6, 1830, at Fayette, New York, Joseph Smith founded the Church of Jesus Christ of Latter-Day Saints (Mormon Church) with 30 members, basing its theology on *The Book of Mormon*, a scripture he had published earlier in the year as his translation of golden tablets he claimed to have unearthed in 1827 at Palmyra, New York. Smith and his fellow Mormons were persecuted everywhere they attempted to settle, and on June 27, 1844, Smith and his brother were murdered in the Mormon community of Nauvoo, Illinois, by outsiders. After this, most of the Mormons followed Brigham Young to a new settlement on the Salt Lake in Utah.

Sobell, Morton (1917–) Sobell was the son of Russian immigrants. He became an engineer for General Electric and Reeves Electronics, working on military contracts. With Ethel and Julius Rosenberg, he was tried in 1951 for passing atomic bomb secrets to the Soviets. Found guilty, he was sentenced to 30 years and was released in 1969.

Solomon, Susan (1956–) Solomon was a chemist working for the National Oceanic and Atmospheric Administration in 1986 when she led an expedition to Antarctica to discover why the depletion of the earth's ozone layer was happening faster than expected and happening especially fast in Antarctica. Solomon discovered high levels of chlorine oxide in the stratosphere over Antarctica, which proved that the human use of chloroflourocarbons (CFCs)—abundant in refrigerants and aerosol products—was largely responsible for the depletion, which threatened the earth's environment. The discovery led to a ban on CFCs—and a great improvement in the condition of the ozone layer.

Soto, Hernando de (ca. 1496/97–1542) This Spanish explorer and conquistador was one of the conquerors of Central America and Peru, then ventured into the region that is now the southeastern United States. He explored Florida, Georgia, the Carolinas, and Tennessee, reaching the Mississippi River (at present-day Memphis) on May 21, 1541—the first white man to do so. Stricken by fever here, Soto was buried on the river's bank.

Sousa, John Philip (1854–1932) The son of Portuguese and German immigrants, Sousa enlisted in the U.S. Marines as an apprentice in the Marine Band and by 1880 was bandmaster. He left the Corps in 1892 to form his own band and became the most famous and sought-after bandleader in the world. Sousa composed 136 military marches, including "Semper Fidelis" (1888), which became the official march of the U.S. Marine Corps, "The Washington Post" (1889), "The Liberty Bell" (1893), and "The Stars and Stripes Forever" (1897).

Spaatz, Carl "Tooey" (1891–1974) A combat pilot in World War I, Spaatz became commander of the 8th Air Force in World War II, in charge of the great U.S. strategic bombing offensive against German-occupied Europe. During 1944, he was commander of U.S. Strategic Air Forces in Europe. After the war ended in that theater, he moved to the Pacific and directed strategic bombing there. Following World War II, he was named chief of staff of the U.S. Air Force, when it was created as a service independent from the army in 1947.

Spielberg, Steven (1947–) Spielberg was obsessed with film all his life and began directing in the early 1970s. His breakthrough was the masterpiece thriller *Jaws* (1957), one of the most profitable films ever produced. *Jaws*, like many of Spielberg's subsequent successes, was the story of an ordinary man confronting the extraordinary—in this case, a killer shark; in the case of *Close Encounters of the Third Kind* (1977), it was extraterrestrials. In his later career, Spielberg reached beyond the adventure and science fiction genres with such films as *Schindler's List* (1993)—about the Holocaust—and *Saving Private Ryan* (1998), set against the events of D-Day.

Speck, Richard Franklin (1941–1991) On July 14, 1966, drifter and sometime merchant marine Richard Speck methodically beat, raped, and murdered eight student nurses in their shared apartment on Chicago's South Side. The senseless brutality of the crime shocked and haunted the nation at a time when many complained about the "sickness" of society.

Spock, Benjamin (1903–1998) In 1946, Dr. Spock published the first edition of *Common Sense Book of Baby and Child Care* (which went through six editions by 1992), destined to be the ubiquitous bible of child rearing. Spock's loving, commonsense approach to raising children influenced generations. During the 1960s, Spock became a high-profile opponent of the Vietnam War and was even convicted in 1968 of counseling draft evasion; the conviction was overturned.

Squanto (died 1622) Squanto, whose Native name was Tisquantum, was an English-speaking Pawtuxet Indian whom Samoset (the first Indian to make contact with the newly arrived Pilgrims) introduced to the Plymouth colony. Squanto became the Pilgrims' key Indian emissary and guide.

Standish, Myles (or Miles) (ca. 1584–1656) Myles was an English military officer who served as the strong military leader of the Plymouth colony. He was immortalized by Henry Wadsworth Longfellow in his 1858 poem "The Courtship of Miles Standish," which relates the apocryphal story of his asking fellow colonist John Alden to propose marriage on his behalf to Priscilla Mullins—who replied, "Speak for yourself, John" and married Alden instead.

Stanford, Leland (1824–1893) Stanford was a merchant who grew rich supplying miners and others during the California gold-mining period and served as California governor from 1861 to 1863. He was a major investor in the Central Pacific Railroad (western leg of the transcontinental railroad) and served as its president from 1861 to 1893. With his wife, Jane, he established Stanford University in 1885.

Stanley, Henry Morton (1841–1904) Born John Rowlands out of wedlock in Wales, Morton later took the first and last names of the merchant who adopted him, Henry Hope Stanley. He served as a Confederate soldier during the American Civil War and in the U.S. Navy and U.S merchant marine, then worked as a journalist in the Far West. In 1867 James Gordon Bennett, publisher of the *New York Herald,* sent him to Africa to cover Britain's war against King Tewodros II of Ethiopia. Bennett next sent him in search of the famed British missionary Dr. David Livingstone, who had disappeared in 1866 while looking for the source of the Nile. Stanley found Livingstone on the shores of Lake Tanganyika in 1871, greeting him with "Dr. Livingstone, I presume?"

Stanton, Edwin McMasters (1814–1869) Edwin Stanton succeeded President Abraham Lincoln's first secretary of war, the notoriously corrupt Simon Cameron, on January 13, 1862. Once in charge, Stanton prosecuted the Civil War with ruthless energy. He was legendary for his ill temper and willingness to provoke disputes with other officials and with military commanders. The attempt of Andrew Johnson (who succeeded Lincoln after his assassination in April 1865) to remove Stanton from the Cabinet triggered Johnson's impeachment.

Stanton, Elizabeth Cady (1815–1902) With Lucretia Mott, Stanton, in 1848 composed the Declaration of Sentiments, a statement on women's rights. In the same year, she pulled together the first organized demand for woman suffrage in the United States and worked with Susan B. Anthony for a half a century toward obtaining the right of women to vote.

Starr, Kenneth (1946–) An attorney and former judge, Starr was appointed independent counsel in 1994 to investigate allegations of possibly impeachable offenses committed by President Bill Clinton in connection with certain real estate dealings. Four years and $40 million later, the "Starr Report" cleared Clinton of wrongdoing in connection with the real estate issue, but detailed his sexual liaison with a 21-year-old former White House intern, Monica Lewinsky. Starr concluded that Clinton had violated his oath of office by perjuring himself in a sworn deposition he had given in a sexual harassment civil lawsuit brought against him by a former Arkansas state employee, Paula Jones. He also alleged that the president had lied about the affair to a grand jury. Based on the Starr Report, Congress voted, along party lines, to impeach President Clinton, who was acquitted on February 12, 1999, in a Senate vote also along party lines.

Steffens, Lincoln (1866–1936) Journalist and social critic Steffens was among the writers President Theodore Roosevelt called "muckrakers," using a term borrowed from John Bunyan's 17th-century allegorical classic, *The Pilgrim's Progress,* among whose characters is a "Man with the Muckrake . . . who could look no way but downward." The term also took on a positive connotation to describe writers who exposed social corruption and injustice. Steffens's 1906 *The Shame of the Cities* exposed the widespread corruption of urban politicians and fueled many of the reforms of the Progressive era in American politics.

Steichen, Edward (1879–1973) Born in Luxembourg, Steichen was taken to the United States as an infant. He became an important photographer, who began working in a pictorial or painterly style, but evolved into straightforward realism, specializing in portraiture of the most influential artists and celebrities of the 1920s and 1930s. In 1955, he organized quite possibly the most ambitious photographic exhibition ever, the "Family of Man," a show of 503 master photographs chosen from some 2 million submitted from all over the world. Enormously popular, the exhibition, which traveled internationally, was seen by an estimated 9 million people and was a declaration of the brotherhood of humanity.

Stein, Gertrude (1874–1946) A former medical student, Stein moved to Paris with her brother Leo early in the 20th century and established a salon that became a meeting place for emerging writers and artists, including, after World War I, expatriate Americans such as Ernest Hemingway and F. Scott Fitzgerald. It was Stein who labeled the writers and artists who had passed through the crucible of the Great War the "Lost Generation." An important avant-garde writer, Stein was a mentor and surrogate mother to that Lost Generation. She was also an important collector of modern art.

Steinbeck, John (1902–1968) Steinbeck produced his masterpiece, *The Grapes of Wrath* in 1939. Narrating the epic journey of the Joad family from the Oklahoma Dust Bowl to what they hope will be a better life in California, the novel embodies the harsh human realities of the Great

Depression. Steinbeck was awarded the Nobel Prize for Literature for 1962.

Steinem, Gloria (1934–) Steinem emerged in the 1960s as a popular writer on feminist subjects. With Betty Friedan, Bella Abzug, and Shirley Chisholm, she founded the National Women's Political Caucus in 1971, the same year she launched *Ms.* magazine, which featured issues of contemporary interest treated from a feminist perspective.

Stetson, John Batterson (1830–1906) A native of Orange, New Jersey, Stetson became a hat maker. In the 1860s, he journeyed to the West for his health and was inspired to make a new kind of hat, suited to the cowboy. He designed and manufactured the high-crowned, broad-brimmed headgear known as the Stetson, which became a symbol of the cowboy. Based on its popularity, the John B. Stetson Company, formed in 1885, became one of the largest hat firms in the world.

Stevens, Thaddeus (1792–1868) Republican senator from Pennsylvania, Stevens emerged during and after the Civil War as leader of the Radical Republicans, the faction that favored harshly punitive measures against the former Confederacy during the Reconstruction period following the war. Stevens was a forceful advocate for the rights of freed slaves.

Stevenson, Adlai E. (1900–1965) As assistant secretary of state in 1945, Stevenson was one of the architects of the United Nations and served as U.S. UN ambassador during 1961–1965, a period highlighted by his showdown with the Soviet U.N. ambassador during the 1962 Cuban Missile Crisis. A popular governor of Illinois (elected in 1948 by the biggest majority in the state's history), he was twice defeated for the presidency by Dwight D. Eisenhower, in 1952 and 1956.

Stewart, Martha (1941–) A former fashion model and stockbroker, Stewart started a highly successful catering business in 1976 and published *Entertaining* (1977), the best-selling cookbook since the work of Julia Child. This was the start of Stewart's career as a cooking and domestic arts adviser to the masses. She hosts her own television show and publishes a magazine, *Martha Stewart Living*, both produced by her company, Martha Stewart Omnimedia. Her corporate empire was shaken by her conviction on charges related to her trial for insider trading. She served five months in prison and was released on March 4, 2005. Although she was compelled to step down as CEO, her company substantially recovered.

Stieglitz, Alfred (1864–1946) Stieglitz was a major American photographer, who also championed the work of others, opening in 1905 Gallery 291 in New York City to exhibit the work of emerging modern photographers. Stieglitz was also an advocate and impresario of modern art in general and was married to one America's greatest modern artists, the painter Georgia O'Keeffe.

Still, William Grant (1895–1978) Educated at Oberlin Conservatory of Music and the New England Conservatory of Music—and also a student of avant-gardist Edgard Varèse—Still was a rare commodity when he began to compose in the 1920s: a black composer of classical music. His symphonies, operas, ballets, and other works were influenced by traditional African-American music and also often evoked black life in America.

Stimson, Henry L. (1867–1950) Stimson was a New York attorney and Republican politician who served during 1911–1913 as President William Howard Taft's secretary of war. During the administration of Calvin Coolidge, he was sent to Nicaragua to resolve unrest there and was also appointed governor general of the Philippines. Stimson was Herbert Hoover's secretary of state from 1929 to 1933. In 1940, President Franklin Roosevelt appointed the Republican Stimson his secretary of war. Stimson served through World War II, continuing under President Harry S. Truman until his retirement after the war in September 1945. Henry Stimson was a major influence on U.S. foreign policy during the first half of the 20th century.

Stockman, David (1946–) Stockman was a businessman and politician (U.S. Representative from Michigan from 1977 to 1981) who became President Ronald Reagan's director of the Office of Management and Budget (1981–1985). Stockman was a leading figure of the era of "Reaganomics," implementing the Reagan budget cuts aimed at dismantling the "Democratic welfare state." Austere and uncompromising, he became infamous for justifying funding cuts for federal school lunch programs by his proposal to reclassify ketchup as a vegetable—since supplying this condiment was the cheapest way to satisfy requirements for vegetable content of federally funded school lunches.

Stone, I. F. (1907–1989) Born Isidor Feinstein, Stone worked as a journalist for the *Philadelphia Inquirer, New York Post, The Nation,* and other publications before starting his own weekly, *I. F. Stone's Weekly* (later *I.F. Stone's Bi-Weekly*) in 1951. The journal was published through 1971 and, although always small in circulation, was eagerly read by the nation's movers and shakers, including the likes of Albert Einstein and Eleanor Roosevelt. Stone was an early advocate of civil rights and an early opponent of McCarthyism and, later, the Vietnam War.

Stone, Lucy (1818–1893) Stone was cofounder of the American Equal Rights Association in 1866 and the New Jersey Woman Suffrage Association the following year. She was a moving force behind the woman suffrage movement until her death.

Stone, Oliver (1946–) Among the defining experiences of Stone's life was his army service in the Vietnam War (1967–1968), which inspired three films about Vietnam—*Platoon* (1986), *Born on the Fourth of July* (1989), and *Heaven and Earth* (1993). These are typical of Stone's cinematic interests, which approach large historical events and social subjects from a personal perspective. His 1991 *JFK* advanced a conspiracy theory concerning the assassination of John F. Kennedy, his 1995 *Nixon* was a dramatic portrayal of that president's rise and downfall, and *World Trade Center* (2006) was the story of the 9/11 terrorist attacks on New York from the point of view of two police officers trapped in the wreckage of the WTC.

Stowe, Harriet Beecher (1811–1896) New Englander Harriet Beecher Stowe saw slavery close-up when she lived for a time on the Ohio-Kentucky border with her Bible-scholar husband, Calvin Stowe. Passage of the Fugitive Slave Act in 1850 prompted her to begin a book she called *Uncle Tom's Cabin, or Life Among the Lowly,* which was published serially during 1852 and appeared as a book in 1853. An international bestseller, its vividly sentimental scenes dramatized the cruelty of slavery, shaking the apathy out of many

Northerners and enraging slave-holding Southerners. When Abraham Lincoln met Mrs. Stowe during the Civil War, he greeted her as "the little lady who wrote the book that made this big war."

Strand, Paul (1890–1976) Strand made a radical break with the pictorial, painting-like photographic styles popular early in the 20th century and created sharply focused "objective" photographs, typically of commonplace buildings or objects shot in ways that simplify them into stark abstraction. Strand conceived photography in terms of photography rather than painting or any other visual art. In this, he was extraordinarily influential on the history of the medium.

Straus, Nathan (1848–1931) With his brother Isidor, Straus co-owned the great R. H. Macy department store in New York City from 1896. During the 1890s, Straus also began his philanthropic work, giving away food and coal to poor New Yorkers and supplying pasteurized milk to children in 36 American cities. By 1920, he had founded nearly 300 milk-distribution depots in the United States and abroad. In 1909, Straus also financed the first tuberculosis "preventorium" for children (in Lakewood, New Jersey).

Straus, Oscar S. (1850–1926) Straus was born in Germany. He was the brother of department store owners Isidor and Nathan Straus. When President Theodore Roosevelt appointed him secretary of commerce and labor, he became the first Jewish member of a U.S. Cabinet. Straus also served as U.S. emissary to the Ottoman Empire (1887–1889, 1898–1900, 1909–1910) and was an adviser to President Woodrow Wilson.

Strauss, Levi (1829–1902) Born in Bavaria (as Löb Strauss), Levi Strauss immigrated to New York City with his family in 1847. With his brothers, he became a dry goods merchant and moved to booming San Francisco in 1853. In response to the need of gold prospectors for more durable trousers, Strauss developed denim overalls. In 1872, he acted on the suggestion of Jacob Davis, a Reno, Nevada tailor, to use metal rivets to reinforce pants at vulnerable points of strain. Strauss and Davis patented this new type of trousers on May 20, 1873, and Levi's jeans were born. They would become an article of clothing symbolic of American popular culture through many generations.

Stuart, Gilbert (1755–1828) Born in North Kingstown, Rhode Island, Stuart (born Stewart) became internationally recognized not only as the finest portrait painter of the new American republic but also its most distinctive, having created a style that drew on English precedents but that was also uniquely American. Of his more than 1,000 portraits his most famous is the unfinished "Atheneum Head," the 1796 portrait of George Washington, which was for generations endlessly reproduced for display in classrooms and other public places.

Stuyvesant, Peter (1592–1672) Irascible and unyielding, Stuyvesant became governor of New Netherland—the Dutch New World colony—in 1647 and tried in vain to rally the colonists to resist the British attempt to conquer the colony. Without the necessary support of his people, he was forced to surrender to the British—who renamed New Netherland New York—and he retired to his Manhattan farm, the Bouwerie (the Bowery) at the edge of New Amsterdam (which was renamed New York as well).

Sullivan, Ed (1901–1974) Sullivan was a Broadway newspaper columnist who became a television pioneer with a variety program called "The Toast of the Town" (1948–1955). This was renamed in 1955 "The Ed Sullivan Show" and, from 1955 to 1971, it was a fixture of Sunday evening programming, bringing into the nation's living rooms a wide variety of popular entertainment. Because Sullivan seemed to have an unerring instinct for "the next big thing," the show became an American trendsetter and tastemaker.

Sullivan, John L. (1858–1918) On February 7, 1882, boxer John L. Sullivan defeated Paddy Ryan at Mississippi City, Mississippi, winning the world heavyweight boxing championship and thereby beginning his rise to becoming a national sports hero, America's first great sporting celebrity.

Sullivan, Louis (1856–1924) Sullivan was a brilliant late 19th-century architect generally regarded as the father of modern architecture and the first great architect to tackle the skyscraper. His leading principle was to ensure that the form of a structure followed its function and was organic to the building, rather than a matter of mere decoration. His early masterpieces were produced in partnership with the Dankmar Adler and include the Auditorium Building, Chicago (1866–1889) and the Wainwright Building, St. Louis (1890–1891). Frank Lloyd Wright was Sullivan's apprentice.

Sulzberger, Arthur Ochs (1926–) The grandson of Adolph S. Ochs, who transformed the *New York Times* into a major newspaper at the end of the 19th century, and the son of Arthur Hays Sulzberger, *Times* publisher from 1935 to 1961, Sulzberger guided the paper from 1963 to 1991, an era during which it became the nation's "newspaper of record," acquiring a reputation as a watchdog on American government, politicians, and big business.

Sumner, Charles (1811–1874) On May 22, 1856, Sumner, a fiery anti-slavery senator from Massachusetts, was savagely beaten with a cane by South Carolina representative Preston S. Brooks on the Senate floor in retaliation for his having maligned the state of South Carolina and one of its senators, Andrew P. Butler, Brooks's uncle. To the North, the caning represented southern brutality at its worst and served to galvanize abolitionist sentiment and to bring civil war closer. As for Sumner, his injuries were so severe that it took him three years to recover.

Sumner, William Graham (1840–1910) Sumner was a disciple of the British philosopher Herbert Spencer, who believed that, in society as in the natural world, the strong survive and prosper at the expense of the weak. Far from being a situation government and society should endeavor to correct, Sumner believed that ruthless economic competition was beneficial to the evolution of society, and both opposed any steps that contributed to the creation of a welfare state.

Sunday, Billy (1862/1863–1935) Born William Ashley, Sunday grew up an orphan and became a Presbyterian minister in 1903. A fundamentalist, he conducted revivals nationwide, reaching as many as 100 million people. Sunday was the precursor of Billy Graham and the later televangelists, whose object was to reach as many people as possible.

Surratt, Mary (1820–1865) Born Mary Jenkins, Surratt ran the Washington, D.C., boardinghouse at which John Wilkes Booth and the other conspirators in the assassination of

President Abraham Lincoln met to plan the crime. She was tried and convicted of complicity in the conspiracy and, on July 7, 1865, became the first woman to be hanged in the United States.

Sutter, John (1803–1880) Born Johann Augustus Suter in Germany, Sutter spent much of his life in Switzerland, then fled bankruptcy by settling in California in 1839. He became a prominent rancher, and, on January 24, 1848, his employee, James Marshall, discovered gold in the race (stream) of a mill on the ranch. The discovery triggered the California Gold Rush the following year, instantly populating the territory and making California statehood an urgent issue.

Swift, Gustavus (1839–1903) Swift was a butcher who founded the meat-packing firm of Swift & Company. He transformed meat packing into a giant industry by commissioning the design of a refrigerated railway car for the mass transportation of meat from his plants in Chicago to the East.

Taft, Robert A. (1889–1953) Son of President William Howard Taft, Robert A. Taft was Republican leader in the U.S. Senate from 1939 to 1953. He represented the most conservative wing of the Republican Party and was a strong advocate of isolationism and a foe of President Franklin D. Roosevelt's New Deal (which he denounced as Socialist). The 1947 Taft-Hartley Act (which he cosponsored) restricted the rights of organized labor.

Taft, William Howard (1857–1930) Taft was handpicked by Theodore Roosevelt as his Republican successor to the presidency. He served from 1909 to 1913, but his conservatism was a disappointment to Roosevelt, who ran against him on the Progressive (Bull Moose) ticket in 1912, and the incumbent Taft came in a humiliating third behind Woodrow Wilson and TR. Wilson's successor, Warren G. Harding, appointed Taft chief justice of the U.S. Supreme Court. He served from 1921 to 1930.

Taney, Roger B. (1777–1864) Taney was the fifth chief justice of the Supreme Court, serving from 1836 until his death in 1864. On March 6, 1857, he handed down the Supreme Court's decision in *Dred Scott v. Sandford,* holding that Scott, a slave suing for his freedom on the grounds of having lived in the free state of Illinois, was ineligible to sue because neither slaves nor free blacks were citizens; Taney further held that the Missouri Compromise (under which suit was brought) was unconstitutional. Taney's decision put the slavery issue beyond peaceful compromise and virtually ensured the coming of civil war.

Tarbell, Ida (1857–1944) Tarbell was a pioneering investigative journalist whose 1904 *History of the Standard Oil Company* charted the rise of a giant business monopoly, chronicling a litany of unfair practices by which the company achieved its success. Tarbell was one of the leaders among the "muckrakers," writers who exposed corruption in American society and whose work triggered the reforms of the Progressive movement.

Taylor, Edward (1645?–1729) Taylor immigrated to New England, studied at the newly founded Harvard College, and became minister in Westfield, Massachusetts. During his life spent in this frontier ministry, he composed 400 pages of poems, most of them religious meditations in elaborate metaphysical style with complex metaphors.

Taylor, Frederick Winslow (1856–1915) In 1911, this former steel plant foreman published *The Principles of Scientific Management*, in which he presented a rigorous system for rationalizing the human element in industrial production. "Taylorism" soon swept American industry, whose managers strove to replace idiosyncrasy and "outmoded" individuality of craftsmanship with strict control of all work procedures and production methods so that the pace of production would never be tied to any particular worker or set of workers. While Taylorism increased productivity, it also created profound dissatisfaction among workers, who felt dehumanized, exploited, and alienated.

Taylor, Maxwell (1901–1987) During World War II, Taylor was one of the creators of the 82nd Airborne Division and was commanding general of the 101st Airborne Division. He pioneered the tactics and doctrine of airborne (paratroop) assault, which was widely used by the United States in World War II and afterward.

Taylor, Zachary (1784–1850) Taylor was a military hero of the U.S.-Mexican War (1846–1848) and was tapped by the Whig Party as its presidential contender in 1848. He took office in 1849 and was immediately faced with the problem of whether to extend or to prohibit slavery in the territories acquired from Mexico. Taylor had little time to deal with this and other problems—including a Cabinet-level financial scandal—because he succumbed to cholera 16 months after taking office. He was succeeded by his vice president, Millard Fillmore.

Tecumseh (1768–1813) A Shawnee chief, Tecumseh traveled extensively in an effort to unite various tribes in order to make effective resistance against white invasion of the Ohio country. He allied himself and his followers with the British during the War of 1812 in hopes of stemming the tide of American westward-moving settlement. Although he succeeded in drawing together more tribes than any previous leader, Tecumseh was killed at the Battle of the Thames (in Ontario, Canada) on October 5, 1813, by troops under William Henry Harrison.

Teller, Edward (1908–2003) Born in Hungary, the Jewish Teller immigrated to the United States in 1935 to escape a Europe increasingly under the sway of Nazi anti-Semitic ideology. Already recognized as a major physicist, Teller taught at Georgetown University (Washington, D.C.) and worked with Enrico Fermi at the University of Chicago beginning in 1941 to create the first self-sustaining nuclear chain reaction. In 1943, he joined J. Robert Oppenheimer's team of Manhattan Project scientists at Los Alamos, New Mexico, to create the atomic bomb. After the war, Teller advocated taking the bomb to the next step, using nuclear fission (the mechanism of the atomic bomb) to trigger a far more powerful explosive release of energy by means of nuclear fusion (hydrogen bomb). The fruit of Teller's labors was successfully tested at Enewetak atoll in the Pacific on November 1, 1952. Teller had given birth to the age of thermonuclear weapons.

Terkel, Studs (1912–) Terkel was born in New York City but grew up in Chicago. He was active during the Depression in the Federal Writers' Project of the Works Progress Administration (WPA) and became a radio script writer and, later, a television personality on early Chicago television. It is, however, for his popular oral histories that he is best known—remarkable books compiled from interviews of mostly ordinary people. His best-known oral histories include *Hard Times: An Oral History of the Great Depression* (1970) and *The Good War* (1985), an oral history of World War II, which won a Pulitzer Prize.

Thalberg, Irving (1899–1936) Sickly and frail, Thalberg worked with the brilliance and intensity of someone who knew he would die young. By the time he was 21, Thalberg was manager of Universal Pictures. Four years later, when MGM was formed, he was head of production and had authority to reedit any film. His management made MGM the most prestigious studio in the world, with such films as *Mutiny on the Bounty* (1935), the Marx Brothers' *A Night at the Opera* (1935) and *A Day at the Races* (1937), and *Camille* (1937).

Tharp, Twyla (1941–) Tharp studied at the American Ballet Theatre School and with Richard Thomas, Martha Graham, Merce Cunningham, and others before joining the Paul Taylor Dance Company in 1963 then forming her own company in 1965. As a choreographer, she created innovative dances, which, in contrast to much modern dance, were also laced with great good humor.

Thomas, Clarence (1948–) Born in rural Georgia, Thomas was raised by his grandfather, educated in Catholic schools, and received his law degree from Yale in 1974. After working in the private sector and in government, he served as a justice on the U.S. Court of Appeals for the District of Columbia from 1990 to 1991, when he was nominated by President George H. W. Bush to replace Thurgood Marshall on the Supreme Court. Both Thomas and Marshall were black, but whereas Marshall (retiring for reasons of age and ill health) was a liberal, Thomas was a staunch conservative. His televised Senate confirmation hearing was bitter, marked by accusations of sexual harassment from Anita Hill, a former colleague. Thomas's appointment shifted the Supreme Court toward conservatism.

Thompson, J. Walter (1847–1928) In 1868, Thompson went to work as a bookkeeper for William James Carlton, who sold advertising space in religious magazines. Thompson became an ad salesman for the company, which he purchased in 1877, renaming it the J. Walter Thompson Company. Whereas advertisers traditionally wrote their own ads, Thompson introduced professional copywriting and illustration, the twin cores of modern advertising. Thompson's company was an advertising giant for more than a century.

Thoreau, Henry David (1817–1862) In the 1830s, Thoreau fell under the influence of Ralph Waldo Emerson and became his intellectual disciple, contributing to the magazine Emerson had started, *The Dial.* In 1845, Thoreau built a cabin on Walden Pond, two miles south of Concord, Massachusetts, on land owned by Emerson. He lived there alone, keeping a journal of his thoughts and observations in what became an experiment in stripping life to its essential core. He lived at the pond for two years, and in 1854 published *Walden*, a masterpiece of contemplative prose, which combined great nature writing with an internal record of Thoreau's experiment in living. Although reclusive, Thoreau was hardly disengaged from society. In 1846, he was briefly jailed for failing to pay his poll tax. He declared that he could not support a government that would wage an unjust war on Mexico (U.S.-Mexican War, 1846–1848), and he wrote his most famous essay, "Civil Disobedience," which influenced generations of activists, from Gandhi to Martin Luther King, Jr.

Thorpe, Jim (1888–1953) A member of the Sauk and Fox tribe, Thorpe was twice on All-American football teams (1911 and 1912) and won the decathlon and the pentathlon in the 1912 Olympics, but was subsequently stripped of his gold medals because he had played semiprofessional baseball in 1909 and 1910. Thorpe played professional baseball from 1913 to 1919 and professional football from 1919 through 1926.

Tibbets, Paul (1915–) Tibbets was an outstanding bomber pilot in World War II and was chosen in September 1944 to command the 509th Composite Group, which would drop the first atomic bombs on Japan. On August 6, 1945 Tibbets flew his B-29, named *Enola Gay* after his mother, from Tinian Island in the Marianas and dropped an atomic bomb on Hiroshima at 8:15 a.m. local time.

Tiffany, Charles Lewis (1812–1902) Connecticut-born Tiffany went to New York City in 1837 and, with John B. Young opened a stationery store that soon also offered jewelry and silverware. By 1853, Tiffany gained sole control of the firm, which he named Tiffany & Co.—today the most famous name in American jewelry.

Tiffany, Louis Comfort (1848–1933) Son of the jeweler Charles Lewis Tiffany, Louis Tiffany became a stained-glass artist in 1875, attaining leadership in the field by the 1890s and fashioning decorative glass that created the dominant look of the Art Nouveau period. Tiffany also went on to create blown-glass works of great artistry, then expanded into lamps, jewelry, and pottery.

Tilden, Samuel J. (1814–1886) During 1865–1875, Tilden reorganized the Democratic Party of New York City, ousting the infamously corrupt Tweed Ring and generally reforming the city's politics. He went on to election as New York governor in 1874 and earned national recognition for his reforms. Nominated by the Democratic Party for president in 1876, he outpolled Republican Rutherford B. Hayes, but the election was contested, and, in a backroom deal, the Democrats conceded the election to Hayes in return for his pledge that he would bring an immediate end to post-Civil War Reconstruction (including military government) in the South. Tilden accepted the deal for what he considered the good of the country.

Tocqueville, Alexis de (1805–1859) A French political scientist and historian, Tocqueville toured the United States during 1831–1832 and produced the four-volume *Democracy in America* (1835–1840), a brilliant analysis of American government, politics, society, and the collective national psyche. It is among the most perceptive analyses of American culture ever written.

Toomer, Jean (1894–1967) Toomer was a leading black literary figure of the 1920s, who wrote poetry and fiction. He is best known for his 1923 novel *Cane*, which used experimental literary techniques, imagery, and symbolism to explore the history of black America.

Tower, John (1925–1991) Tower, a conservative Republican senator from Texas, was appointed on December 1, 1986, by President Ronald Reagan to chair a commission charged with investigating the National Security Council and its role in the Iran-Contra affair, by which arms were to be illegally sold to Iran in exchange for Iran's help in freeing American hostages held in Lebanon; profits from the arms sales were to be illegally funneled to the "contras," the right-wing opponents of the leftist Sandinista regime in Nicaragua. Tower delivered the commission's report on February 26, 1987. To the surprise of many, who expected a whitewash, the report criticized the council and although it did not conclude that the president was aware of the extent of the illegal scheme, it also criticized him for lacking control over council staff.

Travis, William B. (1809–1836) Travis was an attorney and soldier who settled in Texas in 1831 as one of the early American colonists of what was then a Mexican possession. He became an advocate of independence from Mexico and was in command of the Texas forces that garrisoned the Alamo (in San Antonio) when it was attacked by far superior numbers of Mexican soldiers under General Antonio López de Santa Anna. Travis died along with the Alamo's other defenders on March 6, 1836.

Trist, Nicholas P. (1800–1874) Trist studied law under Thomas Jefferson and served as private secretary to Andrew Jackson. President James K. Polk sent him to negotiate an end to the U.S.–Mexican War, and he emerged with Treaty of Guadalupe Hidalgo (February 2, 1848), which ceded to the United States California and most of what is now the American Southwest.

Truman, Harry S. (1884–1972) Truman was a U.S. Senator from Missouri who came to national prominence when his Truman Committee cleaned up corruption and waste among War Department contractors. He was tapped by Franklin D. Roosevelt as his running mate in 1944, and, just three months after taking office, found himself president when

FDR succumbed to a cerebral hemorrhage. It fell to Truman to lead the nation through the last stages of World War II, culminating in his decision to drop two atomic bombs on Japan. Truman then formulated the "Truman Doctrine," a policy of "containing" the aggressive expansion of Soviet (and then Chinese) Communism through economic and military action. The biggest tests of the new doctrine came with the Soviet blockade of West Berlin, which Truman circumvented by the Berlin Airlift of 1948–1949, and the Communist invasion of South Korea, which became the Korean War of 1950–1953. Few pundits believed Truman could win reelection in his own right in 1948, but he defeated Republican challenger Thomas E. Dewey. Largely because of the Korean War (and his firing, for insubordination, of Douglas MacArthur as commander in chief of U.S. and UN forces there), Truman was unpopular when he left office in January 1953, but he lived long enough to see himself reevaluated as one of the great presidents of the 20th century.

Trumbo, Dalton (1905–1976) Trumbo was a successful screenwriter (one of Hollywood's highest paid) and novelist who became one of the "Hollywood Ten," a group that refused to "name names" when summoned in 1947, during the postwar "Red Scare," by the U.S. House Committee on Un-American Activities about their alleged communist ties and the communist ties of their associates. Blacklisted—meaning that no studio would hire him—Trumbo was also imprisoned for contempt of Congress for 11 months.

Truth, Sojourner (1797–1883) This New York slave was born Isabella Van Wagener. Freed when New York outlawed slavery in 1827, she took the name Sojourner Truth in 1843 and became an itinerant evangelist, who combined her religious message with a campaign for abolition and for women's rights.

Tubman, Harriet (ca. 1821–1913) Harriet Tubman was born a slave in Dorchester County, Maryland, and escaped to freedom about 1849. Not satisfied with having achieved her own deliverance, she repeatedly risked recapture throughout the 1850s by journeying back into slave territory to lead some 300 other fugitives, including her parents, to liberty. She was a founder of the "Underground Railroad," the abolitionist network that smuggled thousands of fugitives to freedom before the Civil War. During the war, she risked her life as a spy in Maryland and Virginia.

Turner, Frederick Jackson (1861–1932) On July 12, 1893, Turner, a University of Wisconsin history professor, delivered a speech as part of the World's Columbian Exposition in Chicago in which he presented census statistics that revealed the "closing" of the American frontier; that is, he explained, the population figures no longer demarcated a distinct western limit of settlement. With the frontier closed, Turner declared his belief that the "restless, nervous energy . . . dominant individualism . . . buoyancy and exuberance" traditionally engendered in the American character by the presence of the frontier would now be channeled into ventures abroad, and the United States would enter an age of imperialism.

Turner, Nat (1800–1831) Just before dawn on August 22, 1831, Turner, a slave and lay preacher, led 50 or more fellow slaves in a rebellion in Southampton County, Virginia. Turner and his band killed 60 whites before he and most of the others were apprehended. With 19 followers, Turner was quickly tried and hanged on November 11, 1831. Local whites retaliated against the uprising by randomly killing African Americans in the area. Uprisings such as Turner's were a great fear of white southerners during the era of slavery.

Turner, Ted (1938–) The son of the owner of a billboard advertising company, Robert Edward "Ted" Turner III took over the failing business after his father committed suicide. After making it profitable again, he invested in the purchase of a failing UHF Atlanta television station in 1970 and turned it around. In 1975, he transformed the station into "Superstation" by using communications satellite technology to broadcast to a national cable television audience. In 1980, he created the nation's first 24-hour cable news network, CNN (Cable News Network). Superstation and CNN radically changed the nature of television broadcasting.

Twain, Mark (Samuel Langhorne Clemens) (1835–1910) Raised in the Mississippi River town of Hannibal, Missouri, Samuel Langhorne Clemens learned to love life on the river. He worked as an itinerant printer and journalist, but his favorite job was as a riverboat pilot before the Civil War, a position from which he observed human nature on the rough-and-tumble American frontier. When he began to write humorous stories—his first big hit, "The Celebrated Jumping Frog of Calaveras County" (1865) was a slice of life from California gold country—he adopted the pseudonym Mark Twain, the call of the Mississippi riverboat leadsman indicating a depth of two fathoms, ample for safe passage. As Mark Twain, Clemens wrote often hilarious (and tremendously popular) works that nevertheless portrayed the darker side of human nature and of life on the frontier. His *Adventures of Huckleberry Finn* (1884) is a masterpiece of narrative art, a look at life in America on the eve of civil war through the eyes of a high-spirited, warm-hearted twelve-year-old orphan.

Tweed, William Marcy "Boss" (1823–1878) Boss Tweed was a powerful ring leader for New York City Democrats known then as Tammany Hall. Using his position as city supervisor, he appointed cronies and the party faithful, creating a thoroughly corrupt city government known as the "Tweed ring." The most famous of the 19th-century urban "bosses," Tweed was exposed in the satiric cartoons of Thomas Nast and was ultimately tried and convicted on charges of forgery and larceny.

Tyler, John (1790–1862) Tyler was a Democrat who became president when William Henry Harrison died within a month of taking office. Tyler was the first vice president called on to succeed the president, and this created a crisis. The Constitution did not make clear whether a vice president, upon succession, became president or merely acting president. Tyler asserted himself as president, an assertion that has not been challenged since.

Tyler, Royall (1757–1826) Born William Clark Tyler, Royall Tyler was a Vermont attorney and teacher, who also wrote plays. His 1787 *The Contrast* pits a naïve Yankee against a sophisticated Englishman for the affections of the same girl. A delightful comedy—on a par with the best produced in England at the time—*The Contrast* also created an enduring cultural stereotype in the character of Jonathan, "the Yankee."

Updike, John (1932–) Updike's novels typically focus on small-town, middle-class Protestant American life, using this slice of the nation to explore more profound themes of fidelity and infidelity, religious faith and atheism, and the perennial search for meaning in a society that offers few enduring values.

Vallandigham, Clement (1820–1871) Vallandigham was an Ohio "Copperhead," a Northern Democrat sympathetic to the Confederacy and favoring a negotiated end to the Civil War. Vallandigham and other Copperheads saw Union victory in the Civil War as benefiting only East Coast moneyed interests. Vallandigham's wartime activities were judged subversive by Union authorities, and he was exiled to the South.

Van Buren, Martin (1782–1862) Van Buren had served as a senator from New York, governor of New York, and secretary of state during Andrew Jackson's first term. He was Jackson's vie president during his second term, from 1833 to 1837 and, handpicked by Jackson, was elected president in 1836. Seeking to avoid civil war, he tended to placate the southern slaveholders, although, after being defeated for reelection in 1840, he unsuccessfully ran for president in 1848 as the candidate of the antislavery Free Soil Party.

Vance, Cyrus (1917–2002) Vance was an attorney who served as secretary of the army during the Kennedy administration and as deputy secretary of Defense under Lyndon B. Johnson. Initially in favor of the Vietnam War, he turned against it in 1968, and Johnson appointed him deputy chief delegate to the Paris Peace Talks. As Carter' secretary of state, Vance played an important role in facilitating the Camp David Accords, which brought peace between Israel and Egypt in 1978.

Vanderbilt, Cornelius (1794–1877) Vanderbilt built his fortune on ferry operations between Staten Island and

Manhattan, expanding this to control of Hudson River passenger traffic and then, during the California gold rush that began in 1849, operating steamship service from New York and New Orleans to San Francisco via Nicaragua. After 1850, Vanderbilt became increasingly interested in rail transportation, acquiring control of the New York Central in 1863 and expanding it to connect Chicago and New York. By the time of his death, Vanderbilt was worth in excess of $100 million.

Vanzetti, Bartolomeo (1888–1927) Vanzetti was born in Italy and immigrated to the United States when he was twenty. He became a fish peddler and, angered by the way many immigrants lived in America, he became a committed anarchist. On May 5, 1920, Vanzetti and his friend and fellow anarchist Nicola Sacco were arrested for the robbery-murders of a shoe factory paymaster and a guard. On flimsy circumstantial evidence, they were convicted in 1921. The case became an international cause célèbre as prominent intellectuals the world over protested that the men had been convicted for their political beliefs. On August 23, 1927, after seven years of appeals and incarceration, Sacco and Vanzetti were executed. Subsequent investigation suggested that Sacco was in fact guilty, but Vanzetti innocent. On August 23, 1977, Massachusetts governor Michael Dukakis posthumously exonerated both men.

Vaux, Calvert (1824–1895) Vaux was born in London and came to America in 1850 to work with landscape designer Andrew Jackson Downing in creating the grounds of the White House and the Smithsonian Institution, among many other works. In 1857, Vaux became a founding member of the American Institute of Architects and started a vogue for "Victorian Gothic" architecture. He is best remembered today for his collaboration with Frederick Law Olmsted in designing Central Park in 1858.

Veblen, Thorstein (1857–1929) Veblen took an evolutionary approach to the analysis of economic institutions, publishing in 1899 *The Theory of the Leisure Class,* an economic study that verged on satire and that became a popular sensation with iconoclastic readers. Veblen coined the term—and concept—"conspicuous consumption" to describe spending habits among the well off, who customarily purchase items chiefly to exhibit and demonstrate their socioeconomic status.

Verrazano, Giovanni da (1485–1528) Sailing for France, this Italian navigator ventured to the New World in 1524 and explored the east coast of what is now the United States. He discovered the sites of present-day New York Harbor, Block Island, and Narragansett Bay. His name is commemorated in the Verrazano-Narrows Bridge spanning New York Harbor from Brooklyn to Staten Island.

Vesco, Robert (1935–) Vesco worked his way up from Detroit auto worker to owning controlling interests in companies with more than $100 million in sales by the late 1960s. The U.S. Securities and Exchange Commission accused Vesco of looting investments in one of his companies, thereby defrauding thousands of investors, and in 1973 Vesco was indicted for illegal contributions to the Nixon reelection campaign. Vesco fled prosecution, eventually ending up in Cuba, where Fidel Castro jailed him and refused extradition.

Vesey, Denmark (ca. 1767–1822) Vesey was a self-educated slave who purchased his freedom in 1800 (using $600 won in a street lottery). While free, he read anti-slavery literature and became radicalized. He organized perhaps as many as 9,000 slaves in and around Charleston, South Carolina, in a revolt that called for seizure of arsenals, the killing of all whites, and the destruction of the city. Tipped off by a house servant, authorities crushed the rebellion just before it began. Of approximately 130 blacks arrested and tried, 67 were convicted and 35, including Vesey, were hanged. It was the most extensive planned slave revolt in U.S. history.

Vespucci, Amerigo (1454–1512) This Italian navigator participated in New World voyages during 1499–1500 and 1501–1502 and served Spain as *piloto mayor* ("master navigator") from 1508 to 1512. In 1507, the German geographer Martin Waldseemhller coined the name "America" in his *Cosmographiae Introductio*, mistakenly attributing the discovery of the New World to Amerigo, whose earliest New World voyage was in 1499, seven years *after* Columbus.

von Neumann, John (1903–1957) Born in Hungary and educated there as well as in Germany and Switzerland, von Neumann immigrated to the United States in 1930 to teach at Princeton. He made fundamental contributions to mathematics (including the definition of ordinal numbers) and physics (his 1932 *Mathematical Foundations of Quantum Mechanics* remains standard), then created the field of game theory, with special application in economics. In computer science, von Neumann pioneered logical design.

Wainwright, Jonathan (1883–1953) Wainwright was second in command to Douglas MacArthur in the Philippines at the outbreak of World War II. After MacArthur was ordered to evacuate, Wainwright was in command of the desperate defense of the island against overwhelming Japanese invasion forces. He held out as long as possible, making the invasion far more costly than the Japanese had anticipated, but finally surrendered on May 6, 1942. He and his command were held as prisoners of war under the cruelest of conditions until 1945. Wainwright received the Medal of Honor.

Wald, Lillian (1867–1940) In 1893, this American nurse and social worker founded the Henry Street Settlement in New York City's Lower East Side to serve the health needs of impoverished immigrants. In the process, she singlehandedly created the profession of public health nursing. Her work with children's health also prompted Congress to create the U.S. Children's Bureau in 1912 to oversee and maintain national standards of child welfare.

Walker, Alice (1944–) Walker grew up in a family of Georgia sharecroppers, began writing as a child, attended Spelman College and Sarah Lawrence, then, during the 1960s, became active in the civil rights movement. She also worked as a teacher and started writing for publication. She is a poet and essayist, but her best-known work is her fiction, including *The Color Purple* (1982), about a black woman's coming of age in Georgia. The book won a Pulitzer Prize and was made into a highly successful film by Steven Spielberg.

Wallace, George C. (1919–1998) Wallace was elected Alabama's governor in 1962 largely on his pledge to maintain racial segregation in his state. He served four terms, during which he became a national symbol of southern racism during the Civil Rights movement. In 1968, he ran for president on the American Independent Party ticket, and in 1972, while campaigning for the Democratic presidential nomination, he was shot and paralyzed below the waist. In the 1980s, Wallace not only renounced segregation, but sought reconciliation with the black community.

Wallace, Henry A. (1888–1965) Wallace was an Iowa agricultural editor and expert, who, switching from the Republican to the Democratic Party, delivered predominantly Republican Iowa to Franklin Roosevelt in the 1932 presidential elections. Wallace served as FDR's secretary of agriculture from 1933 to 1940, successfully formulating and administering bold New Deal initiatives in an agricultural economy devastated by the Depression. Wallace became vice-president during FDR's third term (1941–1945), but Democratic conservatives (and others) objected to what they regarded as his increasingly leftist orientation. Harry S. Truman replaced him as vice president in FDR's fourth term. When Truman became president after FDR's death, he appointed Wallace secretary of commerce, but Wallace left the administration in protest of Truman's hard-line anti-Soviet stance.

Walters, Barbara (1931–) Walters began writing for NBC's morning talk show, *Today*, in 1961 and was promoted in 1964 to the "Today Girl," a decorative role she amplified into one of substance. From 1974 to 1976, she co-hosted *Today*, then signed a $1 million contract with ABC to co-anchor the news. This made her the highest-paid journalist of the time. From 1978 to 1984 she co-hosted the TV "magazine" *20/20* and became famous for her penetrating interviews with most of the world's notables, ranging from film stars to world leaders. She enjoyed great success in obtaining interviews even with the most elusive figures.

Ward, Montgomery (1844–1913) In 1872, Montgomery Ward, a prominent Chicago merchant, began distributing a

280-page catalog throughout the rural Midwest, seeking to expand his market to farmers unable to get into the city. The success of Ward's mail-order retailing model inspired Richard W. Sears and A. C. Roebuck to begin their own catalog-based mail-order business in 1889, which became the giant of the new mail-order industry, transforming American retailing—and introducing "urban" goods throughout the country.

Warhol, Andy (1928?–1987) Warhol was born Andrew Warhola, probably in Pittsburgh. He became a commercial artist, an experience that inspired him to create works generally recognized as the first instances of the Pop Art movement. In 1962, he exhibited paintings of Campbell's soup cans, Coca-Cola bottles, and wooden sculptures of Brillo soap pad boxes—all icons of everyday American life. The following year, he added the dimension of mass production to art through silk-screen printing. Warhol challenged the definition of art versus everyday banality by bringing the one to the other. He transformed himself into a Pop culture figure, as his New York studio became the gathering place for a variety of "underground" celebrities.

Warren, Earl (1891–1974) Warren, a California Republican, was nominated as chief justice of the Supreme Court by President Dwight D. Eisenhower in 1953. Eisenhower assumed that Warren would bring a conservative cast to the court, but during his tenure—1953 to 1969—the high court introduced epoch-making social changes of a liberal nature, beginning with *Brown v. Board of Education of Topeka* (1954), which declared public school segregation unconstitutional and including the 1964 *Reynolds v. Sims*, which pegged representation in state legislatures to population, not geographical area, and the 1966 *Miranda v. State of Arizona*, which ruled that police officers, before questioning a suspect, must inform him of his right to remain silent and to have an attorney present. Warren also presided over the controversial Warren Commission in 1963–1964, which investigated the assassination of John F. Kennedy.

Warren, Mercy Otis (1728–1814) Sister of James Otis, an early advocate of American independence, and married to James Warren, a Massachusetts political figure, Mercy Warren was a self-taught writer who drew on her proximity to events and personalities to write plays and poems about the American Revolution—while it was happening. Later, in 1805, she wrote the three-volume *History of the Rise, Progress, and Termination of the American Revolution*, which remains valuable because of its intimate perspective on the conflict.

Warren, Robert Penn (1905–1989) Honored by being named the first official poet laureate of the nation in 1986, Warren is better known as a literary critic and novelist. Although most of his work is literary rather than popular in nature, his 1946 novel *All the King's Men*, loosely based on the life and career of Louisiana's Huey Long, became a bestseller, was awarded the Pulitzer Prize in 1947, and was made into an Academy Award-winning film in 1949.

Washington, Booker T. (1856–1915) Born a slave and impoverished after emancipation, Washington nevertheless managed to acquire an education, become a teacher, and, in 1881, gain appointment to head a newly established vocational school for blacks in Alabama. He transformed Tuskegee Institute into the center of black education in the United States. Washington believed that economic opportunity was more important to black progress than social equality, and he was willing to forgo (at least temporarily) the latter to achieve the former. This so-called "accommodationist" position was appealing to many whites, but alienated many younger black activists (most notably W. E. B. du Bois), who refused to settle for less than complete equality. Despite this, Washington was widely regarded as *the* voice of black America from 1895 until his death.

Washington, George (1732–1799) This Virginia planter turned soldier then national leader richly deserved the title frequently given him: Father of His Country. As a young Virginia militia colonel, Washington fought in the first battles of the French and Indian War, was active in the independence movement, and was chosen by the Continental Congress to lead the newly formed Continental Army. He was overall commander of the American military effort during the revolution. Victorious, he could have become king or dictator, but chose instead to retire to his beloved plantation, Mount Vernon, until he was called on to preside over the Constitutional Convention and then to become first president of the United States under the new Constitution. He served two terms, from 1789 to 1797, in effect creating the office of the chief executive even as he led the nation through its infancy.

Washington, Harold (1922–1987) While in his second term in the U.S. Congress, Washington agreed to run for mayor of Chicago in 1983, defeating in the Democratic primary incumbent Jane Byrne and Richard M. Daley, son of the late long-time mayor, Richard J. Daley. He then went on to defeat the white Republican challenger in the general election, in which voters turned out in record numbers. Washington faced much opposition in the mostly white City

Council, but he was nevertheless elected to a second term. He died in office seven months into that term.

Watson, James D. (1928–) During the early 1950s, this Chicago-born geneticist and biophysicist worked in England with Francis Crick on the puzzle of DNA structure. In 1953, Watson made the breakthrough discovery that the principal DNA components were linked in pairs. This insight led him and Crick to establish the double helix molecular model for DNA, which quickly gave rise to an explanation of how the molecule encodes and transmits genetic information. Watson and Crick (with Maurice Wilkins) shared the 1962 Nobel Prize for Physiology or Medicine.

Watson, John B. (1878–1958) In his 1913 essay "Psychology as a Behaviorist Views It," Watson defined psychology as the science of human behavior, which could and should be studied in the laboratory with scientific rigor—just as one would study the behavior of animals. Watson went on in other works to codify behaviorism as the objective experimental study of the relation between environmental stimuli and human behavior. This approach dominated psychology in America throughout the 1920s and 1930s.

Watson, Thomas J., Sr. (1874–1956) In 1924, Watson, who was president of CTR (Computing Tabulating Recording Company), a maker of tabulating machines, renamed his firm IBM—International Business Machines—and began to lead the company's rise to the position of world's leading maker of innovative electromechanical calculating devices, collation and sorting machines, typewriters, and other machines for business. In 1940, IBM participated in the development of the Mark I, considered the first modern programmable computer.

Wayne, "Mad Anthony" (1745–1796) A brilliant American commander during the American Revolution—his boldness suggested by his nickname—Wayne's military masterpiece came after independence had been won. During 1786–1794, the Shawnee, Miami, Ottawa, and other tribes resisted white settlement of parts of present-day Ohio and Indiana. U.S. Army and militia forces suffered repeated defeat until Wayne formed, trained, and led a new force, winning the Battle of Fallen Timbers (in present-day Ohio) on August 20, 1794. The victory opened the vast Ohio country to settlement.

Wayne, John (1907–1979) Born Marion Michael Morrison in Winterset, Iowa, Wayne first appeared in silent Western films in the late 1920s and, in 1930, first starred as "John Wayne" in *The Big Trail,* directed by Raoul Walsh. From that time until his death, Wayne played (usually) cowboys and other figures of the American West and, especially during and after World War II, soldiers. For millions of fans, he was the image of the strong, stoic American masculine ideal, a man of deeds rather than words, who lived by an unshakeable moral code.

Webster, Daniel (1782–1852) An attorney who argued before the Supreme Court, a U.S. congressman from Massachusetts (1813–1817 and 1823–1827), senator (1827–1841 and 1845–1850), and secretary of state (1841–1843 and 1850–1852), Webster was celebrated as the greatest orator of his day. During January 19–27, 1830, he engaged Senator Robert Y. Hayne of South Carolina in a series of debates on the doctrine of states' rights. Webster held that the individual states were sovereign only where their power was not qualified by the Constitution and further argued that the Constitution and the federal government were not sovereign over the states, but over the people of the United States. The Webster-Hayne debates established the opposing concepts of government that would lead to the outbreak of the Civil War.

Webster, Noah (1758–1843) The first American lexicographer, Webster wrote books that not only endowed American English with an identity distinct from British English, but advanced the proposition that spelling, grammar, and usage were not absolute, but rather based upon living language as actually spoken at a particular time and in a particular place. Webster democratized the dictionary.

Weems, Mason Locke (1759–1825) Often called Parson Weems, Mason Locke Weems was a traveling book salesman and a writer. In 1800, he published *The Life and Memorable Actions of George Washington,* inserting into fifth edition (1806) of this extraordinarily popular work the entirely fictitious story of how young George chopped down his father's favorite cherry tree then owned up to the act because (he said) "Father, I cannot tell a lie." The story caught on as a parable of the incorruptible character of the future "Father of His Country."

Weinberger, Caspar (1917–2006) "Cap" Weinberger served as President Reagan's secretary of state from 1981 until his resignation on November 23, 1987. He presided over an extraordinary expansion of the American military in accordance with Reagan's hard line against what he called the Soviet "evil empire." Recent historians believe that

Weinberger's massive military spending program forced the Soviet Union to overspend its faltering economy in an attempt to keep pace. This weakened the Soviet Union, bringing about, first, a thaw in the Cold War and, ultimately, the collapse of Communism. Weinberger ended his tenure as defense secretary embroiled in the Iran-Contra Affair, the major scandal of the Reagan administration. Indicted for his role in Iran-Contra, he was pardoned by Reagan's successor, George H. W. Bush, before he could be prosecuted.

Welch, Joseph (1890–1960) Welch was a civilian attorney for the U.S. Army when it was under investigation by Joseph McCarthy's Senate Permanent Subcommittee on Investigations. On June 9, 1954, the 30th day of the nationally televised "Army-McCarthy Hearings," McCarthy attempted to smear one of Welch's junior attorneys, implying that he had Communist ties. Welch squashed the attempt, then rebuked McCarthy: "Have you no sense of decency, sir? At long last, have you left no sense of decency?" Welch then cut off McCarthy's bid to renew his attack by demanding that the chairman "call the next witness." The gallery burst into applause, and the American television audience saw McCarthy for what he was: a reckless bully who built his career on destructive innuendo.

Welles, Orson (1915–1985) At 26, Welles directed—and starred in—*Citizen Kane* (1941), based loosely on the life and career of media magnate William Randolph Hearst and considered by most critics of film the greatest American movie ever made. In addition to telling a compelling story, the film introduced innovations in narrative, cinematography, lighting, and editing—all of which exerted a profound influence on film. Although *Citizen Kane* was the apogee of

Welles's career, he had also earned fame—and notoriety—for his radio plays, especially his 1938 adaptation of H. G. Wells's *War of the Worlds*, which used the format of a news broadcast, projecting such realism that it caused widespread panic among listeners who believed the earth was being invaded by Martians.

Welty, Eudora (1909–2001) Welty was born, raised, and lived in the Delta town of Jackson, Mississippi, and created a body of fiction focused on this region. Welty's characters are drawn with realistic precision—she was one of the great writers of regional dialect—but their situations partake of universal aspects of human relationships.

West, Benjamin (1738–1820) One of the most important of early American painters, West reversed the usual situation—in which an American painter studied abroad then returned to America—by getting the bulk of his artistic training in America, supplementing it by study in Italy, then settling in England, where he was celebrated as a painter of historical and mythological subjects. His patron was no less than King George III. West, who was a founder of the Royal Academy in 1768, had an extensive influence on history painting in England.

Westinghouse, George (1846–1914) Westinghouse's first major invention was the air brake, which he patented in 1869 and which made rail travel safe and comfortable. Toward the end of the 19th century, Westinghouse developed the innovation for which he is best known, alternating current (AC) generation, which (against much opposition, including that of Thomas Edison) he deemed far more practical for commercial power generation than traditional direct current (DC). It is thanks to Westinghouse that the United States soon adopted the AC standard.

Westmoreland, William (1914–2005) A distinguished officer in World War II and a rising star afterward, Westmoreland directed military operations in the Vietnam War from 1964 to 1968, the peak years of the conflict. Repeatedly requesting larger and larger forces, he was a lightning rod for antiwar protest. Under his command, paradoxically, the U.S. Army won every battle in Vietnam, yet nevertheless lost the war to an enemy who, repeatedly beaten, would not accept defeat.

Weston, Edward (1886–1958) Weston started his photographic career making "pictorial" pictures, imitative of Impressionist paintings, but by 1915 he began to make sharply focused, straightforward photographs and, in conjunction with this, formulated an entire aesthetic theory of photography. He developed a style of great purity and directness, always using a large-format camera, never enlarging negatives, and never cropping them. His influence over 20th-century American photography was profound.

Weyerhaeuser, Frederick K. (1834–1914) Born in Germany, Weyerhaeuser immigrated to the United States when he was 18. He worked in an Illinois sawmill, which he purchased after its owner was wiped out in the financial panic of 1857. From this beginning, Weyerhaeuser built an empire of lumber forests (some 2 million acres), sawmills, paper mills, and other wood-products processing facilities.

Wharton, Edith (1862–1937) Born Edith Newbold Jones, Wharton lived among the New York City gentry, which became the focus of her most important novels, including *The House of Mirth* (1905) and the Pulitzer Prize-winning *The Age of Innocence* (1920). Within the confines of this select universe, Wharton found boundless emotion to explore as well as the often exquisite tension between the individual and his social milieu.

Wheatley, Phillis (ca. 1753–1784) Wheatley was born in West Africa and taken to America as a slave in 1761. She was purchased by a Boston tailor as a servant for his wife. The couple treated her virtually as one of the family and allowed her to learn to read and write. She began to compose poetry at age 14 and was first published in 1770. A collection, *Poems on Various Subjects, Religious and Moral,* was issued in London in 1773.

Whistler, James Abbot McNeil (1834–1903) Best known for his *Arrangement in Grey and Black, No. 1: The Artist's Mother* (1871)—familiarly called "Whistler's Mother"—Whistler was born in America but studied in Paris and then lived most of his adult life in London, where he achieved his greatest fame. His paintings are often titled quite abstractly—"Symphony in White No 1," and so on—reflecting Whistler's belief in creating art for art's sake, without reference to any other intellectual or moral purpose. As influential as his paintings were—they constituted the avant-garde of his time—even more important were his eloquent critical and theoretical writings about art.

White, Theodore (1915–1986) A distinguished journalist and successful novelist, White is best known for his two insider accounts of critical presidential campaigns, *The Making of the President, 1960* (1961) and *The Making of the President, 1964*

(1965). Intimate histories of the Kennedy and Johnson campaigns, they combine the skill of a journalist and the sensibility of a novelist with the understanding of a historian to present the politicians not as abstractions but as people caught in critical moments of history.

White, William Allen (1868–1944) Born and raised in Emporia, Kansas, White was dubbed the "Sage of Emporia" for his journalism, especially his editorials, which appeared in the Emporia *Gazette,* making this small-town newspaper internationally famous. White embodied the best of small-town America, a mixture of optimism and liberal Republicanism with an outlook that, while parochial, was also enlightened and tolerant. His most famous editorial, "What's the Matter with Kansas?" (August 15, 1896), was a critical attack on populism and was widely credited with helping moderate Republican William McKinley defeat populist Democrat William Jennings Bryan in the presidential election of 1896.

Whitefield, George (1714–1770) Whitefield was an Englishman who came to America in 1738 as a Methodist evangelical missionary. He traveled widely throughout the country, preaching with an emotional eloquence that made him a prime mover of the "Great Awakening," a major revival movement in the British-American colonies.

Whitman, Marcus and Narcissa (1802–1847; 1808–1847) On September 1 1836, Marcus and Narcissa Whitman, together with another Methodist missionary, H. H. Spaulding, and their families, founded the first American settlement in the Oregon Territory. This was the prelude to a torrent of far-western settlement dubbed "Oregon fever"; however, on November 29, 1847, the Whitmans and 12 others were killed by Indians (who blamed them for spreading a deadly measles epidemic). The "Whitman Massacre" drew federal attention and military forces to Oregon, which further hastened its settlement.

Whitman, Walt (1819–1892) Whitman was a mostly self-taught newspaper editor and schoolteacher, whose *Leaves of Grass*, published in its first version in 1855, is perhaps the most original collection of verse ever written. The poems, whose long, unrhymed lines were inspired by operatic arias, embodied the spirit of democratic America, moving Ralph Waldo Emerson to write to Whitman, "I greet you at the beginning of a great career." Whitman spent his life continually reshaping, revising, and enlarging *Leaves of Grass* through several editions until just before his death in 1892.

Whitney, Eli (1765–1825) In 1793, Yale graduate Eli Whitney, who was working as a tutor at Mulberry Grove, a Georgia plantation, patented the cotton gin, a device he designed to automate the removal of seeds from short-staple cotton, making cotton cultivation extremely efficient and profitable. Whitney's invention had two profound effects: it made cotton king in the South, and it increased the demand for slave labor to pick cotton, thereby ensuring the continuation of slavery as a southern institution. Whitney realized little profit from the cotton gin—which was widely pirated—but made a fortune selling rifles to the U.S. Army in 1797, producing them with interchangeable parts, so that they could be rapidly assembled by unskilled workmen. It was a prelude to true mass production.

Whittier, John Greenleaf (1807–1892) Whittier was a New Englander, whose early career, from 1826 to 1832, was devoted to journalism and poetry, and whose middle years

(1833–1842) were taken up with his work as an abolitionist. Later in life, he returned to poetry, producing his most-beloved work, *Snow-Bound* in 1866.

Wigglesworth, Michael (1631–1705) Wigglesworth immigrated from England to America in 1638, graduated from Harvard College, and began preaching in Massachusetts in 1653. He wrote rhymed poetry expounding Puritan doctrine, the most famous of which was the book-length ballad *The Day of Doom: or a Poetical Description of the Great and Last Judgment* (1662), a horrific evocation of Judgment Day, which became a popular sensation in the British-American colonies and was the first American bestseller.

Wilder, Thornton (1897–1975) Wilder focused on small places and specific events to convey universal truths of human existence and human nature. In his 1927 novel *The Bridge of San Luis Rey,* he used the collapse of an obscure Peruvian bridge in the eighteenth century to examine the lives of five persons killed in the tragedy. In his most famous work, the play *Our Town* (1938), Wilder peered into the lives of the inhabitants of a small American town, evoking moving elements of their common humanity.

Wilentz, Sean (1951–) Since 1979, Wilentz has taught at Princeton, where he is the George Henry Davis 1886 Professor of American History. Generally regarded as one of the nation's greatest living historians, he created a sensation with his May 2006 article on President George W. Bush in *Rolling Stone* magazine titled "The Worst President in History?"

Willard, Frances (1839–1898) In addition to founding the WCTU, Willard was a leader of the national Prohibition Party.

Her work helped to create the political climate in which national prohibition was enacted by the Eighteenth Amendment in 1919.

Williams, Bert (ca. 1876–1922) Williams was born in the Bahamas and raised in California. He partnered with another black performer, George W. Walker, in 1895 to create an enormously successful comedy team. Williams's greatest success was in the Ziegfeld Follies, where he played a dim-witted black stereotype character in blackface make-up—because his own complexion was not sufficiently dark for the stereotype. Williams's performances—especially his dryly fatalistic signature song, "Nobody"—were always charged with a poignancy that reflected the racial bigotry in which he worked.

Williams, Roger (1603?–1683) A radical minister in the Massachusetts Bay Colony, Williams broke with orthodox Puritan doctrine by advocating elements of religious toleration. On September 13, 1635, Bay Colony governor Roger Winthrop banished him, and in June 1636, Williams founded Rhode Island on land he legally purchased from the local Native Americans. He established the colony on principles of the separation of church and state ("Coerced religion stinks in God's nostrils," he declared) and as a haven of religious tolerance.

Williams, Tennessee (1911–1983) Despite his sobriquet, Williams was born Thomas Lanier Williams in Columbus, Mississippi—not Tennessee—and he made his Broadway breakthrough in 1944 with *The Glass Menagerie,* a play about social decay, dreams, and disappointment. His next play, *A Streetcar Named Desire* (1947), was an even bigger sensation, setting forth the themes that occupied Williams throughout his career: the portrayal of a world of frustrated desire underlying a surface of decayed Southern romance and genteel manners.

Williams, William Carlos (1883–1963) Williams grew up in New Jersey and became a pediatrician, practicing lifelong in Rutherford, New Jersey, while writing a unique body of poems and prose, in which he revealed within the mundane and even the ugly—the detritus of modern civilization—the beauty of vitality and passion. His masterpiece, the five-volume poem *Paterson,* is a complex vision of this New Jersey industrial city as the embodiment of humankind and of modern man in America.

Wilkie, Wendell (1892–1944) Wilkie left the Democratic Party because he believed President Franklin D. Roosevelt's New Deal brought too many government restraints on business. In 1940, as a Republican, he ran unsuccessfully against FDR, who was bidding for his third term. During World War II, he saw himself in the role of the "loyal opposition" and did much to promote the early war effort. In 1943, he wrote *One World,* a book advocating postwar international cooperation. Wilkie's view helped prevent the kind of Republican isolationism that had swept the country after World War I.

Wilmot, David (1814–1868) Although he was a Democrat, this Pennsylvania Congressman supported abolition, and proposed on August 8, 1846 a proviso (actually originated by Jacob Brinkerhoff of Ohio, but promoted by WIlmot) to outlaw slavery in any territory acquired from Mexico as a result of the U.S.-Mexican War. Wilmot attempted to attach the proviso to various bills, but it was always defeated. Nevertheless, its introduction gave birth to the Free Soil Party, which led to the founding of the antislavery Republican Party.

Wilson, Woodrow (1856–1924) Thomas Woodrow Wilson abandoned the practice of law to become a professor of American history and political science, was a prolific author on these subjects, and rose to the presidency of Princeton University. He was elected governor of New Jersey in 1910 and proved to be such an effective reformer that he earned the Democratic presidential nomination in 1912. He handily defeated both incumbent Republican William Howard Taft and third-party challenger Theodore Roosevelt. During his first term, Wilson introduced a variety of reform legislation, including the Sixteenth Amendment, which provided for a federal income tax. He also steered America on a resolutely neutral course during World War I (the "Great War"), which had begun in Europe in July 1914. Reelected in 1916, however, he led the country into the war (April 1917), in the belief that U.S. participation would give the country (and him) a strong hand in reshaping the world for a lasting peace. After the armistice, Wilson assumed a major guiding role in shaping the Treaty of Versailles, which included the founding of the League of Nations, an international body intended to resolve all future conflicts peacefully (for which Wilson received the 1919 Nobel Prize for Peace). A Republican-controlled U.S. Senate, however, refused to ratify the treaty or the League, Wilson took his case to the public in a cross-country whistle-stop lecture tour, during which he collapsed from exhaustion. After suffering a massive stroke on October 2, 1919, he was severely disabled, leaving his wife, Edith Gault Wilson, to manage many of the affairs of government for the rest of his second term.

Winchell, Walter (1897–1972) Winchell (who originally spelled his name *Winchel*) was a vaudeville entertainer who became a part-time gossip columnist in 1927. This quickly evolved into a full-time job as people responded to his rapid-fire, telegraphic style, which embodied the latest slang. By the 1930s, Winchell was nationally syndicated in the papers and, beginning in 1932, had a national radio program as well. He delivered news and gossip, was highly opinionated, and had access to all the nation's movers and shakers. From the thirties through the fifties, he wielded tremendous influence. He crusaded for social justice (as in his campaigns against racism and the rise of Hitler), but by the 1950s he became an arch-conservative and a major apologist for Senator Joseph McCarthy.

Winfrey, Oprah (1954–) Winfrey was the product of a broken home, but overcame adversity early on to become a TV news anchor at age 19 in Nashville, Tennessee. She rose through jobs in larger television markets, and in 1984 moved to Chicago as host of *A.M. Chicago*, transforming the failing program into a popular hit. In 1985 it was renamed *The Oprah Winfrey Show.*, then syndicated nationally the following year. Since then, Winfrey has built a media empire, becoming one of the most popular and influential figures on television—as well as the publisher of a national magazine and the head of a major production company.

Winthrop, John (1588–1649) One of England's persecuted Puritans, Winthrop joined the Massachusetts Bay Company in 1629 and was elected first governor of the Massachusetts Bay Colony. From the founding of the colony until 1648, he was chosen governor 12 times and was regarded by the colonists as a stern but loving father. Without doubt, his strong hand helped to ensure the survival and prosperity of the colony, but he was also a force for Puritan intolerance and came into conflict with such advocates of liberality and non-orthodoxy as Roger Williams and Anne Hutchinson.

Wirt, William (1772–1834) Wirt first came to national prominence as the prosecutor in Aaron Burr's 1807 trial for treason, and in 1817 President James Monroe named him attorney general. He served for 12 years, through the administration of John Quincy Adams, and permanently transformed the position into a powerful one by identifying and prosecuting important cases for the government. Wirt was also an author of note, publishing in 1817 *The Life and Character of Patrick Henry*, which published for the first time many of Henry's most famous speeches. Some believe that Henry's ringing "Give me liberty or give me death!" speech was actually invented by Wirt for his book.

Wister, Owen (1860–1938) Although he was an easterner, Wister earned his fame as an author of westerns, most notably the 1902 novel *The Virginian*, which introduced into American culture the leading elements of the enduring popular picture of the cowboy, including the cowboy's upright code of ethics, his naïve way with women, and the showdown gun duel.

Wolfe, Thomas (1900–1938) A native of Asheville, North Carolina, Wolfe tried unsuccessfully to become a playwright, then turned to fiction, creating in a very short time four long novels that were based in large part on his own coming of age. Lyrical, rhapsodic, and epic, Wolfe's fiction deals with time and memory as well as growing up in America. William Faulkner thought him the greatest novelist of his generation—rating *himself* second.

Wolfe, Tom (1930–) Wolfe earned instant fame with his first book, *The Kandy-Kolored Tangerine-Flake Streamline Baby* (1964), a collection of essays that reported on (and satirized) American fads and personalities of the early 1960s. This was followed by *The Electric Kool-Aid Acid Test* (1968), a chronicle of the psychedelic drug culture of the later 1960s. These works established Wolfe as a hip, irreverent verbal virtuoso, who applied the techniques of a novelist to journalism, creating what was soon dubbed the "New Journalism." Wolfe continued to apply this technique *The Right Stuff* (1979), about the early U.S. manned space program, and he also wrote more conventional novels, which satirized aspects of contemporary culture.

Wood, Grant (1892–1942) Iowa-born Wood depicted not the impressive landscapes of the eastern or western mountains, but the humbler surroundings of his native Midwest, creating an art movement known as Midwestern Regionalism. His approach was highly stylized, even geometric, and slyly satiric, as in his classic *American Gothic* of 1930, which has become a familiar icon of "middle-American" values and mindset.

Wood, Leonard (1860–1927) Wood began his military career as a civilian contract surgeon, later becoming a medical officer. He served as military governor of Cuba (1899–1902), introducing a host of educational, judicial, and health reforms, then, in 1910, became chief of staff of the army—a remarkable achievement for a medical officer. He bucked the prevailing American isolationism to advocate preparedness after the outbreak of World War I in Europe and set high standards for transforming civilians into soldiers and officers. In 1921, he was named governor general of the Philippine Islands, serving there until 1927.

Woodhull, Victoria Claflin (1838–1927) Born into a family of impoverished eccentrics, Victoria Claflin was part of her family's traveling medicine and fortune-telling show, continuing in this even after she married Canning Woodhull when she was 15 years old. Moved by a vision of the ancient Greek orator Demosthenes, Victoria Woodhull met shipping and rail mogul Cornelius Vanderbilt, who was deeply interested in spiritualism. Backed by him, Woodhull began publishing a magazine and launched into a variety of reform movements, which made her a national sensation. These included woman suffrage, free love, and, finally, what she called "mystical socialism." In 1872, the highly visible Woodhull became the first woman to run for president when the Equal Rights Party nominated her.

Woodward, Bob (1943–) With Carl Bernstein, Woodward made journalism history—and changed American history—with investigative reporting, in the *Washington Post,* of the Watergate break-in, which led directly to the resignation of President Richard M. Nixon in 1974. With Bernstein, he also coauthored a book on Watergate, *All the President's Men* (1974), and an inside account of the collapse of the Nixon presidency, *The Final Days* (1976). More recently, on his own, Woodward wrote two books on the George W. Bush presidency, *Bush at War* (2002), about the war in Afghanistan, and *Plan of Attack* (2004), about the genesis of the U.S. invasion in Iraq. Both contain remarkable "insider" information—a hallmark of Woodward's work.

Woodward, C. Vann (1908–1999) A professor of American history at Johns Hopkins (1946–1961) and Yale (1961–1977), Woodward was regarded as the most important analyst of the post-Civil War history of the South. His landmark 1955 book,

The Strange Career of Jim Crow, demonstrated that legal segregation in the South was not rooted in time-honored Southern custom (as apologists claimed), but was the deliberate product of legislation that followed the defeat of Populism as recently as the 1890s. Woodward's argument provided a cultural basis for the federal desegregation legislation of the 1950s and 1960s by demonstrating that, historically, integration, not segregation, was the norm—even in the South.

Woolman, John (1720–1772) Woolman and his father, English Quakers, immigrated to New Jersey when young Woolman was 21 in 1741. Three years later, John Woolman began the first organized antislavery campaign in America by preaching against slavery throughout the colonies.

Wright, Frank Lloyd (1867–1959) Wright served an apprenticeship with the great architects Louis Sullivan and Dankmar Adler and in 1892 designed his first building, the Charnley House, in Chicago. This structure contained elements Wright developed into the "Prairie style"—perhaps best exemplified in Chicago's magnificent Robey House (1907)—featuring a broad, low roof, strong horizontal lines, and harmonious integration of design elements, inside and out. The Prairie Style became the most influential basis of advanced 20th-century residential design in America, and Wright became the nation's most celebrated architect.

Wright, Orville and Wilbur (1871–1948; 1867–1912) On December 17, 1903, at Kill Devil Hill, Kitty Hawk, North Carolina, Orville Wright flew a 750-pound aircraft he and his brother, Wilbur—partners in a Dayton, Ohio, bicycle shop—designed and built. Its 12-horsepower gasoline engine, which they also designed, propelled the airplane for 12 seconds a few feet above the ground over a distance of 120 feet.

Wright, Richard (1980–1960) Born and raised in Mississippi poverty, the grandson of slaves, Wright moved north during the Depression and began writing under the auspices of the Federal Writers' Project. His two most famous books, the 1940 novel *Native Son* (1940) and his 1945 autobiography, *Black Boy* (1945), were the first books by an African American to embody social protest. They were a prelude to a dominant movement in African-American literature after World War II.

Wythe, George (1726–1806) Wythe was admitted to the Virginia bar in 1746 and became active in the independence movement. A delegate to the Continental Congress, he participated in the Constitutional Convention of 1787. As a chancery judge (appointed in 1778), Wythe was an ex officio member of the Virginia supreme court, and, in *Commonwealth v. Caton* (1782), he was the first U.S. judge to assert that a court could refuse to enforce unconstitutional laws. A great jurist, he was also mentor to great jurists and leaders, including Thomas Jefferson, John Marshall, and Henry Clay.

Young, Brigham (1801–1877) Young was a carpenter in Mendon, New York, near the church Joseph Smith had established. Young read the newly published Book of Mormon and, on April 14, 1832, was baptized into the Church of Jesus Christ of Latter-day Saints, soon becoming a church leader. On July 24, 1847, three years after Smith was assassinated in the Mormon town of Nauvoo, Illinois, Young, now in command of the church, arrived with 148 Mormons—143 men, 3 women, and 2 children—in Salt Lake City, Utah Territory, which he had chosen as the new seat of the faith. This was the vanguard of the great Mormon Trek, a mass Mormon migration, which would ensure the survival of the Mormon religion and open a vast western territory of the United States.

Younger Brothers (Thomas "Cole" Coleman [1844–1916], With Frank and Jesse James, the Cole Brothers were the most celebrated and notorious bandits of the American West, responsible for a decade of brazen bank and train robberies from 1866 to 1876.

Zappa, Frank (1940–1993) Zappa was a prolific contemporary composer-performer more or less in the rock idiom, creating some 60 albums in his 30-year career. His original group, the Mothers of Invention, was founded in the 1960s, and personnel varied over the years. His music was innovative, often satiric, usually subversive of the complacent values of middle-class America, and, by the 1980s, frankly embodied political protest. Zappa took rock and roll traditions—the prevailing American popular music since the mid 1950s—and expanded them to challenging social and aesthetic dimensions.

Zenger, John Peter (1697–1746) John Peter Zenger, publisher of a colonial newspaper called the *New York Weekly Journal,* was arrested in October 1734 on charge of "seditious libel" for printing criticism of the colony's royal governor, William Cosby. Lawyer Andrew Hamilton defended Zenger at trial in 1735, securing his acquittal on the grounds that the truth can never be deemed libelous. The decision was an American milestone in the principle of freedom of the press and figured as a precedent for the First Amendment to the U.S. Constitution.

Ziegfeld, Florenz (1869–1932) Ziegfeld started in show business in 1893 as the manager of Sandow, a strong man, and went on to produce extravagant Broadway revues that became known as the Ziegfeld Follies. Sanitized versions of the Parisian Folies-Bergère, the Ziegfeld shows began in 1907 and were repeated in various versions through 1957. Ziegfeld's chorus lines were intended to "glorify the American Girl," and his extravaganzas also produced a galaxy of solo stars, including Will Rogers, Bert Williams, Fanny Brice, and Eddie Cantor.

Zworykin, Vladimir (1889–1982) Born and educated in Russia, Zworykin immigrated to the United States in 1919 and became a citizen in 1924. While working for Westinghouse, he patented in 1923 the iconoscope—the television transmission tube—and the following year the kinescope, the television receiver. Together, these were the basis for an all-electronic (as opposed to electromechanical) television system and made possible modern television technology.

Printed by the National Geographic Society
John M. Fahey, Jr., *President and Chief Executive Officer*
Gilbert M. Grosvenor, *Chairman of the Board*
Nina D. Hoffman, *Executive Vice President; President, Books Publishing Group*
Kevin Mulroy, *Senior Vice President and Publisher*
Marianne Koszorus, *Design Director*
Gary Colbert, *Production Director*
Ellen Beal, *Project Editor*
Peggy Archambault, *Art Director*
Mike Horenstein, *Production Project Manager*
Cameron Zotter, *Production and Design Assistant*

Library of Congress Cataloging-in-Publication Data available upon request.
ISBN 13: 978-1-4262-0052-6

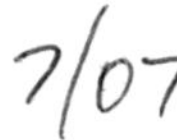

Founded in 1888, the National Geographic Society is one of the largest nonprofit scientific and educational organizations in the world. It reaches more than 285 million people worldwide each month through its official journal, NATIONAL GEOGRAPHIC, and its four other magazines; the National Geographic Channel; television documentaries; radio programs; films; books; videos and DVDs; maps; and interactive media. National Geographic has funded more than 8,000 scientific research projects and supports an education program combating geographic illiteracy.

For more information, please call
1-800-NGS LINE (647-5463)
or write to the following address:

National Geographic Society
1145 17th Street N.W.
Washington, D.C. 20036-4688 U.S.A.

Visit us online at www.nationalgeographic.com/books

For information about special discounts for bulk purchases, please contact
National Geographic Books Special Sales: ngspecsales@ngs.org

First Printing February, 2007

Printed in Mexico

THE LIBRARIAN in the UNIVERSITY:

Essays on Membership in the Academic Community

edited by
H. PALMER HALL
and
CAROLINE BYRD

The Scarecrow Press, Inc.
Metuchen, N.J., & London
1990

British Library Cataloguing-in-Publication data available

Library of Congress Cataloging-in-Publication Data

The Librarian in the university : essays on membership in the academic community / edited by H. Palmer Hall and Caroline Byrd.
p. cm.
ISBN 0-8108-2399-3 (acid-free)
1. College librarians--Faculty status. 2. Libraries, University and college--Relations with faculty and curriculum. 3.Libraries and education. I. Hall, H. Palmer, 1942- II. Byrd, Caroline.
Z682.4.C63L5 1990
378.1'2--dc20 90-21791

Manufactured in the United States of America
Printed on acid-free paper

CONTENTS

Introduction 1

PART ONE: The Librarian in University Governance

Moving Beyond the Library Sphere: Academic Librarians in the Larger Institution *by Michael O. Engle* 9

Expanding and Enhancing the Role of University Librarians: The Views of Academic Administrators *by W. Bede Mitchell* 19

Among Friends: Involvement in Academic Collegiality *by Irene B. Hoadley* 31

Partnership for Quality: Non-Traditional Students and the Librarian *by Susan Swords Steffen* 39

The Librarian as Legislator: An Important Campus Role *by Marilyn Myers* 50

The Librarian in the Faculty Senate *by Joan McCauley* 66

Working with Faculty in an Outcomes-Oriented Curriculum: Observations from the Library *by Terrence F. Mech* 72

PART TWO: The Librarian as Teacher

The Academic Librarian as Classroom Teacher *by Robert Hauptman and Fred Hill* 93

Getting into the Classroom in a Non-Bibliographic Instruction Way *by H. Palmer Hall* 100

Teaching in Rotation as a Member of the Instructional Faculty and as a Librarian *by Taylor Hubbard* 109

Uncharted Territory: Building a Library Instruction Course in Geography *by Robert B. Marks Ridinger* 117

PART THREE: Research, Publication and Networking as a Librarian in the University

Deflating the Oxymoron; or, Searching for a Shoe Beneath the Leather and the Lasts *by Dale R. Schrag* 123

Lighthouses, Mannequins, and Pioneer Women: Serendipitous Encounters with Teaching Faculty *by Caroline Byrd* 138

Social Contact in the Academy: An Indirect Route to Collegiality *by Douglas M. Ferrier* 147

PARTFOUR: The Librarian and the Student: Outside the Library Walls

Librarians and Student Advocacy: A Holistic Perspective *by Gloria Elaine Hilario* 154

The Librarian as Academic Adviser *by Kathy Sisoian and H. Palmer Hall* 159

A Synergistic Supplement: Remedial Writing Instructors & Reference Librarians Teamed to Build Confidence in the Underprepared Student *by Carmen F. Embry* 166

Working with Students: Gaining Perspective as a Faculty Liaison and a Faculty Mentor *by Renee Nesbitt Anderson* 171

PART FIVE: A Recommended Reading List for Librarians in the University

A Recommended Reading List for Librarian Faculty Members *by Susan Hall* 180

Introduction

In reading reams of library literature over the past ten years, the editors have been struck by the lack, until very recently, of any relevant information concerning the librarian outside of the library and in the college or university where he/she works. The profession of the academic librarian is a two-forked profession: it is important, and no one can overestimate how important, to be a highly competent and professional librarian, but it is equally important to be a member of, to be engaged in, the college or university that is the sole purpose for having a library in the first place. Library literature normally ignores this second prong of the academic library profession.

The literature of librarianship reflects the normal work existence and issues of academic librarians -- as catalogers, reference librarians, acquisitions librarians, library directors, and so forth. While professionally involved in, and sometimes obsessed with, the professional tasks which they follow, librarians are not normally a prominent part of their university community. Arguments have been put forth that only library directors have the opportunity to make an impression on the general university community, mostly because of the prominence of their own positions in the hierarchy. That is an easy cop-out. University community members in other areas, department chairs, assistant professors of various subjects,frequently play prominent roles in their universities without having the convenient office for support. What's the difference? Why is it that a junior professor in chemistry or English can have a profound influence on the overall shape of the university and librarians frequently feel that their own positions keep them from playing a significant role outside the library?

Librarians too often fail to serve on important non-library committees, do not often sponsor student organizations, are not normally elected to faculty senates unless there is a "special place" reserved for them, fail to attend all but required meetings of the faculty on campus, and are mostly irrelevant in the day-to-day lives of the students whom they serve, except as purveyors of information. We do not want to underplay the importance of being a good purveyor of information, but there is more to being an engaged member of the faculty and a member of a community of educators than that.

Job satisfaction is a matter of increasing concern to librarians everywhere, but it is too often couched simply in terms of satisfaction within the library structure. Are you happy in your position as cataloger or as a public services librarian? We should look at the question from another vantage point: Are you happy in your community of work? Are you happy with yourself as a member of the educational community of X University? The major question should deal with satisfaction in carrying out the important mission of the university as well as the important subsidiary mission of the library. Just as the faculty member in marketing must see himself or herself as furthering the mission of X University through good teaching and the parallel work of curriculum development and student service through education, the librarian must see herself or himself as furthering that same set of major missions. We are librarians *in* the university, not librarians *at* the library located *at* the university.

The literature of librarianship frequently deals with issues tangential to being a librarian *in* the university. The major issue as far as numbers are concerned is the issue of faculty status. From the outset, we contend that faculty status is *important* to the role of being a librarian in the university community, but it is not the central issue. Faculty status confers certain rights and obligations on the librarian, but it does not require effective participation in the university community.

This book is about librarians becoming full citizens of their academic institutions and has been written by a number of librarians who have gotten involved with the parent institutions of their libraries. They have served on major university committees, taught in the classroom, worked as colleagues with the teaching faculty in research and publication, sponsored student organizations and even lived in residence halls. They are librarians, but they are also dedicated members of their college or university communities.

The first part of the book deals with the major problem of university governance and the role librarians can contribute in collegial governance of their institutions. Michael Engle of Linfield College begins with a discussion of the corporate culture of universities and the unique role librarians can play within the institution.

W. Bede Mitchell of Appalachian State University decided to survey over one hundred chief academic officers of non-ARL, research institutions to find out what they thought librarians should be doing to gain greater recognition within their own institutions. The results were not surprising: librarians have a much better view of their roles than do their chief academic officers.

A series of articles dealing with specifics on how to get involved in university governance is kicked off by Irene B. Hoadley of Texas A & M. Stressing that the faculty are our natural allies on the university campus, Hoadley shows various strategies for getting on university committees and also points out the necessity of making a positive contribution to those committees.

Susan Swords Steffen works with University College of Northwestern University and describes the value of working in an environment where librarians, by virtue of being the largest full-time component of this branch campus, play a major role in curriculum development as well as support and development of the largely part-time faculty who serve University College's non-traditional student body.

Stressing the value of working with the faculty on those committees that are actually responsible for the faculty share of university governance, Marilyn Myers of Arizona State University urges librarians to get out and participate, to become a participant in helping to determine what happens to the university, to the library, and to their own professional lives. Though some are elective, these committee structures are normally appointed and exist within the bureaucratic hierarchy of the institution.

Joan McCauley of California State University - Long Beach discusses the most venerable means of participation in university governance -- involvement in the faculty senate. The senate is the formal route around bureaucratic hierarchies for faculty members to give input to university decision making.

The final section in this first part of the book deals with a growing movement on college and university campuses -- the outcomes assessment movement. Terrence Mech of King's College, one of the leading institutions in the outcomes movement, discusses the opportunities for involvement that are presented through outcomes assessment and some of the drawbacks of such involvement.

The second major section of the book moves from the problem of librarian involvement in university governance and into the classroom. Many faculty members in the classroom argue that the major reason librarians should not have faculty status is that we do not teach and do not share their professional concerns in syllabus building, classroom performance and student evaluation. With the notable exception of those universities that offer bibliographic instruction as a formal course, this argument is persuasive.

In fact, Robert Hauptman and Fred Hill of St. Cloud State University describe librarians as "academic outsiders" for just this reason. They describe the situation at their own institution where librarians do, in fact, teach and are treated as equal members of the faculty -- not just through collegial recognition, but through contract periods, sabbaticals and full participation in university governance as faculty members.

Palmer Hall of St. Mary's University recommends that qualified librarians take the initiative by approaching academic departments and offering their services as adjunct members of the faculty outside the library. Aside from extra pay, this can lead to greater recognition from our peers in the formal classroom.

Taylor Hubbard of The Evergreen State College describes their unique approach to librarians as faculty members and the rotation system that sends librarians into the classroom as subject teachers on a regular basis. Teaching faculty members also rotate into the library to serve as reference librarians, bibliographers and so on. Hubbard argues, like Hauptman and

Hill, that librarians don't have to seek recognition, they receive it because of their roles in the college.

Robert Ridinger of Northern Illinois University describes his teaching as a librarian, but within the academic department for which he was the library liaison. While the course he developed owes its heritage to bibliographic instruction it is offered as a departmental course, not as a course within the library.

All of these librarians feel that it is important that at least some of the librarians at their institutions teach from time to time. It gives the library a new insight into the problems of both the teaching faculty and the students who are the main focus of the library.

Research, publication and social activity make up the third part of this book. The faculty at almost all universities participate in all three and success as a faculty member is marked by attention to all of these as much as it is to teaching.

Dale Schrag of Bethel College discusses the importance of research. His essay shows that research can give librarians both the sense of being a faculty member and a deeper understanding of the role of libraries. The article is an excellent argument for the second master's degree with thesis, as a minimum professional development tool for becoming a member of the faculty.

Publication, of course, goes hand in hand with research. Caroline Byrd of St. Mary's University recommends an excellent way to begin a publishing career. That method requires the librarian to be an active member of the university community and to develop collegial relationships within the teaching faculty. The synergy that can develop in such a professional relationship can lead to publication and presentation of papers.

Doug Ferrier of Texas Wesleyan College encourages librarians to take advantage of a very pleasant side of university life -- the social side. Participation in the social life of the university is a good way to get involved in many other aspects of the university. Through the Faculty Club or informal sessions, librarians become known, meet colleagues, and get the opportunity to participate more fully in the professional life of the institution.

The fourth section of the book deals with the interactions of academic librarians and students outside the library. Moving beyond traditional bibliographic instruction and reference assistance, the authors stress the need for educating the whole student in a variety of ways.

Academic librarians are prime promoters of holistic education asserts Gloria Hilario of Palo Alto College. According to Hilario, numerous ways exist for librarians to foster a holistic environment for students. Sharing with students the personal fulfillment which comes from social service is one such way.

Academic advising, traditionally the province of teaching faculty, is examined by Kathy Sisoian and Palmer Hall of St. Mary's University. The authors discuss why librarians are in an advantageous position to do academic advising and what rewards can come from such activity.

Carmen Embry describes her unusual position at the University of Louisville's Ekstrom Library. In addition to being Coordinator of Bibliographic Instruction, Embry also serves as a remedial writing instructor. Through her dual role, she emphasizes confidence building in the underprepared student.

From California State University at Long Beach, Renee Anderson writes of her involvement with the Faculty-in-Residence Program and with a special mentoring program. As a participant, Anderson lived in a dorm where she did academic advising, tutoring and, later, mentoring as well as interacting socially with the students.

In the concluding section of the book, Susan Hall of Incarnate Word College presents a recommended reading list for librarian faculty members. Based on a survey of chief academic officers, the books selected all deal in some way what with it means to be a faculty member.

The contributors to this book come from a variety of backgrounds, institutions and experiences within their institutions. Despite their differing circumstances, all share a strong image of themselves as librarians and faculty within the broader context of the academy.

To attain that image, each has made a deliberate decision to be faculty *within* the institution. Further, each has pursued specific actions designed to promote that image to their coworkers outside the library. While no one method will work for all librarians, the editors hope that these contributions will inspire other academic librarians to become true members of their academic communities.

H. Palmer Hall
Director of Libraries
St. Mary's University
San Antonio, Texas

Caroline Byrd
Assistant Director/
Systems Administrator
St. Mary's University
San Antonio, Texas

PART I

The Librarian in University Governance

MOVING BEYOND THE LIBRARY SPHERE: ACADEMIC LIBRARIANS IN THE LARGER INSTITUTION

by
Michael O. Engle

Public Services Librarian
Linfield College

One of my strongest points . . . is . . . that academic librarians need to know far more than the technical skills they learn in library school. They need to know especially the social, economic, and political context in which the library operates.

--Edward G. Holley (462)

The reality that academic libraries are part of a larger institution certainly comes as no surprise to the librarians who work there. Most of them were attracted to professional work in an academic setting because of its intellectual richness and variety. "The life of the mind, especially in our information-based society, excites us, and we want to be part of institutions critical to the functioning of our democratic society" (Holley 464). Yet the academic library seems to constitute a separate world, isolated from the hubbub that surrounds it. In spite of the profound interdependence of the library and its parent institution, academic librarians encounter attitudes, values, and organizational structures that inhibit their activity outside the library and undermine the development of an institution-wide academic community. Leaving the library sphere temporarily and becoming active in the larger institution can give librarians a new perspective on library issues and problems. The broader view can be both refreshing and disturbing, a source of new insights and friendships and a challenge to old ways. Such participation is an important element of professional growth and maturity.

This chapter explores the nature of the contemporary corporate culture of American colleges and universities and the place of librarians in it. Each institution has a set of values and ideals that form the background for accomplishing its central tasks of teaching, learning and research. These values are implicit or explicit in various ways, including formal mission statement, the publications of the institution, and the speeches of its leaders. To use an alchemical metaphor, these values, beliefs, and assumptions define the boundaries of a container within which the transformations of social and intellectual growth can occur. Inside the container, the concentration of teachers, learners, and academic resources (of which the library is one important example) is the medium that feeds scholarship and encourages it to flourish.

The container and the medium taken together constitute the corporate culture of each college and university. This culture has two subcultures, one visible and formal, the other invisible and informal. The formal subculture presents the conscious, written and public statements of the institution's mission. Ideally, these formal values and beliefs are articulated in a document created by interested, representative members of the institution. More specific goals and objectives that relate to this overall mission may be developed to guide day-to-day decisions and activities. People initiate or modify programs, formulate syllabi and course goals, purchase books and materials, and select classes and major areas of study within the context set by the overall mission. Individual departments and units may write their own mission statements, as librarians often do in accordance with ACRL Standards. Whether there are written mission statements or not, each institution operates under a set of policies and assumptions, visible in organization charts, governance structures, and publications, that define its formal corporate subculture.

Intimately interwoven with the formal subculture is a much larger, but less immediately apparent, informal subculture. Made up of social, economic, and political dimensions, this subculture is also unique to the institution. It influences the allocation of economic resources, the general nature of social interactions, and the distribution of political power among individuals and departments. The active participation of librarians in both these subcultures is important for the vitality of their professional work and their library.

For example, librarians may make a difference in the formal direction of the institution by becoming involved in the process of formulating a college or university-wide mission statement. Not only is this an opportunity to see that library needs get a hearing, but it also gives librarians a wider knowledge of the health of the institution, a feel for external constraints on its behavior, and a sense of the priority that the institution puts on library services and support.

Involvement in the formal subculture can be very important for establishing equitable, reasonable standards of evaluation for librarians since the evaluation process is often based on existing formal standards that may not take the specific intellectual tasks of librarians into account. But the translation of the institutional mission and standards into actual practice is largely dependent on the workings of the informal corporate subculture.

Significant participation in the formal mission and standards-setting processes by librarians usually depends on gaining a position in and an accurate knowledge of the informal subculture. This is the realm of action that depends on personal relationships -- who knows whom and how well. The social, economic, and political processes of the institution are channelled through this subculture. These informal channels among researchers and scholars are often called the "invisible college." Among administrators and in the political process, they are referred to as the society of "good ol' boys" or the "old boy network." Librarians usually call the process networking. In this informal territory, relationships may satisfy social and intellectual needs, as well as political and economic ones.

Participation in the informal subculture of the parent institution is too important to be left solely to the library director or a few top library administrators; it is the responsibility of as many librarians as can manage it. For example, by attending faculty lectures, or paper presentations by thesis and honor students, librarians make contact with faculty and students with similar intellectual interests. Participation in the question and discussion periods following these presentations often leads to further involvement with departmental faculty and students, such as reading drafts of papers and books being prepared for publication or serving on search committees. Faculty and students are often eager to explain their current research to a genuinely interested enquirer. By becoming visible to the members of invisible colleges, librarians become players in the informal subculture. The challenge to academic librarians is to become members of these research networks outside the library and "fully recognized faculty members of the invisible colleges" (Grover and Hale 14).

Another area of significant participation in the informal corporate subculture is the recruitment, retention, and advising of students. Telephone recruiting of potential students can be very important to the success of tuition-driven schools. Individual contact with current students by librarians can increase retention rates. As academic advisors, librarians have no departmental axe to grind; as vocational advisors, they are a valuable resource to students and local people considering a library career.

There are significant costs associated with increased activity in the formal and informal subcultures of the larger institution, trade-offs between time spent on services in the library and the outside work. But the long-term costs of working exclusively inside the library can also be high: a profound sense of isolation, low morale, and a lack of vigorous external support for the collections and staff of the library.

The isolation of librarians from the larger institutional culture is related to a strong tradition of autonomy and specialization among academics, a tradition that separates them into departments, and, within departments, still further into their areas of specialized interest and research. In the same way, librarians tend to be confined to the library, the realm of their particular professional expertise and interest. The library becomes a separate sphere of activity with its boundaries reinforced by the traditions of academia and librarianship.

Central to these traditions are the ideals of academic and intellectual freedom. According to intellectual freedom, the individual reader is the judge of the worth of the reading material. Decisions about what and how to teach, the proper subject of research, and what to read are individual matters. Autonomy of teaching and research is one of the attractions of the academic life, even though it may not always be true in practice. The solitary researcher has given way to collaborative effort in the world of contemporary science, for instance. Still, the negative consequences of these ideals, with their radical emphasis on the individual or the expertise of the few, lead to isolation, territorialism, and a narrow view of the world. These attitudes inhibit the kinds of learning and growth that can follow the development of the attitudes of cooperation, compromise, and tolerance necessary to the success of a diverse community. The struggle to find a proper balance between the individual and the group, autonomy and community, is an ancient and enduring one.

The very large size of many academic institutions is another factor that makes an institution-wide community elusive. Large groups must break down into smaller ones to function well. The professional staff in large research libraries is bigger than the entire faculty at many liberal arts colleges; involvement outside the library means very different things in these different-sized settings. Activity within one of the colleges of the university may be more nearly equivalent to involvement in the whole institutional structure of a small school.

Giant universities are rich in variety, but they can take on mythological dimensions to the outsider, appearing monolithic and frightening. They aren't called giants for nothing. Giants are massive, clumsy, and slow. Even well-intentioned ones are heavy and strong and can inadvertently squash anyone they step on. Survival depends on staying out from underneath their feet. Smaller institutions may lack the sheer bulk and variety of intellectual resources, but are correspondingly easier to deal with.

Where and how academic librarians find their niche varies, but, in any setting, gaining a foothold outside the library is much easier with the help of an experienced mentor who knows the local culture. And personal contact with the teaching faculty is often a real morale booster because most of them are real library supporters and appreciate the contribution of their library colleagues.

One of the articles of the librarian's faith is "that [a] humane, idealistic institution is better than a cynical, self-committed one" (Finks 356). The creation of a humane institution is a task that confronts the inertia built into large social structures. In an analysis of the political economy of the university, Carrigan cites scholars' descriptions of them as "organized anarchies" in which decision making has become more and more diffused. When the president, the faculty, and other groups all hold veto power over any major action, the tendency is toward "less action, more commitment to the status quo -- the status quo is the only solution that cannot be vetoed" (329).

Institutional inertia breeds an isolation and territorialism that is compounded by the location of the library and librarians in a separate building, by the uncertain status of the master's degree in an environment where the doctorate is the standard credential, and by the absence of librarians from the classrooms and laboratories, the central setting for teaching and learning. The acts of reading, browsing, and searching the literature are normally seen as self-directed, individualistic acts, in marked contrast to the classroom and laboratory experience.

Even the historical circumstances of the rise of professional librarianship during the Victorian era, and the resultant identification of the library with the home, continues to contribute in subtle ways to the isolation of the library and an image of it as a separate sphere. In the middle-class, American culture of the 1870's, all women belonged in the home as mothers, there to create a separate world of spiritual purity and high moral ideals, a refuge from the punishing male world of politics and business. Middle-class, white women who worked outside the home were usually unmarried, and most sought work that the gender ideals of the time claimed were suitable for proper women: teaching children, nursing, social work, and librarianship. In these jobs in safe settings, the superior moral virtues of women could be employed to lift up the weak, the tired, the ill, and wayward.

> Like a visitor to a home, the reader was to be welcomed, to be given kind and individual attention, to be treated with tact and gentle manners. Not the cold impersonality of the business should pervade, but rather the warmth of the well-ordered home, presided over by a gracious and helpful librarian. (Garrison 179)

The modern ideal of the academic library retains some of this ethos -- a refuge for the classroom and committee-weary scholar, a place of intellectual refreshment and retreat with academic librarians as its keepers. But there is danger in this Victorian view of the library as a sphere separate from the business and politics of the institution and society around it. "Librarians perpetuate the myth that librarianship is apolitical" (Birdsall 75), but a separate sphere ideology of librarianship is a political statement itself, a statement that academic librarians are willing to continue to accept being isolated from the policy councils of their institutions (Carrigan 330). The problem of foregoing an active role in the larger institution is this: while they remain only keepers of the library, academic librarians will be the "kept women" of the larger organization.

Another result of this ethos is the expectation that librarians will always be available -- in the library -- to meet the needs of library users, just as the Victorian mother was on twenty-four-hour call to tend the needs of her husband and children in her home. Increasing outside activities requires giving up some time and energy for work inside the library and challenges this expectation of constant availability. Balancing inside and outside work successfully requires support and flexibility from other library staff, including the top administrators. To be successful, involvement in the parent institution must be a central part of the library's mission, and it must be encouraged across the board. When handled properly, these outside activities promote the visibility and the viability of the library and the self-esteem of librarians. When the evaluation system does not adequately recognize college and university service as a significant contribution for promotion and tenure purposes, then the risk can be too great, and the separate sphere ideology is reinforced (Gamble 346).

Even with support within the library, the boundary-breaking involved in consistently moving outside the library sphere entails risk. There is no way around it. With the institution in the hands of another and dominant profession, operating on the turf of the teaching faculty can be daunting (Wilson 183). But new teaching faculty learn the institutional ropes from the ground up, and so can librarians; no one expects new faculty to know it all.

> Every person who works in a library is going to be taking more risks in the next five years. Stepping outside our comfortable hierarchies can be an uneasy move.... We have to participate, we have to say what we think; we have to put some of

> our responsibility on the line and be assessed by the people we work with and that's not so easy.
>
> We have to be open and show initiative and courage, and those are qualities that are difficult at times to develop. (Gapen 360)

Although written six years ago, Gapen's advice is still true today. The boundary-breaking is worth it because librarians have something special to offer the larger institution.

Librarians bring two useful and needed gifts to the academic enterprise: an interdisciplinary perspective and a sense of history. Work across disciplines comes quite naturally to most librarians since they catalog and classify materials and handle reference and research questions in a wide range of subjects on a regular basis. The development and expansion of bibliographic instruction has intensified the cross-disciplinary nature of their work because it requires intimate knowledge of the structure of the literatures and the research practices of many disciplines. Armed with a generalist's approach to knowledge and a research perspective on a variety of specific subjects, librarians can function as bridges among scholars working in very different areas. In committee service, at social gatherings, and in other informal situations, librarians carry the broader vision of the quest for the expansion of human knowledge, the vision of the whole institution working together in a common, but varied, enterprise. It is a vision easily lost in the specialization, turf wars, and autonomy issues of academia.

Cross-disciplinary connections often develop in area or topical studies, including gender studies, ethnic studies, American studies, and international programs. In many cases librarians play a prominent role in these programs, bringing together relevant materials out of various disciplines, organizing them for use and acting as an important contact and intermediary among participants. Librarians sponsor workshops that bring together faculty from diverse departments to discuss course goals and teaching methods and to suggest ways bibliographic instruction can be integrated into courses to further those goals. Not surprisingly, faculty discover common problems and common approaches to their subject matter that enhance their teaching effectiveness and expand the invisible college across disciplinary boundaries.

Involved as they are in retaining and preserving the

cultural record of human civilizations, librarians have a natural contribution to make to academic institutions as cultural and institutional historians. "One of the truly appalling facts about faculty in colleges and universities (not just librarians) is the widespread ignorance of how our colleges and universities became what they are today, what constitutes their general mission, and how the political milieu, on and off campus, affects us all" (Holley 463). As a response to this ignorance, Holley recommends that academic librarians study the background of the history and development of higher education, scholarship, and learning. "While we do not necessarily have to be scholars ourselves (many faculty are not, whatever the pretense), we have to be scholarly persons, with keen intellectual curiosity and have something to contribute to the enterprise beyond what we learned in liberal arts colleges and graduate professional schools ten, twenty, or thirty years ago" (464). Stimulated by this curiosity, librarians will often find the history of their college or university waiting in the library archives and in the memories of current and emeritus faculty. The key to understanding the structure of academic institutions lies in their social, political, and economic history. This historical knowledge helps librarians define the mission of their library, and more clearly analyze the institutional dynamics they confront inside and outside the library. More general histories like Frederick Rudolph's wryly humorous survey of the changes in the American undergraduate curriculum cultivate that larger perspective. Academic librarians are natural candidates for the task of injecting the historical perspective into the consciousness of the parent institution.

It is the unique combination of involvement in and distance from the processes of the academy that makes academic librarians so valuable. Extensive use of bibliographic instruction, returning to graduate school for intensive work in a particular subject, and advising students give librarians needed contract with teaching, learning, and research. When they are most involved with these core processes, librarians are colleagues and peers of the teaching faculty. Yet, it is their different perspective that constitutes their greatest contribution to the academy. Generalists are rare and valuable these days. Building bridges across boundaries is the natural work of generalists, and a much needed one. Academic librarians owe themselves the self-respect and stimulation that can be gained by working outside the library's sphere, as well as within it.

Works Cited

Birdsall, William F. "The Political Persuasion of Librarianship." Library Journal 1 June 1988: 75-79.

Carrigan, Dennis P. "The Political Economy of the Academic Library." College & Research Libraries 49 (1988): 325-331.

Finks, Lee W. "Values Without Shame." American Libraries April 1989: 352-356.

Gamble, Lynne E. "University Service: New Implications for Academic Librarians." Journal of Academic Librarianship January 1989: 344-347.

Gapen, D. Kaye. "Myths and Realities: University Libraries." College & Research Libraries 45 (1984): 350-361.

Garrison, Dee. Apostles of Culture: The Public Librarian and American Society, 1876-1920. New York: Free Press, 1979.

Grover, Robert, and Martha L. Hale. "The Role of the Librarian in Faculty Research." College & Research Libraries 49 (1988): 9-15.

Holley, Edward G. "Defining the Academic Librarian." College & Research Libraries 46 (1985): 462-468.

Rudolph, Frederick. Curriculum: A History of the American Undergraduate Course of Study Since 1636. San Francisco: Jossey-Bass, 1978.

Wilson, Pauline. Stereotype and Status: Librarians in the United States. Westport, CT: Greenwood, 1982.

EXPANDING AND ENHANCING THE ROLE OF UNIVERSITY LIBRARIANS: THE VIEWS OF ACADEMIC ADMINISTRATORS

by
W. Bede Mitchell

Associate Librarian for Public Services
Belk Library, Appalachian State University

Introduction

Academic librarians have long recognized that defining their role in higher education is an ongoing process. Just as higher education evolves in response to and anticipation of societal needs and trends, so do academic librarians' functions evolve in response to and anticipation of the needs and trends in teaching and research. While the broad goals of librarianship remain the same (succinctly stated by Jesse Shera as acquisition, organization, and interpretation and service), librarians today spend their time very differently than did their predecessors of thirty years ago. The ways in which we now attempt to achieve those broad goals have been profoundly affected by new technologies, new learning theories, newly emerging scholarly disciplines, trends in higher education administration, the evolution of librarian faculty status, and advancements in library theory, to name only a few influences. In the future we will need to continue to adapt because education and society are fluid and constantly evolving.

One way of determining the needs which academic librarians should be meeting is to solicit the opinions of university leaders. This chapter will report on just such an effort, a survey of academic affairs officers whose backgrounds in teaching, research, and university administration provide them with unique perspectives on the higher education enterprise. The survey sought the responses of the academic affairs administrators to the question, "How could librarians contribute more fully to their universities than they already do?"

Background of the Study

Fifty-seven academic affairs vice presidents, vice chancellors, or provosts responded to the survey out of eighty who were contacted. The administrators were from universities classified by the Carnegie Foundation for the Advancement of Teaching as Doctorate-Granting Universities I and II. Such institutions grant up to forty-nine doctorates per year.

Twenty-four administrators were interviewed by phone and thirty-three responded to a mail questionnaire. The phone interviews were conducted because the method offers several advantages over mail questionnaires, including the increased likelihood of obtaining responses to specific questions, the ability to probe more deeply into responses, the opportunity to clarify issues and answers when necessary, and the opportunity to elicit opinions through the use of open-ended questions (Dillman;Frey). However, the expense of long-distance phone interviews made it necessary to use mail questionnaires to enlarge the size of the surveyed population.

Responses of the Administrators

The responses to this survey appeared to fall most congenially into three categories which inevitably overlap: the need for librarians to improve certain areas of performance, the need to improve methods for evaluating performance and quality of services, and the need to improve the working relationships between librarians and certain library clients and campus services. I will attempt to summarize those opinions and suggestions which were expressed by more than just one or two respondents, and will conclude with a brief discussion of those responses.

Performance: None of the responding administrators found fault with the job librarians have done in initiating new programs, offering new services, implementing new technologies, and expanding their traditional higher education role. In fact, the respondents generally had little but praise for librarians' activism. However, a number of administrators suggested librarians should redirect some of their energy toward improving certain skills and services.

Many respondents thought that libraries must become more than mere repositories of information. In other words, the broad goal that Shera called interpretation and service appeared to these administrators to be receiving less emphasis than acquisition and organization. Such an opinion may be startling to public service librarians who spend countless hours helping patrons find needed information, but the failure of administrators on some campuses to recognize the public assistance available in their academic libraries may be a function of our inability to communicate the reality of library services. Still, though some of these respondents may have been naive about what librarians really do and how they spend their time, we must not dismiss their criticisms cavalierly. Instead, we would do well to consider the possibility that we are no longer seeing the forest of patron service because of our many trees of bureaucratic details. But if upon careful analysis we reject that possibility, then perhaps we simply are not doing a very good job of communicating our performance to key segments of our constituency. In either case (and both might certainly apply on a given campus), corrective measures would obviously be desirable.

A similar re-examination of philosophy and policy might be the best response to another perception of several administrators, that librarians should spend more time working with faculty to strengthen important subject collections. On further probing it was found that some of the administrators holding this opinion thought the faculty's role in collection development was too small, while others felt the faculty's role was adequate but should be better coordinated with the collection development role of the librarians.

Why might some administrators believe that faculty do not play a large enough role in collection development? Perhaps this perception was caused by the tendency among university libraries to no longer allocate large portions of their book budgets to academic departments. As librarians have assumed a greater role in collection development than they had in the early decades of this century, it is not surprising that the faculty's influence would be thought to have declined. Yet while faculty members may deserve a collection development role by virtue of their subject expertise and need for library materials to support their teaching and research, the problem has always been to determine an appropriate role that is not too large for them to adequately discharge. Why is it not clear to many administrators that current collection development policies attempt to delegate that kind of role? Is it lack of communication with the faculty, or is it because many libraries have indeed failed to determine an appropriate faculty role? Obviously the answers to these questions will vary from campus to campus.

For the respondents who took the view that the faculty and librarians needed to better coordinate their collection development roles, the main concerns were for efficiency and for building upon the complementary natures of faculty and librarian duties. Because these respondents offered few specifics regarding their concerns for efficiency, little can be said about them here except that administrators plainly need to be reassured that our collection development policies and procedures are rational, carefully planned to support the university's educational goals, and efficiently involve all appropriate parties. On the other hand, the respondents had more to say about the general need to build closer working relationships between librarians and faculty; these comments will be considered later in a later section of this chapter, "Developing Closer Working Relationships with Others."

A number of other suggestions related to librarian performance were raised by only one or two respondents and are mentioned here because of their provocative nature. Two administrators said librarians spend too much time doing work that should be delegated to support staff. Such an opinion will rankle with those of us who feel we have no choice but to do certain "non- professional" tasks because of a lack of institutional support to hire the staff necessary to perform those tasks. Of course, it is important to not overreact to such an opinion when it was expressed by only two people. Nevertheless, the perception that librarians do a lot of menial work has been around a long time. It is difficult to avoid the feeling that the rewards for pitching in during a pinch are decidedly mixed when some administrators conclude we spend too much time doing what Peter Drucker calls "donkey work."

A few administrators counseled librarians who wish to enhance their subject expertise and research skills to abandon the second master's degree approach and seek an appropriate doctorate instead. As a scholarly pursuit the second master's was seen as redundant in light of librarians already holding the M.L.S. degree. According to these respondents, those who wish to be subject bibliographers, curators, or subject specialists in reference would be better advised to pursue doctorates because of the different and greater level of scholarship required. Similarly, those who want to develop their management or research skills should seek relevant doctoral degrees, either in librarianship, administration, or the desired research subject area.

A particularly interesting suggestion was that librarians should serve as academic advisors of students. The feeling was that this role would give the librarians greater exposure to and understanding of the needs, goals, and lifestyles of a student body which, at so many universities, is growing more and more diverse. Ideally this understanding would enable the librarians to adapt library services to student needs and habits, just as librarian participation on university committees has long been touted as an effective way for librarians to understand the university educational goals that the library must support.

In addition to making the above suggestions for improving the performance of familiar, traditional library functions, the respondents emphasized the need for librarians to find better means of evaluating the effectiveness of services. While concerns about evaluation can certainly be classified as concerns about performance, the depth of the concerns seems to warrant treatment in a section of its own, a section to which we will now turn.

Evaluation: The most serious and often expressed criticism of librarians was that we have not developed adequate methods for measuring the effectiveness of library services and evaluating the performance of individual librarians. One respondent characterized typical librarian evaluation criteria as falling into the same category as criteria appropriate for administrative secretaries, that is, "How we do a great job greeting and serving patrons."

When pressed for ideas about what librarians should do to improve their evaluation techniques and criteria, few administrators had detailed suggestions because of their lack of background in librarianship. However, they emphasized that the evaluation of services and performance should be more like the criteria used to measure the effectiveness of academic programs and faculty.

It was obvious to the administrators that measuring library services and performance was a slippery subject. Academic libraries are not profit-making ventures. They can no more be judged by the standard criteria for commercial businesses than can universities themselves. But just as education is expected to develop methods of judging the quality of teaching and research, so too must librarians accomplish the same goal within their own field. Unfortunately, it was not clear to many administrators whether librarians have such evaluation methods and criteria.

Several respondents speculated that if librarians have difficulty constructing evaluation criteria that are quantifiable, understandable, and realistic measures of librarian performance and library services, then there may be a need to further refine the field of librarianship. This line of thinking appeared to be based on the premise that it is usually possible to effectively evaluate efforts to carry out a well-defined philosophy and set of objectives. Other respondents did not think that difficulties in evaluation of performance and services indicated a problem with the field so much as it indicated the need for librarians to sharpen their managerial skills.

Further remarks on this topic will be reserved for the section below. At this point focus will be shifted to the final set of comments most frequently voiced by respondents, comments which emphasize the need for librarians to work more closely with certain other segments of the university.

<u>Developing Closer Working Relationships with Others:</u> As if in answer to the questions about communication posed above, many respondents encouraged librarians to be more aggressive in "marketing" their skills, services, and potential contributions to higher education. Students should be made more aware of how much help librarians can be with research projects of almost any kind, class-related or not. Faculty members would not be so inclined to take librarians for granted or regard them as glorified clerks if librarians were more aggressive in demonstrating their potential contributions to the professors' teaching and research functions. It is the relationship between faculty and librarians which the respondents believed is most in need of improvement. One administrator described the educational

process as a triangle whose sides connect the students, faculty, and librarians. Unfortunately, the line between the librarians and faculty is obstructed by misunderstandings and misguided assumptions about relative status and roles.

The best way to remove the obstructions, according to a number of respondents, is to play up the inherent differences between the duties and expertise of librarians and faculty, rather than play them down. These administrators suggested having librarians coordinating more closely with faculty to develop subject collections, having librarians with subject specialties participating in planning meetings of the appropriate academic departments, and having librarians participating in university committees for planning, academic priorities, curriculum, and instructional design. Not only would these various cooperative endeavors improve academic decision-making by ensuring that all relevant parties are involved and informed, but faculty and librarians would inevitably come to better understand the complementary nature of their training and expertise. As this understanding develops, so will many new ideas for cooperative activities.

A number of administrators urged librarians to help define their relationship with campus computer centers, telecommunications offices, and instructional design centers. Plainly there is much overlap as all are ultimately in the business of educational technology and information. What the academic affairs officers want to know is how it should all be integrated into the teaching and research functions, and what should be the administrative relationships? Should these different facilities be merged in some way? How should responsibilities be divided? Advice from librarians would be very welcome.

The foregoing is a summary of the opinions expressed most frequently by the responding academic affairs administrators. A few comments about those opinions are now in order.

<u>Discussion:</u> In general it is safe to say that the academic affairs administrators offered few ideas and opinions that have not already been stated by librarians in our professional literature. Perhaps this is a sign that on the whole librarians have done a pretty good job of anticipating and understanding the higher education trends which will affect libraries. It is also tempting to speculate that many of the respondents' opinions had

been shaped by the librarians with whom they have worked over the course of their careers as faculty and administrators. In any event, even though the administrators may have contributed nothing new in the way of ideas, their comments may be useful in helping us to prioritize our own ideas about the directions academic librarianship should take in the next few years.

It is also interesting to compare the range of subjects raised by the academic affairs officers with the range of subjects considered by Allen Veaner in his ACRL-commissioned working paper "1985 to 1995: The Next Decade in Academic Librarianship." While almost all of the issues mentioned by the academic affairs officers were discussed by Veaner, it is instructive to note the topics which the academic affairs officers failed to mention. None of the respondents referred to academic library governance as an issue, that is, whether librarians should direct the library as autonomous professionals using as their model the way faculty collegially govern their academic departments. Nor did they say that librarians should be concerned with the possible restructuring of the bibliographic enterprise, the likely effects of end user searching on conventional bibliographic control, the need for bibliographic standards, the possible transition of librarians' responsibilities from production to management, or a host of other topics considered by Veaner.

What can be concluded about the failure of the academic affairs officers to raise these matters as areas librarians should be addressing? It does not seem reasonable to expect that non-librarians would even be aware of, let alone understand, many of the issues raised by Veaner. Yet many of those issues are among the most important facing higher education in general, not just librarianship. Therefore it is obvious that the academic affairs officers are dependent upon librarians to translate institutional goals into library goals and find the techniques, technologies, policies, and people able to achieve those goals. It is incumbent upon us to demonstrate to academic administrators that many institutional goals are just as dependent upon the seemingly more arcane aspects of librarianship as they are upon the issues that the administrators themselves recognize.

Turning to the topics that the administrators did raise, one cannot help wonder why the respondents are unaware of so much that librarians have been doing to address those topics. Just to name two examples, document delivery systems have gone a long way on many campuses to make materials even more accessible to busy faculty members and F. W. Lancaster has brought together numerous techniques which librarians have developed to evaluate the effectiveness of services. Of course, not all of the new services, evaluation techniques, and other innovations have been implemented on all campuses. The comments of the respondents to this survey appear to indicate that they would welcome such innovations. But the administrators' lack of knowledge about current trends in librarianship is probably not just a function of whatever innovations have been implemented on their own campuses. The problem may also be symptomatic of the need (expressed by the respondents themselves) for librarians to market their skills and potential services more aggressively. Veaner refers to this as the problem of the "low visibility of the academic librarian."

> Programs are sorely needed to make educational administrators aware of what academic librarianship is truly about. Moffett (1982) reports a series of dismal incidents from librarians and library administrators that illustrate the lack of understanding among faculty and campus administration of the role of the academic librarian. The images are familiar: librarians emerge "somewhere between secretaries and warehouse supervisors," are regarded as "technicians or bureaucrats," but not as peers or collaborators. Concerted efforts at both institutional and national levels are required to combat such damaging misperceptions. (Veaner 211).

The fact that many respondents praised librarians' innovation and activism shows we have been successful in communicating much of what we are doing and what we could do. That some respondents seem unaware of our efforts in the areas of evaluation and innovative information delivery may simply mean that we have failed to communicate about our activities in those areas.

The most general and sweeping recommendation made by the respondents was that academic librarians must improve their management skills in order to better market their potential contributions, to administer complex library services and technologies, and to further develop the evaluation techniques and criteria that the respondents think librarianship lacks. Toward those same ends, the respondents also recommended that librarians refine the field of librarianship. Does this imply that librarians must also pursue more scholarship in their chosen discipline? If so, is it reasonable to think that librarians have the time to be both administrators and scholars? This is a familiar question that has often been raised in the librarian faculty status literature. Many of the administrators believed the two roles dovetailed because each would be aiming to improve managerial skills and library theory. In other words, the administrators considered the dichotomy between the management and scholarship roles to be artificial in the case at hand. The research and experimentation required for librarians to develop theory and management techniques are part and parcel of what managers in any field must do. Thus the administrators seem to view this as a separate issue from the concern that librarians with faculty status must be active researchers while simultaneously performing their daily duties.

Conclusion

Much else might be said to place the comments of the academic affairs administrators in a broader context, but that would require more space and wisdom than I have. A remaining issue which should be dealt with here is the way in which the respondents' comments may have been biased. The respondents were aware that the survey was being conducted by a librarian. It may be that this awareness caused the administrators to express their thoughts more conservatively than they would have to a researcher who was not a librarian. The respondents may have tended to praise librarians more and criticize less out of politeness or a fear that their lack of knowledge about librarianship would make their criticisms appear naive or uninformed.

However, such inhibitions might be more likely to arise among the administrators when interacting with librarians on their own campus as opposed to a researcher who is unknown to them. In other words, one might make a good case that under the circumstances of this survey the administrators were more inclined to forthrightly express criticisms than they would have been to pull their punches. The administrators knew what they would be asked before agreeing to be interviewed. This survey provided them with a soapbox from which to address the library profession at large. It seems unlikely that they would have taken valuable time out of their busy schedules to respond if they were not going to be candid.

To the extent that others may not be convinced by this line of reasoning, what value should they place on the administrators' comments? I offer the same advice that I would offer to those who believe the administrators' opinions were expressed with no reservations. The administrators' observations can serve as valuable aids as we determine our profession's future directions and priorities. The respondents' tendency to recommend avenues for action already anticipated by librarians may indicate that librarians can set their own agendas to a greater extent than they realize, even if not to the extent that they would like.

Works Cited

Dillman, Don A. Mail and Telephone Surveys. New York: Wiley, 1978.

Drucker, Peter F. "Managing the Public Service Institution," College & Research Libraries, 37:4-14 (January 1976).

Frey, James H. Survey Research by Telephone. Beverly Hills, CA: Sage, 1983.

Lancaster, F. W. If You Want to Evaluate Your Library. Champaign, IL: University of Illinois, 1988 .

Shera, Jesse H. "Librarianship and Information Science," in The Study of Information: Interdisciplinary Messages, eds. Fritz Machlup and Una Mansfield. New York: Wiley, 1983 .

Veaner, Allen B. "1985 to 1995: The Next Decade in Academic Librarianship," College & Research Libraries, 46:209-229, 295-308 (May & July 1985).

AMONG FRIENDS: INVOLVEMENT IN ACADEMIC COLLEGIALITY

by
Irene B. Hoadley

Director, Evans Library
Texas A & M University

The basic premise of involvement is to have the parties in interest become an integral part of the activity or program. If this premise is correct, librarians who endeavor to be a part of the university or college environment in which they work must be involved in the general activities and programs of the institution.

As many people who are involved know, getting involved is the easy part. Trying to determine what to be involved in and how to keep up once the commitment has been made are more difficult decisions. Why should librarians (whether they are faculty or not) be involved in university or college activities? After all we are librarians and as such should be practicing our profession and not diffusing our efforts beyond the library! Unfortunately, there are librarians who support such a philosophy.

On the other hand, there is much to be gained by involvement. Perhaps most important is the opportunity to influence what is happening or even to have some input into new ideas and programs. For example, when a new degree program is proposed, a librarian on the curriculum committee can provide information, in a timely way, about what type of library support is available or indicate what will be needed to support such a program. There is, then, a realistic expectation of what resources are available and what it may cost to move forward. Providing information is, therefore, another advantage of involvement. It is also an opportunity to gain an understanding of other parts of the institution, in essence gaining a broader perspective of the institution and how it works. This usually means that there is an opportunity to help improve the quality of the environment. Through involvement, librarians get to know their colleagues throughout the institution, and knowing one's peers can offer the possibility of collaboration. A good example would be a journal cancellation project which requires an understanding and the cooperation of faculty from throughout the institution. Involvement also makes librarians more sensitive to change in the institution because there is a better understanding of what and why something is happening.

On a more practical level, librarians gain recognition from participation. It is an opportunity to become known rather than remaining part of the sea of faceless ones. For librarians with faculty status and for those who want simply to be recognized as professionals, it is a means of legitimizing their roles. If librarians act like faculty, they must be faculty; if they act like clerks, they are probably perceived as clerks. More effort needs to be put into being professionals so that our role becomes solidified.

Having faculty status places a requirement on the individual to perform as a faculty member. One of the requirements expected for promotion and tenure is service to the institution as well as service to the profession. And lastly, it just makes good sense for stakeholders to be participants. Librarians are stakeholders in their institutions whether they realize it or not, and they should recognize the responsibility and contribute to the general efforts of the institution.

If the foregoing are sufficient reasons for involvement in institutional committees and other activities, how does one go about having librarians appointed to committees? Usually the easiest way is to ask. There may already be a precedent which can be used as a foundation on which to build. If librarians have faculty status, they probably serve on the faculty senate which usually has the responsibility of appointing some of the campus committees. Not having faculty status may not be an issue, but it may mean that it could take more time and effort to accomplish the goal through established reporting lines. The library director should propose that librarians be placed on institutional committees, thereby providing a service to the institution and the library. That may be all that it takes. However, if the answer is "no" at that point, the director will have to determine if a less direct method may be feasible. One such approach might be to have the library director serve on committees which then might open the door for others. Another approach would be to select a librarian with a particular expertise that matches the activities of a specific committee and approach the chair of the committee and either ask to have the person appointed to the committee or if that is not possible volunteer the individual as a resource person to work with the committee. There are other similar indirect methods which could be used.

Once membership is obtained, there are a few considerations which should be kept in mind. Recommend good people who will take their responsibilities seriously and reflect well on the library. This can mean many things but some of the most important are that the individual will contribute to the deliberations of the group rather than be an observer; that the person will be prepared for discussions and will follow up when that is needed; and that the person will reflect the point of view of the library when that is appropriate. It is always good when the librarian can achieve a leadership role, but this is not always possible. Unfortunately, leadership often has more to do with politics than with ability.

Choosing individuals to serve on university committees should be done with care, especially if this is an early effort at library involvement in campus activities. Besides choosing someone who has the appropriate expertise, it is important that the person have a proven body of experience to ascertain that he/she is capable of doing what is required. It is also important that any real clashes of personalities or personal styles be avoided if that is possible. This is one good reason why the director should be involved in campus activities -- to insure that this kind of information is either known to her/him or can be easily obtained. Initially, taking care in making appointments will help solidify the place of librarians in university activities.

Having visibility on the campus is an advantage in trying to become a part of university committees and activities. If the library has an active outreach program so that librarians already know their colleagues on a professional basis, it is much easier to take the next step to becoming involved in university endeavors. Such visibility can be achieved in many ways. Perhaps the most common is a liaison program for librarians to keep faculty informed about library services and collections and to obtain feedback from the faculty. This is a common activity in most libraries. Librarians are going to be more acceptable to their faculty colleagues if they are known to them.

Involvement in university activities should not be limited to committees. There are other forums such as student groups, including student government (as an advisor), religious organizations and fraternities and sororities. Another group of activities will center on such faculty or staff organizations as a faculty club, sports activities or professional groups like honorary societies. But whatever the group, the tactics to become involved are pretty much the same:

1. Decide what you want to do
2. Identify the appropriate group
3. Choose a position
4. Know what is allowed
5. Identify the leaders
6. Take part in the process
7. Provide information
8. Build working relationships

What is the purpose of all this effort? It gives the library a role in campus policy formulation. It makes the library a part of the process rather than a beneficiary or victim of it. It also provides the library a forum for airing issues of concern, and it helps to convey library issues beyond the university administration. As a result it helps to build coalitions to assist the library when that is needed. Participation in the governance of the institution is a prerogative in which librarians have a right to share, but it sometimes takes an initial effort to become a part of the process.

If these reasons are the impetus for librarians being involved in campus activities, then what is the outcome of the involvement? Does the investment pay dividends to the library? There are a number of considerations. Recognition and visibility have been mentioned previously. Is recognition advantageous to the library? Although some librarians prefer to be protected by their ivy-covered walls, most librarians want to be and are a part of the active university community. Librarians can toil in their own garden, doing their own thing, but then they have missed the purpose of the library's mission. The purpose of a library is not only to store and protect, but to disseminate and share. If the library fulfills the roles of access and dissemination, it becomes a valuable added service to all the campus community from students to staff to researchers to faculty.

There has been little discussion of the status of librarians or what effect status might have on achieving a desired level of campus involvement. On most campuses little thought is given to the status of librarians by anyone except the librarians. In universities where librarians have faculty status is there a greater likelihood of involvement in campus affairs? Only a survey of those institutions with faculty status could provide current and specific information. Based on the experience at Texas A&M, there are some definite correlations between faculty status and campus involvement. Beginning at the most elementary level, faculty status for Texas A&M librarians automatically opens some doors by providing representation in faculty governance through membership on the Faculty Senate and on many of the University's standing committees. It provides access to research funds which are provided as seed monies by the University to the colleges and the Evans Library.

Beyond such specific points of involvement there are also issues of professionalization. Being involved in a part of the educational process is really why many of us work in academic institutions. A second point is the development of closer relationships with the teaching faculty. Peer relationships are easier to develop and nourish than are tiered or line relationships. It is much easier for one faculty member to approach another than for a subordinate to approach and interact with someone at a higher level.

Third, faculty status often creates higher standards for librarians. Because of the criteria that faculty must meet, the standards are often higher and the staff more motivated. That motivation often comes from having to fulfill the criteria for promotion and tenure. This means that individuals are encouraged to and actually have to publish and do research to meet the criteria for promotion and tenure. Doing research and publishing usually means that librarians are more analytical in viewing their responsibilities. There is more acceptance of experimentation. Standards are also higher because faculty status tends to raise the educational qualifications of librarians because there is more emphasis on advanced degrees.

The visibility beyond the campus also provides visibility on the campus. Librarians' professional accomplishments are reported in the same way as those of other faculty in university publications. This provides recognition to the individuals, but it is also an opportunity to indicate that library faculty are performing the same types of activities that are required of all faculty. They must publish and be involved professionally; they are recognized by their peers by being honored. These activities also bring recognition to the university. Some institutions are recognized for the quality of research, the faculty, teaching or the library. When one thinks of recognition of a library that often means quality or quantity of the collections. However, there are now libraries that are recognized for other reasons. The Evans library has received considerable recognition for the utilization of CD-ROM services. There are libraries recognized for activities such as bibliographic instruction or automated services. Whatever the reason for "star designation," this also means recognition of the institution.

Perhaps another outcome of involvement in university activities is a sense of cohesiveness of purpose and direction. If there is a better understanding of where the institution is going, there can be more focus on how the library can respond to that direction and purpose. It also provides a sense of being a part of the organization rather than being a single cog that makes it go but without any understanding of how it all fits together. Cohesiveness also contributes to camaraderie.

This paper proposes that librarians should be a part of the academic governance of an institution in order to have a better understanding of the environment and because librarians have a responsibility to the institution. In reviewing library literature to determine the professional stance on this issue, it became evident after some time that there is not such a position. A lot has been written about the library asserting its role as the purveyor of information for the campus. But most of the discussions speak of the library as an entity unto itself with the implication that if the library does what it is supposed to do, its role will be enforced and even strengthened. There is some truth in that assumption, but it seems that the role of libraries and librarians is strengthened even more if there is participation in the efforts being made to improve our institutions. And not only by the library administration.

Although involvement in university governance has not often been a concern of librarians, it has been considered a right and responsibility of the faculty. However, there now seems to be some reluctance for faculty to participate in governance. For untenured faculty, participation is not a significant measure to achieve tenure nor does it have any real effect on compensation. There is also a sense in some institutions that the faculty is being excluded from participating in the decision-making process (Watkins, 32; Jacobson, 15). There are, however, others who have a different attitude:

> Rather than blaming others for our difficulties we are beginning to see that solving problems requires the combined efforts of everyone. We are beginning to realize that the skills and talents we use in scholarly work can be applied to the problems we experience in the university. (Tucker, 11)

The academic community should be making its own determinations, and librarians are a part of that community. It is an opportunity to take a leadership role to provide direction and to promote change.

Involvement like faculty status could be debated for a very long time and probably will be. This discussion has centered on the advantages and benefits; someone else can provide the other side of the issue. Librarians have devoted a lot of time debating whether librarianship is a profession. Perhaps if less time had been devoted to talking about it and more to demonstrating how librarians are professionals, the profession would not still be going through an identity crisis. Involvement or service is one way of making a commitment to the profession, while at the same time bringing recognition to what librarians are and do accomplish.

Works Cited

Jacobson, Robert L. "AAUP's Leader Assays Decline in Faculty Morale, Governance." The Chronicle of Higher Education 27 June 1986: 15.

Tucker, Charles W. "Academic Stars and Faculty Responsibility." Academe 73, no.3 (1987): 10-11.

Watkins, Beverly T. "Most Professors Think Faculty's Role in Governance Is Crucial, but Many Won't Take Part, Report Finds." The Chronicle of Higher Education 27 May 1987: 32.

PARTNERSHIP FOR QUALITY: NON-TRADITIONAL STUDENTS AND THE LIBRARIAN

by
Susan Swords Steffen

Director of the Schaffner Library
Northwestern University - University College

Non-traditional students are fast becoming the norm on college campuses. According to the U.S. Department of Education, 52% of all undergraduates and 59% of all students are over 22 years of age and 43% of all students attend classes part-time ("Fall 1987 Enrollment" A24). Meeting the needs of these students while maintaining the academic quality of the continuing education programs in which they are enrolled is a responsibility shared by all segments of the higher education community.

This significant change in the student population presents a major challenge for librarians. The strong library resources critical to the strength of all academic programs are no less important to the quality of continuing higher education programs. Yet because of their own time constraints, evening and weekend class schedules, and weak and outdated library skills, students in continuing education programs often experience many barriers to using libraries. In most cases the institution's library resources are available to all its students, but few academic libraries have taken an active role in meeting the special needs of nontraditional students. After coping with huge budget problems, rapid technological change, and the competing demands of many different user groups, academic libraries rarely have additional energy left to devise library services to meet these particular needs (Fisher 530). So these students and their teachers become quite adept at avoiding assignments that require use of libraries which in turn compromises the quality of their academic experience.

By devoting some resources to the continuing education program of the institution, librarians can significantly enhance its quality. By focusing on the special needs of adult students and the faculty who teach them, librarians can design new services or adjust existing ones to reduce the barriers those students face. But librarians should not restrict their efforts to the provision of library services. Drawing on their experience in working with faculty, in influencing curriculum, and in helping students, librarians can play active roles in faculty development programs, curriculum design, student support services, and program review. By reaching out and working closely with continuing education administrators, librarians can influence the quality of their institution's continuing education program in important ways.

The Northwestern University Experience

In seeking to insure the academic quality of its program, the University College administration, like that of all continuing higher education programs, takes on a complex task. It must create a balance between protecting the intellectual integrity of the institution and meeting the special needs of adult students. It must recruit, develop, and nurture a high-quality faculty drawn from both traditional academic disciplines and the professions. It must design a curriculum which is appropriate to the institution yet is responsive to the broad scope of the interests and needs of adult students and in which both innovative and traditional teaching and learning methods are used. It must create student support services which make the university's programs accessible to all adults who can benefit from them while at the same time acknowledging and addressing the weaknesses of adult students. It must continually and rigorously review the operations of its programs to ensure that adult students and the faculty who teach them are held to standards no less demanding than those required of traditional-aged students (Freedman). It has found librarians to be valuable partners in this enterprise.

At Northwestern University, librarians from the Schaffner Library, a branch of the University Library whose primary mission is to serve the needs of students in continuing education programs, work with administrators from University College to enhance the quality of its academic program. Through its part-time evening program, University College offers several hundred undergraduate credit courses and several degree and certificate programs co-sponsored with the College of Arts and Sciences, the School of Speech, the Medill School of Journalism and the Technological Institute. As the continuing education unit of a prestigious research university, University College is particularly concerned with maintaining high academic standards. Its program is accessible to students with a much broader range of backgrounds than those admitted to the traditional day program at Northwestern. Matriculation into University College is based on performance in the first four courses taken at Northwestern rather than on a previous academic record. So, it is essential that the quality of each course be insured.

To support University College's program, the Schaffner Library provides a wide variety of library services designed to meet the needs of adult students. Schaffner is located on the university's downtown Chicago campus where most of University College's classes meet. A strong bibliographic instruction program which emphasizes computer information sources is supported by a small reference and circulating book collection, convenient document delivery from the main campus and a variety of services. These programs increase students' access to library resources, allow faculty to have expectations for student research and writing and enhance the quality of the academic program (Steffen, "Designing Bibliographic Instruction Programs").

Librarians at the Schaffner Library do not limit their activities to the provision of services within the library. Instead, they move outside the library to work directly with the University College administration in its effort to maintain quality by participating in the support and development of faculty, curriculum planning and ongoing monitoring of the curriculum. Through these activities, librarians have not only made important contributions to the University College program, but have also explored new and fulfilling roles for librarians.

Since the "single most important determinant of the quality of a continuing higher education program is its faculty"

(Freedman 170), librarians have been most active in developing and supporting the University College faculty. All faculty teaching in the University College are employed on a part-time basis. They include ABD graduate students, full-time faculty from Northwestern and other institutions, and persons employed in nonacademic positions. Like most part-time faculty, they experience feelings of isolation and lack of connection with the institution, have no regular or consistent natural channels of communication, possess inadequate knowledge about available support services for themselves and their students, and need to develop and improve teaching skills (Steffen, "Working with Part-Time Faculty"). Because they are not organized into traditional academic departments, the University College administration hires, trains, evaluates, and maintains communication with these faculty, and librarians have been able to take and active role in assisting with this process.

To maintain good communications with faculty, the University College administration holds meetings of large and small groups of faculty throughout the year. Once each semester, the entire faculty meets together with the administrative staff to hear news of developments in University College and discussion about and recognition of good teaching. These meetings create a sense of belonging for faculty who would otherwise see only their own students in their own classroom, while at the same time conveying the educational values of the University College administration. At each meeting, a librarian speaks about new developments in the library followed by encouragement from the administration to take advantage of available resources. These consistent appearances not only keep faculty informed about library resources, but they also establish the library as an integral component of University College and librarians as important sources of support for the faculty.

To counteract the lack of traditional academic departments, faculty teaching courses in the same subject area, such as the organization behavior faculty or the computer science faculty, meet for dinner throughout the year to discuss common concerns about their specific curriculum and about teaching in general. A librarian always attends these dinners not only to present information about the library, but also to participate in curriculum discussions. Unlike faculty who usually teach only one or two different courses, librarians have experience with the entire program and are able to offer a more holistic perspective on many issues.

Because so many of its faculty are novice teachers, University College provides an extensive faculty development program. An introductory workshop for all new faculty conducted by several University College administrators and a librarian presents information about teaching adult students, designing library assignments, and University College procedures. Throughout the year, University College's faculty development coordinator operates faculty seminars covering such topics as motivating students, presenting effective lectures, teaching thinking skills, grading and evaluating, and integrating library skills. Librarians have been involved in both planning the seminar series and in presenting individual sessions on library and writing skills.

The support provided to University College faculty by librarians is not limited to formal meetings and seminars, but also includes work with individual faculty members. Librarians and faculty collaborate to design library research assignments and to provide feedback on student progress as assignments are completed. Instruction for faculty in the use of the online catalog, online searching, and CD-ROM technology assists them in updating their own research skills and makes them more confident about recommending these resources to students. Librarians also help faculty meet their own information needs with research assistance and free online searching. For faculty whose primary employment is in a nonacademic setting, these contacts with librarians provide a connection between their own professional needs and the academic setting in which they teach. To assist faculty in improving their teaching the Schaffner Library's collection includes books on effective teaching techniques and journals in the field of adult education.

Another method that University College has chosen to improve the quality of its program is emphasis on writing skills. The administration believes that good writing skills are essential to becoming an educated person, and that good writing skills can only be achieved through frequent and sustained practice in all courses. To ensure that all students have adequate writing skills to perform satisfactorily in University College courses, University College requires all students to complete at least one writing course within the first four courses that they take in the program. Students who cannot successfully complete this requirement may not be matriculated into degree or certificate programs. Faculty in all courses are then urged to build on this initial instruction and provide opportunities for students to practice writing skills.

Librarians have been actively involved in the implementation of this program in a number of ways. Faculty who teach writing courses and librarians meet regularly to discuss placement testing, course objectives, and appropriate assignments. The information about writing assignments required throughout the curriculum which librarians bring to these meetings has helped to shape the writing program. To encourage all faculty to think about using writing activities in their courses, a major portion of a general University College faculty meeting was devoted to a discussion of writing and a librarian was a key participant in this presentation. The Schaffner Library, in cooperation with University College, sponsors a writing tutoring program which provides support outside of the classroom to students with writing problems. Students may receive help from a writing tutor or may use one of a number of writing software packages to work on improving their writing. The availability of this service reassures faculty that they can require student writing without having to teach writing skills and has made them more willing to make writing assignments. Because the service is located in the Library, the research and writing processes which tend to be viewed as quite distinct have become more integrated.

Librarians also work directly with students both formally in the classroom and informally in the library. Like many continuing education students, University College students' contacts with the institution are often limited to interaction with faculty in the classroom and to (at best) sporadic use of academic advisors. However, whether students are enrolled in one class or a degree program, contact with the library is a constant in their University College experience, and librarians have many opportunities to contribute to its quality. Since adult students often feel considerable uneasiness about pursuing further education, librarians focus much of their work with students on reducing this anxiety and improving their research skills so that they may be more competent and confident students. Bibliographic instruction sessions not only introduce appropriate reference sources, but also address issues of research anxiety and time management. Research consultations with individual students offer as much psychological reassurance that the student will succeed in a research project as bibliographic advice about how to proceed. In their work with individual students, librarians frequently become aware of problems students may be experiencing or skills, such as in writing or use of computers, which need improvement. They can then make referrals to appropriate resources or can alert University College administrators to small problems before they become big ones.

Because librarians are involved in so many aspects of the University College program, they are able to observe its operations on an ongoing basis and share those observations with the University College administration. Each semester librarians review all course syllabi and speak with many individual faculty members to gain an understanding of the type of assignments being made by instructors. These interviews often uncover gaps in information about the University College program, concerns about teaching adult students, and needs to develop specific types of teaching skills. Their contacts with students often reveal frustration with particular aspects of the program or unmet needs, such as for writing assistance or career development information. By sharing their insights with the University College administration, librarians have been able to make valuable contributions to the evaluation and improvement of University College's program.

According to the University College administration, the activities of librarians have strengthened the University College program. The University College administration strongly advocates the development of effective library skills as critical to success in its program. As each faculty member is hired, University College deans make clear that library use across the curriculum is a key part of the University College program and that librarians are ready and willing to assist faculty. According to Associate Dean Louise Love, faculty, though surprised by this emphasis in a continuing education program, willingly agree to raise their expectations for student research because good support is available from librarians. Faculty who have traditionally relied on textbooks, lectures, and exams are beginning to experiment with more student-centered instructional methods that encourage students to search for their own answers and share them with each other. For example, an organization-behavior instructor who previously only lectured on specific cases now requires students to locate and bring to class several current journal articles relevant to each week's topic to shape class discussion. The successful implementation of the new writing requirement and increased practice in writing across the curriculum have been strongly supported by librarians. University College students now write papers in nearly every course, and so have many opportunities to improve their writing skills. In a survey of student needs and attitudes, students rated library resources and assistance received from librarians as very important to their success at University College. According to Donald Collins, Dean of University College, the programs of the library and the activities of the librarians have become such an integral part of University College that it would be difficult to imagine the program without them.

Close cooperation with University College has also increased the quality and effectiveness of the library's programs. With such a strong statement of support from the University College administration, it is easy to schedule bibliographic instruction sessions, and each year librarians present almost 50 sessions to over 1,000 students. These sessions, in turn, generate intense use of other library services including use of CD-ROM tools, online bibliographic searching, research consultations, and document delivery. This high level of activity has enhanced the Schaffner Library's prestige within the larger University Library, and has transformed it from a little-used, little-thought-about outpost to a well-respected, important branch library. The Schaffner Library now not only receives its share of available resources, but is also looked to as a leader in bibliographic instruction, online and CD-ROM searching, and the use of microcomputers.

Librarians have gained important experience from this relationship as well. In a large research library like the Northwestern University Library, librarians often tend to focus on library issues and library problems rather than on larger institutional concerns. Without faculty status, librarians are not frequently in a good position to establish natural relationships with faculty. The librarians from the Schaffner Library, on the other hand, have consistent contact with faculty on collegial basis and have extended their influence beyond the library. Their practical experience with library involvement in curricular change has been helpful to other librarians as the University Library formulates its response to the report of a recent university-wide Task Force on the Undergraduate Experience. As they participate in the resolution of faculty, curricular, and student issues, librarians who work with University College have enriched their understanding of the institution and of higher education in general. During a period of rapid change and uncertainty for the library profession, these librarians have had an opportunity to explore some of the roles librarians are grappling with including teacher, educational reformer, and change agent. They are learning where librarians may most productively apply their talents to make the greatest impact.

General Observations

Clearly, based on Northwestern University's experience, librarians can be an important resource for continuing higher education programs. Nearly every academic institution has librarians experienced in analyzing and designing services to meet the needs of diverse user groups. When applied to the special needs of adult students and the faculty who teach them, these skills can result in an improved curriculum, a better-supported faculty, and more-effective support services. The activities of librarians in collaborating with faculty, participating in faculty development programs, and meeting research needs can provide critical support for excellence in teaching. From their contacts with students and faculty both inside and outside the classroom, librarians can assist in the ongoing monitoring so essential to the maintenance of academic quality. Because they work with many different courses and programs throughout the university, librarians can view the continuing higher education program within the larger context of the institution. Finally, the activities of librarians may also serve to increase the legitimacy of the continuing higher education program within the university. Traditionally, research and the library resources that support it have been important measures of quality in higher education. By presenting evidence of strong library involvement, the continuing higher education program signals that it belongs to the mainstream of the higher education community, and that it upholds the same high standards as traditional programs.

Librarians who choose to collaborate with continuing higher education programs may also expect to benefit. In continuing higher education programs, librarians will find a receptive environment for experimenting with new methods of serving users, expanding their teaching skills, and gaining experience with educational planning beyond the library. Continuing higher education programs operate on the margins of higher education and are generally more flexible than traditional programs. In cooperating with them, librarians encounter fewer barriers to participation, such as lack of faculty status or academic departmental affiliation, and can more easily incorporate their programs into the continuing education curriculum. Administrators, faculty, and students recognize the value of librarians' contributions and welcome them as valued members of the educational team. This gratifying response positively reinforces the efforts of librarians, and they can carry this encouragement into their work with other programs.

The assurance of the academic quality of continuing higher education programs is a complex responsibility which requires the participation of people from many parts of the higher education community. It is a challenge which all institutions offering these programs must meet if the promises of education opportunity for adults are to be achieved. A partnership between continuing education administrators and librarians employs the skills and talents of librarians beyond the confines of traditional library services and brings new resources to the quality assurance effort. For librarians, this association can be a fruitful opportunity to improve services to users, to develop new skills, and to explore new roles for librarians within the university.

Works Cited

"Fall 1987 Enrollment in U.S. Colleges and Universities." The Chronicle of Higher Education. 28 June 1989: A24.

Fisher, Raymond K. in "Academic Libraries and Part-Time Adult Students," New Horizons For Academic Libraries, eds. Robert D. Stueart and Richard D. Johnson, 529-533. New York: K.G. Saur Publishing, Inc., 1979.

Freedman, Leonard. Quality in Continuing Education: Principles, Practices, and Standards for Colleges and Universities. San Francisco: Jossey-Bass, 1987.

Steffen, Susan Swords. "Designing Bibliographic Instruction Programs for Adult Students: The Schaffner Library Experience." Illinois Libraries 70 (December 1988): 644-649.

Steffen, Susan Swords. "Working with Part-Time Faculty: Challenges and Rewards," in Off-campus Library Services Conference Proceedings, Reno, Nevada, October 23-24, 1986, ed. Barton M. Lessin, 306-314. Mt. Pleasant, MI: Central Michigan University, 1987.

THE LIBRARIAN AS LEGISLATOR: AN IMPORTANT CAMPUS ROLE

by
Marilyn Myers

Head, Collection Development
and Bibliographic Services
Arizona State University, West Campus

You cannot rest behind the plate,
The ball has caught the batter's eye
Unmask and be the sport of fate.
--M.D. Feld

Academic institutions don't provide a comfortable existence for their libraries and librarians anymore. With the growing number of costly services critical to the entire campus, libraries compete for both material resources and attention on administrative agendas. The resulting need to do more with less may be healthy in the long term. What is unhealthy is the spreading belief that, in spite of extraordinary efforts, the quality of the library's product is irreversibly diminished. Worse is the pervasive resignation that as an academic librarian one has chosen a profession in which one won't make a difference; leave a mark.

It's time for a few (or a few more) to step outside the safety of the library and apply what they know about service organizations and resource management in the institutional environment upon which the libraries are dependent. It's time to play the game in the major leagues of one's own campus. Whether by accident or by design, a number of librarians are doing just that. But opportunities to compare notes on what's being experienced and learned in institutional environments are rare. Hopefully, what follows can incite dialogue among the veterans as well as recruit new players.

In refocusing one's attention to the broader level, one finds that every university campus is a unique progression of people and events. All are certainly influenced by common external factors -- demographic, economic and political conditions -- but also by strong forces emanating from within. This internal dynamic has its roots in the history of the organization, and derives force from its culture -- reflected in what is done, how it is done and who is involved in doing it. Values and traditions are demonstrated in decisions and actions, as well as in formal and informal communication. Therefore what is true on one campus may or may not be perceived to be so on another. What works in one institution may or may not work in another.

The experience of this author can be described in institutional and professional terms. The institutional perspective is that of medium-sized, comprehensive, urban state universities-- sites of considerable activity and opportunity for anyone interested in a governance role. Governance positions held have included senate president and committee assignments involving curriculum approval, strategic planning, affirmative action, tenure and promotion, personnel grievances, athletics, evaluation of administrators, personnel searches, research support and accreditation. The professional perspective is that of a middle manager in the library who has had responsibility for collection management and bibliographic processing programs, library materials and information access budgets, as well as management of professional and classified staff in both public and technical services.

One individual's experiences must be applied with caution. They can only provide perspective by giving frames of reference within which the reader can seek similarities and differences. It is also the case that in a leadership role one often has only an intuitive grasp of the conditions and influences that enter decision making. Only when the prevailing codes and conventions are broken is one reminded of their presence and power. The leap from personal observation to integration and anticipation of events obviously represents work in progress. Unfinished though the effort to analyze may always be, experience to date suggests that librarians benefit themselves, their libraries, and their institutions by involvement in university governance.

The Decision-Making Environment in Higher Education

Governance in higher education has long been characterized as unorganized and impossibly complex. Observers of these processes of making choices have described them as occasions for "executing standard operating procedures...defining virtue and truth, distributing glory or blame...expressing and discovering *self interest* and *group interest* ...[and] having a good time" (March and Olsen quoted in Bess 5). Hazard Adams outlines operating principles based on what he describes as his personal and quite unscientific observations of academic tribes. Among the most useful to understanding institutional decision making are: (a) The Diffusion of Academic Authority: No one has the complete power to do any given thing. Powers of persuasion and the ability to rally support are essential. (b) The Diminishment of Organizational Allegiance: The fundamental allegiance of the faculty member will be the smallest unit to which he or she belongs. This is usually the academic department, but may be an inter- or intra-departmental research group. (c) The Luxury of Principle, or the Third Law of Academic Motion: To every administrative act there is an equal and opposite reaction. In a group as diverse as university faculty, any position espoused by the administration will generate a reaction founded on principle. A corollary to this says that since faculty and administrators react to one another more negatively in the late months of the academic year, "nothing should be done in May that can be put off to October" (Adams 4-12).

Such descriptions represent a general tendency to underestimate the stable and ongoing nature of university organization. In fact, academic decision-making structures rather effectively process the information generated by the environments in which they operate. That environment accommodates the need for vertical information flows, unit coordination, the exercise of power and collegiality (Bess vii). The most common bodies by which faculty effect decisions or make recommendations on institutional and especially academic matters are senates and ad hoc and standing committees. Senate mechanisms and committee structures serve the vertical and horizontal information needs by bringing together representatives of those impacted by the issues at hand for the purpose of amassing expert opinion and advice. Opinions as to the effectiveness of such bodies revolves around views as to the extent they (1) represent a clear faculty voice as distinct from other campus constituencies, (2) are representative of a cross-section of faculty, and (3) effectively impact decisions of the university's administration. While they may be closely monitored by faculty, responsibility for decisions is spread across the entire group. There are no individual sanctions for poor decisions. Decisions are frequently made on the basis of the exercise of influence with authority held in reserve for purposes of adjudication. Many academic decisions are made by mutual agreement. Only in the presence of conflict is authority invoked.

There is a backdrop of continuity, tradition and expectation on most campuses with respect to problem solving and decision making based on principles of collegiality. Collegiality consists of a (1) cultural framework, (2) decision making structure, and (3) process of behaving (Bess 86). A community is said to be collegial if there is a belief in the rationality and order of its decision-making system. It is assumed that arenas for decisions keep open the rights of participation, and therefore, influence, so that a standing structure for redress exists. When the system is so designed, knowledge is believed to be most effectively utilized, and bias and opinion are less likely to interfere with sound decision making. Such a system is by definition staffed with competent, motivated people who do not need close supervision and whose professional values respect the rights of individuals. Faith in this decision-making structure is substituted for an insistence on complete knowledge and participation. Trust as an ingredient of collegiality presumes that the system succeeds by achieving individual goals, which are coincident with those of the organization. The belief that there is little conflict among individual goals means that conflict resolution focuses on ways to increase the size of the pie rather than how to cut up a fixed-size pie.

The rise of the "corporate university" -- top down management and the adoption of strategic goals -- is viewed with some alarm as being incompatible with collegial expectations and the traditional faculty role (Academe 75, no.1, January-February, 1989). In response to the competitive pressures of the 1970's and 1980's, the collegial traditions are being overlaid by models from the corporate sector for the purpose of managing academic resources. Thus strategic planning processes are being applied campus-wide and serving as a basis for faculty personnel decisions and budget proposals. Public relations offices develop the external image and market the institution, while admissions staff "manage enrollment" and professional fundraisers develop packages to sell to potential donors.

Concurrently, faculty, in competition for fewer tenure-track positions, concentrate on establishing research records and national networks of peers. Newly hired tenure-track faculty are counseled to limit themselves to service within their academic departments and relatively few of the most distinguished senior faculty committees. Academic stars are hired to bring in grant funds and act as entrepreneurs in the development of university-private sector enterprises. Pools of part-time faculty with no governance responsibilities are hired to meet goals of program flexibility and cost effectiveness. Participation of twenty-five percent of the full-time faculty in university service roles is seen as about average for American colleges and universities (Glenn 19). It is no surprise that governance involvement and responsibility is broadening to include more than those in the traditional faculty mold. While acknowledging that all those forces are at work, faculty nevertheless remain basically uncomfortable with the involvement of nonfaculty constituencies in deliberations on many academic matters. Where librarians are seen on the faculty-nonfaculty continuum varies from campus to campus, within a given faculty, and often from issue to issue.

There is little need nor interest in institutional management when conditions are stable, change is incremental and funds are readily available. In conditions of slack, that is, plentiful, resources or in the absence of competitors, the governance structure has little work of substance. These are not the conditions prevalent in higher education today, and the fortunes of higher education are those of their academic libraries.

Institutions of higher education and their libraries must now justify their existence by demonstrating that resources are being effectively and efficiently used, and that their activities support their societal mission. In such an environment librarians need to be able to interpret the library to faculty and students, market services, and justify plans and budgets. Budget recisions are common and place librarians in the position of defending what has already been allocated to support collections and services. Increasingly tough zero-sum decisions on the allocation of resources are made and articulated. Not only the decisions are critical to libraries, but also who is making those decisions and on what basis. Not knowing or influencing who and on what basis is both risky and debilitating.

Librarians and Libraries Can Benefit from Involvement in University Governance

As a body of professionals, librarians want to influence the actions of the organization in which they work and live, and desire influence in all areas of their professional lives--conditions of employment, design of programs, and selection and evaluation of peers. Since the library is an integral part of the academic enterprise, the stake in those issues is naturally shared with the faculty. A strong faculty-librarian bond would be expected.

The bond, if it exists, is not obvious. Librarians are sometimes told (or themselves declare) that they are not faculty, no matter how the institution may classify them. There seems to be a compulsion to confirm the distinctions rather than the similarities. Those for whom the distinctions loom large usually cite the librarians' lack of the PhD, meaning research experience and disciplinary specialization, and the minimal teaching responsibilities, including course and curricula design and student evaluation, as critical differences. In fact, the extent to which fundamental values of higher education held by faculty in academic departments are foreign to librarians is probably small. Concern and responsibility for the quality of the academic programs are felt by both. Many career goals and experiences are common to both--research, publishing, teaching, involvement in professional associations, peer-based evaluation and self governance. Librarians are initially no less uninformed than newly minted PhD's in their first tenure-track positions. The fact that a publisher has been convinced of the need for a how to guide for junior faculty on the early years in academe underscores this (Finkelstein 34).

Adams observes that of all nonfaculty employees, librarians come the closest to faculty. They perplex those who must create tables of organization, and they seem to regard themselves as the most shamelessly exploited. He anticipates that faculty and librarian similarities will more likely unite them than their differences will separate them -- especially where collective bargaining is an issue (Adams 21-22).

Descriptions and principles offered might seem to imply that the faculty is a cohesive unit. It is not. University faculty members value and perpetuate their differences. Physical and biological scientists work in teams. Humanists, although usually independent scholars, work in a common style. Faculty do not necessarily demonstrate their disciplinary theory in their institutional practice. Social scientists, who study individual and group behavior, are paradoxically poorly organized as political groups, defining and redefining themselves on the pure-applied and hard-soft science continuums. Theory-and-practice splits also dominate politics in fine arts where artists challenge the assertions of critics and art historians. Across disciplinary lines, junior and senior faculty may openly disagree about the tenets of tenure and merit-based reward systems.

Meanwhile, with the exception of the library director, there is not a strong record of librarian involvement and investment in faculty governance venues. This is at best, a lost opportunity, and at worst, a strategic mistake on the part of libraries and librarians.

Libraries need to have their professionals routinely involved in these external arenas. Academe's penchant for concentrating on personality and process makes being known a key to empowerment. Academic departments aren't identified merely in terms of their chairs and libraries shouldn't be known strictly in terms of their directors. The librarian's credibility in governance arenas contributes to a halo effect for the library. Each librarian demonstrating competence, good sense and trustworthiness in an external role not only becomes recognized as an individual, but contributes to confidence in the library's capabilities generally. The library as a whole banks the goodwill earned by the individual librarian.

Unique Librarian Qualities Can Advance Faculty Governance

Unless librarians are formally excluded, they are, by the nature of their role in higher education, in a position to contribute some unique qualities of value to faculty governance. First, the complexities of operating an academic library are seldom systematically communicated, so the faculty governance structure may lack the expert input it wants in this area. Further, the line librarian is unlikely to be characterized as "they" in the faculty-administration dichotomy, no matter how administrative one's assignment may be within the library hierarchy. One may therefore establish a library presence in forums that are not open to the head of the library, may carry a separate but equal credibility to that of the director of the library, and may serve as a source of verification for the positions taken by the library director. On nonlibrary issues, librarians may be viewed as more neutral than a faculty member simply because they are not part of an academic department.

Second, the academic-support role perspective is a particularly relevant one and should not be overlooked in institutional deliberations. Strategic planning is one of the newest arenas in which to demonstrate this. Strategic planning processes define and gather the critical players for the purpose of gaining a perspective on the economic, social, political and competitive educational forces impacting one's campus. Valuable questions about the immediate environment and the future that are often neglected in the comforts or pressures of the present are raised (Chaffee and Tierney 184). Strategic planning is also the stage upon which the members of the central administration may articulate their vision for the institution and reveal their preferred implementation strategies. This is an important opportunity to point out to high level administrators the immediate implications of and costs for the library of various institutional strategies. The character of the academic programs, the research support needs of the faculty, the type of student being recruited, and the complementary library services must be reflected in the institution's mission and goals.

Changes in those environmental elements can require costly adjustments in the supporting services. Campus decision makers can also be made more aware of the library proactive roles as a cultural asset in the community, tool in student recruitment, focus for fundraising, and source of vital information to local businesses and the professions. Equally important aspects of this dialogue are the insights gathered on how to cast library needs in terms that complement the institution's goals.

Third, the library is an agency with broad impact within the campus and the librarian holds a position of centrality that offers valuable experience. In fact, librarians are often unaware that they are what Balderson calls "experts in political accommodation" (Balderson 64). For example, interaction with a cross-section of faculty, students and/or the outside community contributes to an institutional perspective. Librarians with multi-disciplinary responsibilities soon gain an understanding of and appreciation for the differences as well as commonalities in research trends and resource needs. Having an advocacy role across departments or colleges establishes the librarian as having an institutional-level stake in resource allocation. Librarians prioritize needs, allocate resources, and justify decisions. Few other professional groups on campus routinely balance their general policy and its application as publicly and successfully.

The librarian's base of relevant experience is not built only at the campus level. Within the confines of the library, success at developing programs and services is dependent upon cooperation and coordination with professional colleagues. Decision-making experience is in the consultative mode with large doses of committee work, operating within a staff and through a reporting hierarchy. These skills are also useful in governance arenas and the experience base can contrast sharply with that of the teaching faculty where each is working in relative isolation from colleagues as teacher and researcher.

The individual and the institution should take advantage of the librarian's position-generated contacts and experience which are naturally broader than that of most faculty. One could further suggest that given their skill-base and shared responsibility for the quality of the academic product, librarians also share responsibility with the faculty for the perceived absence of commitment to running the institution on the part of academics. Libraries are surely sharing the consequences of this absence in tight times.

Costs and Benefits to the Library

Having made a commitment to an active role in governance, the individual librarian and, by extension, the library administration can be called upon to make a considerable investment of time and energy. In the short term, time spent away from one's assigned duties in meetings, preparing reports, gathering information, etc., must ultimately be compensated for by one's colleagues and accounted for in the library's goals and timetables. One of the most common (and positive) outcomes of participating is that the next time a team is chosen, the likelihood of being selected increases. As a result, the responsibility for such activity can get heaped relentlessly upon a few.

On the other hand, the quality of the work environment is enhanced in the long term. The individual librarian's involvement in campus governance provides visibility, recognition, a sense of belonging and a feeling of commitment. Those are conditions that are proven elements of job satisfaction and that contribute to the retention of valuable personnel. Lack of opportunity for promotion within the library can be compensated for by expanded campus responsibilities. Colleagues with such experience work smarter and provide enlightened leadership. The mentoring environment is enriched and junior members of the staff will develop faster.

The service commitment is generally manageable when one's role is to represent library positions and colleagues in senates, committees, etc. The commitment increases sharply in those instances in which the librarian participates as a professional who just happens to be employed in the library. In such cases one's constituency is no longer just the library and the library's priorities must fit into a larger institutional context. A handful of individuals, who have usually been with the institution for a number of years, can be identified as serving this role as institutional statesmen. Within the faculty, that select group will include institutional superstars, those individuals that excel at teaching, research and service, as well as the professional politicians, including individuals perceived as substituting campus involvement for the pursuit of scholarship. To be known to and as a member of the first group is of course preferable as well as useful in getting started.

Playing the Game

Whatever post you assume, do your homework and have something to say. Providing factual data about the library to the campus is the easiest most predictable role. Success at providing that information to the key power brokers in the terms most relevant to them and at the crucial points in the decision processes is more elusive. No opportunities to translate the library's mission and goals into the institutional mission and the faculty agenda should be overlooked --including forums that have nothing directly to do with the library.

Obviously some service roles or contacts carry greater potential payoffs -- for the librarian and for the library-- than others. Those payoffs and costs of participating have to be assessed in terms of each campus. That is a calculation that will need to be reconsidered regularly in light of campus events, or changes in the environment or key players. Participation is driven more by opportunity than by careful design. Be ready to respond based upon who asks you to serve. For example, requests from a member of the central administration are probably not the ones to decline, whatever their timing.

Careful observation and advice from colleagues can help one identify the forums (1) in which campus leaders and opinion setters are active, (2) with which the members of the central administration consistently consult, (3) in which valued resources are allocated, and (4) through which information critical to the institution is channeled. Access to these forums plus the information exchanged there equates with power. This piece of the action may be secured via elected positions or committee appointments. It can also be found in the informal 7:30 a.m. coffee klatch in the student union or on the racquetball court!

A forum dealing with curriculum matters is probably a better investment that one dealing with parking ticket appeals if your goal is to educate others about library programs and plans. Committees with diverse membership -- faculty, students, administrators, members of the community -- can be excellent opportunities to gain understanding of roles, attitudes, values and issues; how they may differ from group to group, and how they vary in their influence in the institution. A forum setting agendas for or making appointments to other bodies is probably more influential than one for which the scope of its charge is limited. For example, experience on a committee making appointments to other committees provides insights on and opportunities to influence the balance of power on campus.

One can't expect to be told who's in charge or who holds power on a campus at an orientation workshop. Melia and Lyttle point out that discussing power is difficult because it changes as soon as one mentions the specifics (Melia and Lyttle 11). If the local paper were to publish information that the president holds titular authority in the university, but the real mover-and-shaker is the vice president for finance whose sister is married to a state senator, the very notification of that fact would change it. The president would try to prove that he isn't just a figurehead and an embarrassed state senator would avoid the vice president. Faculty and staff would seek to prove or disprove the information by pressuring the three individuals in one way or another. Assessing power is also difficult because the people who use power well don't want that fact to be the focus of public scrutiny for the same reasons the vice president for finance and senator desire privacy.

Knowing the system -- structure, climate and culture -- and being known as an individual combines into political savvy for getting things (done) for the library. Where this is done well the library should be successful in securing campus support. That political savvy can also mean getting things (done) within the library. Large organizations resist change and most library program initiatives are expensive and require the reallocation of resources and personnel. Thus, if the library is to progress, support within the library is as critical as that at the campus level. Skills honed in university governance arenas can be applied in the library. The needed leadership skills are attributed to those Perlman calls intrapreneurs -- persons within organizations with an idea who wish to turn that idea into a product or program. Intrapreneurship as a process requires problem definition; working within the organization to build coalitions and gain approvals from the top; pushing the project through to completion; and managing the completed project to ensure its future. Good intrapreneurs build teams, have the ability to lead, tolerate ambiguity, can make decisions often without enough data, trust their feelings, have courage, and demonstrate commitment (Perlman 13-22).

Melia and Lyttle identify roughly the same attributes as critical to success at what they call "operational politics." They go further and offer some insights on why Battin's observation that "Despite the rhetoric about it being the heart of the university, the library and librarians have been for years isolated from the policy councils of most institutions" is true (Battin quoted in Carrigan 330). They suggest that the failure (or inability) to build supportive coalitions or teams is one reason for that isolation. That is in turn due to the fact that the answer to one or more of the following questions may be no.

1. Are leaders judged, and therefore supported, on the basis of their accomplishments rather than on their personalities or values?

2. Can the librarians collectively be counted on to demonstrate loyalty or support on a campus issue?

3. Is the library, having been supported on a matter by some campus constituency, willing to support that constituency when it needs it?

The fact that certain stressful conditions are prominent in women's experiences in academic governance is a further complication (Kirschner 38). The representative that is a woman is often the person who actively supports affirmative action and other feminist issues. Since these issues are often not as high a priority for white male colleagues who dominate higher education, a woman's efforts to emphasize them may interfere with the very relationships she is trying to build. Paradoxically, having created an internal conflict, she is then placed in another traditional female role, as she attempts to conciliate the conflict she has raised. This is of particular concern given that institutions increasingly seek them out for the "women's perspective" and that academic library staffs, which are often predominantly women, are full of potential candidates for such roles.

The "highs" of being involved in projects and processes that make a difference are powerful. Seeing one's views and visions implemented are personal rewards that may be of more lasting value than an annual merit increase. But be prepared to accept decisions that you actively opposed. First, there is some consolation in the observation that big shots are merely little shots that keep shooting. Upon reflection one realizes that in defeats a lot has been learned about "the game" and how things work. For instance, individuals that oppose you on an issue are (probably!) not mortal enemies, and may be part of supportive coalitions on other issues. Today's solutions are not forever. Conditions and players change and new policies create new problems. Further, know that one risks making mistakes. Not only will you make mistakes, other will know you made them and criticize them. Judgments will also be made on how you deal with that criticism.

Standard advice to junior faculty includes the reminder that teaching, research and service are not equally rewarded (Deneef 256-257). They are advised to limit service commitments and concentrate on their teaching and research. Where the criteria for advancement for librarians parallels that of the faculty, this is equally sound advice for them. In the faculty model, service is a weak, third priority in the rank and tenure triad and standards to evaluate the merit of institutional service are largely lacking.

This may be a disservice to the institution, the library and the librarian, and one fact of academic life that deserves reexamination. Chait, for example, points out the irony of the fact that we work in an environment that requires the cooperation of colleagues and in which individual performance is hard to measure. Success as groups is critical, but only individual rewards are provided.

Whatever the causes, the fact of the absence of librarians in governance arenas may in part explain why the librarians' role is not understood, why they are unappreciated, and why they're underpaid. An excellent university service record can not substitute for excellence in the job one was hired to perform. Nevertheless, the institutional service role can only enrich the academic community's understanding and support for the library, one's performance as a librarian and one's sense of personal satisfaction in having made a difference.

Works Cited

Academe 75, no.1 (January-February, 1989), articles by Bilik and Blum, Rollin, and Levinson.

Adams, Hazard. The Academic Tribes. 2d ed. Champaign, IL: University of Illinois Press, 1988.

Balderson, Frederick E. Managing Today's University. San Francisco: Jossey-Bass, 1975.

Bess, James L. Collegiality and Bureaucracy in the Modern University; the Influence of Information and Power on Decision-Making Structures. New York: Teachers College Press, 1988.

Carrigan, Dennis P. "The Political Economy of the Academic Library," College & Research Libraries 49, no.4 (July, 1988), p. 325-331.

Chaffee, Ellen Earle, and William G. Tierney. Collegiate Culture and Leadership Strategies. Washington, DC: American Council on Education/ Macmillan, 1988.

Chait, Richard. "Proving Group Rewards for Group Performance," Academe 74, no. 6 (November-December, 1988), p. 34-35.

Deneef, A. Leigh, ed. The Academic's Handbook. Durham, NC: Duke University Press, 1988.

Finkelstein, Martin. "Review of The Academic's Handbook." Academe 74, no. 66 (November-December, 1988) p. 34-35.

Glenn, Larry E. "The Faculty Senate and the AAUP at Southern Connecticut State University," Academe 73, no. 6 (November-December, 1987), p. 16-19.

Kirschner, Betty Frankle. "Hidden Costs of Women's Works," Academe 74, no. 6 (November-December, 1988) p.38.

Melia, Jinx, and Pauline Lyttle. Why Jennie Can't Lead. Grand Junction, CO: Operational Politics, Inc., 1986.

Perlman, Baron, James Gueths, and Donald A. Weber. The Academic Intrapreneur; Strategy, Innovation, and Management in Higher Education. Praeger, 1988.

THE LIBRARIAN IN THE FACULTY SENATE

by
Joan McCauley

Humanities and Fine Arts Librarian
California State University at Long Beach

There are important benefits to be gained from librarian involvement in academic governance. From the perspective of one who has been involved intimately in such activities on a large university campus over the last twenty years, I'd like to explore the subject a little.

At California State University, Long Beach, the primary faculty representative body is the Academic Senate which exercises many of the powers of the faculty. The Academic Senate is composed of elected representatives from each school, based on the number of faculty in the individual schools of the university, including the library. In addition, representatives from the Student Services Division, staff, administration, and student body are also senate members. At many other universities, faculty senate membership is restricted solely to faculty members.

The Academic Senate has an elaborate structure of standing councils and committees which formulate policy and other recommendations that are brought to the parent body for consent or action. These councils and committees deal with such varied matters as educational policies, personnel policies, resource or financial matters, athletics, library, academic computing, student affairs, scholarly and creative activity, awards, teacher education, and organization and operations of the university. In addition to standing committees, there also are numerous university-wide *ad hoc* committees formed to provide advice on a wide variety of matters.

Why have a faculty senate? Because it is the surest method to provide the faculty with a share in governance of the institution. In most colleges and universities, there remains a sharp hierarchical structure, with faculty member reporting to department chair, department chair reporting to dean (or director), dean reporting to academic vice president, vice president reporting to president and president reporting to the board. If there is academic governance, it is at a very low level. Faculty senates were invented to give the faculty a voice, a focus for faculty opinion to have an influence on how the institution is run. While we are using a faculty model, it is as appropriate to the library model in a large library. The individual librarian reports to a chair, reports to an assistant director, reports to director. In smaller institutions, there may not be such overt hierarchies and true collegiality has a better chance of occurring even if by accident instead of intent. Faculty senates are almost always deliberate constructs, built by the faculty to insure its voice in governance of the institution. It is not true that the hierarchical model, in libraries or elsewhere on campus, gives the individual faculty member or librarian such a voice.

It is important that librarians have representation on such bodies for various reasons:

Collegiality and Friendship

What could the chairperson of a dance department, a Renaissance scholar, and a catalog librarian possibly have in common? Answer: The three are very good friends whose friendship developed and has been sustained over a twenty-year period during which they shared an interest in, a concern for, the total university. All three have served on many of the various academic senate committees and councils, as well as being elected to the academic senate and holding elected positions as officers of the academic senate itself. The first very positive benefit of involvement in academic governance is the friendships one forms with other faculty members.

Involvement in Governance

Who wants to sit around and complain about what is happening on campus? Everyone. Who would be able to do a better job of running things if he or she were king or queen? Everyone. What better way of dealing with these delusions of grandeur, of the feelings most of us have that we could do it better if we were just given the chance, than to involve ourselves in academic governance where we can, perhaps, influence the direction in which things move. Another benefit--direct involvement in the decision-making process. Those involved in the planning process have a much greater interest and investment in the implementation of decisions than those not involved.

Participation in Planning and Budgeting

Learning how the university obtains and allocates its budget, reviewing academic programs, revising documents on selection of department chairs, following the curriculum development process, serving on selection committees for various academic and administrative positions, discussing parking problems, and reviewing the budget of the sports, athletics and recreation program are all among the types of activities in which librarians find themselves participating at this campus when they get involved in academic governance. Involvement in this type of activities forces one to investigate campus life beyond the doors of the library. Knowing how the curriculum is changing allows evaluation of library resources on a "pre-need" basis.

Librarians as Peers

Are we intellectually capable of serving alongside our faculty colleagues? Of course we are. We not only serve, but on our campus at California State University, Long Beach, librarians are found frequently among the officers of councils and committees. Librarians are chosen to chair committees and subcommittees and to serve as steering committee members of various councils and committees. They are also to be found among the elected officers of the faculty union. Librarians make a very direct contribution to the university community through their service.

Helping the Library

Does anyone have any faculty colleagues who complain about the imposition of a requirement for research and publication? Do they feel they lack the time they need to do such research? Does the lament sound familiar to you as a librarian who has recently been faced with a similar requirement? How many of your librarian colleagues are unwilling to participate on councils or committees because they perceive research as more important than service for promotion? Do you hear your faculty friends complain about their colleagues in the same way? How many faculty members bemoan their tyrannical, indecisive or ineffective department chairs or deans? Do you have more empathy than you would like, perhaps from personal experience, for your friends experiencing this unhappy situation?

Working with our faculty colleagues serves to remind or inform us that we all have very similar problems. And, I think, the result is beneficial to us all. A study done in 1987 on our campus by Robert Boice, then Director of the Center for Faculty Development; Jordan Scepanski, Director, University Library and Learning Resources; and Wayne Wilson, at that time Library Director at Chapman College, verified the similarity of the problems encountered by both faculty members and librarians in attempting to cope with the new pressures for scholarly writing. Among the conclusions of the study, one finds, "...librarians can better understand their own struggle with faculty status by looking at the struggles of traditional faculty," and "... librarians are similar to their faculty colleagues: they have comparable attitudes about publishing and a commitment to excellence in service."

There are some negative aspects to participating in academic governance. First, it can be very time consuming. One must prepare for meetings, attend meetings, and probably end up on a subcommittee that requires additional time. One who is out working with faculty colleagues stands the risk of being expected to know something about what is happening in the library. It can be very embarrassing if you have a library director who does not involve librarians in planning for the library's future. Perhaps this uncomfortable situation speaks to the need for an effective and collegial form of governance in the library.

Another little noted requirement of service on the senate is that the senator is not always simply representing his or her area. A librarian on the senate has an obligation to represent the best interests of the whole institution and not just the library. It is possible that such representation may not appeal to a library director who is not an advocate of such collegiality and shared governance. Even if it is unpleasant, from time to time, as a member of the senate, the librarian must place the good of the institution and of the faculty as a whole at the center of interest when serving. Other faculty members have similar relationships with department chairs and deans, but librarians seem more inclined to worry about the "library" than about the institution and to worry about presenting a united front to protect the library than do other senators for their schools. Service on the senate implies a concern that moves beyond the provincial and into the university as a whole.

Works Cited

Boice, Robert, Jordan M. Scepanski, and Wayne Wilson, "Librarians and Faculty Members: Coping with Pressures to Publish," College & Research Libraries 48: 494-503 (Nov. 1987).

WORKING WITH FACULTY IN AN OUTCOMES-ORIENTED CURRICULUM: OBSERVATIONS FROM THE LIBRARY

by
Terrence F. Mech

Library Director
King's College, Wilkes-Barre

The author wishes to thank Judith Tierney, Reference Librarian, King's College, for her comments in preparation of this manuscript.

Introduction

The following is a brief description of an evolving program of library instruction. Upon reflection of the program's initial successes and failures it became apparent that if the program was to grow and become an integral part of the curriculum, the program had to be examined from several different angles within several different contexts. One of the most crucial and pivotal elements in the program's future is faculty-librarian relations.

Teaching library skills as an integral part of the curriculum cannot be viewed in isolation from the larger academic context. The logic, clarity, and strength of the argument for library instruction does not, in and of itself, carry much weight in the current academic arena. While the national and local higher education environment greatly affects the success of library instruction efforts, other issues such as assessment, increased expectations of graduates and faculty, improved technologies, and other issues are also pressing higher education.

Academics face a growing number of demands from both inside and outside higher education. What they concentrate on depends to a degree on their own vested interests and local political forces. One such demand is for improved library and information skills for students living in an information-rich world. Developing faculty commitment for library instruction is a long-term investment with few visible dividends initially. While very few faculty are against libraries and library instruction per se, other issues and perspectives intervene and make them seem relatively low priorities. However as part of a college-wide curriculum reform, library instruction attracts faculty attention and administration support.

Faculty frequently have several different concepts about the nature of college libraries. They do not see the library's transformation from a physical place to a multifaceted service. Emphasis is changing from physical possession of resources to providing greater access to known resources, regardless of location. Librarians must help faculty understand this evolution and its consequences for them and their teaching. However, before librarians can effectively work with faculty, librarians must come to a better understanding of academic culture and the current academic environment.

Traditionally, academic life has been one of solitude with teaching and research conducted in isolation. However, academe is now more susceptible to outside influence. Colleges must now be more responsive to their environments to survive, and their responses are affecting them profoundly. The number and pervasiveness of these environmental forces have increased almost exponentially. When faculty and administrators lose the ability to understand environmental forces and control their institution, the result is confusion. As groups lose their ability to affect their institutions through the implementation of constructive programs, they increasingly tend to assert their influence by acting as veto blocks, thus increasing institutional conservatism (Birnbaum 15). Occasionally groups use their veto indiscriminately. Not so much to block a meritless proposal but to show that the group can still flex its muscle. It does not really matter against who or what the issue is.

Academe is changing; administrators are making more decisions and involving students and faculty less. Administrators lament that faculty appear less engaged in college life, except as it affects their own narrow interests. "The transfer of power from faculty to administration may also be driven by frustrations with faculty's inability to reach consensus and take decisive action. Many officials believe faculty lack not only the will to act but also the necessary expertise to make hard decisions required for a college's survival in an age of competition for scarce resources" (Levinson 23). The traditional spheres of influence and responsibility within academe are shifting. Some groups are expanding and refocusing their perceptions of their purview, while simultaneously fending off an invasion of their purview by other groups.

Assessment in a Historical Perspective

American higher education has undergone two periods of rapid and stressful expansion in the last 150 years: 1918-1928 and 1952-1983. During these periods of expansion, the undergraduate curriculum underwent major changes (Resnick & Goulden). American higher education has grown from a closed corporation, almost exclusively for the professional training of elites, to a relatively open and varied set of institutions, which serve as America's most promising route to career success. The large influx of students and subsequent institutional growth pressured institutions to diversify academic programs, expand teaching staffs, and offer new courses and majors. These changes made it difficult to maintain coherent programs. Toward the end of each expansion period, an assessment movement developed, with the goal of restoring coherence and substance to the undergraduate curriculum (Resnick & Goulden 77-78).

The latest expansion was fueled by a larger number of eligible students and an increased importance assigned to higher education by the workplace and society. During expansion, institutions changed as they grew larger and more varied. Undergraduate programs changed dramatically as the number of liberal arts majors declined and the number of professional majors increased. With the forced relaxation of colleges' authority over students there seemed to be little control over programs, achievement, and social conduct. While expansion was in progress, there was little opportunity to impose control over growth. The knowledge explosion of the last fifty years, which created a multitude of subdisciplines, also fragmented the curriculum (Resnick & Goulden 82, 87). Given the variety of academic institutions and textbooks, and different ways faculty were trained, there was no residual common college curriculum.

Assessment is again being used to help establish a more effective undergraduate curriculum after a period of rapid change. Because of severe economic and fiscal problems, and a growing governmental role in higher education, assessment often appears as an externally imposed practice designed to make institutions accountable. Historically assessment, program review, methods, and learning in higher education have been the responsibilities of the local faculty and administration (Resnick & Goulden 77-78).

Assessment in Higher Education

Numerous national reports lament the quality of undergraduate education and various groups are demanding evidence that higher education is producing educated adults. Indeed, much of the accountability movement in higher education can be explained by the public's loss of confidence in academe's ability to determine appropriate performance (Ewell 12).

Traditionally, quality and excellence in higher education was recognized by institutional reputation, faculty research, size and cost of the physical plant, number of faculty doctorates and library volumes, and retention rates. However, these traditional measures of excellence are not convincing to outsiders who ask for proof that students are actually learning. By assessing student outcomes and making comparisons, institutions can determine the difference between where students were when they entered and when they were graduated. Net gains in knowledge and understanding represent better measures of an institution's educational effectiveness than the traditional measures of quality which generally focus on institutional size and resources. Emphasizing student outcomes gives visible priority to undergraduate education, and is one way to respond to demands for accountability while providing valuable feedback to students and the institution (Halpern 5-7).

Outcomes assessment provides individual students with information to gauge their academic progress. When aggregated, this information can be used to make programs more effective. Faculty are more supportive of change when they participate in the assessment process and when the need for assessment is clearly documented. Improved programs produce better-educated students and lead to greater student and faculty satisfaction (Halpern 7).

Assessment at King's College

King's College is an independent, undergraduate, co-educational liberal arts college founded in 1946. In Fall 1988, King's College had a student population of 2,304 (1,715 full-time and 589 part-time). The student/teacher ratio is approximately 16-to-1, with 100 full-time and 50 part-time faculty.

The following description of assessment at King's College is adapted from material written by Dr. Donald W. Farmer, King's Vice President and Dean for Academic Affairs. The present outcomes-oriented core curriculum at King's College is significantly different from King's previous core curriculum. The earlier curriculum emphasized student choice through distribution reguirements. Within a few years, the curriculum degenerated into a smorgasbord of learning. Featuring freedom of choice for students, the curriculum only vaguely defined the educational philosophy behind it and failed to define specific learning outcomes expected.

Designed by faculty in 1982, the new core curriculum is conceptual and addresses students' educational needs for a more systematic, integrated learning experience. The new curriculum did not emerge from the traditional path of faculty politics and turf wars. All core curriculum courses were designed for non-majors and are not the first courses for student majors. Core courses are managed by faculty project teams and belong to the core curriculum, not to individual departments.

All courses in the new core curriculum had to be completely new courses designed by project teams consisting of faculty from several disciplines who would teach the courses. Only after articulating and reaching consensus about the desired learning outcomes did project teams identify the course content most appropriate for students to realize these learning outcomes. Project teams constructed master syllabi for all courses in the new core curriculum. Teams established common guidelines for reading, writing, and other course assignments or projects. Several teams also agreed on a common text for use in all sections of a course. All new core courses were subject to approval by the Curriculum and Teaching Committee.

Project teams experienced occasional difficulties. Such collaborative effort by faculty from different disciplines was unfamiliar, and sharp discussions and strong disagreements were part of the experience of preparing master syllabi and reaching consensus on appropriate assignments, teaching-learning strategies and texts. Nonetheless, teams which engaged in lively discussions produced effective courses.

Design of course syllabi required identification of appropriate methods to insure students would become active learners. Conscious design of assignments and examinations required the application of fundamental skills to specific disciplines. The concept of cumulative learning required that students experience the curriculum according to a specified scenario. Some specific learning skills are initially addressed in core courses designed for this purpose, while students initally experience others as carefully integrated components in a variety of courses.

Competence Growth Plans

The core curriculum identifies eight transferable skills, which reflect both traditional liberal learning and new technological skills. Students are expected to develop specific levels of competence in: Critical Thinking, Creative Thinking and Problem Solving Strategies, Effective Writing, Effective Oral Communications, Quantitative Analysis, Computer Literacy, Library and Information Literacy, and Values Awareness.

Faculty, who teach within a major, are responsible for designing and revising four-year competence growth plans for their majors. Competence growth plans build on learning in the core curriculum by linking it with learning in a student's major. Growth plans outline the developmental sequence of each of the eight transferable skills first on a generic level through the core curriculum and with further development of the skill by appropriate applications throughout students' major coursework. Growth plans provide a specific plan to develop the level of student competence necessary to meet faculty expectations. Students receive constant feedback on their progress from a comprehensive, primarily course-embedded, assessment program.

Competence Growth Plans specify sequential learning objectives for students to master from freshman through senior year. Growth plans identify courses in the core curriculum and major program that will help students successfully meet these objectives. Plans also identify specific assessment strategies to measure a student's level of mastery. Each growth plan concludes with a comprehensive statement indicating the level of competence expected prior to graduation.

Developing and refining growth plans is an ongoing activity with revisions clarifying teaching/learning strategies and assessment criteria. Assessment criteria are performance-based and provide a means of giving meaningful feedback so students can build on strengths and repair deficiencies. The King's College curriculum is an integrated learning plan designed for cumulative learning rather than a collection of courses. Furthermore, faculty in all disciplines must accept responsibility for helping students master transferable skills.

Library and Information Literacy

The Library and Information Literacy project at King's College is a cooperative effort by librarians and faculty to improve students' ability to identify, access, and evaluate information resources. In 1982 the librarians reviewed their instruction program and prepared a plan that provides for a hands-on introduction to the library. Library competencies modeled after the Collegiate Skills Program at the University of Wisconsin at Parkside were developed. Advanced and specific subject-related instruction are provided at appropriate points in the students' major in conjunction with course projects. The library's plan and the freshmen workbook program formed essentially the basis for the Library and Information Competence Growth Plans that faculty developed for their majors.

In 1984, after a year's experimentation, all students in Core 110, Effective Writing, were required to complete Basic Library Skills, a library workbook. With only four librarians (a fifth librarian was added in 1987) and an entering class of over 500 students, self-paced workbooks were the only practical way to provide a uniform introduction to the library. Once a uniform foundation is developed, faculty and librarians can build upon it within the context of a student's major. In 1985, Library Skills For Student Teachers: A Self-Paced Workbook and The Biology Literature: A Self-Paced Library Workbook were introduced as requirements in their respective majors. In 1986, students in Principles of Marketing were required to produce a comprehensive marketing plan for a new product. In 1987, a project was developed for Methods and Statistics of Social Research, required of all social sciences majors. These and other projects are intended to teach library skills while reinforcing course content. In advanced major courses the library's emphasis is on reseach strategies and the structure of the literature within the discipline.

A series of study guides modeled after those at the University of Texas, covering everything from locating background information to writing abstracts and annotations, are popular because of their flexibility. Study guides are used individually by students or by faculty as part of class assignments. With the study guides, annotated bibliographies have become frequent assignments. Faculty not seen frequently in the library come to the library to obtain study guides for their classes.

Although designed to place as few demands as possible on faculty, a number of changes have been made to the freshmen workbook since 1984 to accommodate faculty. To reach all incoming students in their first semester Basic Library Skills was required in Core 110, Effective Writing, and Core 100, Critical Thinking. All new students are required to take either Core 100 or Core 110 their first semester. Faculty reportedly wanted all students to be able to apply library and information skills to their other freshmen courses right away. Trying to reach all incoming students through two courses during one semester rather than through one course during two semesters caused the library some logistical difficulties and changed the nature of the project. To accommodate their own requests and the library's logistical difficulties, faculty had to surrender some of their autonomy and follow schedules and guidelines set up by the library. Over time faculty chafed. In 1989 after probing discussions with faculty to review the freshmen workbook within the total context of curriculum reform and structured library instruction, a more flexible course-integrated exercise was designed.

Library use has increased significantly, both quantitatively and qualitatively, since 1982. Much of the increase is attributable to changes in teaching styles, course requirements, library instruction, and the introduction of online and CD-ROM databases. With the introduction of the online catalog, librarians believe continued growth will be geometric rather than linear. While traffic into the library has increased only by one percent, other statistics have increased dramatically. Circulation has increased 28 percent, in-building use of materials 112 percent, and interlibrary loan requests by students and faculty 118 percent.

The number of reference questions increased 180 percent since 1982. Reference questions have also become more complex. With access to more information students must sort through more information. This requires more interaction with librarians to explore options and strategies.

Observations

While working with faculty to develop and implement the new curriculum it was possible to make observations about the nature of librarians and faculty, and their relations. Our experience was not always positive, but it was very enlightening. Many of these observations can be made in other institutions and, with some accuracy, in academe in general.

Even when faculty intellectually acknowledge the need to teach and reinforce library skills systematically, many faculty have difficulty making the commitment necessary to make library instruction a reality. Contacts and agreements with faculty must be renewed constantly. They cannot be taken for granted. It was not until some faculty missed appointments with librarians, forgot to inform the library of class changes, and in some cases made nasty remarks that librarians realized the extent of the faculty's unhappiness. While acknowledging support for the program, faculty were reluctant to discuss the underlying nature of their unhappiness. Faculty, in certain courses, felt under pressure to address so many skills that they did not see how they could do all that they felt was expected of them. Another difficulty was that the improvements other faculty noted in upper division students' library skills were not noticeable to faculty teaching freshmen. As a result, consciously or unconsciously, some faculty almost instinctively attempted to remove covertly the library's intrusion into their classrooms.

In the beginning when librarians worked with a handful of faculty to design and implement the freshmen workbook program it was exciting. Librarians felt involved in the educational process. Their expectations were high. As the program was implemented, grew, and involved more faculty the excitement dissipated in the face of a drastically increased workload and some faculty chicanery. Looking back it is hard to determine the extent to which faculty's passive resistance was directed at library instruction primarily, or if the library was simply an easy target for faculty's pent-up feelings about curriculum reform. Although the librarians have faculty status and rank they keep pretty much to themselves. Perhaps if the librarians had spent more time with the classroom faculty before the program was implemented it would have been easier to tap into the faculty grapevine for more informal feedback.

Academic institutions are basically very conservative organizations, where change comes slowly. The academic culture does not permit rapid change. For faculty the pursuit of learning, academic freedom, and collegiality are strongly held values. Faculty's primary responsibility is to be learned, and to convey this learning by teaching, research, and publication. Faculty value freedom and believe that autonomy is necessary to advance learning. Faculty value collegiality that provides mutual support, opportunities for social interaction, and faculty governance (Kuh & Whitt 76).

The academic culture that binds diverse faculty together emphasizes autonomy, professional preparation (academic degrees), altruistic commitment of faculty, belief in serving the cause of knowledge and understanding, in intellectual honesty, and in academic freedom. Within academe, disciplines have varying cultures based on differences in research techniques and methodologies, vocabularies, and substantive and symbolic perspectives. Within the academic culture there are also institutional differences. All institutions have an institutional culture that helps create a sense of community and loyalty. While institutional cultures vary, strong cultures are most likely found on older, smaller campuses with interdependent parts, which have experienced a significant transformation (Birnbaum 74).

Academic freedom is generally not an issue with assessment. What is at issue is the work style and autonomy of the faculty. Faculty prefer to work independently and not be accountable to anyone. That is not possible with assessment. Assessment requires collective thinking and accountability. Some faculty oppose assessment because they fear it will become more important than the curriculum or the faculty. It shocks faculty to think they would not have total control over something that affects their discipline (Magner A12-A13).

While there is a general spirit of goodwill and cooperation between librarians and faculty, there are undercurrents of conflict. Librarians and faculty must admit these conflicts exist so that they can deal with them and get on with their work. By working together, whatever remedies are to be found will be found. Most faculty and librarians perceive the library to be a service organization, but they value certain services differently. Earlier observations by Cameron and Messinger (24-25) are still valid. Faculty feel the library's primary purpose is to provide materials to support classes. While recognizing the need to support classes, librarians tend to emphasize the library's educational potential. Librarians have a greater understanding than many faculty of the library's potential as an educational force.

In Hardesty's literature review, Blackburn and Maurice suggest that librarians and faculty harbor secret jealousies which affect their relationships. Faculty love books and wish to possess them, but because librarians actually possess and control them, faculty are jealous. Librarians are jealous of faculty's "ownership of students." Through assignments faculty control which books students will use. While some faculty are aware how useful books are in educating students, other faculty are not. Librarians, realizing the library's potential as an educational force, wish to be more involved in the educational process.

Librarians tend to forget that reference services, much less proactive cooperative library instruction efforts, are still relatively recent innovations within American higher education. Until the last half of the nineteenth century academic libraries offered very little to faculty or students. "They were usually small collections, open only a few hours a week, with restrictive conditions and policies severely limiting physical access to the books." Not until the early twentieth century were libraries recognized as an essential part of the academic enterprise (Moran 1). Well into the twentieth century the library was still a faculty preserve. Undergraduates did not need to use it and were frequently denied direct access to its collections. Faculty preferred that libraries concentrate on building collections. Reference services did not assume an important role in college libraries until the 1940s and 1950s, and did not become a major activity before the 1960s and 1970s (Miller 461-462).

Negative faculty attitudes toward librarians' assuming a teaching role seem to be historically based. Most librarians have been women whose education "emphasized organizational and programming skills rather than scholarship" (Biggs 185). Faculty resistance to accepting librarians as more than clerks is based partly on male dominance of college faculties and female numerical dominance of librarianship (Miller 463). It is only within the last 50 years that faculty have surrendered management of libraries to librarians. Even today among some academic men, women are still regarded as outsiders. While messages are more subtle than years ago, the assumption is that the real faculty are still men (Toth 37).

Beyond the gender issue, faculty perceive that librarians do not understand and respect accepted methods of scholarly research. A fundamental difference between faculty and librarians is their philosophies of information seeking. Librarians promote information seeking as a science, with logical, efficient, systematic approaches; while faculty believe research is a mystical art form, learned through apprenticeship with a mentor. Faculty often rely more on personal contacts with colleagues than on libraries, on footnotes instead of indexes, and on serendipity. For many faculty, research is a very personal and an essentially intuitively creative process that defies description. Because the research process is evolutionary, results may be very different from what was originally envisioned (Stoan). Library skills and research skills are not the same thing. Research skills center on the quest for knowledge; library skills center on the search for information (Stoan 105).

Some of the negative attitudes toward librarians may be attributed to the academic "caste" system. While faculty have traditionally made distinctions among themselves, they make sharp distinctions between faculty and all others, especially administrators and practitioners of all kinds. Librarians are viewed with the same suspicion faculty view all non-teaching collegiate personnel, whether or not librarians have faculty status or teach, they generally are not considered "real" faculty. This creates a needless barrier between faculty and librarians.

For real cooperation to take place, librarians and faculty must get beyond their own traditional ethnocentric views and accept each other as having something important and distinctive to offer. The academic culture assumes faculty are frequent library users and makes it difficult for faculty to admit that they are not totally familiar with all of the library's resources. Some faculty feel they must maintain the facade of being all-knowing at all times. Faculty seldom feel comfortable admitting they are not familiar with something, especially with students present. Students pick up on faculty's projected omnipotence and tend to accept whatever faculty say as biblical truth.

While faculty may accrue a contempt for librarians for reasons of gender and perceived inferior degrees, librarians react similarly to faculty who send students through the library on ill-conceived hunts. From a librarian's viewpoint the average Ph.D.'s library skills are not much better than the average undergraduate's. Students' library skills remain woefully inadequate because students take their cues about what is important from faculty. Fear of appearing less than all-knowing may keep some faculty out of the library and present an unnecessary obstacle between faculty and librarians.

Actually, librarians and faculty are both right about the research process. Taken to its limit, research as "process" is too slick and superficial. With a certain level of skill, an individual can research a question very thoroughly and know very little about the subject when finished. Research as "art" means much wasted time and a patchwork approach. Not all of the time is actually wasted in the process; some sifting of information is occurring. While information is percolating through the mind, being analyzed, and synthesized, learning is taking place. But learning can take place with much less pain and much more efficiency if good library skills are utilized.

The faculty's graduate education typically did not contain any systematic instruction on how to use the library effectively. Thus, library instruction is frequently not compatible with faculty experiences. Library instruction tends to be process-oriented and student-centered while faculty, traditionally, tend to be discipline-centered and emphasize the accumulation of knowledge. Faculty tend to emphasize instructional methods that are most compatible with their experiences and values, and to de-emphasize methods that are not (Hardesty 20-21).

Librarians have high expectations of faculty. Aware of the library's potential as an educational resource, librarians are disappointed that faculty do not teach in ways that take full advantage of library resources. But librarians need to take faculty off the pedestal and realize that faculty are only humans working in an ill-defined job. Many university-trained college faculty have no formal preparation for teaching. Perhaps because faculty suffered through the insecurity of learning how to teach on their own they are extremely sensitive about their teaching. Because library instruction usually results in some additional work for faculty and students, faculty are also sensitive to student comments about assignments.

Faculty are threatened by library instruction. "They see instruction as their territory and it is common for them to think they are already providing enough library instruction." If further instruction is warranted, many faculty are convinced they should be the ones to do it (Rice 29). Because faculty regard undergraduate library projects as intellectual exercises, rather than true research, they give little thought to the problem of how beginners are to get started (Stoan 106). When faculty are receptive to library instruction for their students they tend to view the teaching of library skills as an end in itself rather than a means to an end. Faculty frequently fail to see that students can use library skills to develop a better understanding of a subject.

Teaching library skills is typically seen by faculty as a "one shot" experience rather than a progression of experiences that enables students to learn on their own. Skills must be taught, used, and reinforced. Skills are learned incrementally as students gain confidence in their abilities to use the library and evaluate information.

Faculty are in a bit of a dilemma. They tend to resist anything that results in their having less control over their classroom and students, especially anything that lessens their position as subject authorities, or places them in the vulnerable position of having to learn about another's field (Hardesty 20). However, faculty are attracted to and yet fearful of what libraries and technology are capable of doing. As technology makes more information available, it threatens to leave students and faculty "adrift in a sea of information." Yet, the teaching methods necessary to enable students to sort, evaluate, and effectively use information give students more control of their learning and give faculty "new roles as knowledgeable guides to the process of research and critical thinking, rather than merely sources of facts." Faculty will need to provide students with the knowledge and perspective students need to evaluate information (DeLoughry A14-A15).

The availability of information forces faculty to stay current in their discipline and will keep some from portraying themselves as omniscient sources of information. The volume of information available illustrates to students that information is not neatly packaged within the confines of one discipline. Students have access to interdisciplinary sources with which faculty are not familiar. Faculty may no longer bluff with impunity and must give up the pretense that they can cover everything.

Technology and increased access to information will not make teaching any easier. They are going to make teaching a lot more complicated. Teaching methods that enable students to take advantage of their access to information underlines the need for librarians and teaching faculty to work as a collective team (DeLoughry A15). While most librarians are used to collaboration many faculty are not.

Neither the library nor the classroom are the heart of the college campus. The heart of higher education is the teaching/learning process, of which the library and classroom are only a part. Most faculty do not realize that more and more of the teaching/learning process is taking place outside of the classroom. With the availability of information and the power of technology, the library provides faculty with a powerful set of tools to facilitate learning. However, if faculty "insist on holding onto the old ground of separation, specificity, professionalism, [faculty are] going to be ground under by the computer." Faculty need to put information into the historical, social, moral, and political perspectives that students need if they are to truly use information (DeLoughry A15). Teaching and learning needs to become more of a sharing process where faculty and librarians guide and facilitate the learning of students and are comfortable learning along with them.

Prescription

Truly, integrating library instruction into the curriculum is a slow process. It is difficult for many faculty and librarians to change their behavior. Most faculty do not adopt library instruction right away. There is a cultural suspicion and hostility towards outside influences[1]. The basic response to change or ideas initiated from outside the faculty is to first discredit it and then discard it. However, there is frequently a gestation period where ideas percolate until they become the faculty's own. Some faculty will silently absorb all that you give them and then present it to students as their own. Academic culture being what it is at most institutions, librarians will remain outside the mainstream unless librarians take some initiative, increase their visibility on campus, and develop a better understanding of the academic culture. Currently, most college librarians are in academe but not of academe.

Each college decides the role of its librarians. That decision is influenced by a number of library decisions. College libraries cannot be all things to all people. The library needs to match its goals with the college's. Librarians' professionalism, the absence of a nine-to-five orientation, and the type of work they perform all contribute to how librarians are viewed on their campuses. Despite faculty opposition librarians must free themselves from the library building if they are to exercise their rights and privileges as academicians and share all the academy has to offer.

Colleges are slowly recognizing that they need a number of specialists (computer, communication, and library) to work with faculty as part of the teaching/learning process. Because of heightened expectations of faculty performance and stiffer tenure requirements on many campuses, untenured faculty are more amenable to assistance from librarians. Assistance with research for a manuscript will become a more frequent type of initial contact between faculty and librarians on many college campuses.

Librarians need to communicate more with the faculty. Personal feelings must not get in the way of working with faculty. Frequently denied many informal contacts with faculty, librarians must exploit their available contacts to increase their visibility on campus. "Lunch is politically essential for women, who are excluded from most of the channels of male communication" (Toth 38). Uncomfortable with ambiguity, librarians are not noted risk takers and often take shelter in the library because they feel comfortable there. Faculty take comfort in their classroom because they are familiar with it. Getting to know and understand each other is difficult for faculty and librarians because the other's turf is unfamiliar. However, in academe just doing your job is not enough.

The personal, professional, and academic qualities of librarians are crucial factors in the kind and quality of library service provided. Traditionally within colleges there is a reliance on personal, rather than professional, relationships. This personal approach to the library is a positive feature when it serves to strengthen the professional and academic rapport among librarians, faculty, and students. It works to everyone's detriment when it is allowed to undermine the professional and academic ends of library service (Miller 465). Informal faculty contacts are important to the library but they are no substitute for formal communications and more structured contacts.

The truth is there is no new secret prescription for improving librarian-faculty relations. However, the same evolution that is traumatizing faculty and transforming their world is also transforming the library. Librarians may be adjusting to the changes easier than the faculty. Changes in technology and the need to evaluate information highlight the basic skills of librarians. Librarians are also perceiving themselves and their work in a more positive light. They are realizing that what they have to offer is unique and vital to the new academy.

The same technological advances and outside forces that faculty perceive as intrusions will be what lowers faculty barriers to what librarians have to offer. The glitz of technology wraps librarians in the authoritative mystic mantle that faculty require to be able to work with librarians. However, librarians must help faculty see beyond the glitz. Otherwise librarians will go from "keepers of the books" to "keepers of the terminals."

Librarians must take advantage of the changes sweeping academe. The roles of faculty and librarians are changing. Librarians can play a major part in shaping those roles provided they are in a position to work with faculty and take a realistic long-term approach to library instruction and faculty relationships.

Realistically, most libraries can not accommodate the waves of subsequent library activity that library-literate faculty and students can generate. It only takes a few well-placed faculty, who are even moderately serious about using the library, to generate more activity than most libraries can currently handle. To maintain service levels in the face of increased activity, librarians must distill their vision into a workable plan that involves interested faculty. Librarians can work with and through selected faculty to improve students' library skills.

Assessment is a results-oriented process; in such an environment resources and status are helpful for what they allow you to accomplish. Librarians must be careful not to become the victims of their own success by raising expectations that exceed their current and potential resources. There is a fine line between generating activity that makes the most use of available resources and generating activity that stretches resources beyond their limits. By making the best use of available resources in the face of increasing activity, it is easier to secure additional resources. While increased activity justifies the additional resources, it is important to secure those additional resources before activity outstrips current resources. If that cannot be done, program expansion and enhancement must be delayed or restricted.

A better understanding of the larger academic context in which librarians work does not, in and of itself, make faculty more receptive to library instruction or to librarians. An understanding of the many facets of academic culture tempers idealism and provides librarians a more realistic assessment of faculty-librarian relations. With that knowledge, academic librarians can influence their environment, their future, and the future of their libraries provided they are willing to make the investment.

Works Cited

Biggs, Mary. "Sources of Tension and Conflict Between Librarians and Faculty." Journal of Higher Education 52, no.2 (1981): 182-201 .

Birnbaum, Robert. How Colleges Work: The Cybernetics of Academic Organization and Leadership. San Francisco: Jossey-Bass, 1988.

Cameron, Samuel H., and Karlyn W. Messinger. "Face the Faculty: Prevalent Attitudes Regarding Librarian-Faculty Relationships." PLA Bulletin 30, no.2 (1975): 23-26.

DeLoughry, Thomas J. "Professors Are Urged to Devise Strategies to Help Students Deal With 'Information Explosion' Spurred by Technology" The Chronicle of Higher Education 8 March 1989: A14-A15.

Ewell, Peter T. "Establishing a Campus-Based Assessment Program." Student Outcomes Assessment: What Institutions Stand to Gain, New Directions for Higher Education, no. 59. Ed. Diane F. Halpern. San Francisco: Jossey-Bass, Fall 1987. 9-24.

Farmer, D. W. Enhancing Student Learning: Emphasizing Essential Competencies in Academic Programs. Wilkes-Barre, PA: King's College, 1988.

Halpern, Diane F. "Student Outcomes Assessment: Introduction and Overview." Student Outcomes Assessment: What Institutions Stand to Gain, New Directions for Higher Education, no. 59. Ed. Diane F. Halpern. San Francisco: Jossey-Bass, Fall 1987. 5-8.

Hardesty, Larry. "Instructional Development in Library Use Education." Improving Library Instruction: How to Teach and How to Evaluate, Ed. Carolyn A. Kirkendall. Ann Arbor, MI: Pierian Press, 1979. 11-35.

Kuh, George D. and Elizabeth J. Whitt. The Invisible Tapestry: Culture in American Colleges and Universities. ASHE-ERIC Higher Education Report No. 1. Washington, DC: Association for the Study of Higher Education, 1988.

Levinson, Richard M. "The Faculty and Institutional Isomorphism." Academe 75.1 (1989): 23-27.

Magner, Denise K. "Milwaukee's Alverno College: for 16 Years, a Pioneer in Weaning Students from Dependence on Teachers." The Chronicle of Higher Education 1 February 1989: A10-A13.

Miller, Richard E. "The Tradition of Reference Service in the Liberal Arts College Library." RQ 25, no.4 (1986): 460-467.

Moran, Barbara B. Academic Libraries: The Changing Knowledge Centers of Colleges and Universities. ASHE-ERIC Higher Education Research Report No. 8. Washington, DC: Association for the Study of Higher Education, 1984.

Resnick, Daniel P. and Marc Goulden. "Assessment, Curriculum, and Expansion: A Historical Perspective." Student Outcomes Assessment: What Institutions Stand to Gain, New Directions for Higher Education, no. 59. Ed. Diane F. Halpern. San Francisco: Jossey-Bass, Fall 1987. 77-88.

Rice, James. Teaching Library Use. Westport, CT: Greenwood Press, 1981.

Stoan, Stephen K. "Research and Library Skills: An Analysis and Interpretation." College & Research Libraries 45.2 (1984): 99-109.

Toth, Emily. "Women in Academe." The Academic's Handbook, Eds. A. Leigh Deneef, Craufurd D. Goodwin, and Ellen Stern McCrate. Durham, NC: Duke University Press, 1988. 36-45.

PART II

The Librarian as Teacher

THE ACADEMIC LIBRARIAN AS CLASSROOM TEACHER

by
Robert Hauptman, Learning Resources Services
and
Fred Hill, Learning Resources Services

St. Cloud State University

> *Faculty have their own kinds of ambivalence when it comes to university governance. They usually are reluctant to volunteer for or to accept university service, and they tend to minimize their work until they get a strong sense of its impact on their own evaluations or the perceptions of their colleagues.*
>
> *--Peggy Sullivan*

Introduction

Librarians are academic outsiders. They are an integral part of the college or university community and they may hold faculty status, but they do not participate fully in institutional service or governance. Academic pariahs whom legitimate faculty may denigrate or merely tolerate but do not generally completely embrace, librarians continue to wage an uphill battle for intellectual respect among colleagues in other departments.

Most commentators agree that librarians do not fully participate in college or university affairs. And this is probably one of the primary reasons that librarians lack the respect they often so desperately desire in academic settings. Lynne E. Gamble, in a recent apposite essay, insists that there is a "critical need" for librarians to include university service in their obligations, especially since this "...service has acquired a new significance in a changing university environment" (344). If librarians do not serve the wider academic community, if they do not contribute, suggest, advise, or help govern, if they do not make themselves, their potential, and their needs known, then they will remain the academic pariahs they often consider themselves to be.

All of this seems patently clear to those involved in the day-to-day working of the university (whose avowed purpose, one should recall, is the education of undergraduate and graduate students and research in all fields of human endeavor). Paul Rux disagrees. He is "fed up," he tells us, "with the gobbledygook about the sanctity of faculty status--the teacher career model--in library circles" (32). This model and its concomitant obligations and perquisites is, naturally, inappropriate in libraries not associated with educational institutions, but in colleges and universities and even in secondary and primary schools, it is perfectly logical for librarians to consider themselves educators. But logic does not seem to matter to Rux:

> Knee-jerk obeisance to faculty status and its variations has blinded many of us to the fact that managerial skills are more important to survival as a librarian today than a string of scholarly publications or being a classroom maestro. Increasingly, tight budgets force us to demonstrate managerial, not academic or pedagogical, skills. (32)

The great scholar-librarians of the past are anachronisms. Scholarship and pedagogy are passé. Now all that matters is how to "manage," and the librarian is transmogrified into a glorified businessperson. This seems to be a most undignified and counter-productive development.

An informal survey of seven library colleagues at other institutions (State University of New York at Stony Brook, University of Oklahoma, Stanford University, California State University at Sacramento, University of Texas at El Paso, State University of New York at Albany, and Bennington College) basically confirms received opinion. Four respondents indicate that librarians at their respective institutions play a small role in college or university affairs; two claim medium participation; and one insists on a large contribution. One respondent observes that fifteen percent of his colleagues are involved in one way or another, but he also notes that even teaching faculty at his institution are apathetic and angry. He concludes: "Realistically, we matter little to the university." Four respondents indicate that they serve the university to a limited extent; two participate fully; and one does not contribute at all. All but one of the respondents consider themselves primarily librarians, rather than educators. Colleagues from other departments view librarians with some respect, according to five respondents and with a great deal, according to two. Finally, six of the seven respondents insist that being a member of the greater college or university community (as opposed to just the library) results in greater job satisfaction. (The single dissenter notes,"...but I know it does for most of my colleagues.")

Organizational Structure

St. Cloud State University, with nearly 17,000 students,is the second largest academic institution in Minnesota. SCSU maintains a faculty of 700, 32 of whom serve in Learning Resources Services. One of the principal strengths of the LRS structure is that faculty render services and also teach. Not only do these faculty teach within their own academic area (a three-track program that prepares graduate students for careers in library science, school library media center management, and business and industry training and development), they also serve as advisors to the students in these programs, as well as to general studies, special studies, transfer, and other students who enroll in general education courses. This latter group consists of those who require extra care and attention, because of their prior academic preparation. Special studies students are usually superior graduate students who, under the guidance of an interdepartmental faculty committee, design their own program. General education students are those who have not yet selected a major direction of study; nearly all university faculty advise these students.

LRS faculty render their services in Learning Resources; they teach in the Center for Information Media. CIM offers an undergraduate minor as well as the graduate programs described above. This graduate student body numbers in excess of 300. CIM is conveniently housed within the LRS building, affording teaching faculty all of the LRS resources, which range from access to the OCLC database to a 28-channel Simulsat satellite receiving dish. Understanding the uses and utilization of these technological resources is advantageous to both students and faculty. Although each LRS faculty member has specific service responsibility, many have a nearly global understanding of LRS and CIM and thus become instrumental in serving the campus and local community. These people are often sought out by university leaders for counsel and resource updates.

Finally, SCSU faculty belong to the Inter-Faculty Organization, a fifteen-year-old bargaining unit that serves the entire Minnesota State University System.

A Special Case

Saint Cloud State University librarians may be unique. Naturally, they wear the traditional or public service hat which entitles them to administer, select, acquire, catalog, classify, and serve their patrons through circulation, reference work, and so on. At the same time, all but two of the thirty-two faculty members in Learning Resources Services teach two or more courses each year in the Center for Information Media's undergraduate and master's programs. SCSU librarians hold faculty rank and are considered equal members of the university community. With the exception of the necessity to spend forty hours (or their equivalent) per week at work, there is no difference between librarians and anthropologists, linguists, psychologists, philosophers, or physicists at this university.

Librarians teach, receive appropriate remuneration and rewards, have the option of a nine-month contract, are eligible for tenure and sabbaticals, fully participate in university service and governance at both the local and system level, and more important, have earned the respect and gratitude of their 700 colleagues on campus. Concomitantly, librarians have the same obligations as members of other departments. These include holding advanced degrees (10 of the 32 LRS faculty hold earned doctorates); performing their normal duties; teaching; serving the university and local communities; guiding, helping and advising students in CIM as well as those without a declared major and transfers from other schools; continuing their education; performing research; and publishing the results.

As a part of the Minnesota State University system, all non-administrative SCSU faculty members are included in the state-wide bargaining unit, whose formal agreement stipulates that only full members (as opposed to fair share participants) may serve on university-wide committees. Thus, those few LRS faculty who opt not to join the bargaining unit may not fully participate in university governance. Most of the others, however, do and with a vengeance. Why this should be the case here but not in most other libraries may be ascribable, at least in part, to the fact that SCSU librarians also teach regular courses. They therefore perceive themselves as faculty in the true sense of the word. Additionally, as Peggy Sullivan points out, those professors educating librarians ought "...to be among the most astute in dealing with the political climate of a university..." (114). If this is true, then these people will, naturally, want to contribute to the wider university community.

Because of the organizational structure at SCSU, there is no university senate; this is replaced by the Faculty Association Executive Council. Most LRS faculty serve on university-wide task forces (Assessment, Racial Harassment, Emeriti); committees (Government Relations, Admissions and Retention, Academic Affairs and Planning, Promotion and Recruiting, Research Grants, Quality Assessment, On the Institution, Master Contract, Intercollegiate Athletics, Nominations and Elections, Summer School, Search, International Studies, General Education, Membership, Appeals); Graduate Council; the Faculty Association Executive Council; and in many other ways, for example, the SCSU Inter-Faculty Organization negotiator for the current system-wide biennial agreement is an LRS faculty member. It is obvious that people may serve on many committees, so this list would have to be greatly expanded in order to give a complete picture of LRS faculty involvement in university governance.

Faculty energies that might be eroded because of territoriality disputes and other petty differences have little place in LRS because of the daily opportunity and challenge of service experiences that become even more critical in the classroom as the LRS faculty teach current issues to a diverse group of students. Energy explosion, not erosion, has been felt across campus as other university instructors have come to realize that LRS faculty can assist them in many academic ways as they attempt to provide outstanding instructional services to their students. Imagine a professor in biology entrusting his or her classes to LRS faculty in bibliographic instruction, biological database searching, and research project formation. This triunal relationship of student, biology instructor, and LRS professor, each providing a critical portion of the student's direction and ultimate success, is practical, profound, and has potential for life-long promise.

An LRS faculty member, who has a particularly keen sense of the political pulse of the campus, holds that as scholars and teachers LRS faculty in toto may not be as highly regarded as the members of some other departments, but they are highly respected individually. Furthermore, it is his contention that in contrast to librarians at other institutions, those at SCSU are perceived by their colleagues in other departments most closely as equals.

Works Cited

Gamble, Lynne E. "University Service: New Implications for Academic Librarians." The Journal of Academic Librarianship 14 (6) (January 1989): 344-347.

Rux, Paul. "Teach or Manage? Career Models for Librarians." Library Journal November 15, 1988: 32.

Sullivan, Peggy. "Faculty Participation in University Policy Formation: The Pleasures and the Peril." Journal of Education for Library and Information Science 29 (2) (Fall 1988): 113-120.

GETTING INTO THE CLASSROOM IN A NON-BIBLIOGRAPHIC INSTRUCTION WAY

by
H. Palmer Hall

Director of Libraries
St. Mary's University

Introduction

Among the many arguments, and the one that they most often fall back upon, that the professoriate make against granting faculty status to librarians is that librarians do not teach and "faculty status" means teaching. "Teaching," as they define it, is much more than a one-hour shot at showing students how to find information in the library. It involves total responsibility for a course: syllabus-planning, classroom management over an extended period of time, formal academic advising, helping students master a specific body of knowledge over an extended period of time, and judging the quality of student work in a formal grading system.

Being a faculty member means many other things than standing in front of three or four groups of students for a semester, of course. It means doing research and publishing -- participation in the scholarly exchange of information. It means academic advising of students matriculating at the university. It means participation in the informal or formal governance structure of the university by working with the faculty senate, by serving on university committees, by involvement in the on-going, less-formal discussion on the role of the university -- the drinks or coffee sessions where rage is frequently vented at the administration or at other faculty members not present at the time. All of this is collegiality and all of it is intrinsic to being a faculty member in the university.

But even though librarians may do all of those things -- except formal instruction in the classroom -- and even though librarians know that the more successful and more highly published a faculty member may be, the less he or she actually stands in front of a class, until, finally, Pulitzer Prize, Nobel, Bollingen, professional chair, whatever awarding committee names the professor a veritable "super star" faculty member, no teaching in front of a classroom goes on at all. Not only that, but the smaller the number of students the faculty member comes into contact with, the higher the salary. *Curiouser and curiouser*: Once achieving that exalted, officially recognized faculty status, the "star" faculty member becomes something of a "reference librarian" -- dealing with students on a one-to-one basis, answering questions and directing research.

Essentially, librarians do, or at least have the opportunity to do, most of the things teaching faculty do. Unless we work in library schools or in universities with required bibliographic instruction courses, we do not, however, have formal classroom responsibilities as a part of our day-to-day professional careers. Many librarians do help to define the curriculum at their colleges and universities by serving on appropriate committees, many do advise students academically, many have served as officers and members of their faculty senates or associations and many do publish and present papers at regional and national conferences. But very few actually teach in the classroom.

Qualifications

As basic requirements for becoming an academic librarian evolve, librarians are becoming better and better prepared to teach in the classroom should they choose to do so. Librarians with a second master's degree or Ph.D. are becoming more and more common in academic libraries and those degrees are the basic requirement for teaching at the college level. The advertisements for academic library professional positions that appear in The Chronicle of Higher Education, C&RL News, Library Journal and American Libraries as often as not state that a second master's degree is at least preferred for employment. Many academic libraries will now employ new librarians with just the MLS only with the clear understanding that the candidate will obtain a second master's degree in a subject discipline within a specified number of years.

While the purpose of this chapter is not to argue that the second graduate degree is essential for all academic librarians, for those who do wish to be considered faculty members or to work in an academic library where librarians have faculty status the additional degree does help considerably. For library directors and other librarians who may be on a new librarian search committee, a thing that is common in libraries with faculty-status librarians, maintaining that status may cause the committee to prefer such a degreed candidate whether the second master's degree or doctorate is a stated requirement of the job or not. That may not seem fair, but such committees in faculty-status libraries have a vested interest in the academic respectability of their new colleagues.

Getting the Job

Once the second graduate degree is in hand, the librarian at most universities or colleges has the opportunity to move into the classroom and teach within the discipline of the second degree. Probably, if the librarian desires faculty status and wants to be considered a real faculty member he or she should take advantage of that opportunity. There are normally two options: (1) the library director may be flexible enough that a course could be taught during normal working hours and those hours could be "made up" at another time (perhaps an extra hour in the afternoon each teaching day), or (2) the librarian could teach an evening class that would not conflict with his or her normal library job. A third option that is less desirable is that the librarian could have a joint appointment with the library and the department.

If the librarian has such desires and the appropriate degrees, there are few obstacles in the way of his or her acting upon them. Academic departments, even in the largest universities, do hire adjunct, part-time teachers and normally at the last minute to avoid over-hiring faculty members. Most would much prefer to have an already-on-campus and well-qualified person to turn to than seek, at the last minute, a candidate whom they may not know. A fringe benefit of this opportunity is that the librarian should be paid (albeit not very much -- the same pay other adjunct teachers receive) extra for teaching the course.

If well qualified, getting the job is relatively easy. Get to know the teaching faculty members in the appropriate department. Let the department chair know your qualifications and that you would like to teach on an adjunct or part-time basis. You might need to give the chair a current resume, but your transcript should already be on campus. Stress the correct reasons for wanting to teach, not just the picayune monetary rewards and not just to enhance your own status. After you have done that, wait. It is not unusual to get a call from the department chair late on the final day of registration. New sections of classes may be opening, another adjunct professor may receive a late offer for a full-time position, any of a number of unfortunate maladies may strike. Any of these events could provide the opening you need. Be prepared to take advantage of them. After a few semesters of student evaluations you have the chance of building a portfolio of excellent student evaluations and developing seniority in your college or university.

One of the major problems with this form of late notification most adjunct professors receive for their first few semesters is the difficulty of preparing syllabi at a moment's notice. If you have made friends with faculty in the department, you can normally borrow a workable syllabus and adapt it for your own use. It is not impossible to change a syllabus once you are well into the course, but it would be better to avoid that if possible.

Why Teach? (I'm Already a Faculty Member)

There are several direct benefits to the library and to the librarian for this little stint in the land of our colleagues. One of the most obvious, for those concerned with faculty status, is recognition as a true faculty member by our teaching colleagues. I can hear some librarians arguing already that they are faculty members because their contracts say they are and that it is up to the teaching faculty to recognize that reality. And, in fact, there is some official recognition. Librarians with faculty status tend to be on the short mailing list for all people called faculty. Some are on the faculty senate and most are eligible to serve. Some are asked to serve on committees and do serve. So, yes, in those circumstances librarians are officially faculty members.

But being officially and by decree a faculty member doesn't make a librarian a real faculty member. Why not? For the simple and perhaps unfair reason that other faculty members do not recognize the status as anything other than a categorization for administrative purposes. There is no visceral recognition. When faculty members talk in the senate about faculty concerns, they are not speaking of librarian concerns. When they demand salary increases, they rarely include librarians -- unless librarians are there to remind them.

Librarians have de jure faculty status, but de facto they are not, in most cases, faculty. It would help status for librarians who do not teach for those who are qualified to teach to do so. Once librarians are seen in the classroom, faculty-ness begins to bloom. So, yes, teach for status.

Teach, also, because it is enjoyable. We hear the moans and groans from the teaching faculty about their students, about the impossibility of doing significant research and publishing while teaching too many classes, about grading papers, and about their perpetual shortage of time. Yet, few of them would change jobs for similar salaries, or even larger salaries, if offered the opportunity. Most of them (the best of them) teach for the sheer joy of sharing what they have learned with their students -- even those who gripe the most about the deteriorating capabilities of those same students.

Librarians may share that joy at the reference desk or in the one-shot assignment in bibliographic instruction. Too often, though, academic librarians lose the rationale for the work they do on a daily basis. Our purpose is not to build the best possible library procedures, to give the precise piece of information needed to a student, to catalog every book just as our peers would want them cataloged, to find the best discounts and rate of delivery of books we acquire. Our purpose is shared with the rest of the faculty: the education and development of our students. Teaching in the classroom reinforces that prime purpose in a very tangible way.

As academic librarians, at our best, we teach students to become independent of us; at our worst, we merely spoonfeed information to them. In neither case are we confronted with the final product of our labors. We do not see how the student uses the information we helped to find. We do not see the student independently doing research nor the product of that research. In the classroom, wc do begin to see the ends towards which we have been working. We see the product of the quest for information and knowledge. That product is the true joy of teaching; it is also the true purpose of academic librarianship.

So, teach for that reason and for other reasons as well. Teach because you get to know your students better. They are your students as much as they are the students of any member of the teaching faculty. They are the reason the university employed you in the first place. At the reference desk, there is little time to get to know the student with whom you are dealing. The student comes for help, but another student is waiting. The librarian too often has to rush his or her relationship with students in order to help other students. It can become a treadmill effect and we count our students off one by one on our reference tally sheets. Some of them come back, request a particular librarian, and enter a kind of client/librarian relationship, but not very many of them. In that relationship, though, when it exists, the non-teaching librarian has the best possible opportunity to establish something closer to the relationship that exists between a teacher and his or her students.

By teaching in the classroom, a librarian grows closer to the whole process of which she is but one part. Such teaching actually brings two major benefits to the librarian: (1) the librarian gets to see the students from a new angle which can lead to greater empathy with student problems in the library, and (2) the librarian comes to a better understanding of faculty library concerns. In the long run, this can be extremely beneficial to the library itself.

Other benefits flow from the opportunity if it is

taken. Librarians who are faculty members should already be expected to do what other faculty members do for promotion in rank and tenure. Those things frequently include university service and student advising. There is no better way to get to know students than in the classroom and the librarian has a much greater chance of being asked to moderate groups from the classroom than by staying in the library at all times. Even part-time teachers are frequently asked to attend departmental meetings where they can demonstrate their own command of the subject discipline. This can lead to departmental committee work and even to shared publications within the discipline. That demonstration of awareness can also lead to cross-departmental assignments on committees. It leads much more quickly than not getting out of the library would lead to mutual respect between the teaching faculty and the librarian.

Benefits to the Library

The library director who discourages such activity on the basis of the library's need to keep librarians at their desks eight hours each day because of the incredible workload and shortage in staffing is short-sighted. Librarians involved in teaching and in the other tasks of the faculty can be extremely valuable to the library by spending a portion of their time in working for the common good of the university even if it means giving up an hour or two of professional library work each week. It is in those groups outside of the library, the informal planning structures of the university, that the library needs a spokesperson. Your teaching in an academic, non-library department may make it possible for you to speak for the library during these early university planning stages.

If a university's curriculum committee is considering recommending that a new program proposed by one of the academic departments be established and no librarian is on the committee, the library director may be placed in a position some months later of arguing against a program that has the enthusiastic support of the faculty but that the library cannot support academically because of fund shortages. It would be much better to have had a librarian, who could present the library's case, on the original committee from the beginning than to be faced with fighting a rearguard action against a popular new program. A librarian who is also a classroom teacher has a much better chance of being on such a committee in the first place. After all, other faculty members see the librarian dealing with the curriculum in the classroom, their turf, and feel more comfortable in asking the librarian to serve.

In seeking support for a larger budget for the acquisition of materials or for new staff members, it is helpful to have librarians on the faculty senate to gather formal support for the library. It is easier to do this when the faculty who elect the senate consider librarians to be real faculty members. Too many of them do so only when they see librarians in the classroom.

There are countless other occasions when de facto faculty status is important, even if we already have de jure faculty status: when faculty pay raises are an issue, when rank and promotion and tenure are voted on, when travel funds become an issue, and so on. In all of these cases, empowerment is easier when the teaching faculty see librarians as "one of us" instead of "one of them." That is the essence of collegiality. And that is certainly one reason we should take advantage of the opportunity to teach if we are qualified to do so.

Conclusion

The academic world is not fair. There are sufficient reasons to consider librarians as faculty members without insisting upon classroom teaching. But political reality cannot be ignored. Librarians who do not consider the teaching/learning experience as the centerpoint of the university probably should not be academic librarians. As librarians in the library, we participate in that process. Graduating students are the product of their classroom teachers, but they are also our product. It is simply not fair that our colleagues who are teaching members of the faculty do not fully recognize our contribution to the education of their students.

If enough librarians get out of the library and into the classroom, even teaching just one course each fall and spring semester, we will borrow the can of paint that colors the label "faculty" on our colleagues. Many librarian realists know that we are borrowing the label anyway; teaching in the classroom simply makes it more legitimate.

Teaching is, of course, only one aspect of a faculty member's professional life. If a librarian does not want to teach, yet still wants to be a faculty member, he or she should participate in some of the other areas that belong to the faculty. The alternative is to give up the faculty-status quest.

TEACHING IN ROTATION AS A MEMBER OF THE INSTRUCTIONAL FACULTY AND AS A LIBRARIAN

by
Taylor Hubbard

Public Services Librarian
The Evergreen State College

Introduction

The six faculty librarians of The Evergreen State College (TESC) in Olympia, Washington, maintain a relationship with their college and its teaching faculty which is probably unique in American academic librarianship. In some ways the relationship is reminiscent of the European scholar/librarian, or librarian/scholar. The rotation system which places teaching faculty in the library and librarians in subject teaching positions has been in place since 1978, and is probably the best documented facet of TESC librarianship.

Features of the TESC rotation system and the related status of librarians may be outlined as:

The TESC Rotation System

1. Librarians are hired through the process used for all faculty hirings. Based on the recommendations of a subcommittee composed primarily of library personnel, faculty librarians are approved through the general faculty hiring com-

mittee and appointment by the campus Provost. One factor weighed in this appointment process is a library faculty candidate's potential contribution to the general curriculum subject matter, in addition to library qualifications.

2. Evergreen has no ranks for faculty or faculty librarians; salaries are based upon years of experience. Contracts for all faculty, including librarians, are nine months with summer options. There is no formal tenure system. *De facto* tenure occurs with an eight-year appointment usually following two three-year contracts.

3. In the current Evergreen quarter system, librarians rotate out of the library for one quarter every three years (one quarter out of nine). The logistics for the librarian is this process means physically (and psychologically) moving out of a library office into a faculty office elsewhere on campus -- new telephone, new support staff, new responsibilities. The process is reversed for faculty rotating into the library.

4. The annual deployment of faculty in the Evergreen system requires considerable advance planning. Programs (courses) are interdisciplinary, subject matter determined by the interest or expertise of the faculty forming the team. Program length can vary from one to three quarters. Individual programs customarily constitute a full course load (sixteen credits per quarter) for students enrolled. Team size varies between two and six faculty members. Teams are formed and program design and content planning begins two years prior to the academic year in which a program will be offered. At this advanced stage a librarian scheduled for rotation during that future academic year identifies a program of interest and negotiates membership in the team designing a program and becomes part of the process. With the exception of some core programs whose content remains focussed (although the faculty change from year to year), team-taught programs disband at the end of each academic year and new combinations of faculty create new programs for the next academic year.

5. Although library instruction is a primary concern among the six faculty librarians, the librarian in rotation is understood to be teaching in a non-library-related subject area. Bibliographic instruction is not intended as a major contribution of librarians to their rotation responsibilities. In this entire process, there is considerable latitude for personal expression and initiative. As with other team members, librarians have considerable subject expertise not formalized as a degree credential which can be incorporated into programs.

6. Whenever a librarian becomes a member of one of the programs, a faculty member replaces her/him in reference. Faculty rotated into the library are solicited by the library from a pool of faculty identified as available (not affiliated with a program) in the two-year advance-planning cycle. The criteria for identifying the faculty to be invited into the library vary considerably; it may depend on expertise needed at the time, collections to be developed to meet changing college priorities, past interaction of staff with the faculty member available, etc. Faculty are enthusiastic about working in the library. A substantial portion of their assignment has typically been learning reference and working at the reference desk, although interest has been expressed in other activities, for example, a music faculty member interested in working on cataloging backlogs in his subject area. The most recent example of faculty rotation is a member of the TESC teacher education program whose rotation was used to develop plans for a curriculum library, work on a computer network study, do book selection in education and other areas of interest, as well as learn reference service. While the evaluations of the library rotation experience have been overwhelmingly positive, there is occasional concern among reference librarians that faculty may not fully appreciate the spectrum of complexities involved in library service; there is, for example, some concern among librarians that reference librarianship can not be fully mastered in one or two quarters as some faculty may maintain. Nonetheless, the sheer quantity of goodwill and participation brought by faculty is important. Since rotating faculty are also involved in the group decision-making processes used in the library, they become more knowledgeable about and sympathetic with difficult administrative and fiscal problems faced by the library.

The benefits of the rotation system are not difficult to identify. In a campus setting of about 3,000 students and 175 faculty, the rotation system brings librarians and teaching faculty directly into one another's area of activity. Being involved in teaching helps focus library service by engaging librarians directly in the mainstream of the curriculum and the context of the learning process at the college. Work with other team faculty builds personal and professional contacts which contribute to weaving librarians and the library into the campus fabric. Participating in the programs allows librarians to use great quantities of information and observations and interests developed in the normal routines of working in an academic library. Requirements of planning, lecturing and leading discussions also provides librarians with a new perspective with which to reassemble or systematize the fragmented bits of knowledge which are the daily fare of reference. Working closely in a faculty team also means being a firsthand observer of faculty methods in developing instructional materials, techniques and objectives, and becoming better aware of faculty interests.

The Classroom Experience

The details of a program syllabus are worked out by team members. Program enrollment is currently predicated on a twenty-two to one student-faculty ratio. Thus, a typical core program of eighty-eight students will have four faculty members. For a full-time program, there will be fourteen or more weekly contact hours, divided between lectures (typically six hours), workshops (typically four hours) and seminars on readings (four hours). Lectures are divided among faculty members. Workshops are skills components of programs; they include activities such as writing, mathematics, statistics, learning computer programs and the laboratory or studio components of science or arts programs. Library activities can and have been planned into workshop periods. Seminars are subprogram groups of (in the example) twenty-two students, each led by one of the four faculty members. Seminars discuss reading assignments, usually trade publications -- textbooks are seldom used in programs.

Librarian team members share equally in the responsibility for all these activities. Lectures by one librarian in recent years have included such diverse subjects as classical themes in literature, Russia in the nineteenth century, the Kuhnian theory of scientific revolutions and discourse analysis. Workshops led by librarians are frequently library-related, but need not be. Being in a program does, however, provide greater opportunity for making fully integrated library assignments. For example, in a unit on discourse analysis, part of a "Ways of Knowing" program, a lecture, a seminar reading and a workshop involving a library exercise to locate and analyze examples of scholarly discourse fit together well.

As a team member, a librarian leads a seminar. Seminars create the closest formal relationship faculty members achieve with students. Seminar leaders generally assume advising/tutorial responsibility for students in the seminar -- monitoring their intellectual development in the program, tutoring them as necessary and preparing lengthy written evaluations of their learning while in the program (there are no grades -- only these written evaluations). The consequence is a close relationship between the students and the seminar leader, one that often lasts throughout a student's academic career at Evergreen.

Classroom and seminar contact between students and librarians tends to encourage the perception among students that librarians are integral and participating faculty members, a perception which undoubtedly adds to the heavy use of the library collection and to the role many library faculty assume as counselors, advisors or, simply, friends of Evergreen students.

Besides the rotation system, there are a number of other related opportunities which integrate librarians further into the college faculty. Among these opportunities is accepting learning contracts with individual or groups of students. There are three kinds of academic contracts at Evergreen: Individual Learning Contracts, Group Learning Contracts and Internship Contracts.

An Individual Learning Contract is developed by a student who wishes to pursue a topic too narrow for a program or some topic not represented in the curriculum at the time. The contract is sponsored by a faculty member who provides consultation or advice. Individual contracts may include such activities as readings, field studies or research papers. They are usually undertaken only by advanced students and vary from partial to full quarter credit, depending on the conditions of the contract. In recent years one librarian has sponsored Individual Learning Contracts on such topics as Expatriate American Writers, Social

Sciences Theory, Questionnaire Design, Writing for Publication, Politics of the Supreme Court, 19th Century American Women Writers and Media Production Studies in London.

Group Contracts involve one or two faculty members, may enroll from twenty to forty students and proceed much as the coordinated studies programs of the general curriculum, albeit with a much narrower focus. One librarian has sponsored a Group Learning Contract on Contemporary Literary Theory. Another this year offered a four-credit library research module as part of a larger sixteen-credit group contract on microeconomics.

From time to time, Evergreen faculty form seminars among themselves outside scheduled programs to study subjects or read works of mutual interest or concern. This year, one of the Evergreen librarians formed what will become a continuing seminar among faculty to begin reading postmodernist works in social sciences. Settings such as this help in the continuing critical reappraisal of the role and nature of the library and academic librarianship, especially in relation to concerns and values which are challenging the academy at large. These settings also place librarians with faculty at the beginning of an intellectual enquiry process which will, in all probability, result in new ideas entering the classroom and, eventually, finding their way into the library, with students as common carriers.

Recently, the bibliographic instruction program of the library was refocused by the reference faculty from in-house instruction to instruction integrated into classrooms outside the library. In practical terms, this meant abandoning a stand-alone four-credit Library Research Methods course offered annually with an enrollment of ten to twenty students. As a consequence, individual librarians have been experimenting with new methods of BI delivery. One experiment has been with direct affiliation quarter-time (eight to ten hours per week) with a general curriculum program. In the event, a limited role was negotiated by the librarian with the faculty team involved, allowing participation in lectures, seminars and other program activities in exchange for developing library activities related to material already planned for the program. In addition to reaching far greater numbers than was possible through the library's own program, affiliation meant personal contact with eighty or more students, identity as a member of the teaching team and far more library research credits than were ever generated by in-house instruction. In addition, the librarian worked individually with students responsible for making background presentations on films, and with faculty by supplying maps, chronologies and other instructional materials used in lectures.

In 1988 reference librarians reorganized and adopted a structure (or non-structure) more akin to other faculty. Evergreen has no academic departments; faculty affiliate with "Interest Groups" which are sort of discussion/planning groups within broad disciplines, for example, social sciences. The title "Head of Reference" has been abandoned in favor of "Convener," as in the faculty interest groups. The position is rotated among reference librarians on an annual basis. Administrative responsibilities, such as supervision of a number of activities (documents, periodicals, interlibrary loan, etc.) have been divided among all reference librarians. The successful efforts to integrate library instruction more effectively into the curriculum have also stirred discussion on further reorganization to allow expanded librarian presence on program teams.

The flexibilities of the Evergreen learning program offer enormous opportunity for librarians to become intensively involved in the activities of the general faculty and the goals of the college. Participation can mean continual engagement in the intellectual vigor of the campus and the larger world of learning.

Works Cited

The Evergreen rotation system has been described in the following two articles:

Hill, Fred E., and Robert Hauptman. "A New Perspective on Faculty Status." College & Research Libraries. 47: 156 - 159 (March 1986).

Huston, Mary M. "Research in a Rotating Librarian/Faculty Program." College & Research Libraries News 46: 13-15 (Jan. 1985).

UNCHARTED TERRITORY: BUILDING A LIBRARY INSTRUCTION COURSE IN GEOGRAPHY

by
Robert B. Marks Ridinger

Bibliographer
Northern Illinois University

Introduction

The role of an academic librarian can be likened to the title character in Dr. Seuss's book The 500 Hats of Bartholomew Cubbins, with each day bringing a different set of challenges to one's professional abilities, knowledge, and sometimes sense of perspective. Nowhere is this more apparent than in the relationship with the academic faculty of client departments if you serve as a subject specialist, reference and collection development librarian at a sizable university. This essay will explore the origin and development of a course aimed at providing upper-division undergraduates and graduate students with library skills for the use of and familiarity with available resources in the component fields of geography.

Prior to any attempt by a librarian to create courses, programs, etc., for a particular academic department, college or discipline, it is essential that a frank and open network of communication be established between the departmental officers and the library. Such a network permits the librarian to be aware of the particular needs and interests of individual faculty members and to gradually become familiar enough with the curriculum (both current and projected) to assist in course planning. In most cases, such an atmosphere can be achieved only through regular contact with both faculty and students. In the case of the course under consideration here, it was the department itself which voiced concerns demanding a response by library instructional programming.

In early 1982, a meeting was called by Dr. Donald Maxfield, chair of the Department of Geography at Northern Illinois University, with several of the senior faculty and myself. One primary concern raised at this meeting was the low level of comprehension of available library resources in geographical subjects evidenced in the research papers being written in upper-division level courses and the complaints of the students when sent over that "there's nothing in the library on remote sensing, meteorology, etc." A formal request was made by the chair for assistance in dealing with the problem.

In response, I shared with them a listing of basic resources in the subjects comprising the discipline of geography which had recently been prepared. Grouping the materials together by format, it had originally been intended solely as an in-house tool for public use. Upon re-examination, I realized that its format lent itself well to adaptation as the framework for a series of classes on these indexes, bibliographies and the statewide online library catalog. After some discussion, it was agreed that an experimental course entitled "Library Materials in Geography" would be offered in the fall semester as a topics course under an already approved course number. This would have the advantages of permitting various formats of class presentation to be tested and avoiding the lengthy procedures required for the establishment of an entirely new course for the department.

Developing the Course

The decision to implement the course having been made, it remained to create suitable curriculum materials. For some academic fields, there exists a plethora of basic research sources and bibliographies whose relevance is clear and whose names are well known to the students. An excellent example of this is Chemical Abstracts. In the case of geography, the first problem is one of definition. Beyond the basic and traditional fields of cartography (and its more recent descendant, remote sensing of the environment), a geography curriculum may include anything from soils science and land management to specific topics courses on the problems facing the planet through the depletion of the ozone layer. Thus choosing a group of sources and their manner of presentation must be tailored to fit the needs of a particular population of students. The initial group of indexes chosen reflected this diversity, ranging from the basic Current Geographical Publications to more exotic titles such as Energy Index and Atmospheric Effect of Environmental Pollutants. Perhaps the most reliable guide in such matters is for the librarians to simply consult the course catalog of the department, to determine what areas of the field are being locally stressed and, also, whether any new courses are in the process of being tried out, as seminars may require a separate class presentation.

A word should be said here about the place of information sources which exist in forms other than the traditional paper. Northern Illinois University is a member institution in ILLINET, the statewide online catalog comprising more than eight hundred libraries of all types within the state of Illinois. In the case of geography, while familiarity with standard sets of microforms are not as needful as in some fields such as anthropology, students enrolled at this institution must achieve a degree of facility with ILLINET to carry out adequate research. Realizing from experiences in reference interviews with students that many of them simply relied on the general public interface for an explanation of how to utilize the system, it was decided that a priority of the initial class session would be introducing participants to ILLINET using examples drawn from the components of geography.

Recognizing that a primary problem would be scheduling this class so as not to conflict with course offerings already in place, a time slot prior to the beginning of the normal class schedule was chosen in conference with the department.

The format of the course was designed as a series of eight lectures, based upon the aforementioned outline of resources. Topics addressed were the ILLINET system and its applications to the field of geography, basic indexes and abstracts (this group included Current Geographical Publications and the Social Sciences Citation Index), specific abstracting and indexing services with application to one facet of geography (such as Environment Index and Meteorological and Geoastrophysical Abstracts), bibliographies on germane subjects such as acid rain and the development of Third World cities, printed catalogs of relevant research collections such as that of the American Geographical Society, general geographic reference volumes such as the Dictionary of Human Geography and some discussion of the structure of the Superintendent of Documents system of classification and federal and state sources of geographic data, including the United States Census.

For each class, a set of fifteen questions was created, combining actual questions received on the reference desk with topics contributed by the teaching faculty. Each group was then discussed at the following class and students were advised to keep the listings as models of the types of research possible in these sources. Grading was done for the course with a take-home final examination of thirty questions, with final grades being determined on a percentile basis. While the number of credit hours granted for successful completion of the course varied from one to three initially, evaluations were carried out under established university guidelines. After three semesters, the course was added to the departmental requirements for all incoming graduate students and newly declared majors by unanimous vote of the faculty.

Conclusion

Teaching the course produced several pieces of information which other librarians may find instructive. It quickly became evident that the students were somewhat baffled by finding a librarian familiar with the various aspects of their departmental courses and speaking their professional language with (depending on the topic) some fluency. The general feeling was "but he's a LIBRARIAN," with the clear implication that librarians were not supposed to be found in the context of a classroom, no matter what the subject being taught. Computer literacy was another area in which it was possible to open a dialogue on topical needs, often using ideas which members of the class were considering working on.

Most importantly, it was clear that the major emphasis of the course, which was to teach the process of how to think about doing research in geography, was rather unfamiliar. Reactions indicated that a librarian was supposed to talk about books, be available on call for emergency help, but not to get into the province of talking about how to plan the most effective way of researching LANDSAT photography.

All these reactions have something to tell us as academic librarians as regards the public perception of our work, whether by the teaching faculty or the students we serve. There is a very definite image problem, with librarians being either ignored entirely as members of the faculty or, at best, relegated to the category of supportive professional staff. Debate on this issue can be observed at length in the various journals addressed to academic librarians, with no clear consensus emerging. It is clearly the choice of each librarian as to how much outreach will be made to the academic disciplines, what form said partnership will take and the degree of integration which can be achieved into the framework of subject instruction. But the choice is well worth making, as it validates our claim to be considered peers of the instructional faculty and opens up new avenues of effectiveness, both professionally and within the wideruniversity community.

PART III

Research, Publication and Networking as a Librarian in the University

DEFLATING THE OXYMORON; OR, SEARCHING FOR A SHOE BENEATH THE LEATHER AND THE LASTS

by
Dale R. Schrag

Director of Libraries
Bethel College

[The following is a slightly edited version of a speech given to the ACRL/New England Chapter in November of 1986. The author was invited to address the question, "What are the issues in academic librarianship?"]

To seek an answer to the question "what are the issues in academic librarianship" is to confront a cacophony of concerns--concerns which are every bit as familiar to you as they are to me. My purpose here this morning, therefore, is not to provide you with some comprehensive catalog of those concerns. My purpose, rather, is to focus only on those issues that I perceive to be of the utmost importance. And I am here to suggest that one of the most critical issues facing academic librarians today has to do with the fact that for all too many in academia, the phrase "academic librarian" is an oxymoron; there is a perceived tension, a pronounced tension, between the adjective and the noun. Moreover, I am prepared to argue that such a perception is not limited to the more supercilious members of the "teaching faculty." Indeed, I suspect that in their deepest heart of hearts, in the most private alcove of their stacks, many librarians would confess to harboring those same feelings. Why?

I submit that librarians tend to feel ill at ease in the academy for a variety of reasons. For openers, there is the problem of degrees. From the very beginning, graduate library education in this country was placed on a virtual collision course with academic credibility. The Association of American Universities reports of 1925 and 1927 strongly advised that tacking 30-some post-baccalaureate hours onto an unspecified baccalaureate degree in no way constituted a legitimate "graduate degree." It represented, at best, a certificate program. In many states, students planning to teach in elementary or secondary schools are required to complete a fifth year of teacher education to supplement their baccalaureate degrees. Upon completion of that fifth year of study, they are not considered "masters" of anything. They are considered certified teachers. Period!! Most librarians, on the other hand, do almost precisely the same thing and then call themselves "masters of library science." This may not be a problem in public libraries, but it spells disaster in academe. The M.A.s in chemistry and history (not to mention the Ph.D.s in those disciplines) can hardly be blamed for looking askance on a "discipline" that requires only one year of education for its "mastery."

I would add, parenthetically, that this minimal exposure to the climate of graduate education helps explain why Ed Holley legitimately sees the need for better understanding of the history, development, and politics of higher education among academic librarians (463-464). We don't understand the context of higher education partly because we do not study it (there's precious little time in one year, after all); but our short tenure in graduate programs is also a contributing factor. The Ph. D. in history has studied at the feet of her mentor for several years, and she comes to campus with a much deeper understanding of the politics of academe.

Exacerbating the problem of the flimsiness of our degrees is the ALA's insistence on generalist training for all librarians. From the ALA's perspective, each new MLS should be able to move into any entry-level position in virtually any library. This, of course, is tantamount to defining academic librarianship as nothing more than an accident of employment. If library school graduate X is offered a job at Pawtucket Public, IBM, and the University of Massachusetts-Amherst, and if he happens to choose the job at U. Mass., even if he chose it only because he wanted to be closer to his parents who live in Hadley, PRESTO!!, he is an academic librarian!! Perhaps any profession which defines itself so irresponsibly gets precisely as much respect as it deserves.

A third source of tension results from the fact that, in rather striking contrast to most other academic disciplines, we come to campus almost without a theoretical knowledge base, without a paradigm. Our training is intensely practical. We find our solace in the world of documents and data, in physical things that we can manipulate, mark and park; we are much less secure in the world of ideas. Little wonder that we feel a bit out of place in a community that is often referred to as the "marketplace of ideas."

A related -- though still distinct -- problem has to do with our intense fascination with process. It has been suggested that "librarians have become so concerned with process that they have confused substance with instrumentation" (Shera "Librarianship and Information Science" 384). Let me clarify by example. Some years ago I attended a conference session on online searching in the small academic library. One of the panelists exulted that when he began doing online searching, "the scales fell from his eyes." It changed his whole understanding of reference work. Now he finds that when he does manual searches, he begins by trying to identify appropriate subject terms and then selecting an appropriate indexing tool. And he owes this remarkable insight to the <u>process</u> of online searching!!! Can anyone tell me how in the name of Melvil Dewey he was doing reference work before he discovered online searching???? At that same session another librarian suggested that online searching would demonstrate in a new way the interdisciplinary nature of knowledge. More than the subject catalog? More than the DDC or LC classification systems? We do love our tools, don't we--the more so if they are shiny, new, and electronic. Well, this is not to suggest that our colleagues in the teaching faculty are unconcerned with process and methods and tools, but I think it is fair to say that most of those disciplines--especially the most respected ones, the core liberal arts disciplines--move very quickly to matters of substantive knowledge.

And speaking of knowledge, here is yet another source of tension. We librarians still seem to much prefer the term "information" (Wilson 82-86 or Swan 25-28). Our teaching faculty colleagues almost uniformly see themselves in the knowledge business, concerned with its extension and expansion; we librarians would rather see ourselves in the "information business." $E = mc^2$ is information, I suppose, but so is the fact that our family dog is named Pepper, and our cat is named Bobby Joe. (Do you still want to be in the "information business"?) I am convinced, incidentally, that this is much more than a question of semantics. I think it colors our perception of our fundamental purpose; I think it helps explain why we focus on quantitative measures rather than quantitative substance; I think it contributes to our all-too-often-unreasonable fascination with technology; I think it even contributes to library buildings that are aesthetic abominations. But we must move on, and my primary point here is that it drives yet another wedge between the teaching faculty and the librarians. The "information business" fixation may not cause real problems for public librarians, but I think it is decidedly deleterious for those of us working in academe.

Finally, and perhaps most importantly, there is real tension between us and our faculty colleagues because virtually all of them have done--and the best are still doing--substantive research, and precious few of us have. In fact, precious few of us seem even to understand the research process--witness Steve Stoan's seminal article on "Research and Library Skills" or Connie Miller and Patricia Tegler's "Online Searching and the Research Process." When librarians do engage in "research" (which is a fairly rare occurrence--of sixty contributed papers at ACRL/Baltimore, only seven were considered "research reports." The vast majority were "position papers," (which is precisely what this is!), it frequently consists of "descriptive studies" involving heavy statistical manipulation, questionable methodology, and results that often cannot properly be generalized beyond the provincial and parochial (Shera "Darwin, Bacon, and Research in Librarianship" 147; Wright 769; Freeman 27-28). To all this, you may add a marked tendency toward presentism (we so much want to be <u>au courant</u>, heaven forbid that we should read anything more than five years old); you may add vestiges of an outmoded social scientific, positivistic, value-free methodology (Harris 518-525), and it is not surprising that our research record does not serve to win us friends and influence teaching faculty colleagues. Little wonder that we agonize about faculty status, lament our continuing image problems, and don't seem to be able to attract the "best and the brightest" into our library schools.

This litany of tensions between the librarians and the teaching faculty in academe has clearly tended to fault the former and glorify the latter, perhaps somewhat unfairly in both cases. But, however superficial the treatment, the issue is anything but superficial. It is, in fact, a critically important issue. Irrespective of how their contracts read, effective academic librarians simply must have credibility with the teaching faculty. Faculty constitute, I believe, our primary constituency--more so, even, than the students. One of the few things our research has shown us is that in case after case, the vast majority of student use of an academic library is generated by the faculty! It is imperative, therefore, that we determine how to resolve this tension between adjective and noun; that we strive to deflate any oxymoron potential in the term "academic librarian." How?

As a possible starting point, I offer two quotations of considerable length and (I think) of considerable substance. The first comes from Socrates by way of W.K.C. Guthrie's The Greek Philosophers from Thales to Aristotle.

> If you want to be a good shoemaker [said Socrates], the first thing necessary is to know what a shoe is and what it is meant for. It is no use trying to decide on the best sort of tools and materials to use and the best methods of using them unless you have first formed in your mind a clear and detailed idea of what it is you are setting out to produce and what function it will have to perform.... Given a proper understanding of the end, the understanding of the means to be adopted could follow, but not otherwise. (72 - 73)

The second quotation comes from Jesse Shera's essay entitled "Librarianship and Information Science," which appeared in The Study of Information: Interdisciplinary Messages, edited by Fritz Machlup and Una Mansfield.

> What, then, is the *shoe* that is the end product of the *shoemaker*, the professional librarian? I submit that there are three components in the concept of a library. First, there is acquisition, which involves knowing what to acquire for a given clientele and how to acquire it. Acquisition implies substantive knowledge of the materials and the uses to which knowledge can and should be put. The second is organization, that is, ways in which the accumulated materials can be arranged and processed for maximum convenience and efficien-

> cy of use. It is here, and only here, that information science makes its contribution to librarianship. The third is interpretation and service, which is the raison d'être of the library, and it is here that information science reveals its greatest threat of dehumanizing the library's function. To express the same idea in another way, the library can be seen as three interrelated spheres: the sphere of optimum content; the operational or mechanistic sphere; and the sphere of maximum context. If librarians persist in sublimating librarianship to the lure of the machine and the all importance of data retrieval, their *shoes* will be very uncomfortable to the user, and they will leak at certain vital points. (385)

I am firmly convinced that, as a profession (and I'm speaking now of librarianship generally, not just academic librarianship), we have consistently tended to violate this Socratic vision; we spend the vast majority of our time at conferences, in the literature, and in the classroom focusing on tools and methods. Many (if not most) of the "issues of academic librarianship" today are issues of process and procedure rather than issues of Socratic substance. It was Shera who said, "Librarians have become so concerned with process that they have confused substance with instrumentation.... Librarians are, or should be, characterized by their knowledge, not by their instrumentation" (Shera "Librarianship and Information Science" 384). Why do we focus so exclusively on the latter?

This is neither the time nor the place to undertake a comprehensive study of the history and development of library education in this country. Suffice it to say that in its earliest manifestations (thanks, in no small part, to Melvil Dewey) library education was painfully practical. This situation changed markedly in the 1920s, when--in response to the Williamson reports, recommendations of the ALA's Board of Education for Librarianship, and a whole lot of money from the Carnegie Foundation--library education moved into its present "graduate" phase. The undisputed institutional leader in that effort was, of course, the Graduate Library School at the University of Chicago. The GLS faculty consciously set out to construct a theory of library science. Much to the dismay of the many resisting humanists in the profession, it drew heavily upon the social sciences for constructing such a theory. The attempt was only partially successful in terms of theory building, but the GLS was soon flattered by imitation as other GLSs began sprouting up all over the country in an attempt to recreate THE GLS. To this history has been added in the last two decades a special emphasis on "information science," so that now most GLSs are GSLISs or some initialistic facsimile thereof. Thus endeth our capsule history of library education in America. So what does it all have to do with "Searching for a Shoe Beneath the Leathers and the Lasts"? How does it relate to the problems of academic librarianship recounted above?

I think that this may explain the root cause of most of those problems. In his provocative (if mistitled) article "The Dialectic of Defeat: Antimonies [I think he means "antinomies"] in Research in Library and Information Science" (518 - 525), Michael Harris argues that if the GLS experiment failed to establish a significant body of theory, it did succeed remarkably in setting the agenda and method for subsequent library research. And the success of the GLS in setting the research agenda landed librarians smack dab in the pools of positivism (which is where a lot of social scientists were swimming in the decades of the thirties, forties and fifties). But whereas social science generally has recognized the inherent problems of positivism and moved beyond that frame of reference, the librarians have so insulated themselves from other disciplines (we are insecure, remember?) that they are still stuck in this inadequate mode of social science research. If Harris is correct, (and his thesis is controversial) it may help to explain why so much of our professional research appears to be fixated at the infamous neo-Freudian stage of early "physics envy." It explains why, to quote H. Curtis Wright, "the methodology of librarianship and library education [is] controlled by the numerate data mongers, mathematical wizards, and statistical button counters of physical science" (769). It explains why library science has so totally abandoned its humanistic roots and rashly jumped on the information science bandwagon (although I think the insecurity of presentism plays a role here). And it explains why our research and our theory (such as it is) tends to focus on leathers and lasts rather than on shoes. Because it is this area, the area of tools and processes--"instrumentation," to use Shera's word--that is most amenable to positivistic research methods. Yet this is also the area that contributes mightily to the chasm between librarians and teaching faculty. And I am convinced that if we focus our search for unifying theory here (as we have), we are bound to come up short.

Why? Because we still have to account for the additional two-thirds of Shera's model of the shoe. Instrumentation can account for the operational or mechanistic sphere, but then we're stuck. The sphere of maximum context (interpretation and service) obviously invites the use of social science methodology, but we had best take some cues from the cutting edges of social science research and move beyond positivism. Harris suggests a methodology which is holistic, reflexive, empirical, and dialectical (522 - 525). At the risk of vastly oversimplifying him, what he appears to be calling for here is a healthy re-infusion of humanistic perspectives to temper our scientism. He suggests, for example, a return to the study of the history of libraries and librarianship, a reaffirmation of values. (Please note that Harris is not proposing abandoning the social sciences in favor of the subjectivism of the humanities. The goal here is balance.)

And what of the Shera's final sphere, the sphere of "optimum content," that sphere of acquisition that requires "substantive knowledge of the materials and the uses to which knowledge can and should be put"? Here we confront, it seems to me, the exciting reality that all knowledge is the province of the library-- and the librarian. H. Curtis Wright goes so far as to proclaim that

> librarianship is totally interdisciplinary. It is not a subject matter: it is a way of relating to subject matter. It has a direct relationship to every discipline there is, which means that the supportive disciplines of librarianship include everything in the liberal arts curriculum as a bare minimum, and much else besides. (769)

What if we took Wright seriously? What if we determined that we are spending far too much time focusing on the world of leathers and lasts as we educate future librarians, and far too little time focusing on the shoes of substantive knowledge, all knowledge? Would we fall immediately into the hopeless trap of encyclopedism as Abraham Kaplan suggests? (14). I think not. No one would be so naive as to suggest that academic librarians can or should learn all that there is to be learned. But I think there are some things that are within our grasp. They are things that could not be done in one-year programs, but they could be done. We could, for example, insist that every potential academic librarian receive a thorough grounding in the history of ideas; we could, for that matter, insist that every potential academic librarian receive a thorough grounding in the history of libraries. (This, of course, we used to do, but I sense we've backed away from it.) Remember my earlier comment about our marked tendency toward presentism? Why is this? In part, I think, because we focus on tools, and the tools have indeed changed markedly over the years. But, to quote Jesse Shera yet again,

> A catalog entry on the face of a cathode ray tube is essentially the same entry devised by Charles A. Cutter, and the fact that it has been transmitted across the continent in a fraction of a second may be a convenience to the user, but it does not alter the character of librarianship or transform it into a science. ("Librarianship and Information Science" 385)

We could insist that every potential academic librarian have a basic grasp of the sociology of knowledge; and we must--we simply must--demand that every potential academic librarian engage at some point in his or her educational pilgrimage in substantive research--<u>in any discipline</u> (for we are no longer bound to focus on the narrow specialty of library science).

In the September 1986 issue of <u>College and Research Libraries</u>, Dale Montanelli and Patricia Stenstrom argue that "research is beneficial to the individual librarian" for two reasons: (1) it "promotes advancement," and (2) "it provides recognition when advancement is not possible" (483). And you think we don't focus on process??? Why not because it advances knowledge? Why not because it makes us better librarians? I, for one, am absolutely convinced that it does.

Allow me to try to make my case by example. I have a very dear friend who is also an academic librarian. She recently completed an MA in history, and in the process wrote a substantial thesis on a topic in medieval history. The thesis was 232 pages (leaves, if you're a cataloger) in length; it included more than 650 footnotes; it contained a bibliography of 348 items, fewer than two-thirds of which were English-language titles, the remainder being German, French, and Latin. It was clearly a work of substance which made a legitimate contribution to knowledge. I asked her to evaluate the significance of that thesis for her career as an academic librarian.

She responded by saying that--with the obvious exception of going to library school--it was without doubt the single most important thing she had ever done to prepare for academic librarianship. When questioned further, she explained why. "I had written a 'research paper' in virtually every upper-level course I took as an undergraduate," she said. [How many current library school students can still say that???]

> Two of them, in fact, were in excess of fifty pages in length. In library school, I was one of the few students who took elective courses which demanded research papers. I thought I knew what research was and how to do it. But it was not until I wrote that thesis that I truly learned the research process; it was not until I vowed to track down every possible appropriate citation (provided it was in English, German, French, or Latin) that the truth of Steve Stoan's article on "Research and Library Skills" hit home. In the course of researching that thesis I never once used <u>Historical Abstracts</u> for any purpose other than to see if I had missed something--and I never had. Like most academic librarians, I had participated in the snide criticisms of teaching faculty that so often characterize our gossip, but the thesis gave me a new respect for and understanding of faculty concerns. I knew why they were incensed when our library underwrote part of the direct costs of online searching but insisted that patrons bear the direct costs of interlibrary loan. Given my topic, the former service did nothing for me; the latter was absolutely essential. I also knew why faculty continue to insist that our most important service is our collection; I could not have written the thesis without tremendous support from interlibrary loan, but when you are doing intense citation chasing (as I was), receiving a book three weeks later, when the particular creative spark that drove you to order it in the first place has died, the book you borrowed gives you something of a sense of yesterday's scrambled eggs. Finally, and most importantly, I believe that thesis made a legitimate contribution to knowledge, and those teaching faculty who were on my committee agreed. I cannot overemphasize how important that has been

> for me. For the first time, really, I felt like I was truly part of the enterprise of higher education, not an adjunct--however important--to it, but a central and essential part of it. I had finally paid my dues. That dose of confidence did wonders for me. I already had "faculty status," but now, for the first time really, I considered myself a legitimate colleague of the teaching faculty. (Personal correspondence with the author)

There, I submit, is an academic librarian in the best sense of the term. The MLS made her a librarian, but that thesis made her an academic. And I am convinced that academics make better academic librarians. They make better academic librarians in the first instance, because they understand more completely how scholars--in at least some disciplines--go about the process of research. Second, they understand more completely the psychological needs of persons engaging in research. They can empathize with the patron who "simply must have that article by next Thursday" in a way that the non-researcher cannot. Third, they are more self-confident, more likely to engage teaching faculty in dialogue, not only about library issues, but about any issues. And I would argue that this third advantage accrues most significantly if the research is not done in "library science" narrowly defined, because, as I stated earlier, teaching faculty don't quite trust that "discipline."

I would propose, then, that we deflate the oxymoron by making academic credibility the issue, not faculty status. And one gains credibility with the teaching faculty by demonstrating competence in the world of ideas, by contributing to the expansion and extension of knowledge, by exhibiting exceptional skills in written and oral communication, by demonstrating over and over and over again an understanding of the information needs of faculty and *the willingness to serve those needs.* (Please be advised that supercilious dilettantes are precisely what we don't need. Librarianship is still a service profession, and we simply cannot afford librarians who are unwilling to serve.) We desperately need academic librarians who are considered colleagues by the teaching faculty, but such consideration must rest, finally, on substance not on form.

Well, have we now solved all the problems of academic librarianship by insisting on research, by strengthening our degrees, by shifting our understanding and focus of the discipline of librarianship from instrumentation to all of knowledge? Obviously not. Even if our analysis is accurate, problems would remain. This would not solve the problem of library administrators who will refuse to pay the salaries demanded by the graduates with more years of education and more substantial degrees; this would not solve the problem of job situations which do not allow the time to exercise the research abilities that must be present (although I should add here that I would not argue that every academic librarian must be doing research constantly; I am merely suggesting that every academic librarian must have done it at some point); this would not solve the critical issue of personality--we have all too many librarians with the best degrees who leave a trail of hostility and alienation wherever they go. But despite these problems, I think it is an idea worth considering.

In a 1983 essay published shortly after his death, Jesse Shera suggested that "the great need of the library profession today is to formulate a professional philosophy...." "This need," he said, "lies at the base of every other problem of librarianship ..." (Shera 50). We will not build that philosophy on information science alone, not even on social science alone. Such a philosophy must include, I believe recognition of what Abraham Kaplan called the "humanistic basis of library education." It seems to me," said Kaplan,

> that this humanistic basis includes not only a certain appropriate set of beliefs about what men are like and what they are up to, and how they make use of ideas, but also a certain appropriate set of values. It seems to me that every profession, if it is to be meaningful, at least to its practitioners, must always be something of a calling, something to which we are impelled from within, that is--literally a vocation and not an occupation. I would think that an inculcation of the love of learning, of the love of ideas, of the love of truth, and even of the love of books, is an entirely appropriate part of the training in this profession. (12)

There is no positivism in Kaplan's comments. It is value-laden from beginning to end, but those values are values entirely consistent with those of our colleagues on the teaching faculty who are in the "knowledge business." I submit that this new, expanded view of librarianship, or, more correctly, this old, time-honored view of librarianship, is a shoe well worth trying on once again.

Works Cited

"Diagnosis: A New Year Collection of Views on Some of the Major Problems Which Still Face the Library Profession," Library Journal 88 (1 January 1963): 50.

Freeman, Michael. "The Simplicity of His Pragmatism; Librarians and Research," Library Journal 110 (15 May 1985): 27-28.

Guthrie, W. K. C. The Greek Philosophers from Thales to Aristotle. New York: Harper & Row, 1960.

Harris, Michael. "The Dialectic of Defeat: Antimonies in Research in Library and Information Science," Library Trends 35 (Winter 1986): 518-525.

Holley, Edward G. "Defining the Academic Librarian," College & Research Libraries 46 (November 1985): 462-468.

Kaplan, Abraham. "The Age of Symbol--A Philosophy of Library Education," in The Intellectual Foundations of Library Education, ed. Don R. Swanson. Chicago, IL: University of Chicago Press, 1965.

Montanelli, Dale S., and Patricia F. Stenstrom. "The Benefits of Research for Academic Librarians and the Institutions they Serve," College & Research Libraries 47 (September 1986): 482-485.

Shera, Jesse. "Librarianship and Information Science," in The Study of Information: Interdisciplinary Messages, eds. Fritz Machlup and Una Mansfield. New York: John Wiley, 1983.

Shera, Jesse. "Darwin, Bacon, and Research in Librarianship," Library Trends 13 (July 1964): 147.

Swan, John. "Information and Madness," Library Journal 113 (1 February 1988): 25-28.

Wilson, Pauline. "Mission and Information: What Business Are We In?" Journal of Academic Librarianship 14 (May 1988): 82-86.

Wright, H. Curtis. "The Symbol and Its Referent: An Issue for Library Education," Library Trends 34 (Spring 1986): 769.

LIGHTHOUSES, MANNEQUINS, AND PIONEER WOMEN: SERENDIPITOUS ENCOUNTERS WITH TEACHING FACULTY

by
Caroline Byrd

Assistant Director/Systems Administrator
St. Mary's University

It had been one of those weeks that most academic librarians experience: an avalanche of endless committee meetings; a flood of administrative demands for obscure statistics; a trickle of retired professors wanting to check out the most-used reference books. And of course, the usual hysterical patrons, absent student assistants, failing photocopiers, and crisis-stricken co-workers.

"Another week like this," I muttered. "And I'll be ready to retire to a very remote lighthouse."

The person who heard my threat was the chair of the English/Communication Arts Department. We had grabbed a few precious minutes to review library resources for a graduate course on Twentieth-century Women Writers.

As teaching faculty, the professor could empathize with my woes; after all, she dealt with many of the same constituencies. However, she wasn't a native Texan, so she expressed some good-natured skepticism about finding a lighthouse anywhere near Texas.

Since I had been required to take Texas history from birth, I knew better. Not only could I recall a few dim historical facts about Texas lighthouses, I could remember actually touring such a structure as a child.

The next thing I knew, my colleague and I were ambling along the Texas coastline in search of lighthouses. My faculty friend (a water-loving Pisces) saw this quest as an opportunity to visit the Gulf of Mexico. I saw a chance to try out a new camera. Certainly neither of us foresaw the lighthouse trips as the beginning of a long and fruitful collaboration.

Somewhere along the way, we learned that the Texas American Studies Association was sponsoring a conference focusing on the Texas coast. A study of lighthouses seemed a likely prospect for this conference. Having visited and photographed all extant Texas lighthouses, we now journeyed to the state archives, general research centers, and a number of academic and public libraries. We wrestled with brittle microfilm and disintegrating newsprint. We perused the laws of the Republic of Texas and obscure reminiscences of coastal setters.

From these efforts we wrote a short history of Texas lighthouses and submitted an abstract to the Texas American Studies Association conference. Our paper, and accompanying slide presentation, was accepted by the association, and we set forth to Lamar University in Beaumont, Texas.

The first time is the hardest, no matter what you're doing. My colleague was an experienced hand at these activities, but I was a rank novice and really felt it. (It didn't help that another presenter was a former instructor of mine. Was I going to be graded? Was I going to fail?)

I consolidated all my stage fright around the operation of the slide projector. No matter that I had taken "how to" audiovisual courses both as an undergraduate and as a graduate student, nor that I had had six years of hands-on experience as a secondary school teacher. I knew the basic law of AV: if equipment can go bad, it will.

Imagine my surprise when the projector worked perfectly. Imagine my horror when I realized our carefully assembled slide presentation had to be shown in broad daylight in a room with huge windows and no curtains. Imagine my heartfelt relief when various presenters assumed scarecrow-like positions in front of those windows to block the light.

Having survived that first presentation relatively unscathed, I didn't flinch when my professor friend sent me a call for papers from the Gulf Coast History and Humanities Conference. One aspect of this conference dealt with the architecture and archaeology of the Gulf Coast. We reworked our original lighthouse paper to highlight the regional Gulf Coast connection and submitted an abstract.

Within a short time, we were driving through East Texas, Louisiana, Mississippi, and Alabama to Pensacola, home of the University of West Florida and site of the conference. No doubt, it was easier the second time around. The room was appropriately dark for the slide presentation, and I began to appreciate how much I could learn from these interdisciplinary conferences. In the course of a few days, I was introduced to a wide variety of topics, including New Orleans brick types, the Florida Chautauqua, and a fascinating film based on a Kate Chopin short story.

From a rather offhand (make that serendipitous) beginning, my teaching colleague and I had presented papers at two conferences. I had gained some necessary confidence and had been introduced to all sorts of fascinating topics. On a more practical level, the Gulf Coast History and Humanities Conference had actually paid us to attend. And even better, we had a bona fide publication: the lighthouse paper appeared in a book, Threads of Tradition and Culture Along the Gulf Coast, published by the conference.

In our small university, faculty publications are displayed in the main hall of the Administration Building. While having one's work displayed here is not precisely equivalent to having a star on Hollywood Boulevard, it is a public acknowledgement of achievement. So when I saw Threads of Tradition opened to our lighthouse article, I felt a flush of accomplishment. I also felt a sense of amazement: how, exactly, had all this come about? Serendipity?

For a while both my collaborator and I were involved in various separate projects. I was completing a second master's degree and writing a thesis. Our library was embroiled in automating, and I became administrator for the integrated system. I was serving on more library and university committees.

The English professor, of course, had a large department to chair, classes to prepare and teach, papers to grade, committees to serve on, etc. She was also doing interdisciplinary research with faculty from the departments of psychology and sociology. They were using psychological, sociological, and literary theories to explore what it means to be female in the late twentieth century. Obviously, we were all very busy and involved in our work.

But late one Friday evening, we found time to gather at a favorite Mexican restaurant over a pitcher of margaritas. I was recounting a recent (and rare) foray to the malls.

"I mean, I can't believe this. Last week, I saw two female mannequins in negligees tied together with silver rope."

A jumble of voices. Pornography! Sexism! S and M! Fashion fascism! Women as sex objects! But remember the First Amendment!

In the midst of this feminist, academic tumult, the English professor turned to me and said, "The Popular Culture Association is open to things along these lines." Whatever it was, I was hooked.

But where to begin? We weren't interested in doing a history of fashion or a study of mannequin manufacture. We had a sense that the ways in which mannequins were dressed, displayed, and used represented some societal views of human women.

Rather than doing the kind of archival research required for the lighthouse project, we read, analyzed, and interpreted a large body of readings from various disciplines. Such activity resulted in lengthy and lively discussions.

However, things really got lively when we did our "field research." Armed with my trusty camera, we staked out various department stores. As unobtrusively as possible, we took picture after picture of female mannequins -- mannequins with anorexic bodies and video monitor heads, mannequins with giraffe necks and cascading manes of hair; and yes, even mannequins with nipples. (And no, there's nothing anatomically correct about male mannequins.)

In time we put together a proposal for the Popular Culture Association. Our proposal was accepted, and we were on our way to the conference in Montreal. Even before we got to the conference, we began receiving responses to our paper. As soon as the conference program was published, several newspaper reporters called to inquire about our topic: "Mannequins: Enforcers of Sex-Role Stereotypes." (As all advertisers know, anything with sex in the title, sells.)

I'll never forget taking a call from a Dallas reporter at the reference desk. As a wide-eyed patron eavesdropped, I replied, yes, they're young, scantily clad, tied up, etc. Yeah, I have lots of pictures. Well, so much for the image of librarians as prune-faced prudes.

Our presentation at the conference was well received and actually fun. Once again, I was able to pick up considerable esoteric information about Salem Witches, Jewish Shtetl, and detective novels, among other topics. After the conference, we received numerous requests for copies of the paper, including requests from a fashion museum curator, feminist scholars, semiologists, and even a few mannequin groupies. Like all new converts, we wanted to share our experiences and do a bit of proselytizing. The National Women's Studies Association Conference presented such an opportunity.

Our goal was to promote librarian/teaching faculty collaboration. To this end, we reviewed the various ways librarians and teaching and faculty interact in their professional roles. Prior to our collaborative research and writing, my colleague and I engaged in more traditional means of interaction. Subject coordination is one such means.

As subject coordinator, I act as the liaison between the library and the English/Communication Arts Department. Subject coordination involves much more than merely routing Choice cards and publishers' catalogs to the department. Properly done, subject coordination requires the librarian to have a thorough understanding of the department's mission, course offerings, and future goals.

In addition, it is important to know that Professor X is interested in radical American writers of the 1930's; Professor Y is dazzled by Latin American imaginary realism; and Professor Z wants everything by and about Doris Lessing.

With subject coordination comes bibliographic instruction. I do most of the BI for upper division courses in the English/Communication Arts Department. Such courses include American Romanticism, Mass Communications, Minority American Literature, and Southern Writers.

Currently the most challenging courses for BI are the advanced composition courses. Required for all junior or senior students, these courses emphasize research and writing skills for non-English majors. Topics are limited only by the instructor's imagination. Recent topics include the United States and Nicaragua, world hunger, career exploration, and AIDS. Such diversity keeps me on my toes professionally and brings me into contact with a number of English professors.

These traditional interactions -- subject coordination and bibliographic instruction -- have served to "introduce" me to the teaching faculty and to develop mutual professional respect and trust. Respect and trust, combined with general "hanging out" together, have led to collaborative efforts beyond the traditional.

Our tracing of librarian/teaching faculty interaction culminated in a proposal to the National Women's Studies Association to speak on "Librarian/Teaching Faculty Networking." We delivered our paper in Minneapolis to a mixed group of librarians and teaching faculty.

Their responses were enthusiastic. Librarians spoke of their frustration at being either ignored or patronized by some faculty. They voiced their desire to work <u>with</u> faculty <u>as</u> faculty. Teaching faculty expressed their gratitude and excitement at finding intellectual allies with different but compatible training and talents.

In addition to the positive response we received, I was also pleased by two other serendipitous events which occurred at this conference. The first was the formation of the National Women's Studies Association Librarians Task Force. Meeting with other librarians committed to librarianship and feminism was extremely heartening. We shared many of the same concerns, including a desire to promote increased collaboration between teaching faculty and librarians.

The second serendipitous event resulted from my attending a panel entitled "Women in Academe: Difficulties and Challenges." One of the panelists was a librarian who delivered a thought-provoking paper on academic librarians. After the session, we began a free-wheeling discussion that led to a post-conference correspondence.

This correspondence, in turn, led to my being appointed to her graduate advisor committee for her second master's degree. For her thesis, this librarian is researching methods of integrating feminist materials into college curricula. She asked me to serve on her committee because she identified me as a librarian with a special interest in and professional knowledge of such materials. Serving on such committees is the stuff of "real" faculty, and I was delighted to have such an opportunity.

The women's studies conference had been an exhilarating experience, and we looked forward to continued collaboration. Once again, though, I was immersed in automation. The library was installing an on-line catalog and automated circulation system. As systems administrator, I found that my days were very full with little time for other projects.

One project I had to find time for was the completion of my thesis for a master's degree in history. In our university, the second master's degree is mandatory for librarians seeking faculty promotion and tenure. Completing that degree was not just a personal goal; it was an absolute necessity for professional advancement. Eventually, I finished the degree. Just when I thought I might have some time on my hands, the English professor appeared with a new project.

She and a business school professor were planning to team-teach a course on pioneer Texas businesswomen. The students were to research early Texas businesswomen and write essays on the contributions of these women. Scholarship money was available for the authors of the best essays. The essays were to be published in a local newspaper, and course participants were to be honored during the annual Business Week ceremonies.

The English professor's role was to polish the writing skills of the students. The business professor's task was to emphasize the business contributions of these women. My job was to introduce students who had had little experience with such primary sources.

After meeting with the students in a seminar setting, I continued to meet with them individually throughout the semester. Since I had recently spent considerable time learning to do historical research for my thesis, I enjoyed the opportunity to share this kind of knowledge. I particularly enjoyed the sustained contact with the students. Traditional reference service just doesn't offer such contact.

As in all teaching situations, the enjoyment came not just from what I taught, but also from what I learned. Through the students' efforts, I became acquainted with a fascinating array of businesswomen: the woman whose small general store became a grocery empire; the woman who invented Liquid Paper; the woman whose little circus became part of "the Greatest Show on Earth."

When the English professor and I began to recount the worthwhile aspects of this project, we realized we wanted to share our experiences with a larger audience. In time, we created a proposal entitled "Contributions to Texas Culture Made by Businesswomen: A Student Research Project." The Popular Culture/American Culture Association accepted our proposal; we presented our paper at their annual meeting in Toronto in 990.

Since I first began working in academic libraries, I've had a firm sense of the importance of <u>being</u> faculty. I knew I had to pursue traditional faculty activities -- presenting papers, publishing, serving on university committees, etc. Rather than being merely burdensome, most of these activities have contained an element of joy.

In particular, my collaborative work with the English professor has been the best of all possible worlds. Aside from the obvious resume fodder it has provided, this work has also enhanced my proficiencies (and images) as a librarian. I've had to hone my research and writing skills, and I've had to learn to speak to large groups of diverse academicians. And not to be discounted, these collaborative efforts have afforded me the opportunity to travel, meet interesting people, and take some rather unusual photographs.

Lest anyone think it's been nothing but fun, photography, and travel, be assured that I've also been pursuing more traditional means of academic advancement. I completed my second master's degree. My thesis dealt with the development of community property law in Texas. As a result of the thesis, the editors of the Handbook of Texas invited me to write the primary article on community property law for the new edition. I also wrote an article describing our library automation system for the alumni magazine.

I've been appointed to the Student Conduct Committee and the President's Peace Commission. I'm a member of the editorial board of Communitas, the faculty journal. I've been twice elected by the faculty at large to serve on the Faculty Senate -- certainly a measure of collegial acceptance. And, of course, I socialize with the teaching faculty whenever possible because these informal encounters are important bridge-builders.

If the tone of this piece seems relaxed, the author is not always equally relaxed. Sometimes it seems there are too many hats to wear, too many balls to juggle. I'm adamantly convinced that librarians should pursue (and earn) faculty status. However, I'm concerned that some forms of traditional librarianship, that is, reference desk service, must be curtailed if one avidly pursues faculty status. Quite simply, I can't be at the reference desk for a four-hour shift if I have two university committee meetings during that time period.

Nonetheless, if I were to give advice to a beginning academic librarian, I'd say, "Go for it." Be faculty and all that that means.

But be sure you have a director who is willing to offer encouragement and the necessary flexibility in your schedule. And it would help immensely to be surrounded by understanding co-workers and a support staff who works miracles. (An adequate travel budget would be nice, too.)

If all -- or even some of it -- falls into place, then make contacts, work very, very hard, and try to relax.

SOCIAL CONTACT IN THE ACADEMY: AN INDIRECT ROUTE TO COLLEGIALITY

by

Douglas M. Ferrier

Dean of the Eunice and James L. West Library
Texas Wesleyan College

Introduction

Librarians need to consider how they are perceived by their various audiences and how to position themselves in response to these perceptions. More importantly, librarians need to learn to assert themselves as professionals. The image they project to others and among themselves affects the way in which they are treated, and thus, their effectiveness in performing their jobs. Being a professional is more than dressing the part and having the proper credentials. It is an attitude about meeting the challenges of the job in such a way that the audience is aware the librarian is in control and is capable of dealing with the situation.

Libraries and individuals vary, but an attitude of assurance and confidence can go a long way in projecting a professional demeanor without being stilted or haughty. Librarians should continually address the question of how the major audiences of academic librarians view us and search for ways to make these views more positive and professional.

In the academic world, librarians are in a unique position. Regarded by library patrons (i.e., students) as a combination gatekeeper/watchdog who scrutinizes their behavior and informs them when they have overdue items, these same individuals are seen by college administrators as some sort of hybrid faculty. The classroom faculty view them with a mixture of reactions (ranging from that of colleagues to a type of professional servant), while the campus computer professionals see them as upstarts in a field in which they have little background and in which they can only cause trouble. The non-professional staff of the library often view librarians as fellow employees and view their supervisors with attitudes ranging from respect to "how did this clown get here?" Most troubling of all is how librarians view themselves, for this jumble of perceptions affects how we project ourselves and how we are seen by our peers.

Social Life of the University

A very important aspect of presenting a professional facade can be accomplished through the indirect method of attention to the social life of the university and to the various elements that compose that social life. Other chapters in this book discuss what may seem to many the various, more **important,** images of the professional librarian as a member of the faculty, but without paying attention to the social interaction of the campus, librarians will never really attain peer status and recognition.

Librarians should be a part of the interaction that occurs on the average campus and, by taking part in that social contact, present an image of professional congeniality that will affect the more formal aspects of their jobs. Librarians should expect to socialize with other faculty by participation in the faculty club and less formal gatherings, by taking part in faculty colloquies, and by attending convocations as well as other campus events. Socialization should also be utilized in related events like service organizations and professional groups that can help project the image of a professional actively taking a role in the life of the campus and the profession.

The Faculty Club

The faculty club may seem an unlikely place to attain professional equality with faculty, but it is actually an excellent location. Membership is limited to faculty, and by partaking of that limitation, librarians can tactfully remind the teaching faculty that librarians are indeed full-fledged members of that group. The very presence of librarians in that location is a realization that they are faculty. The conversations that begin over coffee can lead to questions that might not otherwise be asked. The presence of librarians in that setting can develop into a fuller understanding of each other's skills that can be utilized to the productive benefit of the individual and the institution. If for no other reason than the fact that a teaching faculty member can put a face with the name of a librarian, visits to the faculty club become worthwhile. For those campuses without a faculty club, librarians should make every effort to find out where the faculty gather and join them in conversation and joke telling in order to facilitate communications with peers.

Getting out of the library to socialize on a limited basis is as important a part of the job as answering reference questions or checking out material. By establishing that equality through socialization, it is easier to maintain it on a professional basis in the work environment. Sharing a cup of coffee or a soft drink with non-faculty people on campus can also help. Getting to know the campus maintenance personnel and the campus computer people can pay dividends in getting jobs done faster and in finding out information that is important to your operation. Making these social contacts can really help when a crisis develops and you need help fast. You are no longer a faceless name on the library roster, but an individual others know and would like to help. This is an important fringe benefit of faculty recognition.

Extra-Professional Campus Activities

Librarians should also participate in the extra-professional activities of the campus. Librarians should attend faculty colloquies to demonstrate an interest in the endeavors of the teaching faculty. (Some are interesting in and of themselves even without the hidden agenda of faculty peer recognition.) Librarians should use these opportunities to show they are also among the group that contributes to the advancement of knowledge by participating in the discussion that such colloquia generate, even by giving programs themselves. The library profession hosts a variety of scholarly problems that faculty colleagues should be sharing. Certainly high among these are the following possible colloquium topics: preservation of our cultural heritage, journal pricing and the cost of scholarly communication, bibliographic instruction, and many others. Each could be the focus for a major colloquium.

Librarians should particularly consider giving programs about new developments in the library. Such programs help explain the job librarians perform and how it relates to and benefits the entire campus. However, giving such programs may not be possible if librarians do not participate when others sponsor colloquia.

Student Extra-Curricular Activities

Also librarians should make every effort to attend other campus events, like art shows, musical performances, sporting events, and plays. No, it is not in the average librarian's job description to attend such gatherings, but it does serve a very valuable function. Attendance at such events conveys a sense of interest in the campus life to all parties. To the faculty, it shows an interest in their work that goes beyond the eight-to-five routine. To the students, it conveys an interest in them as individuals, not just as clients. To the administration, it shows an interest in your work that means it's more than a "job"; it is professional, important enough to spend your own time supporting it.

Yes, this might be called socializing because it is beyond the typical job description of a librarian to spend time being entertained at campus functions. But what should be kept in mind is that being an equal member of the academic community means more than reporting to work on time and doing your job as a librarian. What it means is breaking through the segregation that has kept librarians in the library and participating as an active campus community citizen in the world outside the library doors.

If librarians expect to be treated as full-fledged faculty members, they should also expect to spend that extra time showing they want to be a part of campus life; even with the extra time such events can require, enjoyment can be found in doing them. The same thing might be said about commencement and faculty convocations. These are symbolic celebrations in the academic year, and while participation by librarians also might be considered symbolic, it is more than that. When librarians take part in these activities, they are acknowledging and expect to have acknowledged that they are indeed a part of the social fabric that comprises the academy. It might even be seen as a type of communion service within this unique congregation.

Extra-University Social Contacts

Social contacts can also be useful in those activities that touch upon the academic world, but are not really a part of it. Membership in service groups such as Rotary or the Lions is a wonderful opportunity to practice social contact. Being a member of these groups is an opening to educating non-academics about the services and activities available in the university world. Using these contacts can help to make friends and raise support in the local community for the college or university and to acquaint them with the benefits that accrue to the community by the presence of the university.

Such relationships are also golden opportunities to maintain contact with alumni and help keep them interested in supporting their alma mater. A big part of alumni affairs centers on maintaining contact. There is no reason librarians cannot help with this activity, and perhaps reap some of the benefits in the form of gifts and contributions.

Perhaps a word of caution should also be inserted here, for in the words of the cinematic philosopher Obi-Wan Kenobi, "there is a dark side to the force." Social contact should not be seen as a replacement for competent professional librarianship. There is no substitute for knowledge of how to do the job, although it can certainly be improved upon and made better through the systematic use of improving relations through social contacts, both on and off the campus. Care should also be exercised so that individuals do not use personal contacts for unfair advantage or to short-circuit established procedures, but this is seldom a problem with competent professionals.

The use of social contacts does have a definite place in the academic library. It is another tool in the arsenal of management techniques to help the librarian attain the position of equality with the teaching faculty, a position the librarian should not shrink from attempting to attain. When used in conjunction with professional knowledge and aggressive work habits, being a part of the social and intellectual life of the university will help the librarian attain a position of true professional equality. We can take pride in our profession, and we should also take pride in doing it in a way that shares with others the joy of being who we are. Librarians are an important part of the academic world, and we need to strive to help others understand that role.

PART IV

The Librarian and the Student: Outside the Library Walls

LIBRARIANS AND STUDENT ADVOCACY: A HOLISTIC PERSPECTIVE

by
Gloria Elaine Hilario

Director of the Learning Resources Center
Palo Alto College

Introduction

There are many voices on college and university campuses who lay claim to representing students in one or the other areas of academics, but few who contend to be proponents for the holistic education of students. In a holistic framework of education, students as learners are afforded the opportunity to develop personally and interpersonally. Students are encouraged to think critically and creatively. Experiences and instruction are provided which emphasize the relationships and interdependencies of all spheres of knowledge, of all peoples, of the universe. Education is global, synergistic, and confluent. The holistic educator, as Caroline Neal defines this individual, is one who is more consciously aware of what learning is -- its relationship to theory, to immediacy, to life and to the possibilities of growth and change.

Academic librarians are the incarnation of the holistic educator possessing that peculiar combination of the careful eclectic and the conscientious iconoclast who never stops observing, learning and growing. As holistic educators we are in a unique position to create an environment and climate for learning throughout our campuses. How can librarians either as individuals or collectively accomplish this? Let me count the ways.

The Academic Environment

Some librarians are already involved in teaching, either in bibliographic instruction or as adjunct professors in other academic departments. Many are currently recruited to act as academic advisors to undeclared or liberal arts majors. Librarians serve as liaisons to academic departments. As departmental liaisons, are you asked to serve on curriculum committees? Several of my colleagues and I have requested such an assignment and at least one librarian serves annually on a college-wide Curriculum Review Committee at Palo Alto College, a community college in San Antonio, Texas.

Some library faculty members have been elected to serve on Faculty Senates. In addition to running for Senate posts and to addressing the needs of the faculty, faculty governance bodies often provide representation on departmental and university-wide committees charged with producing recommendations for changes which impact students. Have you offered your services as a researcher or active participant for any such committees?

Working with Students On Campus

Athletic scholarships at a small private university where academics and athletics are both given priority were in serious jeopardy a decade ago. As a direct result of a great deal of research done by the library faculty member of the College Athletics Scholarship Committee (and of collegial work with students and other faculty members in presenting that research), the scholarship program was retained. In 1989, the scholar athletes at St. Mary's University of San Antonio, Texas, won the NAIA national basketball championship -- an unanticipated but welcome reward for the committee's efforts.

Another St. Mary's University committee in which a librarian actively participated dealt with the problems of student retention, especially of minority students, and produced a subsequent study and findings report to the university on both recruitment and retention. Many of the recommendations were implemented and the study was included as an ERIC document. Yet another librarian was one of a five-member committee that set the guidelines for a form of holistic, personal, academic advising on campus that also paid major dividends in student retention.

Working with Student Services

Many academic librarians often supervise college work-study staff or student assistants who help keep an academic library functioning. But what is the level of involvement with students outside of the sphere of the work environment? The Student Services component of any college or university is always in need of faculty members to assist in sponsoring an organization, in mentoring the activities of both individual students and groups, and in assisting in providing equanimity in student grievance and redress proceedings. Have you approached the Dean of Students or the Vice President for Student Affairs or any student services administrator to lend your assistance?

Librarians have a variety of interests, are a treasure trove of information, and can be totally impartial when called upon to do so or can be vocal advocates for a specific cause. Librarians at St. Mary's University have served as moderators for social sororities and honor and service fraternities, club sponsors (e.g., German Club, L'Alliance Française), and members of the Student Disciplinary Committee. At Palo Alto College, librarians have co-sponsored the International Students Organization as well as moderated other student groups.

Working with Students and the Community

The collegiate experience, if it is to be a time of learning and growth, is not limited to the confines of the ivory tower. As such, students need to experience the community within and without its walls. Are you as a professional librarian involved in other professional and community activities with which you can provide bridges to the greater community for students? If your interest is art, have you worked with the art faculty and others on campus to establish a juried art series for continuous exhibits in your library? Such a series was begun several years ago at St. Mary's University at the suggestion of a librarian and with support from the library director. Though it began and remains a small endeavor, most of the younger, contemporary artists who are achieving prominence in South Texas have had their first one-person shows in the Academic Library. At Palo Alto College, librarians sponsored a Cultural Literacy essay contest to coincide with an area newspaper's series on cultural literacy/illiteracy. Four scholarships which the librarians personally funded were awarded to currently enrolled students.

College students have often not reached the stage at which they realize the importance of social service and the personal fulfillment and gratification which comes from knowing that one has performed a needed or ennobling task. Have you as a librarian helped to identify social service agencies which need volunteer help and made this information readily available to staff and students? If you are personally involved with any such activity are you encouraging students to help, too? At St. Mary's University, librarians were actively involved in recruiting and organizing volunteers to assist with Special Olympics activities and in the annual fundraising campaigns for Muscular Dystrophy Research and Easter Seals services. At Palo Alto College, librarians coordinate United Way campaigns, work with students as Elf Louise Christmas elves, and as volunteers for Habitat for Humanity and the local homeless shelter.

Librarians can be integrally involved in enhancing all aspects of academic life and in creating a holistic environment. The only essential ingredients needed are librarians who will seek out activities in which they can provide leadership or support roles and who will request non-library assignments, and supportive, proactive library directors who are committed to a philosophy of full library integration and participation in university life. Most college and university administrators appreciate and utilize the services of faculty and staff who willingly assume additional duties and responsibilities.

To truly be an advocate for students, one must be a proponent for learning in all its myriad forms, its diverse endeavors, it complex functions and to be actively involved in educating the whole person. This advocacy requires that each one of us serve as a channel, medium, catalyst, nurturer for the ongoing development of the intellectual (intuitive, imaginative, creative, deductive, analytical, rational, constructive, configurational), psychological, physical, social and personal abilities/skills of students.

Socrates stated that "the unexamined life is not worth living." It behooves us as librarians to perform some self-examination to see whether or not we are the holistic educators our profession warrants (still observing, learning, and growing) -- "learners, not teachers involved with other learners."

Enhancing Librarian Status

The best reason for doing these things "away from" your library is that they are worth doing. No other reason is needed. Yet working with students in such activities can lead to greater professional recognition as well as great personal satisfaction.

It is not, simply, the teaching faculty that we as librarians must convince concerning our credibility as faculty members. Our primary audience in our professional careers is the student body of our institutions. I realize that that is debatable, especially at some of the leading research libraries where service to the faculty might take precedence. But it is almost beyond debate at community colleges and smaller universities.

We need the students, not just the teaching faculty, to recognize the value of librarians as academics. For our vanity, yes, but more importantly to enable us to help them in their personal and holistic development.

THE LIBRARIAN AS ACADEMIC ADVISER

by
Kathy Sisoian, Director of Academic Advising
and
H. Palmer Hall, Director of Libraries

St. Mary's University

Introduction

One of the more difficult tasks facing any faculty member is academic advising for hordes of students who would like to matriculate as rapidly as possible. Normally, librarians are not involved in this part of the faculty profession; mostly because faculty members in the departments are jealous about advising their own student majors.

Some universities, though, do ask librarians to serve as faculty advisers. And the students they advise are among the most difficult groups of students and the ones most needing professional advising of any on campus -- the student who has not yet decided on a major field.

Why Librarians?

One major reason librarians are occasionally asked to advise this group of students is that we are less likely to proselytize for a particular major field than are faculty members in the academic departments. Faculty members might be tempted, and are, to recruit the brightest of the undeclared majors to their own departments.

Another reason is that there are simply too few faculty members on the typical campus to do much of anything other than assembly-line advising. Universities moving to a more holistic approach to the advising process cannot use assembly-line techniques and hope to do a job even approaching adequacy in advising. In the sciences, especially, which feature large lecture-style classes on most campuses, there are rarely enough faculty members available to advise even their own students, much less pay attention to students who might not even decide to major in one of the sciences.

A third, political, reason for librarians to serve as academic advisers is related to the second. If additional advisers are needed (and they almost always are), librarians make up a very logical group to do the job. They almost always report through the director to the institution's chief academic officer, the person who is responsible for the advising process. They have gone through at least the first graduate degree. And they have been attracted to academic work. If not, they would not be working in the university.

Political Reality

If librarians on your campus have not been asked to work as academic advisers, that's probably because no one has thought to do so. Library directors may be somewhat reluctant to bring the possibility up at meetings of dean's or academic councils where such things are frequently discussed. The reason for that reluctance is the time needed to do a good job of advising. The typical advising session may take anywhere from fifteen minutes to an hour and if one librarian has ten advisees, that might mean losing a good day of work each month. Part of the reason for that is the time needed to prepare for advising: study of test results, review of courses taken, research on possible major fields.

The amount of time taken per advisee is different for every adviser and is dependent upon the attitude taken towards advising by the adviser. If a faculty member sees advising as simply checking a degree plan against a student's transcript, followed by a quick series of signatures or initials, then very little time will be spent with each student. If, however, advising means **advising**, then it becomes much more than just a signature game.

It is especially critical when dealing with students who are undecided about their career plans. Part of the job of the adviser to a student who has not yet declared a major field is to work with that student to help determine a career field or subject specialty. This can involve hours of discussion that could otherwise be devoted to cataloging more books, developing a class for bibliographic instruction, or any of the other professional tasks that librarians need to be doing.

And yet, we are academic librarians because of our students. Not just because we are attracted to library professional work. If that were not the case, we should not be lobbying for faculty status. We should be content to find our place in the university with other members of the professional staff. The fact that so many of us are not content with that kind of status, that so many of us argue for faculty rank and status is an implicit argument that we want to do the things that faculty do, not simply steal their status. One of the things good faculty members do is to advise students.

What Is Involved in Academic Advising?

Academic advising is much more than an exercise in schedule preparation. And although academic advising is neither a highly desirable academic responsibility nor highly regarded (Walsh 446), the quality of advising is a major factor in student retention and overall student satisfaction with an institution (Habley 46).

Academic advisers need a variety of skills and competencies in order to be successful in their role. A thorough understanding of an institution's academic policies and procedures is of primary importance because advisers are the most accessible members of the academic community and students will readily learn to rely on them for information and assistance. From the very first meeting an adviser can give students the impression they are available and knowledgeable; both factors will determine if a student will return for additional assistance or not. This task requires advisers to keep informed about academic policies and relay accurate and appropriate information to advisees.

Students expect academic advisers to know academic requirements as they relate to course selection and prerequisites. This advising responsibility is readily accepted by academic advisers, but it causes the most conflict for students if mistakes are made. A concerted effort to provide current and accurate information to student advisees helps ensure that they can progress academically at a pace that is appropriate for them. Unfortunately, some students will receive inaccurate information and the adviser should be knowledgeable about the procedures students must follow to rectify mistakes.

Assisting student advisees with the development of realistic career and educational goals is a responsibility advisers are more reluctant to perform. The resistance seems to stem from time constraints, although in some cases advisers are reluctant to discuss goals unless a student initiates the conversation. Preparing a life plan is a very real part of what a student needs to accomplish as an undergraduate, and students without goals are more inclined to leave an institution before they graduate (Tinto 152).

The development of career and educational plans is a process that varies with each student. Some students will have very specific and realistic goals that need little more than support, encouragement, and academic planning. However, other students may need the adviser to get more involved in the establishment of goals.

Students who need assistance with establishing career and educational goals can benefit from a discussion of their skills and interests. Discovering what students like and dislike can provide clues about their interest areas and this information can be related to careers. Students should also examine and clarify their values as they relate to career interests and quite often will benefit from an honest discussion with their advisers. The key seems to be to work at the student's pace and assist with the career decision-making process by asking questions that help students clarify for themselves what direction they want to take.

All of the advising responsibilities discussed require that the advisers be knowledgeable about campus resources. Sometimes the best thing advisers can do for students is to recognize their own limits and make appropriate referrals to other campus offices that are better equipped to deal with a student's specific concerns. This may mean referring a student to the career counseling center where interest tests can be taken and interpreted -- providing a student with information most academic advisers are unable to give.

The responsibility of establishing a positive advising relationship must be shared between the student and the adviser. The adviser must be accessible to the students, and the students must seek out their advisers and go to advising sessions prepared with questions and concerns.

Administrative support for an advising system is probably the most important factor which will contribute to the overall satisfaction of the advising experience for students and advisers. A clear and coordinated system for the delivery of advising services should be established. The institution must develop a statement of philosophy concerning academic advising and clearly state the adviser and student responsibilities in the advising process. The administration must also monitor the adviser-to-student ratio so that advising tasks are realistic and can be accomplished.

Finally, faculty development opportunities should be provided so that advisers can develop the skills they require to perform competently. And probably most importantly, advisers must be valued and recognized for the contributions they make to the quality of a student's educational experience and the impact that their work has on retention. Advising evaluations that affect promotion and tenure decisions could change the perception of advising responsibilities and place advising tasks in their appropriate place.

Conclusion

There are many reasons for librarians to serve as academic advisers. Perhaps the best is that in academic advising, librarians can have a lasting effect on students. The one-to-one advising sessions give an opportunity to get to see what your university is doing in its educational programs from a fresh perspective -- that of the client, the university's customer. Most advisers who take the role seriously develop greater empathy for student problems when they see the problems directly affecting their own student.

At the risk of sounding Pollyannaish, the best reason to serve as an academic adviser is that it is a worthwhile thing to do. Students, especially those who have not decided on their career or life goals, need active, responsive and professional advice and consultation in making decisions that they will live with for decades.

Librarians who become academic advisers need to be prepared to devote time for preparation for the role they will be playing. If a university takes a systematic approach to advising, provides training and workshop experiences, librarians who serve as advisers must be prepared to dedicate the necessary hours to learn to advise well. The teaching faculty are our partners in this learning task. Very few of our colleagues in the classrooms have had anything other than on-the-job training for this critical job.

Works Cited

Habley, Wesley R. "Academic Advisement: The Critical Link in Student Retention." NASPA Journal 18 (1981): 45-50.

Tinto, Vincent. Leaving College: Rethinking the Causes and Cures of Student Attrition. Chicago: University of Chicago Press, 1987.

Walsh, E. Michael. "Revitalizing Academic Advisement." Personnel and Guidance Journal 57 (1979): 446-449.

A SYNERGISTIC SUPPLEMENT: REMEDIAL WRITING INSTRUCTORS & REFERENCE LIBRARIANS TEAMED TO BUILD CONFIDENCE IN THE UNDERPREPARED STUDENT

by
Carmen F. Embry

Coordinator of Bibliographic Instruction
University of Louisville

Introduction

In the midst of demystifying sentence structure, subject/verb agreements and those ubiquitous commas, instructors for the underprepared student can reel in yet one more confidence-boosting component -- the reference librarian. Because I am fortunate to be both a remedial writing instructor and Coordinator of Bibliographic Instruction for the University of Louisville's Ekstrom Library, I have witnessed the synergistic results of ventures between the two academic units.

It continually comes home to me, from both professional corners, that what these students need most is confidence, a feeling they belong in a university setting. The library, the very "heart of academe," is just the unit they must embrace in order to attain self-reliance and to successfully complete their studies. Yet the library too often remains the most intimidating, and therefore remote, structure on campus.

Although Ekstrom Library is located in the center of U of L's Belknap Campus, its sheer size is intimidating. Its 183,700 square feet of net-assignable space, its holdings of more than one million volumes, its subscriptions to more than three thousand periodical titles, frequently keep the underprepared student at bay.

Building a New BI Program

In order to remedy this, we at Ekstrom have worked very closely with the remedial writing instructors this year to create a library supplement to be offered to all underprepared students. While constructing the program, both groups remained aware that this would become yet one more component in bibliographic instruction, a reference service that includes approximately two hundred classes a year. In order to meet this sector's needs and, at the same time, not duplicate other offerings, careful planning was essential. We immediately knew what we did **NOT** want.

This included the content of two programs offered continually throughout each semester: Campus Culture and University Orientation, which receives instruction for MINERVA, our libraries' on-line catalog, and English 102, which receives instruction for Ekstrom's CD-ROMs. Because of these factors, it was imperative that what we created for remedial writing students be unique, tailored for their needs. In order to do so, we reviewed their program requirements carefully.

Several weeks into the semester, as part of the remedial writing curriculum, students are asked to select a topic. After the exploration process, which involves discussion, interview options and encyclopedic supplements, periodical articles extracted from <u>Readers' Guide to Periodical Literature</u> are introduced to provide more detailed information.

At this point, the writing instructors contact the Reference Department to select a date for the fifty-minute library program. Scheduling thirty-some-odd remedial writing classes can be difficult; matching those classes with seven reference librarians can also be difficult -- especially when one considers we are also providing this service for 170 other classes at the same time. Fortunately, the Director of the Writing Center was quite appreciative of these factors and worked closely with the department in organizing the procedures.

Since several classes met at the same time, she suggested the instructors who shared these slots arrive at an agreeable date BEFORE contacting the Reference Department for an appointment. Many were able to do this, making scheduling much easier for those who could not. All were able to abide by the guidelines of making appointments at least one week in advance.

This procedure allowed the reference librarians structure. It offered the remedial writing instructors time to prompt students toward an essay topic that would be conducive to the selections offered in Readers' Guide. In the days preceding the library program, students were asked to explore their selected subjects in general sources, such as encyclopedias.

Teaching the Class

When the bibliographic instruction time arrives, the instructor brings the class to the library instruction room. Here a reference librarian welcomes them to the facility and prepares the students for the first portion of their session -- the orientation video.

This twenty-minute presentation, entitled "Louisville Today . . . The Sports Page," uses humor and contemporary scenarios to make search strategy more appealing. A Howard Cosell-type narrator pits contestants against each other as each proves expert in using the card catalog and Readers' Guide. The activities are interspersed with "commercials" about library services and facilities, including those designed to teach students how to use non-print items in the Multi-Media Department and other resources. The video, written and directed by two of our reference librarians, has continually proved to be an informative and entertaining way of introducing Ekstrom.

After discussion of the program, seeking and answering questions, the librarian then distributes a Readers' Guide worksheet created by remedial writing instructors and reference librarians. Students follow the librarian's explanation of this popular tool via a concise, three-step process outlined on the front of their sheet. Through Step One, they learn how to look up their subject, how to read a citation, how to decipher periodical abbreviations, etc. Step Two illustrates the Serials List, the library's alphabetical roster of periodical holdings. Students learn the various codes and call-number assignments that will enable them to locate their selected sources. Step Three involves the physical arrangement of current and bound periodical sections. Directions to these areas are accompanied with practical details concerning copy facilities and change machines.

When the explanation is completed, students are asked to turn the sheet over to the exercise which asks them to use the index to select four citations relating to their previously selected topic. At this point, the librarian circulates superseded copies of Readers' Guide among the class, asking students to begin the exercise. This activity, held while the students are still in the instruction room, allows both the librarian and writing instructor the luxury of observing the research process. In addition, it allows students an excellent opportunity to ask questions and seek feedback from professionals. And this is how the students see them -- as two colleagues, coming together to teach.

After successfully completing at least one of the four citations, the student can then proceed downstairs to the Readers' Guides located in the Reference Department. After all four entries are completed, the student selects and photocopies an article to be incorporated into the upcoming essay. Because of the photocopy lines, periodicals being removed from the shelves, etc., the writing instructor usually arranges for another class period to be set aside to complete the library activities.

Working with Students in Less Formal Settings

But the bibliographic instruction is far from over. I see many "repeat customers" who remind me time and again that I taught their FIRST class: I introduced them to the library. They are coming back as experienced users to seek help from a faculty member who has given them confidence-building skills. And in return, they have allowed me the opportunity to share their scholastic lives from the ground up, making me a better librarian and a better remedial writing instructor.

Current and future students will seek me out once they pass through the library doors. They have a speech to deliver, a paper to write, a resume to put together. In the classroom they often will question me about sources for academic tasks outside my course. In either setting, they find me the same.

Both of my offices are "decorated" with clippings, articles, posters that have been selected by my students. These change continually with other faculty or students borrowing from the collection and later replacing the items with the same or ones of their own choosing. And while we share information and the printed word here, we've come to share much more.

But, obviously, I am only one person and can hardly keep up with the student population that seems yearly to increase by leaps and bounds. As part of my responsibilities as a member of a collegial situation, I help them understand that I am not the ONLY one who can help, that there are other librarians willing and perhaps more capable of helping them meet their needs. Thus the trust is transferred once again, and the students' experience and opportunities broadened to another level.

The perfect scenario would have a librarian with time and inclination to go beyond the walls, attend sports events, arrange for job interviews, and get involved with extracurricular activities. Several of us here at Ekstrom have been able to do so, and the experiences have enhanced our ability to be instructors, mentors, interactors. We've seen our population of over 21,000 students lift from the college bulletin to become what they should be -- real people. And that gives me confidence to continue doing what I do, riding the line of both professions, giving these underprepared scholars what they deserve: the knowledge that they belong.

WORKING WITH STUDENTS: GAINING PERSPECTIVE AS A FACULTY LIAISON AND A FACULTY MENTOR

by
Renee Nesbitt Anderson

Senior Assistant Librarian
California State University, Long Beach

Introduction

When I began my career as an academic librarian, I was faced with a number of decisions concerning the role I would play in the library and in the university community. The decisions concerning my role in the library were easy to make because I had senior librarians to guide me through the decision-making process. However, the decisions concerning the role I would play in the university community were not as easy. Although a number of librarians were involved in various university committees and councils, there were very few, if any, involved in student-related activities or programs.

When searching for areas in which teaching faculty were involved in student-related activities, I discovered the Faculty-in-Residence Program. This program involved faculty living in the residence halls with the students. Upon inquiring about the qualifications for participation, I found that one had to be a faculty member (librarians are faculty) and be interested in working with students. I was accepted into the program in August 1987 and was the first librarian (and woman) to become a participant. I was active as a faculty-member-in-residence for one and one-half years.

Because of my participation in the Faculty-in-Residence Program, I was asked to apply for the Partners for Success Program, which involved faculty serving as mentors for students from underrepresented groups. I was accepted into the program in January 1990 and plan to be a participant for the fall 1990 semester. I have outlined my experiences in both programs in the following pages, ending with a summary of the benefits I received and those received by the students.

Faculty-in-Residence Program

The Faculty-in-Residence Program began in 1986 and was designed to facilitate informal channels of communication between students and faculty and to promote the intellectual growth of students. Participants in the program are full-time members of the university faculty who reside in the residence halls and serve a liaison function between faculty and students. Each residence hall houses approximately 96 students, a resident assistant, and a faculty member. The faculty member serves as an academic advisor and tutor in his or her subject area(s) and is responsible for planning informal educational programs. Most of these activities take place in a consultation room provided for the faculty member, who dedicates at least ten hours per week to the program. In addition to the consultation room, the faculty member receives free housing and board.

The Faculty-in-Residence Program offered an excellent opportunity to increase and strengthen students' use of library resources and to assist the students in developing lifetime skills in library research techniques. Having lived in the residence halls as a student only a few years earlier, I thought it would be a great opportunity to learn more about the students and the campus. I also thought it could be a great opportunity to show students that librarians have expertise in other areas than library science.

Many librarians have undergraduate and graduate degrees in other areas than library and information science. My undergraduate degree was in statistics and I tutored students in algebra, trigonometry, calculus, and statistics. Many of the students I tutored were surprised that a librarian could have a degree in statistics. When I told one business student that one of our librarians had an MBA, to say he was shocked would be putting it mildly. Sometimes we forget that we have expertise in other areas from which students can benefit.

During the course of the semester, the number of students needing help in mathematics increased dramatically. To help ease the heavy tutoring load, the director of the Residence Hall program implemented a study group program. The program allowed students taking the same courses or experiencing similar problems to be tutored together. Along with the students, I developed schedules to accommodate the various study groups which met in the consultation room. During the first few tutoring sessions, I led the discussions; later, I selected students to be group leaders. The leaders were responsible for conducting the tutoring sessions and for contacting me when necessary to assist with problems. At this point, I served as a resource person.

Another feature of the tutoring program I implemented was online bibliographic searching via informal, online searching workshops in BRS/AfterDark and Knowledge Index. This involved helping students acquire techniques in bibliographic searching, both manual and online, for their immediate needs and for their future uses as educated individuals.

Instruction in manual bibliographic searching included term paper workshops that covered basic steps in research. Students were then better prepared to locate and retrieve pertinent information. The students used a personal computer loaned from the library. The informal workshops were given in the consultation room with the number of participants ranging from one to six students. Students either came during the scheduled office hours or made appointments.

The instructional process involved a series of steps. In step one, I introduced students to the basic concepts of online searching. In step two, we discussed their topics. This involved identifying the major concepts in the topic, using Boolean logic to connect the concepts, and deciding on the system that the students would use to perform their searches. In step three we discussed the commands of the system selected. I would then demonstrate a sample search. Students spent approximately fifteen minutes online to familiarize themselves with the system and to retrieve a few citations. They were then referred to the Online Searching Room in the library to make an appointment to perform their own searches.

Many students talked about their searching ability and inquired about the organization, functions, and responsibilities of the library. For example, an undergraduate student had earlier assumed that the library subscribed to all of the items listed in abstracts and indexes. When the student discovered his misconception, he grew concerned about how the library chose the magazines and journals to which it presently subscribes. A number of good ideas and suggestions came from these discussions. For example, one student stated that sometimes the signs in the reference area were confusing (difficult to read). This idea along with other ideas and suggestions were relayed to other librarians for consideration and response.

Later in the year, I implemented a library referral system which provided students with references to librarians with expertise in specific subject areas. Identification of these subject specialists enabled students to make personal contacts for subject-related library assistance. Referring students to a specific librarian helped to diffuse any apprehensions students may have had.

The students seemed to react positively to my presence; they invited me to participate in extra-curricular activities. During my first semester in the program, I judged a talent show and a lip-sync contest. During the second semester four other faculty members and I participated as a guest act in a lip-sync contest. I also joined students on movie nights, at holiday parties, and outdoor barbecues.

Partners for Success

The Partners for Success program began in 1988 and was designed to create an environment in which faculty members would work directly with students from under represented groups to provide a sense of direction with their career plans, personal adjustments to the university, family-related issues, financial consultation and referral to the resources of the larger university. The program was directed by the Associate Vice President of Student Services and the Assistant Vice President of Program Development and Strategic Planning. Faculty who participate in the program receive three units of assigned time or funds for either student assistants or supplies and services. I became a participant in January 1990.

Participants in the program are called faculty mentors and are divided into cluster groups with one of the faculty mentors serving as the cluster leader. The cluster groups provide a forum for faculty to share experiences about their interaction with students. Topics of discussion have included new resources of the university that were discovered, how a particular student problem was resolved, ideas on how to improve the program and how to get more students to become involved.

The faculty mentor is responsible for recruiting students to participate in the program. Because I did not have regular contact with students in the classroom, I was in a dilemma as to where I could make these contacts. Somehow asking students who came to the reference desk did not seem appropriate. After doing a lot of brainstorming, I realized that the library probably hires more student assistants than any unit on campus. Problem solved. I spoke to several student assistants who worked in the library's online searching room, located in the library reference center, and recruited five students on the spot.

The rewards of participating in the mentoring program are not one-sided. I have received a number of benefits from my participation. For example, one day as I worked on an article that I planned to submit for publication, one of my mentees noticed that I appeared to be under a tremendous amount of stress and offered her assistance. I asked her to review the article and give her opinion. The look on her face was one of amazement. She could not believe that I valued her opinion. I explained to her that her opinions were important and that I would be honored to have her review my article.

Summary

My participation in the Faculty-in-Residence Program was a positive experience, not only for the students but also for me. The students' learning experiences were enhanced not only in subject-related areas, but also in the use of the library and its resources. My interaction with the students provided a valuable informal teaching experience in which to use specific subject area and library instruction expertise with individual students and with small student groups. They also were able to relate to a librarian in a surrounding other than a library.

The rewards I received from participating in the Faculty-in-Residence Program were numerous. I gained an insight into students' perception of the library and its resources. To them, the library is a foreign country where they do not know the language; and for fear of showing their lack of knowledge, they keep silent. Being aware that students sometimes feel intimidated by the library has made me and my colleagues more sensitive to their needs when working at the reference desk.

Participation in the Partners for Success Program provided an opportunity to interact with other faculty, exchange ideas and concerns, and learn more about each other on a personal and professional level. Many of the faculty in my cluster group were excited to have a librarian participate in the program. They viewed the library as an integral part of the students' educational process.

Being actively involved in these two programs was an exciting adventure. I especially enjoyed the interaction with the students and with other faculty. I highly recommend exploring all the possibilities that working on a university campus can offer. Becoming a part of the total teaching/learning/advising experience can make a librarian even more aware of and excited about the end purpose of the work she is doing.

Suggested Readings

Caruso, Richard. "Mentoring Relationships in Higher Education: An Empirical Study." Campus Activities Programming 21 (1988): 50-54.

Colwell, Bruce W. "Faculty Involvement in Residential Life." Journal of College and University Student Housing 13 (1983): 9-14.

Erkut, Sumru, and Janice R. Mokros. "Professors as Models and Mentors for College Students." American Educational Research Journal 21 (1984): 399-417.

Franken, Mary L. "Residence Halls as Educational Environments: A University Committee Study of Campuswide Perceptions." Journal of College and University Student Housing 13 (1983): 13-19.

Keleher, Jean, Deborah Tenofsky, and Robert Waldman. "The Residence Hall Libraries at the University of Michigan."College & Research Libraries News 51 (1990): 222-225.

Kuh, George D. "Suggestions for Encouraging Faculty-Student Interaction in a Residence Hall." NASPA Journal 22 (1985): 29-37.

Merriam, Sharan B. "Mentoring in Higher Education: What We Know" Review of Higher Education 11 (1987): 199-210.

Miller, Donald E. "Live-in Faculty: A Modest Proposal for Higher Education." Futurist 17 (1988).

Oltmanns, Gail, and John H. Schuh. "Purposes and Uses of Residence Hall Libraries." College & Research Libraries 46 (1985): 172-177.

Schuh, John H., and George D. Kuh. "Faculty Interaction with Students in Residence Halls." Journal of College Student Personnel 25 (1984): 519-528.

Tacha, Deanell R. "Advising and Interacting Outside the Classroom." New Directions for Teaching and Learning 25 (1986): 53-63.

Witucke, Virginia. "Off-Campus LIbrary Services: Leading the Way." College & Research Libraries News 51 (1990): 252-255.

PART V

A Recommended Reading List for Librarians in the University

A RECOMMENDED READING LIST FOR LIBRARIAN FACULTY MEMBERS

by
Susan Hall

Associate Professor
Incarnate Word College

Introduction

While earning one or more graduate degrees is a prerequisite to becoming a faculty member, attending graduate school does not in the fullest sense teach us how to become faculty members. As we earn graduate degrees we attain some expertise in our disciplines; we may even acquire some experience in teaching that discipline or in its bibliography. It is unlikely, however, that many of us, regardless of our disciplines, develop any sense of what faculty membership entails. Observers who discuss this phenomenon note that in American higher education becoming a faculty member usually entails a kind of on-the-job training. While this is generally true for new faculty members regardless of their disciplines, it may be especially true for librarians. In the library, the tradition of faculty membership is newer and mentors and models may, therefore, be scarcer.

This essay offers a reading list for librarians making, or thinking about making, the transition to faculty status. A group of college administrators randomly selected from the microfiche collection of college catalogs was polled. Each was the chief academic officer for his or her institution; typically they were academic vice presidents, but titles varied from campus to campus. Each was asked to recommend reading material to librarians making the transition from library school student or staff member to faculty member. Specifically, they were asked to list "books dealing with the meaning of higher education and the responsibilities of a faculty member." The number of administrators involved in this survey -- thirty -- was small; the return rate was unimpressive. Clearly no claim can be made that these individuals are a representative sample of the chief academic officers of American colleges and universities. Neither can it be claimed that the resulting group of texts represents the suggested reading list of academic vice presidents. Nevertheless this list -- a list of recommended books rather than the list -- offers provocative reading for those thinking about what it means to be an American college or university faculty member today.

The thirteen recommended books are similar in that none is a text addressed only to those in a single discipline; they are all in some sense generalists' books, Although some of the texts, such as Gilligan's and Kanter's, are rooted in specific disciplines, they speak to wider audiences. The books listed here can be divided into four groups, albeit somewhat arbitrarily and with some overlap. The first group includes books that might be termed reformist texts; they all grow out of and report on the period of self-appraisal American education underwent in the 1970's. The second group of books deals primarily with issues of curriculum and assessment. Each in one way or another asks the questions "What should American undergraduates learn and how will we know if they have learned it?" The third group focuses on academic culture. Just as businesses have their corporate cultures, so academia has its; these books examine the social and psychological issues that help determine academic culture. The final group examines the issue of faculty development. The past twenty years have been ones of retrenchment, retrenchment made more obvious when compared with the dizzying growth of the postwar years. Because relatively few new faculty members were hired during the past twenty years, development of existing faculty has come to be seen as crucial to any efforts of reform.

Reformist Texts

One group of works cited by the academic vice presidents might be named "reformist texts"; each work in this group was either the report of a commission on educational reform or a commentary on such a report. As a group, these works are critical of American undergraduate education, noting a lack of cohesion in the curriculum as well as meaningful institutional accountability for student performance. Although it did not focus on higher education per se, the most discussed of these works is probably A Nation at Risk, the report sponsored by the Reagan administration and reporting on the status of American education at all levels.

The National Commission for Excellence in Education studied "the quality of teaching and learning" in American education (1) and found them wanting. In perhaps its most famous sentences, the report declares,

> If an unfriendly power had attempted to impose on America the mediocre educational performance that exists today, we might well have viewed it as an act of war. As it stands, we have allowed this to happen to ourselves. . . . We have, in effect, been committing an act of unthinking, unilateral educational disarmament. (5)

A Nation at Risk touches upon "four important aspects of the educational process: content, expectations, time, and teaching" (18). For each aspect, the report discusses findings which the commissioners feel contribute to educational mediocrity and also makes recommendations to improve performance.

In the area of content the commission described a minimum curriculum, which it termed the New Basics and which called for strengthened requirements in English, mathematics, science, social studies, computer science, and foreign languages. In the area of expectation, the commission called for colleges and universities to raise their admission requirements as a means to improving students' performance in both schools and higher education. In addition it called for "more rigorous and measurable standards" (27) at all levels. The commission recommended that more time be spent on education, by lengthening the school day or the school year, or by using existing time more efficiently. Finally, the commission claims that prospective teachers are drawn from the lowest quarter of their classes. Lamenting this situation, the commission recommends improving teacher preparation and making teaching "a more rewarding and respected profession" (30) by instituting changes such as career ladders, improved salaries, and master teachers.

A Nation at Risk argues for lifelong learning for all citizens and makes a humanistic argument for the importance of developing each individual's talents. Nevertheless, the driving force behind the document seems to be economic. The Commission for Excellence in Education notes that the world has become one of "ever-accelerating competition and change" (13) and that Americans are losing their competitive edge in the world economy because of a mediocre educational system.

Involvement in Learning: Realizing the Potential of American Higher Education, issued a year later than A Nation at Risk, resembles its predecessor in being a federally sponsored examination of American education; however, its scope is much narrower. The report concerns itself principally with undergraduate education, and its authors argue that

> the quality of undergraduate education could be significantly improved if America's colleges and universities would apply existing knowledge about three critical conditions of excellence -- (1) student involvement, (2) high expectations, and (3) assessment and feedback. (Study Group on the Conditions of Excellence in American Higher Education 17)

The study group maintains that the first of the three conditions, student involvement, is "perhaps the most important for purposes of improving undergraduate education" (17).

Involvement in Learning consists of brief recommendations for increasing student involvement, for realizing high expectations and for providing assessment and feedback. Despite their brevity, the 27 recommendations are far-reaching. Under the rubric of increasing students' involvement, for instance, the report touches upon issues as far-flung as budgeting (increasing the faculty and other institutional resources allocated to lower division students), hiring practices (consolidating many part-time positions into full-time ones), teaching methods (moving away from lecture to other methods which "require that students take greater responsibility for their learning" [27]), and patterns of institutional organization (forming small and effective learning communities within colleges and universities). The authors argue that each of the changes they suggest, while seemingly unrelated, would work to increase student involvement.

Discussing their second theme, high expectations, the authors argue that colleges and universities must explicitly articulate statements of "the knowledge, capacities, and skills that students must develop prior to graduation" (39) and then use proficiency assessments to assure that these goals are met. The study group takes pains to point out that the model they advocate, one of explicitly stated goals and carefully focused assessment, should not be used to unduly narrow the curriculum. It should, for instance, include at least two years of liberal studies for all students. Additionally, the authors argue that goals for students should include not only mastery of information about various fields of study, but also require that students be able to communicate this knowledge and to integrate knowledge from various sources. Finally, while the report acknowledges that faculty involvement is crucial in the selection, development, and administration, and scoring of assessment instruments, its authors also emphasize the need for systematic programs that "can assess the knowledge, capacities, and skills developed in students" (55). They caution that care be taken when selecting or changing instruments to insure that those chosen are appropriate both to the institutional goals and to the characteristics of the students.

Recognizing that colleges and universities do not operate in a vacuum, the study group addresses various external groups such as graduate schools and accrediting agencies, suggesting policies which will encourage undergraduate institutions to implement the recommendations to Involvement in Learning.

Published in 1985, Integrity in the College Curriculum: A Report to the Academic Community is a report sponsored by the Association of American Colleges to assess the baccalaureate degree in the face of the widespread criticism of American education in the immediately preceding years. The centerpiece of the report is the study group's description of a minimum required curriculum. Noting that the bachelor's degree needs a framework "sturdier than simply a major and general distribution requirements and more reliable than student interests," the authors suggested nine essential experiences: (1) inquiry, abstract logical thinking, critical analysis; (2) literacy; (3) understanding numerical data; (4) historical consciousness; (5) science; (6) values; (7) art; (8) international and multicultural experiences; (9) study in depth. The report eschews a split between the process of learning and the content learned. However, it does emphasize issues of process because in the authors' view American education often "offers too much knowledge with too little attention to how that knowledge has been created and what methods and styles of inquiry have led to its creation" (Project on Redefining the Meaning and Purpose of Baccalaureate Degrees 24).

Integrity in the College Curriculum takes note of several obstacles which must be overcome in order to reform the baccalaureate degree. First, in individual institutions the faculty as a whole must take back ownership of the curriculum; it cannot be divided piecemeal among departments. Second, college teaching must come to be seen as a profession in and of itself. This means that teaching, as well as research, must have status and legitimacy on campus. Moreover, graduate education should include a systematic introduction to the profession of teaching. Finally, colleges and universities must become accountable for their performance without surrendering independence and diversity: "The colleges themselves must be held responsible for developing evaluations that the public can respect" (33).

The Carnegie Foundation for the Advancement of Teaching sponsored College: The Undergraduate Experience in America, the only work recommended by more than one academic officer surveyed in this study. While writen by Ernest Boyer, College involved a team of sixteen observers who in 1984 visited twenty-nine campuses representing "the full spectrum of institutional types" (xii). Boyer pulls together many portraits of individual campuses, programs, and individuals; he tries "to use their examples only as they illustrate, with accuracy, a larger point" (xiv). In addition to insights gleaned from the site visits, Boyer uses information obtained from a specially commissioned national survey of 4,500 undergraduates and 500 faculty members. Similar surveys had been conducted in 1969 and 1974-75, and throughout the book Boyer contrasts the 1984 survey results with the earlier ones .

While College notes both strengths and weaknesses in the American system of undergraduate education, the book concentrates on the problems, or "points of tension" as Boyer terms them, because the latter appeared with such consistency and seriousness on campuses of all types. The eight points of tension Boyer discusses can be quickly enumerated:

> the transition from school to college, the goals and curriculum of education, the priorities of the faculty, the condition of teaching and learning, the quality of campus life, the governing of the college, assessing the outcome, and the connection

between the campus and the world. (6)

These points of tension, however, do not form the organizational structure of the book. Instead, each individual chapter, whether dealing with how students select their colleges, with general education, or with life outside the classroom, to cite only three examples, deals with any of the points of tension as they apply to the topic under discussion. Particularly noteworthy sections of the book include the three chapters devoted to the academic program and individual chapters dealing with faculty roles and college governance.

Boyer's discussion of curriculum notes the pull between career preparation and the traditional liberal arts, a pull which the author feels colleges encourage by treating general education as "the neglected stepchild of the undergraduate experience" (83). To lessen this tension Boyer suggests greater attention to integration. Thus, general education, what he refers to as an "integrated core" should introduce "students not only to essential knowledge, but also to connections across the disciplines, and, in the end, to the application of knowledge to life beyond the campus (91). Furthermore, the integrative thrust of the core should be continued in the major.

This continuation can be achieved in two ways. First, the major should be conceived of anew, as an "enriched major," which not only allows students "to explore a field in depth," but also to place the chosen field in a wider perspective by examining its "history and traditions," by understanding its "social and economic implications," and by confronting its "ethical and moral issues" (110). Second, the courses which make up the general education component should be intertwined with the major rather than always preceding it.

In discussing both the role of faculty members and college governance, Boyer notes the power of institutional culture. Noting that "the American professoriate is a profession with many cultures" (128), Boyer argues for greater flexibility in the ways various institutions strike a balance between the demands of research and teaching. While not denying the importance of the Germanic ideal of the professor as a disciplinary specialist rather than a teacher, nor the applicability of that ideal to the research university, Boyer argues that its imposition on all types of campuses has denigrated teaching and weakened the undergraduate experience for many students. He suggests that in this matter colleges should be truer to their own individual missions and institutional culture.

Similarly, Boyer relates the issue of college governance to institutional culture. He touches upon the difficulties of committee structures and departmental turf, the strains engendered by the needs both for efficiency and for broad consultation, the typically moribund status of student government, and importance of a president's style of leadership. Tying all these strands together is an insistence upon personal involvement. Only through involvement in "purposes and procedures that cut across the separate departments and divisions" can individuals enter into "the common purpose" of their particular institutions (250).

Somewhat more difficult to summarize than either of the preceding works is Excellence in Education: Perspectives on Policy and Practice edited by Altbach, Kelly, and Weis. Noting that "in 1983 and 1984 over a dozen major reports on the state of the nation's schools appeared" (31), this collection of sixteen essays addresses critically the notion of crisis in American education. The collection has two real strengths. First, it treats the many reports as a single phenomenon. Altbach and associates point out that the most influential of the educational reports returned repeatedly to a few common themes: increased math and science instruction as a means to strengthen America's economic competitiveness, greater "quality, autonomy, and pay" for teachers, better linkage between the schools' curricula and the needs of industry, greater and earlier emphasis on foreign language instruction, and increased time devoted to schooling (19-20). Second and probably more importantly, the book provides a rich social, historical, and economic context for the reports. Various of the authors discuss both the costs and the likely economic results of the proposals; others put the proposals in the context of other attempts at educational reform, especially those of the 1960s; still others attempt to predict which social groups will benefit and which will likely suffer if the reports' recommendations are implemented.

What Students Learn

The second group of texts recommended by academic officers all touch upon issues of curriculum or assessment. These works implicitly ask two questions: What should students learn, and how will the college know if they have learned it? Whether addressing curricular or assessment issues, none of these works proceeds along narrow, disciplinary lines. Thus, instead of asking what a business major or a history major should know, these studies all ask what an educated individual, regardless of specialization, should know.

E. D. Hirsch's Cultural Literacy: What Every American Needs to Know draws connections between findings of psychological research, especially in the area of psycholinguistics, and American educational practices. In making these connections, Hirsch criticizes what he terms "romantic formalism" (110) and its influence on American educational theory since the days of John Dewey. Hirsch argues that Romantic formalism de-emphasizes content in favor of skills, that it "conceives of literacy as a set of techniques that can be developed by proper coaching and practice" (112). Drawing on findings of psycholinguistics, Hirsch argues that this skills-intensive view of learning is overly simple and that learners, especially when reading and writing, necessarily draw upon background knowledge. "Every text, even the most elementary" according to Hirsch, "implies information that it takes for granted and doesn't explain" (112). He maintains that romantic formalism has failed because it has prevented educators from systematically teaching students needed background knowledge. Hirsch points both to the declining test scores among the highest achieving groups of students and widespread academic failure among low-income and minority students as evidence.

Hirsch uses the term "cultural literacy" to indicate the kind of background knowledge he feels individuals must have to become truly literate:

> To be culturally literate is to possess the basic information needed to thrive in the modern world. The breadth of that information is great, extending over the major domains of human activity from sports to science. It is by no means confined to"culture" narrowly understood as an acquaintance with the arts. Nor is it confined to one social class. (xiii)

Hirsch notes that knowledge comprising cultural literacy varies from one culture to another, but that within a nation it is an important unifying force because it facilitates communication. A shared body of cultural literacy allows writers to "assume a 'common reader,' that is, a person who knows the things known by other literate persons in the culture" (13). While he admits that no individual could perfectly describe or master his or her culture's essential knowledge, Hirsch also points out that those who write for a mass audience "show a remarkable consistency" (13) in the assumptions they make about their readers' background knowledge.

Perhaps the most famous, or infamous, aspect of Hirsch's book is the appendix which attempts to outline provisionally what literate Americans know. Hirsch, along with his University of Virginia colleagues Joseph Kett and James Trefil, compiled the list to "illustrate the character and range of the knowledge literate Americans tend to share" (146). It is intended to be descriptive rather than prescriptive, an attempt to illustrate the concept of cultural literacy.

While Hirsch sees early elementary school as the time when the notion of cultural literacy could most profitably be used in American education, his book has also sparked discussion on college campuses. Among faculties reviewing their curricula, it leads to debates about what texts and what information are, in fact, central for educated Americans. Conversely, some have argued that Hirsch's notion of culture literacy tends to perpetuate a white, male view of cultural and tends to undercut attempts to broaden the canon of literary texts typically studied by undergraduates.

<u>The New Liberal Learning: Technology and the Liberal Arts</u> by Lisensky, Pfnister, and Sweet consists of three essays all attempting to further the study of technology in liberal arts institutions. In the first, Allen Pfnister defines technology as "preeminently a social process," albeit one "that employs scientifically and empirically based tools, techniques, knowledge, resources, and systems to affect the human environment and its organization" (4). Pfnister argues for the presence of technology in liberal arts institutions both as a subject of study and as a methodology. First, the social nature of technology and its impact on society make it a fit subject for study at institutions which have traditionally offered "value-centered education"; in Pfnister's views such schools should offer their students opportunities "to assess the possible moral and social implications of our technology" (6). Second, the analytical approaches which typify

technology are not exclusive to it; in fact, they are "the kind of thinking expected of the liberally educated person" (12). The second essay, by Lisensky, uses three cases studies to discuss ways in which technology is being taught at liberal arts colleges. Despite differences in the three programs, Lisensky notes common themes among the three cases: all arose out of individual faculty members' personal interests, all benefitted from sustained administrative support, and all have a multidisciplinary dimension. The final essay, Sweet's, is a bibliography. She has put together an annotated bibliography of resources on technology -- books, journal articles, and items included on course syllabi. Sweet has subdivided the bibliography both by format (book or journal), and by the aspect of technology treated (artificial intelligence, ethics, computer literacy, etc.). Essentially, the authors of The New Liberal Learning argue for the inclusion of technology in the liberal arts curriculum not so much as a single isolated course, but as a way of thinking that can be woven into an entire array of courses.

Alexander Astin's Four Critical Years: Effects of College on Beliefs, Attitudes, and Knowledge is a considerably broader work. An attempt to measure and discuss the manifold effects of college upon students, the book presents the first ten year's results of a major longitudinal study, the Cooperative Institutional Research Program (CIRP). The data were gathered from over 200,000 students at 300 institutions. Astin's study reflects the complexity of the issue. Using 80 different measures of outcome, he discusses a range of college effects, including, of course, academic achievement. However, Astin also examines the effect of college on students' beliefs and attitudes (such issues as political liberalism, altruism, or religious affiliation), on their patterns of behavior (issues such as drinking, academic involvement, or marriage), on career development, and on satisfaction with college.

Astin makes careful attempts to distinguish among various types of colleges as well as to distinguish effects likely caused by student maturation or by larger social change from those caused by attending college. In his final chapter, Astin discusses the contrast between his findings and public policy for the last twenty years. While he finds that smaller, private institutions seem, on the whole, to have stronger and more positive effects on their students, American education has moved toward large, public institutions. While Astin's study suggests that resident students benefit more than commuters from the collegiate experience, American higher education has deemphasized dormitory construction. While single-sex institutions produce high positive effects on both men and women, they are largely disappearing from the American educational scene. Astin concludes that debating these larger issues of public policy is more important than evaluating the effectiveness of any individual institution.

Academic Culture

Quite correctly, Ernest Boyer points out that there is not one academic culture but many. Nonetheless, the authors of the books cited in this section all deal with patterns of institutional organization and leadership either unique to the academic world, or at least applicable to it.

Searching for Academic Excellence: Twenty Colleges and Universities on the Move and Their Leaders by Gilley, Fulmer, and Reithlingshoefer arises out of a conscious decision to reject the conventional wisdom of the 1980's. The authors disregarded the notion that the future of the academy was in doubt and "that discipline must be imposed on higher education from outside its ivied wall to ensure quality" (5). Doubting that increased centralization was the key to excellence, the authors opted to "look at what is happening at the grass-roots level," and chose the methodology popularized by Peters and Waterman, In Search of Excellence. They set out to "identify, study, and learn from outstanding and successful institutions" (Gilley, Fulmer, and Reithlingshoefer 7).

Searching for Academic Excellence, then, consists of twenty case studies of colleges and universities that are "on-the-move" (7), as well as a discussion of the elements these institutions share. The diverse institutions include small, church-related institutions such as Alverno College, two-year colleges such as Oregon's Lane Community College, and large state universities such as the University of Maryland system. Despite their differences, Gilley and his associates identified ten characteristics common among "on-the-move" institutions. Such colleges and universities have a "well-defined and widely disseminated" statement of mission, a supportive board of trustees, and a president who is "the key factor in the forward movement" (12). They are institutions that value both teamwork and individual initiative. Their faculty and staff are unusually committed to the institution, which in turn shows notable concern for them and for students. These institutions effectively maintain close relationships with their external communities, are "opportunity conscious," and strive for excellence (13). Searching for Academic Excellence documents the authors' process of selecting the twenty notable institutions, shows how different campuses with varying missions weave many of the same characteristics into their institutional cultures, and discusses ways in which others in education can learn form these examples of excellence.

Working from a Biblical framework, Robert Greenleaf in Servant Leadership: a Journey into the Nature of Legitimate Power & Greatness discusses the nature of leadership. He advocates what he calls the servant leader, the individual who serves others first, and in the process of doing so leads them. Such a leader is superior, Greenleaf argues, because he or she

> is more likely to persevere and refine a particular hypothesis on what serves another's highest priority needs than is the person who is **leader first** and who later serves out of promptings of conscience or in conformity with normative expectations. (14)

Greenleaf addresses his book primarily to trustees of large institutions because of his belief that the caring he advocates is now mediated mostly through institutions rather than individuals. Society, he contends, will be improved if trustees can improve the quality of their institutions, raising "*both the capacity to serve and the very performance as servant*" (49).

A major point made in Servant Leadership is that the hierarchical structure found in most organizations, the situation "that places one person in charge as the lone chief atop a pyramid" (61), is counterproductive. Greenleaf marshals a vast array of arguments against hierarchies. He makes moral arguments, charging that power lodged in a single individual is usually corrupting. He makes psychological arguments, contending that the lone chief often comes to suffer from loneliness and burn-out. He makes pragmatic arguments, arguing that hierarchies, paradoxically, are indecisive and that they prevent prospective leaders from emerging. Greenleaf notes that the hierarchical model is usually advocated for pragmatic reasons; yet interestingly enough his critique of that organizational pattern is pragmatic as well as ethical. He contends that a decentralized pattern, what he refers to as a system of primus inter pares, is most likely to enable organizations both to be good and to do well.

In Men and Women of the Corporation, Rosabeth Moss Kanter argues for a corporate culture similar to that envisioned by Greenleaf, one that is less hierarchical and more empowering for the individuals involved. Nonetheless, it is a very different book from Servant Leadership. Kanter notes that her book has three sources: her interest as a sociologist in "how both men and women are the products of their circumstances -- if not mechanically 'manufactured' by their jobs, then at least limited by them" (xi), her desire to write an ethnography of a single corporation, and her interest as a feminist in understanding "the fate of women as well as men in organizations" (xi).

Kanter has conducted an ethnographic investigation of an industrial conglomerate she refers to as Industrial Supply Corporation or Indsco. Spending over 120 days on-sight, conducting lengthy interviews with over 120 individuals, and gathering survey data from over 500 people, Kanter studied all types of individuals involved with the corporation. She often lets them speak for themselves as she fills in her portrait of Indsco.

In Kanter's view, Indsco is both a fairly enlightened corporation and one with problems typical of industry. The company is generous to its managerial employees. Nevertheless, many in midcareer feel, as they discover promotions don't come fast enough, that the corporation has exaggerated the opportunities it provides. Clerical workers report feeling cut off from any opportunities for advancement. Minority and women newly figure among the managers and are sources of tension as the corporation seeks to adjust to new realities.

Kanter refers to these issues as problems of "blocked opportunity, powerlessness, and tokenism" (266). She argues that these phenomena explain much otherwise inexplicable behavior and that dealing with these problems will strengthen the corporation. While Kanter describes policies which are useful to corporations because they "enhance opportunity, empower, and balance the numbers of socially different kinds of people" (267), she is ultimately pessimistic that the problems she discovered can be best dealt with by large bureaucracies. She contends that size limits reform and that the ultimate answer to providing more humane and more productive workplaces is to develop "viable alternatives to large, overly hierarchical organizations" (286).

In a Different Voice by Carol Gilligan does not address the nature of colleges nor even the nature of bureaucracies, except in the most tangential manner. Instead, it examines the apparently different ways in which men and women view relationships and moral issues. In a Different Voice surveys existing theories of psychological development, especially those of Freud, Erikson, and Kohlberg. Gilligan notes that these theories derive almost exclusively from the examination of men and their behavior; she argues that the exclusion of women has resulted in various developmental schemata which typically deal with the failure of women to "conform to the standards of psychological expectation" by concluding that "something is wrong with the woman" (14). In addition she contends that the omission of women from research in life-span development has resulted in a view of human development which is skewed. As a result, "there seems at present to be only partial agreement between men and women about the adulthood they commonly share" (172).

Gilligan bases her conclusions on three studies she conducted: a college student study which investigated the "experiences of moral conflict" among male and female sophomores enrolled in a course in moral and political choice, an abortion decision study which involved pregnant women deciding for or against abortion, and a rights and responsibilities study which involved both men and women from ages six to 60. From these studies Gilligan derived two major findings. First, men and women tend to envision relationships in different ways, men seeing relationships as hierarchies and women seeing them as webs. These contrasting images

> inform different modes of assertion and response: the wish [among men] to be alone at the top and the consequent fear that others will get too close; the wish [among women] to be at the center of connection and the consequent fear of being too far our on the edge. (62)

Second, Gilligan found that her male and female subjects conceive of morality differently, with the men couching moral issues in terms of rights and justice and women expressing them in terms of care and connectedness. She argues that a truly adequate explanation of human psychological development must both acknowledge the different starting points and explain the paths each sex must travel "to a greater understanding of both points of view and thus to a greater convergence in judgment" (167). While Gilligan's primary interest is psychological theory, In a Different Voice ultimately concerns itself with issues of institutional culture, especially as colleges and universities adapt to greater numbers of women professionals. Gilligan notes that a more inclusive sense of moral development in adults should lead to dialogue that will lead to "a more comprehensive portrayal of adult work" (174).

Faculty Development and Evaluation

Determining Faculty Effectiveness by John Centra is a painstaking review of research in aspects of faculty evaluation. Centra considers assessment of teaching, research, and service, but gives greatest attention to teaching. Centra surveys the types of evaluation practices which are followed nationwide, drawing distinctions among various types of institutions. He then critically analyzes available research to discuss the uses and limitations of the various procedures. Issues surrounding student ratings of professors get lengthy consideration. Centra discusses questions that often arise about student ratings, questions ranging from what content should be included on rating forms to whether various characteristics of the students or their class can influence the rating given to a professor. He also includes a chapter which describes various available rating forms.

Determining Faculty Effectiveness also examines methods of evaluation other than the familiar student rating. These alternatives include self-assessment, evaluations by colleagues, and measurement of student learning. In each case, the method's uses and limitations are discussed. In determining uses and limitations, Centra always remembers the possible purposes of an evaluation. Thus, he draws careful distinctions between methods suitable for summative evaluation -- essentially a procedure leading directly to decisions about hiring, firing, or promotion -- and those suitable for formative evaluation -- a procedure leading to faculty development.

While his primary focus is on the evaluation of effective teaching, Centra also includes chapters on the assessment of the other faculty responsibilities -- advising, research, and public service. In addition he includes a discussion of legal considerations and of methods of integrating bits of information about a faculty member into a system for decision making. While Determining Faculty Effectiveness is carefully grounded in the available research, Centra does not prescribe "a specific system of assessment," but rather he discusses "general principles and guidelines and make[s] suggestions for colleges to consider in developing their own approaches to evaluation" (ix).

Inspired in part by John Centra's work, Personalized Faculty Development: Rationale, Application and Evaluation by Paul K. Preus and Douglas F. Williams describes an attempt to move beyond the most common model for faculty development activities -- what the authors refer to as "'all hands' activities" (6). Rejecting the notion that a single developmental activity is likely to benefit all faculty members, Preus and Williams describe a model for faculty development that is decentralized and individualized. They then present a case study to illustrate how model might be put into practice. The case involves a partnership between Auburn University and eighteen Alabama junior colleges. The program brought representatives to the Auburn campus for an intensive summer workshop, during which they would identify development needs at their own campuses and planned activities to meet those needs. The participants were termed KATS or "catalytic agents," a term which reflected the planners' desire that the community college faculty members chosen for the project would be change agents for their entire campuses. The book describes the activities of the summer workshop and the projects implemented by the KATS on their own campuses; the book includes evaluation of the changes produced both among the individual participants and on their campuses.

Conclusion

This small number of books does not tell the whole story of the current state of university affairs. No such listing can, for universities, like the libraries that are a part of them, are organic, changing institutions. But these books do make up a starting point for learning more about some of the higher education issues being discussed in the top administrative offices of many colleges and universities. A librarian who wants to be a part of the on-going conversation that is integral to higher education should be familiar with the ideas being discussed in these and many other books on higher education.

Any faculty member, whether in the library or in a teaching department, should make it a part of his/her concern to understand the larger institution that includes the library. Through such understanding, the librarian can become a player in the whole life of the institution instead of remaining just one small part of a subdivision of a larger being.

Works Cited

Altbach, Philip G., Gail P. Kelly, and Lois Weis. Excellence in Education: Perspectives on Policy and Practice. Buffalo, New York: Prometheus Books, 1985.

Astin, Alexander W. Four Critical Years: Effects of College on Beliefs, Attitudes and Knowledge. San Francisco: Jossey-Bass Publishers, 1977.

Boyer, Ernest L. College: The Undergraduate Experience in America. New York: Harper and Row, 1987.

Centra, John A. Determining Faculty Effectiveness: Assessing Teaching, Research, and Service for Personnel Decisions and Improvement. San Francisco: Jossey-Bass, 1979.

Gilley, J. Wade, Kenneth A. Fulmer, and Sally J. Reithlingshoefer. Searching for Academic Excellence: Twenty Colleges and Universities on the Move and Their Leaders. Macmillan Series in Higher Education. New York: American Council on Education, 1986.

Gilligan, Carol. In a Different Voice: Psychological Theory and Women's Development. Cambridge, Mass.: Harvard University Press, 1982.

Greenleaf, Robert K. Servant Leadership: A Journey into the Nature of Legitimate Power & Greatness. New York: Paulist Press, 1977.

Hirsch, Eric D., Jr. Cultural Literacy: What Every American Needs to Know. Boston, MA: Houghton Mifflin, 1987.

Kanter, Rosabeth M. Men and Women of the Corporation. New York: Basic Books, 1977.

Lisensky, Robert P., Allen O. Pfnister, and Sharon D. Sweet. The New Liberal Learning: Technology and the Liberal Arts. Washington, DC: Council of Independent Colleges, 1985.

National Commission for Excellence in Education. A Nation at Risk: The Imperative for Educational Reform. Washington, DC: U. S. Government Printing Office, 1983.

Peters, Thomas J., and Robert H. Waterman, Jr. In Search of Excellence: Lessons from America's Best-run Companies. New York: Harper & Row, 1982.

Preus, Paul K., and Douglas F. Williams. Personalized Faculty Development: Rationale, Application and Evaluation. Bear Creek, AL: CESCO Press, 1979.

Project on Redefining the Meaning and Purpose of Baccalaureate Degrees. Integrity in the College Curriculum: A Report to the Academic Community. Washington, DC: Association of American Colleges, 1985.

Study Group on the Conditions of Excellence in American Higher Education. Involvement in Learning: Realizing the Potential of American Higher Education. Washington, DC: National Institute of Education, 1984.